2007

Happy ♡

Kevin

Love, Mom

SHOWDOWN

The Struggle Between
the Gingrich Congress
and
the Clinton White House

ELIZABETH DREW

A Touchstone Book
Published by Simon & Schuster

TOUCHSTONE
Rockefeller Center
1230 Avenue of the Americas
New York, NY 10020

First Touchstone Edition 1997

TOUCHSTONE and colophon are
registered trademarks of Simon & Schuster Inc.
Manufactured in the United States of America

1   3   5   7   9   10   8   6   4   2

The Library of Congress has cataloged
the Simon & Schuster edition as follows:

Drew, Elizabeth.
Showdown : the struggle between the Gingrich
Congress and the Clinton White House / Elizabeth Drew.
p.   cm.
Includes index.
1. United States—Politics and government—
1993–   . 2. Clinton, Bill, 1946–   .
3. Gingrich, Newt. I. Title.
E885.D74   1996
973.929—dc20   95-26197
CIP
ISBN 0-684-81518-4
0-684-82551-1 (Pbk)

For F

Introduction

After the 1994 election, I believed that the country would be facing a struggle between the Presidency and the Congress—now to be dominated by different parties—greater than any we had seen in our lifetime. I understood enough about Newt Gingrich, the new House Speaker, to know that his leadership of the House would be anything but dull, and to take him seriously when he said that he wanted to destroy the welfare state.

At the same time, Bill Clinton, having suffered a huge blow in the midterm election, had to revive his Presidency if he was to be a major force in the coming struggle, and anything but a crippled reelection candidate.

It was clear that there would be a contest over large questions about the role and direction of government, a debate of the sort that this country hadn't had for a long time. Programs that affected every American were up for grabs.

I thought it would be most interesting to be there, on the battlefield, talking to the contending forces, to see what they were thinking at any given moment, what premises they were acting on, what calculations—and miscalculations—they were making, what decisions were reached, and what they meant.

The House Republicans' assault on the Executive Branch was to be total, on every front, and without precedent. Doctrines long considered unassailable, and long-standing assumptions, would be challenged. The total war was meant to scatter the enemy, divide its strength, confuse it. And for a while, this strategy worked.

What no one could have foreseen were the dimensions of the drama that would accompany these events, or the stunning switch in the situations of Clinton and Gingrich. Like a lot of other people, Gingrich underestimated Clinton's wiliness and also the power of the Presidency. The struggle turned out to be a Constitutional test as well as one over policy. The personal strengths and idiosyncrasies and defects of both Newt Gingrich and Bill Clinton played a strong role in this, but so did the new political dynamics set forth by the changing nature of politics and by the struggle itself. Much of what happened was brand new. Experienced politicians were in places they had never been before. Observers had to discard old assumptions about politics and how the Congress worked.

The battle over this country's future turned out to be one of the most extraordinary stories I have ever covered in Washington. In this book, I set out to trace what happened and why, and what it meant to the lives of the citizens, and point to what it may mean for the future.

ELIZABETH DREW
Washington, D.C.
February 1996

1

OPENING DAY

"A Whole New Debate"

In the afternoon of January 4, opening day of the first session of the 104th Congress, Newt Gingrich, the newly sworn-in Speaker of the House, was striding across the Capitol Plaza, and giving a disquisition on power. It was one of the few bitterly cold days of Washington's winter, but Gingrich wasn't wearing an overcoat. Washington's biggest and newest star, trailed by family members, aides, and security detail and preceded by a covey of photographers walking backward, was in an understandably ebullient mood, happily acknowledging the greetings and congratulations of people he passed. He had great reason to be pleased: more than any other factors, his efforts and exceptional long-sightedness had brought about what had until very recently seemed most unlikely to almost everybody but him—the Republican takeover of the House of Representatives after forty years, and his installation as Speaker. Until that moment, Gingrich had been widely known as a "bomb thrower," a man more interested in upsetting than observing the regular order, often to the distress of the more mannerly and traditional members of his own party. Next to the takeover of the House, the Republican recapture of the Senate after eight years seemed almost routine. But Gingrich had had a plan.

The opening day of the new Congress was being afforded all the excitement and attention of a Presidential Inauguration. The broadcast networks had brought their anchors to town. Tickets to the galleries—especially the House gallery—were precious items. Overflow crowds watched the opening events on closed-circuit television in Statuary Hall. In a sign of the new times, radio talk show hosts—almost all of them conservatives and strong allies of Gingrich's and an important factor in his triumph—were given special quarters in the Capitol. Rush Limbaugh's substitute (the popular conservative talk show host was on vacation) worked out of Gingrich's own office. Lobbyists handing out cards crowded the hallways. In the Ways and Means Committee room in the Longworth House Office Building, some Houston oil men threw a lavish reception for their representative, Bill Archer, the new chairman of the tax-writing committee.

Now, shortly after four o'clock, Gingrich, universally referred to as "Newt," having slipped out of the Speaker's chair, was on his way to a reception in the Longworth House Office Building for the families of new Members of Congress, where the leading attraction, courtesy of Gingrich, was the Mighty Morphin Power Rangers, stars of a highly popular children's program. Gingrich said he had asked his five-year-old nephew, Kevin, who was trailing along, whom he would most like to meet.

"I work on four models," Gingrich said, when I asked him what he expected to have accomplished by the end of this session of the Congress, "vision, strategy, tactics, and planning." He continued, "We may have a more limited success in terms of bills, but the whole language of politics will be in the midst of transformation. We'll be building a bow-wave of change." The former history professor cited as earlier examples the change that took place from the McKinley administration to Theodore Roosevelt and the Progressives, which led in time to the Wilson administration. Then came the New Deal, which Gingrich called "the most fertile period in our history." The conservative, even radical Gingrich revered Franklin Roosevelt. Gingrich said, "The real breaking point is when you find yourself having a whole new debate, with new terms. That's more important than legislative achievements." While Gingrich may have been trying to lower expectations of what he would achieve legislatively, it seemed also that this was the visionary in him speaking. "We'll know in six months whether we have accomplished that," Gingrich said. "Reagan didn't quite pull it off."

Gingrich soon reached the cafeteria in the Longworth Building, where a couple hundred people—parents and children—had gathered. Six Power Rangers (they weren't actually the ones that appear on television, but the children seemed none the wiser), dressed in white, black, blue, pink, red, and yellow space suits, were standing on a stage. Gingrich took his place beside them, and seemingly a million flashbulbs went off. Gingrich spoke to the crowd for only a couple of minutes, telling the assembled children that "You're probably more interested in them than in me," and he was soon out of the room, on his way back to the Capitol. Gingrich was rarely so laconic, but his schedule was crowded and little time was needed to accomplish his aim at the reception.

Resuming our conversation, Gingrich said, "I gave a paper to the freshmen in which I described the role of a leader. The first job of a leader is to set and create a focus; second, be a symbol—go places where the simple act of being there communicates. That's what the Power Rangers was all about. It was a pro-family statement. Three, gather resources in the society at large. Four, using the resources of the federal government, govern. The traditional leader would focus on the fourth part. Reagan did the first part. F.D.R. did all four; he's the greatest leader we ever had."

In his talk to the freshmen on November 30, Gingrich, typically, gave them a list of books to read, most of them popular theories about the future and management, and said, also typically, "Economic opportunity and technological opportunity will be available if we can stop obsolete political elites and an obsolete welfare state from blocking the future and protecting the past." He spoke, as he so often did, in global and visionary terms. Whether or not it all stood up to scrutiny, it was clear that Gingrich would be a different kind of congressional leader.

Asked if he was going to try to do all four, Gingrich replied breezily, "Sure. Because that's the idealized leader. If you fall short you're falling short of the ideal. If you think of yourself as a transformational leader, you have to try all four. F.D.R. left the Democrats such a powerful base that it could support them for a long time. Now you have a decaying structure and an obsolescent ideology."

Along the way back, Gingrich obliged a couple from upstate New York who wanted to take a picture of him holding their small child. While doing so, he said to the gathering spectators, "His future is what it's all about."

When I asked him, as he resumed his march to the Capitol, what he was most worried about, Gingrich replied, "The biggest thing I'm worried about is being blindsided, which by definition is something you didn't think of." Gingrich tried to think of everything. "After that," he continued, "is the sheer scale of what we're trying to do. Third, the day-to-day job of creating a new order. Fourth, the established order's ability to thwart things, day by day. It's everything from the *New York Times* editorial board, the network executives, the managing editor of *Time*, who was just here." Gingrich was sensitive to criticism, and he spoke and dealt not in terms of people who disagreed with him but of enemies, including "the established order" and "the forces of the status quo."

As he made his way through a large crowd back to room H 209, just off the House floor—the large ceremonial office recently vacated by former Democratic Speaker Thomas Foley, who had been defeated for reelection —where he would pose, along with his wife, Marianne, for three hours for pictures with new members and their families, Gingrich remarked, "I'll be doing hours and hours of pictures. This is my point about symbolism. It creates a web."

•

Gingrich's speech to the House, after taking the gavel at 1:30 P.M., had surprised a lot of people, but not those familiar with his thinking. (In the past, Congress usually met only pro forma until the President gave his State of the Union address, but Gingrich wasn't waiting for anyone.) While many interpreted Gingrich's praise in his speech of the liberal wing of the Democratic Party for its accomplishments on civil rights—"The greatest leaders in fighting for an integrated America in the twentieth century were in the Democratic Party"—as a magnanimous reaching out, it was, in fact, a reflection of Gingrich's pragmatic long-term strategy of trying to win over more of the black vote to the Republican Party. Vin Weber, a former Republican Member of Congress and close friend and adviser of Gingrich's, said a few days later, "Newt has always believed that politically we need to break into the black community." This was, of course, a strongly held and more openly expressed view of Jack Kemp's. Gingrich had once been a Rockefeller Republican, in part because of his belief that the party should be more committed to civil rights. During the 1980s, Gingrich had ordered up a study by the National Republican Congressional Committee, whose purpose was to elect Republicans to the House, of black attitudes toward the Republican Party. Weber said, "The data showed us that there was a strong basis for a bigger black vote for the Republican Party. The line about civil rights wasn't a throwaway line. It's a vision he has held for fifteen years. How well developed that vision is, I don't know."

Gingrich's speech to the House lasted forty-three minutes rather than the fifteen predicted by his press secretary, Tony Blankley. As usual, Gingrich spoke from notes and winged much of the speech. Gingrich was no great orator, and he was normally garrulous, so his speech was rambling, as most Gingrich speeches were—but effective nonetheless, touching on several themes he had been developing. Another point of the speech, in which Gingrich said, "The balanced budget is the right thing to do, but it doesn't, in my mind, have the moral urgency of coming to grips with what's happening to the poorest Americans," was, Weber said, to show that a conservative leader was saying that domestic policy is as important as macroeconomics. "How can we not decide," Gingrich continued, "that this is a moral crisis equal to segregation, equal to slavery, and how can we not insist that every day we take steps to do something?" He stamped certain issues which Republicans as a whole had never cared much about—health care, the cities, education—as now matters of their concern. This was an important, even historic, statement—if it was genuine. Weber said that Gingrich was proceeding on the theory that unless the conservative party offered an alternative domestic vision to that of the liberal party, it couldn't be competitive. Weber said, "He wants the country to think of the Republican Party as attacking social ills. If it does, the realignment is complete."

Gingrich's going on to say that "If you cannot afford to leave the public housing project, you are not free. If you do not know how to find a job and do not know how to create a job, you are not free. If you cannot find a place that will educate you, you are not free" sounded too close to traditional liberalism for some conservatives, who later let Gingrich know of their unhappiness.

But despite the generally positive reviews of Gingrich's speech, there remained questions about whether he had the steadiness, the maturity, and the discipline to be an effective Speaker. That he had a taste for power was without question. He and his party took power with a lot of rage in them, based on the not completely invalid feeling that the Democratic majority had oppressed them. But beyond that, Gingrich, his momentary ebullience notwithstanding, seemed to have a lot of anger in him.

Bob Dole, the new Senate majority leader, knew that the opening day belonged to Gingrich, and he had to make the best of it. Dole and Gingrich, being of different temperaments—Dole the more traditionalist, institutionalist, and at heart more of a centrist, even if he had moved right in recent years with the Republican tide and his Presidential ambitions—had never been comfortable allies. Dole, whose tongue could be sharp, had already taken some swipes at parts of Gingrich's program, and, in a most uncollegial way, poked at a controversial book deal Gingrich had recently made. (Referring to Gingrich's having gone after former Speaker Jim Wright for questionable arrangements regarding a book, Dole said, of the fact that House Democrats were now attacking Gingrich's book deal, "You live by the sword, you die by the sword.")

But Dole, planning to run for the Presidency, knew that he couldn't afford to alienate Gingrich and his followers—who constituted a substantial portion of the nominating force of the Republican Party. When Dole in January hired as his campaign manager Scott Reed, then the executive director of the Republican National Committee and considered a good catch, they agreed on two things: that Dole would be in synch with Gingrich, and that Dole's majority leader office would be in synch with the campaign. Dole's Senate allies were discouraged from openly criticizing Gingrich, on the ground that that wouldn't be helpful to Dole. On opening day, Dole took steps to seemingly align himself with the new star, including going to the House Chamber for Gingrich's speech (this drew more attention than if he had stayed in the Senate). He did introduce four bills on foreign policy, which, as he had hoped, did get him some notice.

Dole was under growing pressure from within the Senate Republican caucus, which had in recent years become increasingly conservative and activist, in large part because of members coming from the more rambunctious House, several of them allies and co-troublemakers of Gingrich's. The eleven Senate freshmen, seven of whom had served in the House, added to that pool. The newer senators showed less respect for their elders than had been Senate custom and were impatient with the "upper body's" rather creaky ways.

The culmination thus far of this trend was the election, in early December of 1994, of Trent Lott, a conservative activist from Mississippi and a former House member and ally of Gingrich's, as majority whip, ousting Alan Simpson, of Wyoming, a Dole ally. Lott argued that an important election had occurred, that the Senate Republicans should show that they had got the voters' message, and that he would be an "agent for change" in their leadership. He added that he would work well with the new leader of the Republican House. Like his House counterpart Tom DeLay, of Texas, Lott had campaigned for Republican challengers, and won the support of many of the freshmen. Gingrich's being in charge of the House, and the House Republican ranks being more conservative than before, brought still more pressure on Dole.

The House Democrats, under now–Minority Leader Dick Gephardt, still in shock at finding themselves in the minority for the first time in forty years, were a fractionated and unhappy lot, blaming the various factions among them, as well as President Clinton, for their reduced circumstances. Most of them had had to face the loss of friends who had gone down to defeat in November; had had to fire staff members, many of whom they had grown close to (some two thousand committee staff members were laid off) and now could not help—Democrats weren't in great demand in Washington's lobbying and law firms; had been demeaned and demoralized by losing office space. They were having difficulty adjusting to the loss of status. Former powerful committee chairmen were suddenly toothless and irrelevant. (Later, the Democratic caucus would rule that the former barons couldn't serve as ranking member of both a full committee and a subcommittee. For such former almighties as John Dingell, of Michigan, who had been chairman of both the Energy and Commerce Committee and its Oversight Subcommittee and had used his subcommittee as a platform before which CEOs and bureaucrats cowered, this was a tremendous blow, robbing him of his congressional identity, as well as numerous members of his staff.) Several House Democrats weren't pleased with continuing to be led by former members of the leadership, on whom they placed at least partial responsibility for the disastrous election results.

Gephardt wasn't in a particularly strong position within his own caucus. About sixty members backed Charles Stenholm, a Texas conservative, for whip over David Bonior, of Michigan, the incumbent, who was returned to his old post. Several Democratic members—not just conservatives and moderates—grumbled at Gephardt's and Bonior's tendency to cast issues against the Republicans in terms of class warfare, a strategy they saw as outdated and irrelevant.

Senate Democrats, now under the leadership of Tom Daschle, from South Dakota, a pleasant man but an untested leader, were still in a daze. The Senate Democratic caucus had chosen Daschle, a protégé of former Majority Leader George Mitchell, who had had the foresight to retire, over the feistier and more articulate Christopher Dodd, of Connecticut, by one vote. Therefore, Daschle was very much on trial within his caucus, had yet to prove that he was a leader.

President and Mrs. Clinton, who at 2 P.M. on the opening day of Congress returned to Washington from a brief vacation in Arkansas, were still angry and hurt by the results of the midterm elections. In his post-election ragings to increasingly concerned friends, Clinton blamed the press, his staff, his consultants. He didn't much blame himself. A prominent Democratic senator said, "He gets p.o.'d when someone blames it on him." Clinton had a more than ample capacity for self-pity, which didn't help him see his problems clearly, and when expressed publicly even in its less extreme forms didn't convey leadership. Whining isn't Presidential. When one friend said that his mood was doing him no good, that he should pull himself together and get on with the Presidency, Clinton screamed some more. Clinton felt that the main problem was that the public didn't know about and didn't appreciate his accomplishments in his first two years in office. One evening in late November, in a four-hour session in the White House residence with Cabinet officers and other advisers who had been in or managed political campaigns (Clinton particularly valued advice from such people), Clinton blew his top. When one intrepid soul suggested that the President hadn't taken enough strong stands, Clinton shouted, "Don't ever say that to me again!" He said that he *had* taken strong stands on such issues as NAFTA (the North American Free Trade Agreement), cutting the deficit. "The problem isn't that I haven't taken strong stands," the President went on. "It's that I don't have any help around here." Red-faced, he said, "They treat me like a f—ing pack mule around here. They use my time poorly. They schedule me to make calls to individual Members of Congress, not understanding that the role of the President of the United States is message." Leon Panetta, his Chief of Staff, bravely pointed out to Clinton that when the staff scheduled two or three hours off, "You say, 'Is this the best use of my time? Don't people here have anything for me to do?' " As late as two months after the election, Clinton was still reported by some as "screaming" over the telephone—telling friends that the press had "f—ed" him, had done him in. To many in the White House as well as to the President, the election results represented a failure to communicate Clinton's accomplishments, and a failure of the Democratic Party to organize for the election.

The atmosphere in the White House was, one staff member said, "bunker-like." He added, "There is a tendency to see the election results and the criticisms of the President as the malevolency of an unjust world—a tendency to grasp at tactical answers rather than look for deeper reasons."

Panetta, who had been brought in the past July to try to impose some order on the Clinton White House, had taken several steps to bring more discipline to the place, and to the President himself, but now Clinton was angry with *him* for not having fixed things enough. The main problem, of course, was Clinton, who had become unpopular with the public and would accept only so much discipline. Panetta was still having trouble getting decisions out of the President.

Aides said that often when the President did calm down, Mrs. Clinton would start in with her own anger. Hers was in many ways the most dramatic human story of all. An extraordinarily bright woman who had been so praised by so many (including much of the press) that when Clinton first ran for the Presidency he'd say, "Vote for me and get one free," had been brought so low, especially by the debacle over the Clintons' health care program, that toward the end of the previous session of Congress she was virtually in hiding. She had to face the fact that she had been part of the problem. In January, after the 1994 election, her approval ratings were below even those of the President, a rarity for First Ladies. In an NBC/ *Wall Street Journal* poll, her approval rating was forty percent, while her husband's was forty-four percent. Mrs. Clinton now was in a quandary about what her role should be in the next two years. Her new situation caused another problem, because in the past it was often Mrs. Clinton who stepped in in a crisis. Now she had to be careful about any appearance that she was taking charge.

At the same time, the President was holding extensive meetings with his staff, with Mrs. Clinton participating, on a strategy for the coming struggle with the new Republican Congress, as well as for his reelection. A number of meetings were held to discuss what the President should say he had stood for all along, and to the extent aides told the press that this time Clinton's positions would "come from his core," they undermined the idea that he did have a core.

His Oval Office address to the nation on December 15, in which he called for a "Middle Class Bill of Rights" and offered a tax cut and other benefits for the middle class, was controversial among Democrats and even within the White House, because to many it looked panicky, and it also went against his earlier efforts to bring down the deficit. Several Democratic operatives thought that Clinton should lie low for a while, be a little mysterious, and then come bursting before the public in his State of the Union speech, in late January; but Clinton, and others, felt that the State of the Union speech was too far in the future, and that he had to "get back in the game." A President shouldn't have to "get back in the game." On the day after the Oval Office speech, in a long and strange press conference,

Clinton led his Cabinet officers in a round of self-criticism, the Cabinet officers confessing what parts of their departments weren't necessary after all, and vowing to abolish them. Vice President Al Gore's project for Reinventing Government was given new vigor. As in the case of the tax cuts, Clinton was trying to catch up with the Republican parade.

Thus the Clintons, smart people who had come to Washington nearly two years before amidst such high hopes, were hurt, bewildered, and floundering. Within the administration, spirits were low. A senior official said, "The administration is facing a total collapse of morale."

As the various participants in the new drama took their places, the stakes were tremendous. There was to be a war of ideas. Fundamental questions about the role of the federal government would be argued over. Assumptions of the past thirty years—since Lyndon Johnson's administration, or even since Franklin Roosevelt's New Deal—would be challenged. Budget and spending priorities would be reexamined. The rationale for many programs would be questioned. The powers of the Presidency would be challenged on virtually all fronts. It was to be the greatest legislative onslaught on the executive branch in modern history. There would be struggles over consumer and environmental protection laws, and over the economic power of the private sector. There would be a cultural war as well. Gingrich and his allies in and out of Congress—the conservative talk show hosts, the Christian Coalition—were bent on challenging the morals and mores that had been fashionable among many Americans since the 1960s. It would be a war on both the elites and the counterculture—which weren't necessarily the same thing. Before the new Congress assembled, Gingrich had called the Clintons "McGoverniks" (he insisted later that the word he used was "McGovernites"). He charged (without substantiation) that there had been extensive drug use by members of the White House staff before they came to government. The cultural war had been building for years, but now the counter-counterculture had attained unprecedented power.

Gingrich believed that the 1994 election was the most portentous one since the one in 1860, which elected Lincoln and caused the formation of the Democratic and Republican parties. Gingrich was a self-styled revolutionary, bent on radical change—on fundamentally revising the role of government and overturning the established order. The obvious pent-up rage and the revolutionary temperament led a number of people to think of him as "Robespierre."

Some Republicans, Gingrich included, believed that the year 1995 could be their own 1933. They also believed that they had little time—six or eight months—to establish their hegemony and bring that about.

Alongside these struggles, the question of whether the Democrats or Republicans would next occupy the White House seemed almost incidental. But that question was very likely to be heavily affected by the big struggles of 1995. This year, in a most unusual turn, the Congress would set the agenda. In times past, there sometimes seemed little difference between the two major parties. This time it would be different.

And the stakes were great for certain individuals. Would Clinton or Gingrich be seriously damaged—or strengthened—by the events of 1995? What would the conflicting pressures on Bob Dole, as majority leader in an institution where his powers were limited, and as Presidential candidate trying to persuade the public that he was a strong leader, and as essentially a traditional conservative being pushed to the right, do to his roles both as majority leader and Presidential candidate?

Finally, would the Republicans understand the mandate of the 1994 election, or would they go beyond it? And how would the American people react?

2

TAKING OVER

"He Wants to Change the Way People Think About Government"

Before virtually anyone else, Gingrich had seen the possibility of a Republican sweep in 1994, and on the day after the election he was ready.

The Republicans had picked up fifty-two House seats, eight Senate seats, and eleven governorships. Senator Richard Shelby, of Alabama, with whom the Clinton White House had picked a fight in the early days of the administration, switched to the Republicans the day after the election. No Republican incumbent was defeated. Republicans now controlled the House 230–204 (with one Independent) and the Senate 53–47. These weren't enormous margins—the Republicans held only fifty-three percent of the seats in each chamber, not enough to shut off a filibuster in the Senate (which requires sixty votes), and the House leaders could afford to lose only twelve votes on a piece of legislation. (Gingrich was very conscious of this historically low margin, and wanted to add to it in 1996 so as to be in a good position in the *next* midterm election, when the incumbent majority usually loses seats.) But conservative Democrats, largely from the South and Southwest and particularly down on Clinton for putting them in such a jeopardized position, could well decide to vote with the Republicans. More than a dozen House Democratic conservatives were quietly threatening to change parties if Clinton's political situation didn't improve within a few months. Moreover, most of the fifty-two House seats the Democrats lost had been held by moderates, resulting in a more polarized

House Democratic caucus—between liberals and conservatives—than before.

As usual, there were various interpretations of the election, and, as usual, various people saw in the election results what they wanted to see. There are no objective criteria. Elections are always part situational and in some cases partly the result of a historical trend. The 1994 election was both: a referendum on Clinton's Presidency, but also part of a Republican, conservative trend interrupted by Watergate and the Presidencies of Jimmy Carter and Clinton (both Southerners, neither of them having run as liberals), and kept in check by Democratic Congresses resting on the power of incumbency. Clinton's unpopularity had only in part to do with ideology —the feeling on the part of many that the "centrist" candidate of 1992 had governed as a liberal. But Clinton's 1992 campaign had been less centrist than centrists later claimed; he still believed in an activist government, and was full of ideas for government programs. Another interpretation focused on the stagnation of wages for the middle class or below over the past twenty or so years—which Clinton had promised to do something about —and the fact that as a result of this and Clinton's "governing left," sixty-two percent of white males voted Republican. This gave rise to the "angry white male" theory of current American politics. Conservative, Republican-leaning white males came out in larger proportion than did many other segments of the electorate, particularly those with Democratic leanings— the low Democratic turnout was itself a political statement.

The long-term trend interpretation of the 1994 election was that it had been coming for a long time: a reaction against "big," "intrusive" government. According to this theory, the movement began in the late sixties, in reaction to Lyndon Johnson's Great Society and other forms of "social engineering." By this theory, the 1994 election was a seminal one, changing American politics for a long time to come. The disarray and discouragement among Democrats, their lack of a coherent philosophy or strategy, would serve to help the Republicans maintain and even increase their power. Some said that the "revolution" Gingrich espoused began in 1964, when the Goldwaterites—the outsiders—took over the Republican Party. The next such victory came with Reagan, who also stood apart from the party's establishment; the Goldwaterites expanded and elected Reagan. Gingrich, as it happened, had now become the torch-bearer for the Goldwater-Reagan revolution.

The shorter-term trend theory—held even by some Republicans—was that the main trend in politics was volatility, born in large part of impatience. In this theory, the voters had thrown out the Democratic Congress because they felt that it wasn't responsive to their needs, and that if they felt that the Republican Congress didn't meet their needs they would throw it out, too. One of those who believed this was Newt Gingrich.

A possibility was that after two more years the public would decide that neither party was satisfactory, and turn in a new direction: perhaps to Colin Powell if he chose to run, perhaps to a demagogue. Republicans were thus under pressure to produce recognizable change—and produce it fast.

The practice of politics itself in Washington was undergoing a profound change. Many politicians were finding their role, and the act of governing, increasingly difficult—and over the course of the year several would decide not to run again. Early in the year, William Cohen, a fifty-four-year-old, third-term Republican senator from Maine, one of the most thoughtful people in the Senate, said, "At one time there was a sort of mystique about being an elected politician—that people elected you and if you didn't do the job they liked they would throw you out. Now, because of technology, C-SPAN, people feel they're just as knowledgeable as you are. They don't hold us in the same regard. We're moving to an electronic town hall. We are governing by overnight poll. We're fashioning policy around what words we can use to get people to react positively in polls." Addressing the charge that Congress was out of touch, he replied, "We couldn't be any more in touch. The problem isn't we're not listening—we're listening without paying enough attention to the consequences of what we do."

Gingrich had been plotting for a long time. In August of 1989, not long after he was elected House minority whip, he presided over a six-week-long seminar, sponsored by GOPAC—a political action group founded in 1979, originally to help elect Republicans to state legislatures, and which Gingrich now headed—at a mountaintop retreat in Colorado owned by Howard (Bo) Calloway, a former congressman from Georgia, talking about starting a revolution. Republican politicians and strategists came to the mountaintop to meet with Gingrich. Some argued that it was premature to try to overturn the established order: a Republican (George Bush) was in the White House, and another (Bob Michel) was the House minority leader. But Gingrich was impatient.

Gingrich had double reason to be grateful to Michel, his predecessor as House Republican leader. For one thing, the genial-seeming Illinois congressman had systematically played others in the leadership against each other, reducing the ranks of claimants to leadership posts. For another, Michel didn't retire until 1994, so that by the time he did—feeling that he couldn't control the process anymore and was likely to be challenged by Gingrich (Michel had seen other Republican leaders dumped)—Gingrich faced no real rivals. In the end, Michel unintentionally facilitated Gingrich's rise.

Nancy Johnson, a moderate from Connecticut and unabashed Gingrich admirer, said that Gingrich's whip strategy team (a first), of which she was a member, "met with Newt every Wednesday for an hour for a couple of years." She continued, "We talked ideas, what are our goals, what's our strategy, what are our tactics. He talked about how to develop the systems and technologies of activism in a democratic body. We discussed these things at a retreat in 1994. People got tired of hearing him go on like this but we came out of it with a collective understanding of how we establish our goals and tactics and strategy." Like his baby-boom counterpart in the White House, Gingrich favored gab sessions and retreats—complete with facilitators. At the retreat, in Salisbury, Maryland, in January 1994, House members lived in dorms and talked all weekend about how to develop a common vision and the attitude of—and perhaps become—a majority. When Gingrich ran for whip in 1989 the argument was, If you're frustrated with being in the minority, vote for Newt.

A colleague of Gingrich's said, "He was a factor in '94, but there are always a number of factors—in this case, the missteps of the Clinton White House, the tendency of any White House to lose seats in the midterms, the debacle of health care. Otherwise we wouldn't have taken control. The smart thing Newt did was to say out loud, from the beginning, that we'd take over the House."

Gingrich had large goals. He was out to destroy the entire force behind the idea of an activist federal government. In an interview in the *Washington Times* which appeared on the opening day of the new Congress, Gingrich said, "What I can do between now and Easter is break up the Washington logjam, shift power back to the fifty states, break up all the liberal national organizations—and make them scramble to the state capitals in Texas, Georgia, and in Missouri."

For some time, Gingrich had had a vision of what he called an "opportunity society" to replace the "welfare state"—a vision he spelled out in his opening day speech. It was Gingrich who had come up with the name Conservative Opportunity Society (C.O.S.) for a group that he, Weber, and Robert Walker, then a fourth-term Republican of Pennsylvania, founded in 1983. The idea was to break with traditional conservatism, which had little positive to offer, and get the government out of the business of "handouts," and provide individuals with "opportunities" instead. This approach was also a way of ending a whole slew of federal programs—and of breaking the power of their backers. The C.O.S. also had the purpose of trying to shake the House Republicans out of a "minority mentality."

Vin Weber said that Gingrich's talk of repealing the New Deal and smashing the liberal interest groups "is more a political strategy than an ideology." Weber continued, "He wants to change the political dynamic that was put in motion at the time of the New Deal. He believes that to triumph politically you have to smash 'tax-and-spend liberalism,' which has dominated our domestic politics for sixty years. It is an ideological alignment in the sense that it's discrediting a way of problem solving. He puts it in terms of 'the welfare state,' 'bureaucracy'—it can be defined more objectively. He wants to change the way people think about government."

In an interview later, Gingrich said that a demographer had told him that "the coalition Nixon put together in 1972 was ninety-five percent identical with the coalition Reagan put together in '84. It's ninety-five percent identical with the combined Bush/Perot vote of '92. So, you've had this sort of anti–Great Society majority which has not been able to translate into Washington the policies of its politics—if that makes sense. And what I have tried to do over the last twenty years is think through what are the necessary steps to actually translate the political majority of 1972 into an effective working majority inside Washington. And what you're watching is the first act of doing that. Part of that is to transfer power back to the states and to local governments and back to families. And back to nonprofit organizations. And this is all a very deliberate strategy that says that the Great Society overcentralized and it's not sustainable."

Despite his rhetoric, Gingrich wasn't as ideological as others in the House leadership, in particular, Dick Armey, of Texas, the new majority leader, and Tom DeLay, the new majority whip. Gingrich had a pragmatic streak that was at times to help him, at others to put him at odds with a large swath of the members of the House Republican conference—especially the highly ideological freshmen.

Because Gingrich was less ideological than the other leaders, Republican moderates in the Congress felt they could approach him and get a hearing. But, for all his power, Gingrich wasn't always free to practice pragmatism, even if he wanted to. The House Republican conference—made up of all House Republicans—leaned strongly to the right. Of the seventy-three freshmen, more than half had been endorsed by the Christian Coalition, a 1.5-million-member group that campaigned on such issues as school prayer and federal vouchers for private school attendance, and abortion (against), and which had become a powerful force in state parties—exercising considerable or complete control in over half of them by early 1995 —and therefore at the Republican National Conventions. It constituted a powerful force in the new Congress. The freshmen and the fifty sophomores between them, along with some like-minded seniors, virtually controlled the Republican conference. Gingrich was to frequently find himself caught among the conflicting forces within his party.

According to Bill Paxon, a forty-year-old representative from New York, who had become chairman of the National Republican Congressional Committee in 1992, Gingrich was crucial to the 1994 victory. When Paxon took over the N.R.C.C., it was more than $14 million in debt, and most of the staff had to be laid off. Paxon, an enthusiastic man, said one afternoon early in 1995 in his office in the Mussolini-style Rayburn House Office Building, "Two years ago, this couldn't have possibly happened. We had a group of dispirited and despondent individuals—that started with the 1990 budget vote." (He was referring to the split within the Republican Party over whether to support tax increases Bush had agreed to in a budget compromise with the Democratic Congress; Gingrich had successfully led House Republican opposition to it, and Bush eventually signed a different version into law.) Paxon said, "I was unopposed for the N.R.C.C. chairmanship—no one wanted the job. I was saying 'We can win it by '96.' We picked up twenty seats in '92, though Bush lost, but few members had positive feelings about what would happen in '94 or '96."

But as a result of his extensive traveling in 1993, and his growing sense that Clinton was misreading the public mood—as Gingrich saw it the public wanted lower taxes and a smaller government—and that Clinton was promising more than he was delivering, Gingrich began to say, with passion, "We can do it in '94." By that September, the N.R.C.C. didn't have enough money to pay salaries, but a significant number of Republicans were volunteering to run for Congress. Then Gingrich did a typical thing: he redefined traditional assumptions. Paxon said, "Newt said, 'You're thinking old paradigm—that fund-raising has to come first. Get with the new paradigm.' " Gingrich and Paxon went to elected members and convinced them to make contributions.

In late 1993, Gingrich began to say to some of his colleagues, "Capitol steps in September." He had been bouncing around ideas for the House Republican candidates' making a dramatic statement of what they stood for. This ultimately led to the "Contract with America," the statement of ten legislative proposals that would be brought before the House in the first Hundred Days, plus a number of changes in the House rules that would be considered on opening day. Tony Blankley, Gingrich's press secretary, said that in specifying the Hundred Days, Gingrich was borrowing not just from F.D.R., but was also thinking (oddly enough) of Napoleon's hundred-day regime after he returned from exile. The idea was audacious, but audacity had long been one of Gingrich's weapons. Actually, the idea of a Capitol steps event in 1994 preceded the idea of the Contract. Gingrich had been aching for a Capitol steps event ever since 1980, when he had convinced Republican leaders to stage one with Ronald Reagan, where they pledged to enact the Kemp-Roth, across-the-board tax cuts. Gingrich believed that that Capitol steps event was critical to the Republicans' winning the Presidency in 1980. (There were, of course, a lot of other factors, including Jimmy Carter.) But after 1980, Republican White Houses didn't want the congressional Republicans to set the agenda, so Gingrich had to suppress his desire for another such event. Now, Paxon was skeptical about the Contract, and Weber thought it was a bad idea, and tried to kill it. Weber said later, "I thought it would give the Democrats some ammuni-tion—an issue for them to talk about rather than having to talk about Bill Clinton. And it did—but it didn't matter."

Tony Blankley said, "Sometime in the spring of last year Newt began planning on the assumption that we'd win the election. He recognized it would be a substantial task to take over when the party hadn't been in control for forty years. By the time of the election, we had an operational plan for the transition."

To Gingrich, the Contract was a means of unifying the Republican Party. "The Contract served three purposes," Blankley said. "One, it was a device for nationalizing the election. Newt has long believed that you have to nationalize a campaign in order to get a big turning. Obviously, you couldn't do it after Bush raised taxes. Now we had the right situation, with the Democrats in the White House." Blankley, a pear-shaped, chain-smoking, high-living man with a mat of wavy black hair and a partial English accent (his parents were English but he came to America when he was three), enjoyed mischief making and also his own new prominence. Sometimes a wicked grin crossed his face as he tossed a grenade into the mix. He continued, "Two, it was a way of defining our agenda after the election. We had gone through months of vetting our issues with incum-bents and challengers. Three, it was a way of advancing the policy we believed in." Blankley said that the issues—which included a Constitu-tional Amendment calling for a balanced budget, welfare reform, revision of the crime bill passed in 1994, tax cuts—were chosen because of their popularity. "I don't think there's one in there that didn't have a sixty-five percent approval, and most of them were at seventy-five, some in the eighties."

Blankley was engaged in a bit of "spin" that had characterized the de-scription of the origins of the Contract from the beginning—that the items had been chosen for their general popularity, as tested by a pollster—an explanation that was generally accepted. In fact, the items in the Contract were selected by the Republican leadership and their staffs and were also based on a canvass of incumbent representatives as well as challengers. Frank Luntz, then a thirty-two-year-old pollster working with Gingrich, was given the task not, as widely believed, of determining the relative popular-ity of various proposals for the Contract but of finding the most saleable language to describe the ten Contract items that had already been selected. But because, as one Republican figure put it, "Newt wanted to get across that this wasn't something drawn up by politicos," various people were ordered to "spin" that all of the Contract items had "the support of the American people." Luntz himself did such spinning for three days, and, dismayed that the press reports—inevitably—said that the Contract had been written by a pollster, complained to Republican National Committee officials, who ordered him to continue the spinning. The most important thing, he was told, was to say that the Contract had been approved by the American people; this was more important than whatever damage arose from the point that the Contract had been drawn up by a pollster.

In order to give the Contract wide distribution, Gingrich arranged for it to be published in *TV Guide*, at a cost of $275,000, paid for by the Republican National Committee. Gingrich was particularly drawn to the idea that the magazine would open to a detachable card containing the Contract.

Some of the Contract items were aimed particularly at the voters who had supported Ross Perot in 1992—the major swing group in American politics. Luntz had been Perot's pollster. According to Luntz, the Republicans' biggest gains in 1994 came from working-class Americans, and Perot voters supported Republican candidates two to one. "That means the Contract worked," Luntz said. At the behest of mostly Perot voters, a clause was added to the *TV Guide* version of the Contract that said, "If we break this contract, throw us out." Later in 1995, Robert Walker described the Contract as "a collection of items we thought would be popular."

Dick Armey said, " 'Doability' was one of the criteria for something getting in the Contract."

But there was more than that behind the items in the Contract. They reflected a combination of the ideology of the most conservative and even radical wing of the Republican Party and the desires of interest groups—philosophical and commercial—that backed the party. A number of the proposals—including a line-item veto, term limits, a requirement of a three-fifths vote to raise income taxes—involved new and questionable interpretations of the Constitution. And there was a fair amount of deceptive packaging involved in presenting the Contract to the American people. The Contract that the public saw contained the ten items, each with a brief description as prescribed by Luntz. But the legislation to enact these items, hastily drafted by committee staffs and others, under the supervision of Armey, went a great deal further—containing numerous items not contained or even hinted at in the version of the Contract that was presented to the public.

The actual day-to-day supervision of the writing of the legislation was done by aides to Armey, by a representative of the Republican National Committee, and by Joe Gaylord, a consultant whose role as virtually full-time adviser to Gingrich was to become controversial. When Luntz suggested putting something about education in the Contract, Gaylord rejected it. The drafting of the bills offered opportunities for various individuals or groups to get their hobbyhorses into the implementing legislation. Most members, busy campaigning and not seriously thinking that the Republicans would take over the House, didn't closely examine or question the actual legislation. Someone involved in the drafting said, "The legislation was done very quickly, and quite often had little nooks and crannies hidden deep inside that didn't originate with the Contract."

Among the items in the legislation but not in the publicly advertised version of the Contract were: a capital gains tax cut; funding of the Reagan-era space-based Strategic Defense Initiative (S.D.I.), or "Star Wars," which Democrats had significantly cut in 1992; restoration of the "gag rule" prohibiting doctors and other counselors paid by Medicaid from discussing with women the option of abortion (this had been killed by Clinton by executive order). The legislation on welfare reform was significantly harsher than the *TV Guide* language on the subject. There was no mention in the original Contract of legislation on "takings"—guaranteeing compensation to property owners whose holdings lost value because of federal action—nor had there been any noticeable public clamor for such legislation. Neither were takings or S.D.I. mentioned in a summary of the legislation that was distributed to the public. Thus, a lot of issues that were later brought up in the House of Representatives in the name of the Contract went way beyond the words of the original Contract. A Gingrich ally said, "Some Contract items have constituencies more important than the polling results." While some of the items in the Contract sounded benign, they were the instruments for a radical assault on existing government programs and ways of doing business in the House of Representatives.

The implementing bills were given such felicitous names as "The American Dream Restoration Act" ($500-per-child tax credits); "The Job Creation and Wage Enhancement Act" (the capital gains tax break and tax breaks for business). Behind them lay the most powerful forces in Republican politics. (This would probably have been true of any Democratic "Contract.") While some of the Contract items represented the wish list of business, large and small, others reflected the views of large ideological interest groups that had gained an ever-stronger hold on the party. According to key party strategists the most important Republican constituencies in the 1994 elections were small business organizations (especially the National Federation of Independent Business, N.F.I.B.); the National Rifle Association ("it dwarfs all the others," one strategist said); the term limits movement (which had shown remarkable ability in a brief amount of time to organize at the grass roots); and the Christian Coalition. Some Contract issues, such as the Balanced Budget Amendment and crime, weren't so much constituency-driven as representing Republican macropolitics. The Balanced Budget Amendment had become Republican boilerplate, but it would also provide a Constitutional sanction for cutting back or eliminating large numbers of federal programs. The purpose of the crime provisions was to take back the issue from Clinton, who had—despite Republican barriers—gotten a bill through Congress in late 1994.

According to a key Republican strategist, the welfare reform issue was also an important one to take back from Clinton, who had made it one of his New Democrat issues and was planning to push it in 1995. (His failure to do so in 1994 was very costly.) But the welfare issue was also important to the Republicans' efforts to maintain the support of the Christian Coalition, because, the strategist said, "you don't get very far into welfare without getting to illegitimacy." Welfare, according to this thinking, could be framed as a "values" issue, one that didn't threaten to "blow up" the Republican Party, as abortion and school prayer had in the past. The $500-per-child tax credit was *the* preeminent issue for the Christian Coalition. In mid-January, leaders of the group met with Gingrich and pledged to spend a million dollars lobbying for the Contract. Ralph Reed, its baby-faced executive director, said, "The way you win political capital for the social agenda" is to win other battles first. He cited, by contrast, Clinton's allowing gays in the military to become his first major issue. (Conservatives, including talk show hosts, had made much of this in the 1994 election.) S.D.I. was in the Contract because of ideology, as were other national security issues. Though Gingrich and Walker, both of them science and technology buffs, were personally committed to S.D.I., it also had a cult following among some other Republicans. The Contract measures to roll back regulations, and to provide certain tax incentives, were designed mainly for small business. Four key pieces of legislation—none of them mentioned in the Contract or the summary of the legislation—to roll back environmental laws were of great interest to developers, utility companies, and property owners, particularly in the West. Legal reform was there largely for small business.

Gingrich himself made the decision not to put in the Contract such divisive social issues as prayer in the schools and abortion, in the well-founded belief that these would draw particular press attention and, Blankley said, "cloud the clarity of our message." To the dismay of a number of Republicans, repeal of the ban on assault weapons in the 1994 crime bill wasn't put in the Contract because it was too controversial—dividing Republicans—and might draw a Presidential veto that couldn't be overturned. The Republican leaders wanted as few vetoes as possible during the Hundred Days. Blankley said, "We were obviously looking for legislation that we could all, or virtually all, agree on and that we thought was popular and would pass and was useful for the nation. We weren't looking for opportunities to have needless fights on marginally winnable cases." The original Contract item on term limits was stronger than the subsequent summary description, which promised only a "first-ever vote" on the subject. This was redundant, because the Contract itself promised only that these issues would be brought to the House floor for a vote, not that they would necessarily be approved. And there was, after all, a Senate. But, to the frustration of Republican leaders, this distinction was largely lost on the public. Term limits were strongly opposed by many incumbents and particularly by Judiciary Committee Chairman Henry Hyde, of Illinois, and Gingrich himself wasn't keen on the idea. Yet because the term limits movement was such a strong force in the 1994 election, and ardently backed by a number of Republicans running for Congress for the first time, it had to be included in the Contract. Some of the items in the Contract had been debated before; some—such as the highly popular proposal that the Congress be governed by the same laws that it imposed on the public— had, as it happened, been passed by the House in 1994 but blocked by the Republicans, so as not to allow Clinton and the Democrats to take credit for it.

The Contract also included a list of procedural and other changes to be made on the first day of the 104th Congress.

Blankley said that the Democrats' decision in the 1994 election campaign to attack the Contract was "manna from heaven," because until they did, a couple of days before the Contract was unveiled, there was to be little coverage of the signing, in front of the Capitol in September. Jim Nussle, a thirty-four-year-old, third-term congressman from Iowa, whom Gingrich had put in charge of the transition, said that the fact that the Democrats— and Clinton in particular—attacked the Contract "just amazed us." Nussle continued, "Clinton fell into the trap. He legitimized the Contract." But the Democrats had little of their own to say.

The main vulnerability of the Contract, which the Democrats landed on, was that it called for tax cuts but suggested no way to pay for them, and also appeared to call for increased spending for defense and a balanced budget. (The defense item was ambiguous.) To the Democrats, this opened the way to charging that Republicans would cut Social Security and Medicare, and go back to "Reaganomics." But these weren't fresh arguments. And Reagan was popular once again.

Three hundred and sixty-seven Republican incumbents and challengers signed the Contract. Three Republican members declined to do so, as did three potential freshmen. The signing wasn't actually on the Capitol steps, but on an esplanade in front of the west side of the building, facing down the long expanse of the Mall.

Out of necessity, the Contract metamorphosed from a campaign document into something else. Weber said, "The closer we got to the election, the more Newt saw the Contract as a device for managing the first six months." Before the election, Gingrich had worried that if the Republicans did win the House they wouldn't have an agenda.

So, though polls taken shortly before the election indicated that only twenty-four percent of the public was aware of it, and only four percent said that it would make them more likely to support the Republican candidate, and even though the Republican victory margin was narrow, Gingrich declared the result a mandate for the Contract. No one else was ready, or in a position, to gainsay him.

Clinton and his staff were caught utterly flatfooted by the election returns. Mark Gearan, the director of communications, had taken an internal poll on election day, and not a single White House aide predicted that the Republicans would win the House. Therefore, Clinton and his people were most unready to deal with the new situation. This problem was compounded by the Clintons' hurt and anger.

It took the President's aides some time to adjust to the fact that their party was in the minority on Capitol Hill, and that the White House wouldn't be setting the agenda. But even before the election they hadn't contemplated a large legislative push in 1995. The President's flurry of legislative activity in his first two years in office was predicated on the principle—a sound one—that a President's first two years is when he is most likely to achieve things, and that after that, Presidential election politics takes over. After a round of meetings, Clinton's advisers came up with the concept of putting Republican proposals into three "baskets." First were the areas where the President would cooperate with the Congress. This included the line-item veto, giving the President the power to veto a particular item in an appropriations bill; curbing unfunded mandates, in which the federal government orders the states to do various things, but doesn't send the money to do so; and welfare reform. Next were the "yes-buts"—issues on which Clinton would work with the Congress, but demand some changes. The third were "hell, nos"—issues he would fight the Republicans on: repeal of the assault weapons ban, or cutting back on education funding, or on health and environmental protection measures already enacted. Another item in the third category—adding to the deficit—soon gave way to other imperatives.

Clinton's advisers realized that, as one put it, "We will be on the receiving end of congressional initiatives. We don't have many cards to play."

Typically, the Clinton people decided that one lesson of the election was that they hadn't got their "message" out. This had been a refrain for nearly two years, and though there was some truth to it, it far from explained Clinton's troubles. In any event, a new "message" had to be honed. So, another threesome, decided upon in December, was that the President had to be seen as fighting for working families; that he had to be seen as seeking political reforms, not as standing for the status quo; and that Clinton had to come across as a leader with a vision for the future. The idea was to show, by contrast, the Republicans as fighting for the privileged, as taking a slash-and-burn approach to government, and as having no vision of the future. On foreign policy, the Republicans would be painted as isolationists. A Presidential adviser said in mid-February, "There have been a lot of baskets."

On the day after the election, Gingrich, in his district in the suburbs of Atlanta, Georgia, made a conference call to various members he had tapped to work on specific parts of the transition. A lot of work had to be done by opening day. Putting Nussle in charge of the transition was a highly symbolic move, because in 1991, during the uproar over alleged abuses of the House bank, Nussle had appeared on the House floor with a brown paper bag over his head, to symbolize, he said, the need "to unmask this institution." David Dreier, a forty-two-year-old, eighth-term Californian, was put in charge of reorganizing the overall committee structure, with the goal of cutting the number of committees and subcommittees, which over the years had grown like kudzu.

Gingrich, a military historian, often thought and talked in military terms, and pictured himself as a military leader. He had said the movie *The Sands of Iwo Jima* was "the formative movie of my life." Gingrich explained later that he identified with the John Wayne figure, Sergeant Stryker, the tough drill officer who, knowing the fierce combat that lay ahead, molded his men into a fighting force. Stryker understood that even if the men didn't understand, it was necessary to be tough—and his men came to appreciate him in the end. Gingrich saw that organizing his troops would be a huge undertaking, and sometimes he considered George Marshall, the Army Chief of Staff during the Second World War, as his management model, and sometimes Dwight D. Eisenhower, who molded a unified fighting force out of the Allied countries' troops.

In January, when Gingrich and the key House figures on the budget met for dinner in the Speaker's dining room in the Capitol—Gingrich said it would be the most important dinner of the year—he used the analogy of General Ulysses S. Grant, whose picture he had hung on a wall in his office. Framed along with the picture were Grant's signature and a quotation about the Battle of the Wilderness: "I propose to fight it out on this line if it takes all summer." Gingrich cited this quote to his budget team. After hearing some of his lieutenants' concerns, Gingrich said, "Having looked at these numbers, I have only one question—are you up to it?" All present said that they were. Gingrich added, "I'm prepared to stake everything to get to a balanced budget."

He had often spoken with friends about the concept of doctrine as used in the military, so that when crunch time came, everyone knew how to behave. He had wanted the Republican conference to proceed according to that doctrine. He was trying to change the culture of the conference as well as that of the House as a whole.

•

Gingrich had talked with allies for many years about changing the "culture of the House." He saw the existing culture as a means of maintaining the status quo, of both parties' maintaining themselves in office and changing things only at the margins. He would ask, "What is the technology of activism in a democratic body?" Weber said, "Newt felt that if they were to achieve a real realignment of the country, it would take more than gaining a majority. It would mean changing the expectations and the behavior patterns of Members of Congress in a very fundamental way. It would mean changing their expectations about their schedule, their work habits, and ultimately their expectations about what is possible politically. The Contract was most importantly a way of changing the culture."

During the transition, Gingrich and his lieutenants took a number of historically important steps, the most significant of them the effective abolition of the seniority system, which had been in place since the beginning of the twentieth century. In three instances, Gingrich skipped over a committee's ranking Republican, placing the chairmanship in the hands of someone he saw as abler—and more reliable. In the past thirty years Democratic insurgents *within a committee* had dumped seven chairmen, but Gingrich's moves constituted a new and highly important use of a Speaker's power. In the case of the Appropriations Committee, Gingrich skipped over four people—one had been indicted and the other three epitomized old-style pols lacking the proper revolutionary ardor, or energy —and turned to Robert Livingston, a fifty-one-year-old member from Louisiana (at least ten years younger than the others), more modern, reform-minded, and presumably more responsive to the leadership. The seventy-two-year-old Carlos Moorhead, of California, who didn't exude great dynamism, was skipped over for the chairmanship of both the Commerce and Judiciary Committees. In another break with tradition, three freshmen were made chairmen of subcommittees. Gingrich further broke with the past by putting freshmen on such key committees as Ways and Means, Appropriations, and Commerce—thus guaranteeing himself loyalists where they counted most. Also, chairmen of the Appropriations subcommittees were asked for letters pledging that they would support the Contract.

For Gingrich, these actions were both a way of gathering more power unto himself and a dramatic demonstration of the fact that things were going to be different. In a conversation in December 1994, Weber said, "Newt and I talked about a year ago about the necessity, when he became the leader—the Speaker or majority leader—of dumping some committee chairmen to change the culture of the House, to show change, to say, 'Don't expect the past patterns of choosing a chairman will prevail.' It was much more complicated than a 'power grab.'"

Paxon said, "Newt puts more emphasis on members, less on committee chairs. Power has been dispersed, reallocated away from committee chairs to individual members and the Speaker." A Contract provision limiting the terms of committee chairmen to six years was another instrument for moving power away from committee chairmen. (So as not to exempt himself, Gingrich limited a Speaker to eight years in the office, long enough to install the next chairmen.) In times past, some Democratic committee chairmen wielded more power than the House leadership, or even a President of their own party. Under Gingrich's rule, there would be no barons to challenge him. Gingrich essentially ran the House with the assistance of the Speaker's Advisory Group, which was made up of the inner circle of the leadership—plus Walker—and met once or twice a week. Gingrich also appointed "task forces" for dealing with various subjects that cut across committee jurisdictions—which lessened somewhat the power of chairmen of standing committees vis-à-vis the leadership, but also was a useful way (to the chairmen as well) of picking up early signs of potential problems on the floor. (Freshmen were placed on the task forces.)

Another form of Gingrich's tightened grip was the rearrangement of the modus for making committee assignments—a matter of great importance to members. A Gingrich aide said, "We reconfigured it to give Newt absolute power."

Also during this period, the special interest caucuses, most of them Democratic, or largely so—the Black Caucus, the Hispanic Caucus, the Women's Caucus, and the Democratic Study Group (a liberal organization that among other things put out a much-read newsletter about pending legislation)—had their funds cut off. (The Black Caucus already had support from outside.) Some of the caucuses—known formally as Legislative Service Organizations—reconstituted themselves with outside funding. The argument for lopping off the L.S.O.'s—that public funds (in the form of contributions from members' offices, and office space in the House office buildings) shouldn't be used to support special interest groups—had a certain plausibility; but the real objective was to break the power of the liberal-oriented organizations. (There were Republican caucuses as well, but they were of less political significance—and they weren't in Gingrich's way.)

The freshmen were eager for these and other changes—and even challenged Gingrich's new arrangement for assigning committee membership, but then backed down. A Gingrich associate said, "It was a little bit much, even for Newt."

The new members brought stylistic changes of their own. A number of them, unwilling to move their families to Washington (or carry the cost of maintaining two homes), slept in their offices. Gingrich gave his approval.

Gingrich had mastered the art of power-by-inclusiveness. He had developed a participatory style that led other Republicans to believe that he was truly listening to them, and sharing responsibility. As he acquired power, he didn't dominate meetings, and for the most part didn't choose to run them—but would sit back and listen attentively, taking notes. He accumulated indebtedness by handing out responsibilities—"hand out the monkeys," he would say—and letting people run with them. He kept a lot of things in his head, wasn't followed around, as many members were, by staff members taking notes. After an interval of, say, three weeks, he would ask a member how such-and-such a project was going. Paxon said, "You only let it slip once, because you want to be part of his team. And the more you prove you can do it, the more responsibility you get."

David Dreier ran into more difficulty in abolishing committees than he had bargained on. The serious and handsome Californian (a bachelor) had for some years concerned himself with reforming the rules and nature of the House, but his efforts had run up against the intransigence of the previous majority. Now he had the imprimatur of Gingrich, and the help of Gingrich's staff. Proposals to abolish—Dreier preferred the term "merge"—committees and even subcommittees would go straight at members' bases of power, and numerous House Republicans, as ranking committee members, had long eyed, even if they didn't expect, chairmanships. Suggestions that they now forgo them weren't greeted warmly. Further, various committees had long-standing alliances with the interest groups that came within their jurisdiction—an arrangement that overrode partisanship. In the end, only three committees—Merchant Marine and Fisheries, the District of Columbia, and Post Office and Civil Service—were abolished. The Veterans' Affairs Committee, with the backing of veterans' organizations, successfully resisted Dreier's efforts to abolish it, as did the Small Business Committee, backed by the party's small business constituency. An important test of the new Republican majority would be whether it was any more successful at resisting its interest groups than the Democrats had been.

According to Dreier, fifty-two Senate and House committees and subcommittees claimed jurisdiction over programs dealing with children and families, ninety over the Environmental Protection Agency, a hundred and seven over the Pentagon. "My goal here," Dreier said, "was to increase the accountability. When ninety committees and subcommittees have jurisdiction, who is accountable?" Dreier did succeed in eliminating thirty-one House subcommittees out of a hundred and fifteen, and in perhaps the biggest battle of all, he reduced by twenty percent the jurisdiction of the old Energy and Commerce Committee, formerly headed by Dingell, which had had authority over forty percent of the legislation that moved through Congress. The new chairman, Thomas Bliley, of Virginia, and his staff were not pleased. Much of the resistance Dreier encountered was from committee staffs, who guarded their own power at least as zealously as did their bosses. Many shouting matches preceded the ultimate decisions.

For good measure, and adding much confusion, Dreier changed the names of ten of the nineteen remaining major committees.

These changes were significant if not radical, and at the least the notion was established that in the Gingrich Congress such changes could be made.

One advantage Gingrich had in starting his Speakership grew out of his having spent years molding the House Republicans into a united party, shaping its vision. He had successfully courted some moderates ("Gypsy Moths," so called because of the Northern states they came from). Some moderates had supported Gingrich's rise within the party ranks. Nancy Johnson was one of the first moderates to support Gingrich for whip.

And, as the new 104th Congress began, most of the House Republicans felt that they owed their majority status to Gingrich. A very large percentage of the freshmen felt that but for him they wouldn't be in the Congress at all. But that didn't make them his slaves.

The unity of the Republican Party was on display on opening day, when it pushed through the House a package of rules changes, some of them highly significant, and some of them more than mere rules changes. Gingrich wanted to show right away that the House had changed. Several of the changes were long overdue. Even some Democrats thought it was high time to sweep away some of the barnacles. The Contract had specified that the rules changes would be passed on opening day, and in following through on that Gingrich was both getting the word out that the Republican-controlled Congress *would* be different, and applying a major shock to the institution—changing the culture of the House.

Since not a single Republican member had been in Congress when the Republicans last controlled the House, everyone had a lot to learn. Before the Congress convened, Republicans had rehearsed for their new role, with practice sessions conducted on the House floor, under the guidance of Robert Walker, one of Gingrich's closest allies during the resurgence. Walker knew so much about floor maneuvers that in the rehearsals, where he played the role of new Minority Leader Gephardt, he repeatedly tied the new majority in knots.

The rules changes included cutting the number of House committees; cutting committee staffs one-third (members' staffs were untouched); requiring that all committee meetings be conducted in the open, or justify in writing the reason for not doing so; banning proxy voting; and limiting the terms of committee chairmen and the Speaker. Gingrich told friends that he didn't feel he could keep up the pace and momentum of the job for longer than that, anyway. He said that he could walk away from the job anytime and be content running a museum, or teaching. They didn't believe him. But Gingrich did feel that he couldn't maintain the pace or the controversy he engendered for more than eight years.

The changes were bulldozed through the House, the Democrats not allowed to offer alternative proposals—a procedure that they complained about vociferously but was a familiar tactic of theirs when they were in power. According to Walker, the new leaders had decided to take up the changes separately, so as to not appear to be ramming through one large package of rules, as the Democrats had, and also to draw attention to the kinds of changes that were being made. In another innovation—announcing a new day—the Republican leaders allowed freshmen to help present each proposed change.

One rules change that gave some Republicans pause, even deep misgivings, was a requirement of a three-fifths vote of the House to raise income tax rates. Such a requirement of a "super-majority," ardently backed by most of the freshmen, was seen by these Republicans as a formula for minority rule, and for blocking potentially necessary tax increases. To them, it was a disturbing kind of detail to put in the House rules. A three-fifths vote to raise income taxes was also proposed in the Contract as part of the Constitutional Amendment requiring a balanced budget—which suggested that it was of more importance than a mere rule. But it was being made a rule as insurance against failure to win it as part of a Constitutional Amendment.

Some Democrats had argued in the caucus that they should oppose the three-fifths rule on principle, but, one said later, "We were met with blank stares or no response from the leadership on that." He continued, "Some of us wished we had put it to a vote in the caucus."

The Republican order of the day on opening day was unity, and some Republican moderates went along with the rules change, but at the same time let the leadership know that they would oppose such a change when it came up later as part of the proposed Constitutional Amendment. Dreier was among those bothered by both the three-fifths rule and a Constitutional Amendment for a balanced budget. Marge Roukema, a moderate from New Jersey, held out for some time on the three-fifths rule. But great pressure was put on any potential holdouts and the rule was adopted by a vote of 279–152, with no Republican dissenters.

The decorousness of the first hours of opening day, when Gephardt graciously handed over the gavel to Gingrich (Gingrich substituted one of his own, which he said had been sent to him by a Georgian, and which was larger than the traditional gavel) and Gingrich's speech was received politely by the Democrats, soon gave way to an undercurrent of anger between the Democrats and Gingrich—a tone that was to remain through much of the session. Most of the Democrats felt a dislike, even hatred, for Gingrich, based largely on his past tactics. His method had been to undermine the House itself—shut it down, paralyze it—in order to inherit it; his invective had been apocalyptic and often mean. He had stirred up some of the scandals that the Democrats had endured. And now he was bent on destroying their handiwork. Their shock at seeing him actually take the gavel gave way not to paralysis but to a deliberate attempt to undermine his authority.

The House Democrats had debated in their caucus the day before opening day over how to deal with Gingrich—how aggressively to take him on. Some Democrats, concerned about the possible effect of another crisis of legitimacy, which could be brought on by another round of warfare, and which would further damage the image of the Congress, had misgivings about going after him on every issue, and about highlighting the issues raised by the book deal Gingrich had made, and other Gingrich activities. David Skaggs, a fifty-one-year-old fifth-term Democrat from Colorado, said in an interview a couple of days after the new Congress opened, "As righteous as our cause is, as indignant as we are, we have got to deal with our responsibility to restore the Congress in the minds of the people. We've got to worry about whether this government can hang together and rely on the legitimacy that only the consent of the governed can give it. It would be the ultimate sacrifice to let these issues go but I'm worried about what the collateral damage would be." But the more aggressive members of the caucus prevailed. Gephardt and Bonior themselves were of an aggressive nature, Bonior more the pit-bull, and other key members of the caucus—Barney Frank, of Massachusetts, Rosa DeLauro, of Connecticut, and Steny Hoyer, of Maryland—shared their view.

The House Democrats were facing a role crisis. Skaggs said, "The overriding thing is the sense that we have to be saying something. It's almost the act of being on the stage rather than yielding the stage. That's a big piece of our motivation right now. The theme on Wednesday [opening day] was supposedly let's show their hypocrisy. There's some validity to that but also a bitterness that runs through all of us right now. Rather than book envy there is a certain terror that the momentum is theirs and we haven't figured out a game plan. I can only figure out what's in me. It's hard to force a good idea. I think as we go through this and settle in there will be revelations. So that gives me a certain patience. But in the Democratic caucus right now there isn't much patience; if we're not fully engaged there's a sense of failure."

Gingrich was already angry at the Democrats, and the press, for criticism of his having made a deal with HarperCollins, announced in December, to publish two books in 1995 for an advance of $4.5 million. (Another book, a novel, was being brought out separately.) In late December, under pressure, Gingrich had resentfully given up the advance (saying he would accept only one dollar) at the urging of some of his allies, particularly Walker. An unstated reason for his reluctance to give up the advance was that his wife, Marianne, was very much opposed.

The problem for Gingrich was that the book deal, while to all appearances legal, gave the impression that this self-styled agent of change, this tribune of the common man, was cashing in on his new celebrity. Moreover, the deal had been made with a company that was part of Rupert Murdoch's empire, and Murdoch had regulatory issues before the government. The opportunity this gave Democrats to go after Gingrich was all the more delicious because of Gingrich's having driven Speaker Jim Wright from Congress over a questionable book deal. The Democrats were out, of course, not just to undermine Gingrich but also the program he was pursuing.

On the Tuesday evening before the opening of the Congress, Gingrich, in a meeting in his office with Gephardt, asked him to keep the Democrats from bringing up the question of book royalties—which Gingrich would still receive—on opening day. (Bonior had taken charge of undermining Gingrich, and had been harassing him on the book deal.) Gephardt was noncommittal. Democrats, in order to get under Gingrich's skin, planned to offer on opening day rules changes to place a limit on royalties as well as to reform the lobbying laws. A lobby reform bill had been passed in 1994 by the House and the Senate, but was killed at the last minute through efforts by Gingrich and his talk show allies. Though the new Republican leadership paid lip service to reform of campaign financing and the lobbying laws, neither issue was in the Contract or high on the agenda. A Gingrich aide said later, "It [the limit on royalties] was offered twice during the rules votes, so that tells us that Gephardt is aboard this strategy." (Members of Gephardt's staff did tell Gingrich aides that the attack was coming.)

Gingrich had shown his anger and sensitivity to Democratic criticism of the book deal by calling the motion a "pathetically narrow partisan gimmick," a "cheap and nasty" strategy. This simply encouraged the Democrats.

At 11:15 P.M. on opening day, Gingrich gathered in his new suite of offices in the Capitol with Majority Leader Dick Armey, Whip Tom DeLay, Walker, Paxon, Susan Molinari (also a representative from New York, and Paxon's wife), Joe Gaylord, Weber, Connie Mack (a former House ally and now in the Senate), and some of his relatives, including two daughters from his first marriage. Gingrich was happy. He thought the day had gone well, and he talked with Walker and Weber about how it could all be traced to their founding of the C.O.S.

Gingrich was highly amused when Weber told him that that day a taxi driver had said of Gingrich, "I like this guy. He reminds me of an African tribal leader." Weber knew that Gingrich would like to be seen that way— as having power based on more than official responsibility, based on culture and shared values. Another of his favorite movies was *Zulu*.

At 2:24 A.M., after a session that had lasted fourteen hours and twenty-four minutes, Gingrich reclaimed the Speaker's chair and declared that it had been "one of the most productive sessions for any single day in House history." Through shock treatment, he had succeeded in his attempt to get the House off to a fast start, to show the country that the House would now be a different kind of place. It was a good beginning for him.

3

GINGRICH TALKS

"A Nutty Idea
That I'm Just Tossing Out"

Gingrich wasn't as prepared for his new status as he had thought. The limelight, which he craved, was a dangerous temptress. Suddenly Gingrich was cock of the walk, his every utterance taken down and televised. In the early days of the new Congress he was a dervish, appearing everywhere, offering his prescription for everything—sometimes having in short order to take back what he had said.

He also wasn't prepared for the close scrutiny of many of his acts, present and past, or for the attacks from Democrats for some of these acts. Nor was he used to having his free-floating ideas taken so seriously, and examined.

Several of Gingrich's ideas had already stirred controversy before he assumed this new role. In the fall, he had suggested that Woody Allen's leaving Mia Farrow for one of her adopted children, and the drowning of two young boys by their mother, Susan Smith, in October, were the results of Democratic Party rule. And Gingrich continued to stir up controversy when he argued (on *Meet the Press*) that under some circumstances children should be put in orphanages.

While even Tony Blankley said later that some of these became a "distraction" from Gingrich's message about the Contract, they were quite deliberate.

A Gingrich associate said, "Nine times out of ten he knows exactly what he's doing. And he's willing to take the flak and tough it out. Most politicians wouldn't want the firestorm that resulted from his comment about the White House staff and drugs. For Newt, this is just the next step, and there are twelve or fifteen more steps. At the end of the day, most of the American people will have heard that one-fourth of the Clinton White House had used drugs. When he relates Susan Smith with the Democratic Congress, to him it's not a cheap shot. He's gone through a thought process that connects them—the decline of personal responsibility and the rise of a gratification-seeking population. To him, the liberal sensibility is always rejecting responsibility and looking for underlying causes." But Gingrich didn't always think through his comments. And he sometimes made off-the-cuff policy statements that took his colleagues by surprise.

Some of Gingrich's rhetoric could be traced to a GOPAC memo about language as a mechanism of control. Drawing on focus group tests, Gingrich advised Republican candidates to speak of Democrats with the words "pathetic" and "sick" (two words Gingrich often used). "Corrupt," "liberal," and "waste" were other key words. Republicans were to be associated with "change," "moral," and "family." Some of Gingrich's friends had argued to him in the past that he shouldn't spend so much time vilifying the Democrats. But Gingrich believed, according to one friend, "that everyone who has effected realignment in the United States has thoroughly vilified the opposition. For him it's not a chess game or an Oxford-style debate—though he likes them. It's an ongoing struggle. There is victory and there is defeat, and there's not much in between."

For Gingrich, attacking the counterculture was a device for undermining the Democrats by tapping into various class and cultural resentments. Though they had not been hippies, the Clintons were sufficiently identifiable with the counterculture to provide Gingrich with a prominent symbol (as wouldn't have been the case with, say, Dick Gephardt, or Bill Bradley, the senator from New Jersey). The Gingrich friend continued, "In politics, defining your opposition is the most important battle. Maybe he has to take a hit today so that a week and a half later he takes the next step, and his opponents don't keep up with him."

In suggesting orphanages as a way of dealing with illegitimacy, and keeping up such talk and even hosting an airing of *Boys Town* on TNT in mid-December and providing a running commentary, Gingrich had a very deliberate purpose: to smash the current welfare system. Of course, the saccharine portrayal of an all-white Boys Town, where everyone but the Mickey Rooney figure behaved (and eventually he did, too), and Spencer Tracy's all-wise Father Flanagan presided almost single-handedly, bore little relation to reality. And though Boys Town began as an orphanage, it soon turned into essentially a refuge for troubled children. (At the time of all the talk about orphanages, the head of Boys Town, Father Val J. Peter, wrote an Op-Ed piece saying, "Please do not embrace this idea as *the* solution to our problems.")

Gingrich and his allies were bent on shifting the welfare debate from one concerning work to one concerning illegitimacy, which should be treated punitively. By using extreme examples—a girl who left her baby in a dumpster, or a five-year-old boy who was fatally thrown off a balcony in Chicago—and posing the question of whether an orphanage wouldn't be preferable, Gingrich was trying to move the welfare debate.

In a meeting with Weber and Gingrich that went on for three hours at the Sheraton Carlton Hotel, on the day before Gingrich's *Meet the Press* appearance, William Bennett, the conservative theoretician and former "drug czar," suggested that Gingrich pivot from his talk about orphanages to talking about Boys Town. Weber said later, "If you get to the point where you've had a serious discussion of the need for orphanages, you have destroyed the standing of the welfare program. Newt used orphanages to illuminate his rejection of the existing welfare system. It highlights the worst problems of the welfare system. Conservatives believe that the heart of the welfare system is that it's encouraging out-of-wedlock births, and that those children have a lot of pathology."

Conservatives, using only partially representative images—though the facts were sobering enough—tried to draw Democrats into admitting that there might be some circumstances to which orphanages would be preferable. Ways and Means Chairman Archer drew Health and Human Services Secretary Donna Shalala into such an admission in a hearing in early January. Weber said, "It's like discussing the eight-hundred-dollar toilet seat as a metaphor for the Pentagon. [Democrats had made much mockery of such an item during the Reagan years.] There's some truth to it, but you use one striking example to make the case."

This turned out to be an only partially successful strategy. Democrats—including Shalala and Hillary Rodham Clinton—struck back, citing costs of orphanages and playing on the point that a lot of people don't want to see a child taken from a parent. In early February, Frank Luntz sent Republicans a memo saying that "orphanage" wasn't a good word to use, that "foster home" or almost any other term was preferable. In Luntz's view, based on his polling, "work" was the issue most on voters' minds. Gingrich stopped using the term "orphanage." Democrats were gleeful, feeling they'd pushed Gingrich back on this issue.

Tony Blankley said, "The 'orphanage' issue is fairly typical of the way Newt operates. He drew the contrast between a dumpster and Boys Town. 'Orphanages' is a word that communicates very well. Over time, we win the larger policy debate on welfare; it sharpens the focus on the existing program. It puts our opponents in an untenable position."

Some of Gingrich's utterances showed that he had a lively and far-ranging if not a very deep or disciplined mind. He was an unusual combination of the roughneck politician and the politician of ideas. He took himself seriously as a man of ideas, and badly wanted to be considered to have *gravitas*, but because he was glib, and he sometimes said silly things, and because his ideas were so scattershot, he wasn't taken as seriously as he would have liked. His mind hopped and skipped about, from idea to idea, snippet to snippet. He was familiar with contemporary social analyses, some of them serious, some of them problematic—and he didn't always make the distinction. No detached scholar in pursuit of objective truth, he drew on the ones that suited his political purposes. His ideas were in service to his politics. He sometimes found in these prescriptions more than was there, conferred on them excessive relevance to contemporary problems. He obviously had a high IQ, and though he did continue to read history, he wasn't the serious scholar he presented himself as. (He didn't get tenure at West Georgia College.) But he was perhaps the most imaginative person in contemporary politics, and it was in part his imagination that made him a leader.

He made new combinations of the things he saw and read. Some of his ideas about the future sounded odd, but not all of them were. Just as he thought long in politics, he thought long about the world beyond politics —and how that could affect politics. Gingrich was an unconventional politician. Many people misread what he was up to, or misgauged his prospects, because they judged him by conventional standards. Gingrich was usually thinking ahead. Not unlike his counterpart in the White House, Gingrich was eager to show off how much he knew. His presenting himself as a visionary was also part of his politics, believing as he did that the conservative party had to offer a positive vision. If some of the specific visions supported his political purposes, so much the better. As a fan of technology and the space program, Gingrich believed that certain new technological developments—in communications and in biomedical science—could transform society and, important to his politics, reduce the role of government.

Gingrich was constantly giving his audiences reading assignments. The list ranged from the Declaration of Independence to Peter Drucker's *The Effective Executive*. His bible was *The Third Wave*, by Alvin Toffler, a formulaic proposition—that the world was moving from an industrial-based society (Second Wave) to one based on technology and information and that this had profound consequences for society and government. (The First Wave was the agricultural economy.) Toffler and his wife, Heidi, who collaborated on his works, argued that Third Wave societies must be decentralized—a theory that fit Gingrich's politics.

Gingrich argued that the early expansion of the federal government had met a need of the industrial society but now those bureaucracies stifled creativity and hindered progress. Therefore, the bureaucracies and the laws, and the political forces that sustained them—from the New Deal on —should be destroyed. This, in turn, fit the political and financial interests of his party. (The Tofflers, though, did say that Republicans weren't sufficiently concerned with the dislocations caused by the Third Wave.) Gingrich wrote in a preface to a paperback recently issued by the Tofflers, "The failure to apply the Toffler Third Wave model has kept our politics trapped in frustration, negativism, cynicism, and despair."

Gingrich talked a lot about the information age and cyberspace, and was in fact one of the first politicians to understand the possibilities of new technological capabilities—just as he had been one of the first to understand the possibilities of getting one's message out, and creating a following, through C-SPAN. Combining this understanding with his understanding of the use of symbols, on the second day of the new Congress he participated in the introduction of a program, called Thomas (after Jefferson), at the Library of Congress, which put the *Congressional Record* and several other congressional proceedings on the Internet. Actually, Clinton and Gore, two other aficionados of the new technology, had in 1993 introduced in the White House an e-mail system and a program offering speeches and other government documents. But Gingrich made off with the "futurism" theme.

Another book Gingrich purveyed in order to make his point was *The Tragedy of American Compassion,* by Marvin Olasky, first published in 1992 and reissued in paperback in early 1995 after Gingrich heaped praise upon it. The book, which fit Gingrich's purposes nicely, argued that private institutions such as charities and churches had done a better job of helping people than subsequent public programs begun in the 1960s had. (Olasky overlooked the changed and enlarged clientele for such help.)

In an appearance before a conference in early January on "virtual America" convened by the Progress & Freedom Foundation, which among other things sponsored the televised college course he still taught and his weekly program on the conservative cable channel, National Empowerment Television, Gingrich gave a rambling tour of history, citing Adam Smith, de Tocqueville, and Pitt the Younger. He said, "Virtuality at the mental level is something I think you'd find in most leadership over historical periods." In an appearance before the House Ways and Means Committee on the second day of the Congress he did something characteristic. Prefacing with "I'll give you a nutty idea that I'm just tossing out"—thus taking himself off the hook—he suggested that the poor be given tax credits for purchasing laptop computers. Though the poor may have had more immediate needs, and weren't in a position to receive tax credits— and Republicans were planning to reduce other benefits—the idea wasn't as ridiculous as much of Washington pronounced it to be. Gingrich was getting at something—the need for new skills if people were to qualify for jobs that took them into the middle class. But the idea was so mocked that Gingrich, in a rare show of humility, later took it back. (Gingrich's proposal wasn't as spontaneous as he suggested: he had made a similar proposal several years ago, to an executive of a major technology company, and had been told it wasn't feasible.)

When Gingrich made a speech, his immense energy and his apparent self-confidence filled the room. He gave off energy, and the self-certainty with which he spoke cast a spell on willing believers. Others could be alarmed; some just dismissed him—which was a mistake. When Gingrich spoke, he projected more magnetism in the room than came across on the television screen. The great self-certainty was part of his power.

Sometimes he made factual mistakes—using examples of some horror or other that turned out to be inaccurate. On *Meet the Press* in December he displayed a heart pump that he said was being held up by the Food and Drug Administration. But it turned out that the Danish company that made the device hadn't applied for F.D.A. approval, and there was some question of whether the pump worked any better than other forms of resuscitation. But Gingrich was on an anti-F.D.A. crusade, and in 1995 proposed that it be abolished. Gingrich tossed out so many ideas that sometimes they got lost in the flood. A statement to the Progress & Freedom Foundation forum in early January that it was time to "transform Medicare" went largely unnoticed. Gingrich repeated the idea in a speech to the American Hospital Association three weeks later. This time, his statement got a lot of attention. Tony Blankley said that Gingrich was "more satisfied."

Overlooked in his Ways and Means testimony was an important, and ominous, Gingrich trait. In talking about a luxury tax on boats that had been passed in 1990 and then repealed in 1993 because boat builders complained that their business had been destroyed, Gingrich said that "the same socialist bureaucrats" who had been consistently wrong had been wrong again. Even when he was trying to appear the reasonable, even affable, leader, a tamed Newt, this dark side of his nature came out. If people got in his way, or needed to be got out of the way of his agenda, Gingrich would vilify them. Sometimes it seemed reflexive, at other times, especially when he felt cornered, he called upon it—and he also called upon it as a preemptive action. He dealt in terms of enemies, real and conjured. He branded his opponents as defenders of the "old order," of the "welfare state," of the "status quo." When, in late December, he announced that he would take only the one-dollar advance for his book, he said that he didn't want to give an opportunity on opening day to "the embittered defenders of the old order." He talked about "the elites" and "the pervasive cynicism in the culture of Washington."

There was a mischievousness to Gingrich, but sometimes the mischief was serious. During his sixteen years in the House before he became Speaker, he enjoyed being a troublemaker. Even after that he enjoyed lobbing a hand grenade here or there, for the sheer fun of it. Sometimes the grenades could cause real damage. He wasn't a particularly warm man, and conversation with him could seem like conversation with an act. He was lacking in social graces. At times he flashed a boyish, even cherubic, grin. Sometimes the grin was a friendly gesture; sometimes it meant real trouble. He didn't come off as a settled person; like his counterpart down Pennsylvania Avenue he seemed somewhat unmatured. Next to Gingrich, Clinton came off as the more mature figure.

Also like his counterpart, Gingrich had a powerful temper.

The many similarities between the two men—Gingrich at fifty and Clinton at forty-eight—were striking: both were bulky (Gingrich the bulkier) and brilliant political strategists; both were hard scrappers, and the engineers of their own rise to great power (no patrons); both had high intellectual powers and were interested in ideas; both came from middle-class backgrounds and dysfunctional families (including missing fathers, adoring mothers and problematic relationships with adoptive fathers) and were exemplars of the meritocracy; both were garrulous; both had to show off; both had deep flaws and histories of infidelity.

During this opening period, the story of Gingrich's book deal grew: in January it was disclosed that he had met with Murdoch in late November, and that a Murdoch regulatory problem was raised. Borrowing a page from Gingrich, a group of Democrats, led by Bonior, used the opportunity to make one-minute statements during the "morning business" period, before the House took up legislation, to attack the book deal. A circular process began, in which the more Gingrich showed that he was thin-skinned about the book—by lashing out at the Democrats during his daily pre-session televised press conferences (another innovation)—the more they poked and prodded and needled.

Though several of Gingrich's colleagues were urging him to give up the book deal—arguing that it was a distraction from the serious work of enacting the Contract, and from expounding their message of change— and letting reporters know how they felt about it, Gingrich dug in, for reasons known only to a very few people. A primary one was that Gingrich knew that the Democrats would come at him with a variety of charges, and that if they weren't focusing on the book deal they would focus on something else.

A number of questions had already been raised about the financial-political network that Gingrich had established or supervised. GOPAC, which he had headed since 1986, didn't reveal its donors until November 1994. Even then, it disclosed only twelve percent of its contributions— whereas contributions to federal candidates had to be revealed. (The *New York Times* said on December 18, 1994, that of $2 million spent by GOPAC in 1994, only $20,000 went to direct contributions to candidates.) In early October 1995, the *Washington Post* reported letters from Gingrich to potential contributors that indicated that GOPAC had become involved in campaigns for congressional seats before it was legally allowed to do so (when in 1991 it registered as a federal political action committee). The Federal Election Commission brought a suit against GOPAC in 1994, and in November 1995 it said that GOPAC had helped "support" Gingrich's 1990 race (a very close one).

The Progress & Freedom Foundation, headed by Gingrich's close ally and adviser Jeffrey Eisenach, was another conduit for contributions to Gingrich's causes, and it funded the course, "Renewing American Civilization," that Gingrich taught at Reinhardt College, in Waleska, Georgia. It also distributed (for purchase at $250) videotapes of the course. (Eisenach was a former executive director of GOPAC.) The foundation's role in the course raised the issue of whether tax-exempt funds were used for political activities. (The dean of the business school at Kennesaw College, in Gingrich's district in suburban Atlanta, where he originally taught the course until the Georgia Board of Regents withdrew permission, and Gingrich moved to the private college, told the *Los Angeles Times* later in the year that he had long believed that Gingrich's course was politically inspired.) In keeping with the intricate web these people wove, Eisenach had served as a consultant to Kennesaw College when Gingrich taught the course there. And, according to the *New York Times*, Joe Gaylord, as a highly paid consultant to GOPAC, helped establish the lecture series. Contributors to other Gingrich causes, such as GOPAC, were solicited for donations for the course. Some contributors were singled out in the course for praise. The Progress & Freedom Foundation also underwrote Gingrich's weekly call-in program on the conservative cable network, National Empowerment Television.

There were thus a number of avenues for incurring Gingrich's gratitude —and for circumventing the federal campaign finance laws.

Charges were filed with the House Ethics Committee about various Gingrich activities: his promotion of the tapes on the House floor (giving the 800 number). Bonior said, "C-SPAN isn't the Home Shopping Network." Bonior himself filed a charge concerning Gingrich's past promotion of GOPAC in speeches to the House. The committee was also looking at the donation of airtime for the course by a large cable television company, and Gingrich's promoting the course to interest groups before which he appeared. It was also examining a charge that Gingrich violated House rules when he used GOPAC and tax-exempt foundations, as well as the resources of his own congressional office, to help set up his course. Another charge before the committee was that Gingrich had improperly intervened in a regulatory matter by urging that the Food and Drug Administration approve an AIDS-testing kit, the manufacturers of which later contributed to the Progress & Freedom Foundation.

At the same time that Gingrich was giving speeches critical of the F.D.A. (as he did in 1995), the Progress & Freedom Foundation was drawing up plans to overhaul the agency—and drug companies were contributing to the Progress & Freedom Foundation. Another foundation project, called "Cyberspace and the American Dream," which advocated deregulation of telecommunications, closely paralleled Gingrich's utterances about the possibilities of the "Third Wave," and his keen interest in deregulation legislation (which was passed by the House later in the year). The foundation received contributions from corporations seeking such deregulation.

According to a close associate, Gingrich was particularly worried that if attention were drawn away from the book deal, it would turn to Joe Gaylord's role. Gingrich also felt that the matter went to his strength as Speaker. He told friends, "Am I really going to let these guys make me give in?"

Gaylord was funded by some organizations closely connected with Gingrich—including GOPAC, the National Republican Congressional Committee, Friends of Newt Gingrich, Gingrich's own campaign fund, and the Republican National Committee. House rules prohibited the use of private resources for official purposes. Beyond that, federal law prohibited the use of private funding to support official activities. Gingrich's patronage was a valuable thing. According to reports filed with the Federal Election Commission, in 1994 Gaylord earned $326,000 from various political sources, and in a conversation in the fall of 1995 he said that he expected to earn about the same amount that year, too. The top staff positions in Gingrich's office earn $122,932. A close Gingrich associate said, "Joe is really the chief of staff," and another described Gaylord as Gingrich's top adviser. (According to one Gingrich associate it was Gaylord who arranged the book deal. Gaylord denied this, but said in that same conversation that he did work with the publishers on Gingrich's subsequent book tour.) A close associate said, "Joe Gaylord has line authority for everything in Newt's life." Another said, "Gaylord has complete control over Newt's schedule" —and then he added, "along with Dan Meyer." Dan Meyer was officially Gingrich's chief of staff. Gaylord was Gingrich's chief political strategist, and was also known to chair substantive meetings on matters of interest to Gingrich. A close associate said, "Newt delegates to Joe, and Joe calls other members of Newt's staff and gives instructions. Joe sits in staff meetings where he's present and Newt is not, and the next ranking person in the room is Dan Meyer." In the conversation, Gaylord himself described his

role as, "I do his political coordination, and with someone like Newt political coordination is a huge job—from his base in Georgia through his
interactions with the various political committees." Gaylord, an amiable if
elusive figure who very rarely spoke to the press, had silvering straight
hair, a prominent, beaked nose, and closely set hazel eyes. He continued,
"I handle his out-of-Washington schedule. What he signs politically and
doesn't sign politically comes through me." Gaylord said that he also made
the calls on Gingrich appearances in Washington that were political in
nature—which was, obviously, a high proportion of them. When there was
a substantive issue that involved politics—and few didn't—Gaylord was
often in the room. Gaylord had become Gingrich's closest friend and con-
fidant following the death in 1993 of Gingrich's closest friend since high
school. One Gingrich associate said, "The core of it is Newt relies on Joe
emotionally." According to Gaylord, they usually spoke on the phone at
the beginning and end of each day. Though Gaylord officially kept an
office at the Republican National Committee, in times past he was a near-
constant presence in Gingrich's own office. In 1995, aware that eyes were
on his role, Gaylord's physical presence was reduced, but not his influence.
Gaylord's situation continued to worry some Gingrich allies.

Gingrich was especially concerned that he would face an open-ended
investigation by an independent counsel appointed by the House Ethics
Committee—just as Wright had. In January, Nancy Johnson, one of his
closest allies, was put in charge of the Ethics Committee, on which the
parties had equal representation. (Two of the five Republican members,
Porter Goss, of Florida, and Jim Bunning, of Kentucky, had connections
with GOPAC—Goss's campaign donated $5,000 to GOPAC in 1994, and
Bunning said he was the first candidate to receive a GOPAC contribution
when he ran for the Kentucky state senate in 1979.) Johnson had submitted
her resignation from the Ethics Committee in early December of 1994, but
Gingrich convinced her to go back on it.

Yet Gingrich knew that even having a friendly chairman might not be
enough to protect him from a broad inquiry. When he charged in his press
briefings that the Democrats were "out to destroy" him, he meant just that
—and he was correct. "I think a strategy based on the personal destruction
of somebody is pretty amazing," he said in one of his briefings. He was
also correct when he charged that through damaging him, the Democrats
hoped to undermine the Contract. For the time being, the Democratic side
of the Ethics Committee was willing to let the charges accumulate, hoping
that press and public pressure for the appointment of an outside investiga-
tor would build to the point that it couldn't be resisted. But Gingrich would
resist mightily.

So, for all his public bravado, by late January Gingrich was alarmed. A
close associate said, "He sees from day one of the Congress a united

Democratic Party out to destroy him. That scares him." Gingrich was frightened that the attacks on him would totally preoccupy him.

Because of Gingrich's anger and anxiety over the Democrats' attacks on the book deal, his House allies, acting on what they thought he wanted, made a big mistake. After the new Congress opened, Gingrich said to his colleagues almost daily, "Dammit, every day I'm out there I'm under attack and no one is defending me." On January 18, Carrie Meek, a black Democrat from Florida, who was using the one-minute time to attack the book deal, said, "Now more than ever before the perception of impropriety, not to mention the potential conflict of interest, still exists. . . . News accounts tell us that while the Speaker may have given up the $4.5 million advance, he stands to gain that amount and much more. That is a whole lot of dust where I come from. If anything, now how much the Speaker earns has grown more dependent upon how hard his publishing house hawks this book." Bob Walker, Gingrich's closest friend in the House, thinking he had heard Gingrich to be saying "Will no one rid me of this turbulent priest," moved to "take down"—that is, strike from the record—Meek's words. The taking down of a member's words was, of course, an archaism in the days of C-SPAN, and Walker's move guaranteed that they would be replayed many times.

Gingrich's staff realized right away that Walker had made a well-intentioned mistake. All hell broke loose on the House floor—the deep tensions on both sides erupting. Dan Meyer, Gingrich's chief of staff, went to the House floor at once, to try to calm things down. He could see a story coming on that night's television news about the book and about Democrats charging that they were being gagged. Democrats challenged the ruling of the chair that Walker's move was in order, and Republicans rolled over the challenge, showing their muscle in the roll call vote that followed.

The event was a transforming one for some House Democrats. Harold Volkmer, a sixty-three-year-old tenth-term congressman from Missouri, theretofore a nondescript figure, was suddenly yelling, as he appealed the ruling. The former almighty and until now dispirited John Dingell was on his feet bellowing: "This is not the Duma, this is not the Reichstag. This is the house of the people."

Late that afternoon, Walker, Armey, Paxon, Nussle, and some members of Gingrich's staff met to discuss what to do about the increasingly partisan and disputatious situation. There was a difference of opinion. Armey felt that they should let the Democrats keep pushing, let things get totally out of hand, and then clamp down hard. The Democrats were already using the opportunity handed them by the Republicans, use of the "open rule," under which legislation was brought to the floor without any limits on amendments—Republicans wanted to show how different they were from their predecessors—to hold up legislation. Walker disagreed, arguing that he didn't come to the majority to invoke the same "tyranny of the majority" that Republicans had suffered under. Walker was also concerned about the idea of letting the Democrats have their head for a while so that it wouldn't look as if the Republican leaders were "gagging" the House. Walker said in an interview later, "My problem with that is that you encourage people to be more and more outrageous and in violation of the rules." The decision was to defuse the situation, bite their tongues, and see where the Democrats were headed. The story was, of course, on the television news that night.

The brouhaha on the House floor had lingering effects. Some members, such as Volkmer, remained angry and, as in his case, felt liberated—and from then on often rose to challenge the Republican leadership. Weber said, "They really made a mistake in response to Carrie Meek. They fell into exactly the trap that we hoped every day the Democrats would fall into when they were the majority."

The outbreak over the book was the first of two reverses in what turned out to be a bad week for Gingrich and his aides. Gingrich himself made the second mistake. At a meeting in his office on Friday morning, the twentieth, he and his advisers discussed the speech he would give later that day to the Republican National Committee, which was meeting in Washington. All of them—including Gingrich but with the exception of Gaylord—agreed that the speech should be about the Contract, that Gingrich should stay away from the subject of the Democrats' attacks on him, especially on the book deal. But then Gingrich went before the R.N.C. and gave an angry speech. A friend said, "He went into that speech and lost control, frankly." Gingrich struck out at this target and that. He sniped at Mrs. Clinton's having made a large profit in cattle futures and at Jim Wright ("Jim Wright was a crook").

At times in the speech to the R.N.C. his face seemed filled with hate, the anger deep—the cherubic smile was gone. Gingrich could be disciplined —as the long march showed—but there was a streak of irresponsibility that worried his friends. There was also the brawler in him, the alley fighter. Gingrich liked to tell friends that his natural father was a barroom brawler; he would describe him as a big man who got into barroom fights that his mother would have to stop. (His mother left his father after three days of marriage, and before Gingrich was born.)

A House Democrat who requested anonymity but was one of the more fair-minded members, remarked on Gingrich's seemingly dual personality. He said, "All of us have the state and the private modes but with him it's more dramatic. In previous years he was following the Vietnam 'burn the village in order to save it' strategy, or calling in the artillery even if you took out some of your own people. The military metaphors come easily about him. There's something sociopathic. I don't use it casually. The attributes of that personality are intelligence and charm and a fundamentally amoral willingness to use whatever mechanisms, including amoral ones, that are expedient to get the job done. Expedience and opportunism. As compelling as his rhetoric is about matters of principle, I just mistrust what's really there."

Gingrich's staff—especially Meyer and Blankley—were very down by the end of the third week in January. They felt that two big mistakes had been made. They felt that there was no system for getting the right decisions made and carried out, that they had given the right advice about the speech and now were taking the heat for how it had turned out, that they had lost control of the agenda, were set back in their plans. Gingrich was outwardly unrepentant.

Other events created material for ridiculing Gingrich. A tape of one of his classes at Reinhardt College, in which he said that women couldn't stay in trenches for more than thirty days because they got "infections" and men weren't good at sitting in an office because "males are biologically driven to go out and hunt giraffes," was circulated by, among others, the White House, and gave the Democrats useful material for one-minute statements. Gingrich was actually talking about the role of women in the military, but, per habit, he wasn't disciplined in what he was saying, and let his fertile mind and desire to show off take him down some strange paths.

Gingrich dealt quickly enough with the problem of having hired as House historian Christina Jeffrey, who had, as consultant to the Department of Education, criticized a junior high school curriculum on the Holocaust on the grounds it didn't reflect "the Nazi point of view." The issue didn't have much staying power because Gingrich fired her the same day that the memo was revealed. Jeffrey insisted later that Gingrich had known about her controversial comments—which had been the subject of a congressional hearing in 1988—and said that she had told Gingrich's staff about them in December.

Gingrich's extraordinary hold on his Republican flock stemmed from both his pragmatism and his ruthlessness. He listened, but he could also punish. His lieutenants were less flexible. Armey was a large, friendly, beefy man with a deep, sonorous voice who favored cowboy boots and aphorisms. ("The market is rational and the government is dumb.") Like Gingrich, Armey had been a professor at a small college—Austin College in Sherman, Texas. Armey was the true ideologue. A colleague said, "Dick's not manipulative. He just doesn't want to compromise." A key Armey staff member was Virginia Thomas, wife of Supreme Court Justice Clarence Thomas, herself a strong conservative. Armey wasn't complicated; he was known for being blunt to a fault. He turned out to be an able legislator and majority leader, carrying a heavy burden for Gingrich—which Gingrich appreciated. He appreciated people who could make things happen.

DeLay had nosed out Gingrich's close friend Walker for whip by raising a lot of money and campaigning for the 1994 challengers—to the point of hiring someone just to look after their campaign needs. DeLay said in an interview, "I wanted them to think of me as their brother." And most of the grateful incoming freshmen backed him for whip. DeLay—short, compact, with slicked black hair, a big laugh, and a mean streak—said that Gingrich had remained neutral in the leadership race because DeLay had been part of the leadership team before (he had plotted the rejection of the Bush budget agreement), because he was very partisan, and, DeLay said, with a laugh, "he knew that I make a terrible enemy."

A Gingrich ally said that Gingrich would have preferred Walker, and let people know that, but didn't work on Walker's behalf because "it would have taken a lot of his political capital." DeLay and Gingrich had a somewhat edgy relationship: DeLay had worked for Gingrich's opponent in the whip race, knew that Gingrich preferred someone else to be his own whip, and considered Gingrich to be not as conservative as he should be.

Armey was perhaps the most ideological of the three leaders, and he would often weigh in when Gingrich sought to compromise to keep order among his troops—and to secure enough votes. One moderate said, "You can talk to Newt. He'll listen. Talking to Armey and DeLay is like talking to a wall." Gingrich made a point of attending with some frequency the "Tuesday Lunch Bunch" of Republican moderates, and hearing them out. Gingrich had to pay attention to the moderates, who numbered about forty, because of his twelve-vote margin. Often, however, the moderates had to settle for much less than they had asked, something that fell short of even "face-saving." They developed various ways of rationalizing this.

Gingrich's modest-sounding motto was "Listen, learn, help, and lead," and though he sometimes followed it, he also from time to time reminded members of his power over them. When, in early February, Charles Taylor, a Republican from North Carolina, appealed a ruling issued by Gingrich from the chair, and in a vote on the appeal fourteen Republicans didn't support Gingrich, they heard forthwith from Gingrich, Armey, DeLay, Livingston, and some of Gingrich's staff. "You're voting the wrong way," the errant Republicans were told. At one point when there appeared to be twenty Republicans prepared to buck the Speaker, some were told, on the spot, that this was a "career-breaking vote"—that they could lose their committee or subcommittee chairmanship. Appropriations Committee Chairman Bob Livingston got involved because a few of the heretics were on his committee.

A leadership aide said later, "We can control that committee pretty well, and Livingston will help us. If any of them want something spent on, or an appointment, or other rooms, they'll be at the end of the line." The aide said, "It was so serious that the day after the vote, the Steering Committee —which made appointments to the standing committees—met to discuss whether subcommittee chairmen who balked at the Speaker's ruling should have their positions threatened." Gingrich himself warned the apostates against any repetition of their action. The aide said, "It was made clear that you're only granted one mistake, and some individuals will be treated with disfavor from now on." One member was denied an appointment to a board, as well as a place on a conference committee to iron out legislative differences between the House and the Senate on a particular bill.

Gingrich was a listener, and he delegated a lot to Armey, but there was no doubt as to who was in charge of the House.

4

THE SECOND TRANSITION

"I'm Talking to the Smartest People I Know"

The first meeting between the President and the bipartisan leaders of the new Congress, in the Cabinet room on January 5, was largely ceremonial, but it also portended some things to come. Gingrich, sitting to the President's right, was all cordiality. He talked of wanting to make the relationship with the White House work, saying that he thought there was a window of opportunity before the politics of 1996 took over. "The people want results," he added. The President, similarly eager to display a cooperative spirit, told the Republican leaders that he was willing to sign bills making Congress live under the same laws that the private sector had to, giving the President the line-item veto, and limiting unfunded mandates.

The blunt-spoken Armey (in 1993 he told Clinton that his economic program would make him a one-term President) said he appreciated the courtesy shown by the President and the House Democratic leadership, given the "disastrous" results in November. He praised them for "coping" with it so well. Tom DeLay, complaining that the administration had issued 1,700 regulations since the election, proposed a moratorium on new regulations—which was rejected by the President and Panetta. Panetta said that a six-month moratorium during the Bush administration had created havoc and was more expensive than not doing so. Gingrich suggested that they try to work something out. Vice President Al Gore said that perhaps they could work together on the regulatory reforms he was making in his Reinventing Government project. The Republicans were seeking far more than that. Dole, seated on Clinton's left, talked about the importance of bipartisanship in foreign policy—of speaking with one voice—even though he had already introduced legislation to overturn some administration policies.

The White House was still feeling its way along in the new situation. Panetta recalled, "The thing that told us that drawing the line on Congress would give us momentum was the issue over national service." In mid-January, on Martin Luther King's birthday, Clinton, speaking in Denver, blasted Gingrich for his recent criticism of the national service program—probably the one closest to the President's heart. (Gingrich said it wasn't a "volunteer" program, but it was "coerced volunteerism . . . a gimmick," because the volunteers were paid.) That same day, White House aides quickly laid on a press conference, featuring national service workers. While this seemed a bit of overkill, the President's advisers took note of the fact that, as one aide put it, "The President got more press on this issue than he does signing a bill into law." He added, "It was clear that the press and the public were interested in the fight, that if we picked our fights we could get attention."

But it was to be a long time before the White House truly broke through and captured public attention on its differences with the Republican Congress.

The complexity of the relationship between Gingrich and Clinton stemmed from the fact that each had conflicting imperatives, and they had a mutual imperative. Both had to show that they stuck to principles, and both had to show that they could get things done. In Gingrich's case, he had to thread his way between the views of his most avid and ideological troops —particularly the freshmen—and the necessities of reaching agreement with both the less-ideological Senate Republicans and, on certain issues, with Clinton. The Contract was the wish list of the most conservative wing of his party. Not every bill could be something that Clinton was sure to veto. Gingrich had to show results.

And so did Clinton. His task was complex because he had yet to demonstrate to many Americans that he *had* principles. Both Gingrich and Clinton made more purring noises at the beginning than their conflicting positions might have suggested. Gingrich had to demonstrate that he wasn't simply a narrow partisan. For this reason, Gingrich, like Dole, immediately agreed to Clinton's request, in a White House meeting on January 12, for support of action to provide a $40 billion loan guarantee to strengthen the Mexican peso, which was quickly losing value, threatening Mexico's economic and political stability. The peso matter was one of those issues that imposes itself on the agenda, distracting leaders' time and attention. Though in the meeting Gingrich took the only position he thought he could, he did foresee problems on Capitol Hill, and he asked a number of specific questions. He also suggested that Federal Reserve Board Chairman Alan Greenspan, who was at the meeting, call Rush Limbaugh to explain the necessity for this action. (Greenspan complied.) Later, when the White House wanted to work directly with Jim Leach, of Iowa, the chairman of the House Banking Committee, on the issue, Gingrich made it clear that the work was to be done with *him*. Similarly, when the President in January sought to meet with some House Republican moderates, Gingrich told the members that he didn't want to see that happen during the first Hundred Days.

In January, Panetta went to Capitol Hill to see Dole and Gingrich. Gingrich told him that he thought it was in their mutual interest to work together on some issues, that they both needed to pass things rather than produce gridlock, that he and the President were in the same boat.

Because of the competing imperatives, Panetta said later, "The President felt that it wouldn't make a lot of sense to confront them right off the bat —that we should see if there weren't places where we could work out legislation, recognizing that there would be points of combat later." Clinton and Gingrich had to show the voters that Washington wasn't simply a battleground, where there were no clear outcomes.

In his floundering around for a new definition of his Presidency, Clinton reached in a lot of directions. Clinton, his wife, and Gore spent a lot of time talking in the White House residence about what to do. Gore's political life was every bit as much on the line as Clinton's, and this Vice President, who already had more influence than any in history, was to take an even more aggressive role in the overhaul of the Clinton Presidency.

All three decided that the President needed some new advisers—that the current ones, in the White House and out, had failed him. In January, the Clintons reached for some motivational gurus, whom—to the embarrassment of some of the staff—they invited to Camp David. They also convened there on Saturday, January 14, a seminar with social scientists, political thinkers, and historians. The list was drawn up by Bill Galston, a White House aide formerly associated with the Democratic Leadership Council (D.L.C.), the centrist Democratic group which Clinton had helped found, and which was now vying for a greater voice in his Presidency. At that Camp David meeting there was much talk about the need to rebuild "our civil life." One of those who attended the Camp David meeting was Robert Putnam, the director of Harvard's Center for International Affairs, who had recently published an article called "Bowling Alone," which said that people were bowling more than ever, but not in teams. It was said at the Camp David meeting that another sign that civil society was breaking down was that the P.T.A. was declining as a force. There was a lot of talk about the need for Clinton to move from legislator to President. Clinton, who, like his wife, remained largely quiet throughout the meeting, did refer to a time "back then when I was legislator in chief." Some of the Camp David talk was to turn up in Clinton's next State of the Union address.

Clinton was in effect going through his Second Transition. In the first one, mistakes were made—such as the belated selection of the White House staff, with a preference for inexperience—that haunted Clinton's first two years. In the Second Transition, he had to prepare for leadership in a dramatically new climate, and establish his Presidentialness. The President, his wife, and his staff understood that the loss of stature that he had both endured and helped bring about in his first two years was now his deepest problem. Further, surveys indicated that the public didn't see Clinton as a moral leader who reflected its values. And first impressions, reinforced over two years, were hard to erase. That was Clinton's biggest challenge. It was recognized at the White House that the fact that Congress had changed hands could make it easier for Clinton to extricate himself from the role of legislator in chief, which he and many of his advisers belatedly saw as one of his problems. Now it wouldn't be for him to struggle, lobby, and wheedle for passage of his own legislative initiatives but to respond to those coming from the Republican Congress, entering in negotiations on some.

Freed from having a Congress to try to enact things through, he had an opportunity to say clearly what he was about. Panetta said, "The bright light that came out of the darkness was the opportunity to define ourselves." The question was whether Clinton could define himself, and whether he could stick to it. So the election was both a repudiation of Clinton and potentially his liberation.

There was never much question that in the second half of his term Clinton would "go back to the center" in order to recapture the identity that might help him get reelected. But in a long—nearly five-hour—political meeting held in January in the first-floor Map Room of the White House residence, attended by the President and his wife, Al and Tipper Gore, and several political advisers, including Cabinet officers who had been in politics, one conclusion reached was that Clinton had to nurture the liberal base of the party. It was agreed that the base's low level of enthusiasm (and turnout) had defeated New York Governor Mario Cuomo for reelection in November. Therefore, "the base" had to be enthused as it watched Clinton move away from it. Another conclusion was that the Republicans had succeeded because they had gone back to what Gore termed original principles, that Gingrich the history student in particular seemed to have a way of putting present battles into historical context, making them battles over principles, even if they were really about feeding the lobbyists.

Clinton faced dual pressures—just as he had in the campaign and in the first two years of his Presidency—leading to a confusion as to who he was. The battle over Clinton's identity continued between his advisers, such as George Stephanopoulos, his thirty-four-year-old close adviser, and Harold Ickes, deputy chief of staff in charge of Clinton's reelection efforts, who came out of traditional Democratic politics, and those, such as Al From, the president of the D.L.C., White House aide Galston, and chief speech-writer Don Baer, who saw moving to the center as Clinton's only chance for reelection. Stephanopoulos, who used to work on Capitol Hill, was seen by some of Clinton's more centrist advisers as too close to the congressional view, and as reflecting Old Democratic politics. Panetta, a former congressman, wasn't long on vision, and, anyway, Clinton was down on Panetta. Following the election, former Representative Dave McCurdy, who had gone down to defeat in Oklahoma, told Clinton in a harsh Oval Office meeting that he should fire Stephanopoulos. Al From gave similar advice. But Stephanopoulos was valuable to Clinton because he was smart and could read Clinton's mind and foresee the political impact of various actions.

Since the election, unbeknownst to almost all of his staff, Clinton had been conferring regularly with Richard Morris, a political consultant who had engineered Clinton's gubernatorial comeback in 1980 (he had advised Clinton even before that, but the two had had a falling out). Morris had continued to advise Clinton through the 1980s as Clinton was developing his theories of how a progressive Democrat could govern in a Southern state, or could win the Presidency. In recent years, Morris had advised Republicans, including Trent Lott in his 1988 and 1994 Senate campaigns. Still, both Clinton and his wife associated Morris with Clinton's salvation in 1980 and now Clinton was more than ever in need of salvation.

Clinton and Morris had met eight or nine times during Clinton's first two years in the White House (in the residence, so that Morris wouldn't be spotted) and they spoke a few times on the phone. Morris said in an interview that a week before the election he told Clinton that the Democrats would lose both the Senate and the House. Clinton had phoned Morris after returning from a trip to the Middle East. Morris said, "I told him, 'Your ratings are up, go back abroad.' I meant he should work Presidential issues." Clinton's response was that since his ratings were up, he could go out and campaign for Democrats—several of whom had made it clear that they wouldn't mind if he didn't show up for them. Morris said that after the 1994 election "the relationship accelerated."

Later, Morris said that his interpretation to Clinton of the election when they spoke shortly afterward was that "the cosmic reason for the outcome was not that he had failed but because he had succeeded and used up his mandate." Morris explained, "This happens to people in other political jobs." He pointed out that Winston Churchill was turned out of office after winning the Second World War; that after Lyndon Johnson got the Great Society enacted he was turned out over Vietnam; that Nixon ended the Vietnam War and fell over Watergate; that Carter restored the integrity of the office of Presidency and then fell over the hostages in Iran; Bush won the Gulf War but had little to say about domestic economic problems. Similarly, in Morris's view, Clinton "ended the recession and then was faced with second-tier issues."

Morris, at forty-seven, fast-talking and cocksure, had straight brown hair that stood up, a flattish face and a large mouth, and he came across as having few doubts. He also had a quick mind, and he was a salesman. He wove multiple and elaborate theories, some of which didn't seem to hold much water, and seemed to believe in every one of them. His little history lesson had some truths and some stretches, but he offered it forcefully, in his machine-gun way of speaking. He seemed to share the Clintonian confidence that he could talk his way past most anything, and convince people of what he said.

On a less cosmic level, Morris believed that a large number of House Democrats were defeated in 1994 because so many of them were relatively new, having replaced senior members who had retired—over the House bank scandal or for other reasons. To explain this, Morris used the image of oaks (the senior members) and saplings (the recently elected ones who had an opportunity to grow). Morris favored metaphors—especially ones about rugs and football.

Another reason for the outcome, Morris said, was that while Clinton had won the Presidency with forty-three percent of the vote, the Democratic candidates in 1994 had to win fifty-one percent of the vote, in an off-year election when the turnout is often low "and the people who don't turn out are Democrats."

And then Morris mentioned the theory for which he soon became known, that "Clinton became too oriented toward traditional Democrats." Clinton embraced this theory—that the problem was that he had too much accepted the dictates of the Democratic congressional leaders. It was a convenient theory. Morris said that when Clinton first met with the Democratic congressional leaders (after the 1992 election, in Little Rock), "his worry at that point was that he'd be marginalized by the Congress." Morris continued, "When he found that Foley and Mitchell were willing to block for him, help him, he was delighted and relieved. They were loyal to him, but this scrambler, this intuitive, imaginative player became dependent on them, and he was in the pocket, throwing balls. In this process, he didn't realize at the time that the majority on which he depended would be more and more tenuous as various groups in the Democratic caucus had to be appeased. Because the Republicans gave him total opposition, he had to govern with only Democratic votes, and as he tried to get every last vote on the Democratic side he was pulled to the left." Morris also pointed out that because of the Republicans' frequent use of the filibuster, Clinton needed to get sixty votes in the Senate for almost everything of significance —"something he hadn't expected."

Concluded Morris, "When a candidate becomes dependent on a congressional base he becomes their hostage."

Morris's prescription was that Clinton had to get back to the center, and find his voice: "He needed to reach down in himself and find his own approach, his own style." More effort toward this end went on in the ensuing months than people generally realized. Morris said later, "The core idea was that he needed to take back control of his Presidency himself, to be able to guide more according to his own views than the consensus of the Democratic Party. It was terribly important for him to articulate his core ideas, which were different from the orthodox Democratic view or the orthodox Republican view. He needed to become a third force."

Clinton knew Morris well enough that, in reaching for him, he was aware of what sort of advice he would receive. Morris understood the neither-left-nor-right, "third way" politics that Clinton had been searching for and sometimes had practiced. He understood post-Perot politics. According to Mike McCurry, Clinton's press secretary, Morris "has a window on the angry white male." Shortly after the election, Clinton asked Morris to conduct some polls for him (which Morris did through the polling firm Penn & Schoen, with which he was closely connected). Clinton felt that his advisers in the White House and some on the outside had pulled him too far left, and he realized that his approach to the 1994 campaign—mainly charging that the Republicans would cut Social Security and Medicare—reeked of "old politics." Morris's role, besides helping Clinton get back to the center, was to bring more of a strategic sense to a White House that tended to think in terms of day-to-day tactics. McCurry likened him to the late Lee Atwater—Morris's hero—the pugnacious Republican strategist who had a talent for spotting the big issues (usually negative ones) that would move people. According to another White House aide, Morris was "willing to accept a lot of cost" to Clinton for going in some new direction if he thought that the President's new position would help him politically. "He's very up-front about it," this aide said. "He believes that issues drive it." One of the costs could be a reinforcement of the impression that Clinton didn't have fixed views.

A friend of the Clintons' said that they had a pattern of reaching for people as their saviors—David Gergen, Ira Magaziner. This friend said,

"They're always looking for someone who can save them rather than trying to understand the ambiguity. Dick Morris is just the latest of them." It was a sign of Mrs. Clinton's ultimate pragmatism where her husband's career was concerned that, whatever her own political views, she concurred in calling in the centrist—or perhaps someone with no political views at all —who could help the cause. (Just as she had concurred in calling in David Gergen in 1993.) In early 1995 Clinton told an aide, "My first two years here, I was totally absorbed in getting legislation passed. I totally neglected how to get the public informed. It was my fault and I have to get more involved in crafting my message—in getting across my core concerns. Now I'm talking to the smartest people I know." Clinton wanted help with his message and his politics; he wanted people who could think strategically.

Another person Clinton started calling not long after the 1994 election was Bill Curry, former state comptroller of Connecticut who ran unsuccessfully for governor in 1994 and whom the Clintons had known since 1992. The Clintons made two trips to Connecticut during the 1994 campaign, and Mrs. Clinton was said to have been particularly impressed with Curry. In 1992 Curry had thought that Clinton represented the best hope for refashioning the new Democratic Party, and he endorsed him. Like a number of people at the time, Curry was attracted by the fact that Clinton was serious-minded enough to have read the literature on contemporary problems, and could discuss them in some depth. After the 1994 debacle, Clinton urged Curry to talk to Morris, who, as it happened, had advised Curry's primary opponent in his race for the governorship—but the two men had been in touch after that. They didn't get into serious conversations until the President suggested that they do so. Morris and Curry shared the view that a large part of what had gone wrong in Clinton's first two years was the result of taking too much heed of the liberal Democratic Congress. This view was to have large consequences.

Morris and Curry were to play a major but clandestine role in the crafting of Clinton's 1995 State of the Union speech—the first of a series of collaborations.

Clinton's lengthy (an hour and thirty-one minutes) but effective State of the Union speech on January 24, his third, reflected the growing influence of the centrists around Clinton, and of Morris's encouraging him to "wing it" when he felt like it. Clinton was "a verbal guy," Morris said with considerable understatement. Inviting Clinton to wing it was courting trouble at the same time that it might liberate him. Trouble accepted the invitation in his State of the Union speech.

Some parts of the speech were written through the normal staff procedures. Then, on the day of the speech, the Clintons added material Al From had sent the White House that morning, in response to a draft of the speech he had seen the night before. From's addition resuscitated the "New Covenant" theme that Clinton had used some in his campaign, but little in his Presidency. Speechwriter Don Baer was also a strong advocate of reviving the New Covenant. And then material from Morris and Curry was added. Their contribution was mainly visionary talk at the beginning of the speech about the challenges other Presidents had faced, what had been accomplished in the Clinton Presidency, where he hoped to see the Presidency go, and the need to "forge a new social compact."

It wasn't unusual for the Clintons to edit and rewrite a major Presidential speech almost up to the moment it was to be given. But what was unusual was for them to add whole globs of copy seemingly from nowhere. Virtually no one on the White House staff knew the origin of the Morris-Curry material. Panetta told reporters that the Clintons themselves had lengthened the speech. And Clinton lengthened it further in his delivery of it, interpolating numerous remarks. Morris said later that almost half the speech was extemporaneous.

The New Covenant theme—the idea that with opportunity came responsibility—had grown out of Clinton's involvement with the D.L.C. The New Covenant was associated with the most successful period of Clinton's political life, his Presidential campaign. But it never really captured public imagination. Still, it now offered not only a much-needed retouching of Clinton's political identity, but also a response to the Contract with America.

The term "New Covenant" had hardly appeared since Clinton's acceptance speech in 1992. Many of his aides thought it a clunker, and it was hard to explain. But nothing else seemed to work. (An aide looked up the number of times during his Presidency that Clinton had used the term: he found two.) In the new political climate, it was a way to set himself apart from both liberals and Gingrichites. It fit Clinton's position that not all government is bad, and also said that government shouldn't indulge the people it was helping. In this, as had happened in the past (on his economic program), Clinton had a more complex case to make than his opponents did, one that was harder to get across.

Clinton made several attempts in his State of the Union speech to show that he was in the mainstream. He pointed out that because of reductions made through Gore's Reinventing Government program and other efforts, "We will have cut a total of more than a quarter of a million positions from the federal government, making it the smallest it has been since John Kennedy was President." Though Clinton had made this point many times, it didn't seem to seep into the nation's consciousness.

Addressing the Republican drive to turn over many programs to the states, Clinton said, "Let us remember that there are certain fundamental national needs that should be addressed in every state." Whether this would be recognized and whether Clinton would fight for this principle were among the biggest questions of 1995.

He touched on some popular issues—immigration and terrorism, such as the foreign-bred attack on the World Trade Center, in February 1993—promising legislation on both subjects. Aware that a common interpretation of the 1994 election was that it was a rejection of the status quo, he called for reform in the campaign finance and lobbying disclosure laws—subjects to which he had given little attention in his first two years.

He made only one explicit veto threat: to not allow the repeal of the ban on assault weapons passed the year before. This was by design; the idea was to avoid a list, with people asking why this or that wasn't on it. So he picked one of the more popular issues. He also said that he would fight for continuance of the national service program. He did say that he would oppose a Republican tax cut if it didn't "build the middle class and shrink the underclass." He pushed his own "Middle Class Bill of Rights," first unveiled in the December Oval Office speech, to provide tax deductions for all education and training after high school, and permit withdrawal tax-free from I.R.A.'s for education, health care, first-time home buying, or caring for a parent. It also would offer retraining vouchers for laid-off workers, which had been the subject of a long dispute within his administration. Clinton also proposed an increase in the minimum wage. This wasn't expected to be passed by the Republican Congress, but it was expected to be good politics.

The two apologies in the State of the Union speech about having "made mistakes" in the first two years of his Presidency were at least one too many. There was a lot of talk about values and society, which bordered on making the speech a mishmash—there was even some Newtonian talk about "moving from the industrial age to the information age." Clinton's prescription for meeting the new political situation contained a swipe at the Republicans: the government, he said, should be "leaner, not meaner." Clinton alternatively took such swipes and spoke earnestly of his desire to work with the Republican Congress. Saying that "government still has important responsibilities," Clinton, perhaps inescapably, went into a long list of programs he felt were worth preserving. This section of the speech also reflected a sense of what the Capitol Hill Democrats wanted to hear. (During his speech, Republican freshmen waved copies of the Contract, like Little Red Books.)

White House aides said that Clinton understood that if his new approach was to be effective, he would have to be consistent—the themes he enunciated in his State of the Union speech would have to be repeated. They said that from then on all of his public appearances would be tied to his efforts to do more for the middle class. But, as before, between events intervening—such as the Mexican peso crisis—and Clinton's lack of discipline, there was less consistency than had been hoped for. Early in the year a three-part test was applied to any potential Presidential public event: does it show the President as a reformer, as addressing middle-class interests, and looking like a leader—a "stature event"? Asked in mid-February what had happened to that approach, a Presidential adviser replied, "Time passed."

After a long personal search, Mrs. Clinton took up a role far less public, and far less publicly political, than before, and more heavily laced with traditional activities of a First Lady—showing off the redecorated Blue Room, lunching with the food editor of the *Washington Post*. It was definitely decided that she wouldn't head any more legislative efforts, as she had on health care. She would take on relatively uncontroversial issues, such as women's health (she pushed mammograms) and children. A little later, she took an interest in the "Gulf War Syndrome," the mysterious disease suffered by Gulf War veterans. And she took a highly admired trip to South Asia, with her daughter, Chelsea, along. But, behind the scenes, Mrs. Clinton was still very much a force in policy deliberations—not only on the State of the Union but also key policy questions and, as before, any important political or personnel decisions. In part as a result of this, and of her insistence on diversity, a number of White House and other political jobs, open or known for months to be coming open, remained unfilled in the opening months of 1995.

The election, and the Clintons' angry reaction to it, played a large role in Clinton's first decisions on his 1995 budget, in which he walked away from his earlier commitment to reduce the deficit. His successful effort to do that was widely considered his biggest achievement in the first two years. Now Clinton and his wife had lost interest. In a key meeting on the subject in early December 1994, not long before the President's December 15 Oval Office speech, both Clintons expressed the view that the President hadn't received credit for his earlier successful effort to reduce the deficit by $500 billion, so why bother? The President said angrily, with his wife concurring, that this is one of those times when you see that good government is bad politics.

Clinton's budget, unveiled on February 6, was touted by his aides as representing clever politics—let Congress cut such politically loaded programs as Medicare, veterans' benefits, and agriculture programs. A senior White House official said, "It was better to let *them* take on their constituencies, since they kicked the hell out of us on our five hundred billion." Another said, "The decision was made not to cut Medicare, because we knew that they would have to."

Perhaps the President's proposal was clever short-term politics, but in giving up the pursuit of ever-lower deficits, Clinton surrendered the high ground he had attained, with great effort, in 1993. Going after the deficit had shown character, and Clinton now needed all the character credits he could lay his hands on.

In the 1994 campaign Clinton not only didn't receive credit for his deficit-reduction program, but was battered for having proposed tax increases —according to the Republicans, "the biggest tax increase in history." (This was an arguable point: the program signed in 1982 by Reagan was larger.) Though most of the 1993 Clinton plan's tax increases were on the wealthiest one percent of the public, plus a small increase in the gasoline tax, and tax increases made up only about half the deficit reduction, the Republicans, to the President's great frustration, had won the rhetorical battle. This was to affect the President's thinking in the ensuing months. A senior White House official said, "If you get serious about raising revenue, you lean into mortgage deductions. Having fought that battle of deficit reduction, including tax increases, before, there's not much interest in going through that again."

Some of the President's advisers shared this view. But others—including Panetta and Alice Rivlin, Panetta's successor as director of the Office of Management and Budget—felt that he should continue on the deficit-reduction path. But Panetta didn't say much about this in the meetings on the subject, and was cautious about taking bold deficit-reduction steps. Rivlin argued strongly, and virtually alone, for not proceeding with the tax cuts, and for continuing on the deficit reduction path. She told the President that through genuine courage he had made some real changes in the budget and that he *would* get credit for it, and that he shouldn't walk away from such an important theme. She argued that the tax cuts would make little economic difference to the recipients but would have real consequences on the deficit. Her arguments were brushed aside by Stephanopoulos.

Some other advisers encouraged Rivlin in her resistance to the tax cuts, but left her out there alone. This reticence was a result both of fatigue and of the President's and his wife's anger. A Presidential adviser said at the time, "In this atmosphere, it's fairly hard for contrarian views to be raised." One troubled senior official said to another, "There's no point in opposing this. But if you want to, you can." According to an official, Mrs. Clinton's mood "took the form of iciness and even anger at things said around the table. She may not have meant it to sound as harsh as it did. But the result was that the atmosphere was more intimidating than in the health care meetings."

An incident in the election campaign itself had fed Clinton's new inclination. He was thrown on the defensive by a memorandum by Rivlin that had leaked to the public in late October 1994, laying out the President's options for further deficit reduction. It included tax increases, limiting mortgage deductions, capping Social Security for wealthier recipients, and cuts in Medicare—all very sensitive issues. The President argued that the memo didn't reflect policy, and that he ruled out increases in taxes on Social Security or Medicare cuts, except in the context of health care reform. A Clinton adviser said, "He got dug in at that point." Clinton's new budget, which, while making some cuts, came out with deficits of about $200 billion projected until the end of the century, reflected Clinton's and his wife's view that his earlier efforts hadn't been appreciated.

While the decision to abandon the deficit reduction path was justified later by advisers who pointed out that the deficit was now 2.5 percent of the Gross Domestic Product, a manageable level, down from about five percent when Clinton took office—an argument that had been made internally as well—and there was some concern that further deficit reduction risked a contraction of the economy, the ultimate decision was a political one. The new terminology was that the deficit was "under control."

The issue of whether to pursue further deficit reduction was essentially settled when it was decided, in early December, to go for tax cuts for the middle class, as proposed by Clinton in his Oval Office address.

The political argument, made in White House meetings principally by Stephanopoulos, was that the Republicans would pocket any controversial spending cuts, such as in Medicare—the fastest-growing entitlement program in the budget—that the President put on the table, and then Clinton both wouldn't get credit for the cut and couldn't attack the Republicans for cutting Medicare. This was one of the main reasons no new health care proposal was put forward by the administration. Another was the power of the elderly. A Presidential adviser said that "seniors" make up twenty percent of the electorate, and in 1992 had given Clinton his highest margin of any age group, but in 1994 had significantly swung toward Republicans, splitting their vote evenly between the two parties. Seniors had come out against Clinton's health care proposal in 1993—a big blow. In his State of the Union speech, the President conceded that in the health care proposal he and his wife had put forward in the previous Congress they "bit off more than we could chew," and when the new budget was released, officials said that any reductions in Medicare would have to be in the context of health care reform. But if they proposed a new reform with Medicare cuts, it was argued internally, the Republicans would take the cuts and not do health care reform. Therefore, no health care reform—and no cuts in Medicare—would be proposed.

In the budget discussions, Rivlin also raised the possibility of abolishing some Cabinet departments—the Departments of Transportation, of Housing and Urban Development, and of Energy were put before the President —but, said a colleague, "You tend to get shouted down with that proposal." Those who sympathized with the idea understood that it wouldn't necessarily save a great deal of money—that some programs would simply have to be shifted to other departments—but they argued that this would be an important symbolic move. (At the last minute, HUD Secretary Henry Cisneros fought off a proposal to abolish his department by offering to radically strip it down.) The only agency of even minimal significance Clinton ended up proposing to abolish was the Interstate Commerce Commission. A Clinton adviser said, "The President has flashes of intuitive brilliance—he can jump to an understanding of things, and articulate it. But he doesn't organize his thinking in a way that looks at big alternatives. You can't take them to him. It gets dismissed out of hand."

The President also walked away from the opportunity to cut the deficit by taking slices out of what Labor Secretary Robert Reich had termed in a speech in late November "corporate welfare." Reich was referring to the various subsidies to business through entitlements (agriculture) and other spending programs and through the tax code. The term caught on. The numerous items that fell in this category had been spelled out in a report, issued in early 1994, by Robert Shapiro, an associate of the Progressive Policy Institute, the research arm of the D.L.C. Shapiro pointed out sixty-eight such subsidies, and proposed reductions and reforms that would yield $225 billion over five years. He proposed that proceeds of the cuts go both to "investment" in government programs, such as education and training, and private investment. This "cut-and-invest" proposal was along the lines of part of Clinton's 1993 economic plan, but this time it would draw heavily for funds on government subsidies of the private sector. Reich, who was making a series of speeches on what he termed "the anxious class" (the middle class), argued that the wage-earning differential between those with education and training and those without it was growing wider and wider, threatening "a split society."

Clinton was intrigued by the idea of further steps in the cut-and-invest approach, talked about it a lot privately, and also mentioned the possibility not only in a speech to the D.L.C. in early December, but also in his State of the Union address, in which he said that he would offer cuts in "special interest subsidies."

But by the time of the State of the Union speech the subject was essentially moot. In the end the President balked, because half of the subsidies came through tax breaks and he feared that any elimination of those would be treated as tax *increases*. This point was made forcefully by Stephanopoulos. Of the other half—out-and-out subsidies—the President proposed changes that amounted to only about ten percent of his spending cuts. He had been burned in the past by taking on Western interests by proposing increases in grazing fees, and the imposition of fees on mining on federal lands—issues that remained unsettled. So he proposed a few cuts in business subsidies, one of which—to privatize the Power Marketing Administration, which provided subsidized power from publicly owned dams—soon came under attack from largely the same Western senators who had tied up his mining and grazing proposals. (When these Western senators went once again to see Clinton, he seemed in a very bad mood.) Lloyd Bentsen, his Secretary of the Treasury, as chairman of the Senate Finance Committee had played a role in putting several of these breaks in the tax code, and he denigrated Reich's idea publicly and privately. Later, Reich, feeling liberated by Bentsen's departure in December 1994, kept up the drumbeat for cutting "corporate welfare."

As the new House minority leader, Dick Gephardt faced a great challenge and had a complicated set of equations to resolve. Gephardt, fifty-three, a shrewd politician, one of the new, cool generation of Democrats who entered Congress in the 1970s, was accustomed to making unsentimental calculations, and now he had a load of them to make. He had to find a way to rally his troops out of their state of dispiritedness—some were in a depression—and make them relevant, both as the opposition party and as an alternative voice. He had to mold into something coherent a caucus that contained such disparate spirits as the conservative Charles Stenholm, of Texas, and the liberal Charles Rangel, of New York. He had to figure out how to regain majoritydom, and in the process decide how closely to work with the Clinton White House and how much to have his flock be identified with Clinton himself. Moreover, Gephardt's own Presidential ambitions hadn't died. His unsuccessful run for the 1988 nomination and his sitting out the 1992 race, which had begun with George Bush seeming invincible, had done anything but bank the embers. He could not of course take Clinton on frontally, at least not at this point. But he could, and would, as would a few others, get ready, just in case.

In this pursuit Gephardt preempted Clinton's December tax cut speech with one of his own, and shortly after the new Congress convened he offered testimony on both a flat tax and his own version of welfare reform, and not long after that made a speech on raising the standard of living of the middle class—which received less attention than he had hoped. The Clinton White House, spooked, kept a Gephardt watch, which was somewhat complicated by the close relationship between Stephanopoulos, who had worked for Gephardt, and Gephardt's staff, and by the fact that the White House needed Gephardt. Gephardt's calculation, made along with David Bonior, was that the House Democratic Party had to show some independence from the Clinton White House, make clear that it was not in lockstep with it. A top House Democrat said, "We're different entities and we have different political imperatives and we feel there has to be some space there." After all, many House Democrats blamed Clinton for their lowered status, believing, with good reason, that numerous former colleagues had gone down because they were too closely identified with him, and had cast votes for some of his controversial proposals. While Gephardt believed that it would be all the more difficult to regain control of the House in 1996 if Clinton went down to defeat, there would be no plank-walking on Clinton's behalf.

Gephardt now functioned out of a warren of seven cramped offices, with four staff members working at desks in the narrow hallway, on the second floor of the Capitol Building on the opposite side of the Capitol from Gingrich's offices. His familiar chiseled features betrayed no aging, his strawberry-colored hair no sign of gray, his demeanor as controlled as if he wasn't the slightest bit pressured. Yet, in his effort to find consensus within his philosophically and temperamentally widespread caucus, he was conducting meetings day and night. Having concluded that the only way to get back to majority status was to be inclusive, and having been under pressure from the various wings of the caucus to include them in the party's deliberations, Gephardt had expanded the leadership group to nearly thirty members (more than three times its previous size), who met every day at 5:00 P.M. The entire caucus met once and sometimes twice a week.

In an interview in late January, Gephardt said, "Because we are presenting an alternative, and we need to present a message to people, since we're not going to pass legislation, we've been struggling with how you centralize policy into the caucus and into the leadership. We're used to having the committees have the main say on what policy would be. Now we're trying to include the committees and work with them but expose their ideas to the whole caucus and almost have the whole caucus decide what the policy would be, which is a revolution."

Gephardt continued, "We meet all day and all night—I mean, just constant meetings. It's a very collaborative effort; we're trying to get people to think not so much that they're legislating but that they are creating a message or an alternative that can be expressed to people over time, so that we can define Democrats and the Democratic Party in a positive and constructive way." Gephardt talked about leadership in terms remarkably similar to Gingrich's: both talked about leading by including, and about giving authority from the bottom up instead of just from the top down (and both were reducing the role of committee chairmen). These same current theories animated Vice President Gore's Reinventing Government project. Gingrich, of course, went further, and handed out reading assignments on the subject.

Then Gephardt conceded, "We are yet to find what we believe the vision is." He added, "We are working on that, and it will be at least four to six months before we can get there." But it was to take longer than that.

One question was whether this effort would result in anything with edge or in mush. Another was whether the Democrats, if they had a message, could find ways to get it across. Democrats, including Gephardt, envied Republicans for having moved into a new generation of communications, going around the traditional ones with the right-wing radio talk shows, and through such groups as the Christian Coalition and the National Rifle Association. Groups such as organized labor, which used to carry the Democratic Party's message to its members, had become weaker over the years. Democrats, obsessed with Rush Limbaugh, desperately searched for their own alternative. Mario Cuomo started a radio program in early June. Limbaugh's effectiveness, they realized, came in part because he was entertaining. Market analysts the Democrats brought in told them that rather than appealing to the politically unaware, Limbaugh pushed already committed people further, got them energized, and turned them into activists. During the indoctrination sessions for Republican freshmen before the Congress convened, Vin Weber told them that the most effective way to get their point of view across was to go to the roughly seven hundred conservative talk show hosts. But if the Democrats wanted to compete effectively with the Republicans on the airwaves, they had to have something to say.

A House Democratic "communications group" headed by Richard Durbin, of Illinois, and Kweisi Mfume, of Maryland, met every day to figure out what the Democrats' message should be on various issues, and how to make the best use of the one-minute statement or the Special Orders period, of which Gingrich and his group had made such effective use when they were in the minority. The Democrats' approach was to have at least one comment about Gingrich each morning, and one about an issue before the House. The communications group was given rudimentary equipment to work with, and as of mid-February still didn't have a "blast fax" capacity, as the Republicans did, to send message faxes to hundreds of recipients simultaneously. But they were working on getting the up-to-date fax capacity, and getting on the Internet. A policy group, headed by George Miller, of California, and John Spratt, of South Carolina, and including people not just from the relevant committees, was to bring policy initiatives to the leadership, who would, if they approved, take them to the caucus.

According to Durbin, Frank Luntz's early-February memo (the one that had warned off using the word "orphanages") gave Democrats their strategy by showing that the Republicans' weakness was their vulnerability to looking "mean" and "uncaring." (Luntz also advised the Republicans to cast issues in moral terms—thus all the Republican talk about cutting funds for one thing or another in order to make the future brighter for the nation's children.)

Lacking a message of their own, the Democrats' derivative and negative strategy would have to do. And it did work for a while. The more the Republicans by their actions on the Contract played into the Democrats' hands the more they used this strategy. The opportunities caused some members to blossom. Rosa DeLauro, the chief deputy whip, became a major figure in thinking through and executing the one-minutes. (She was the wife of Stan Greenberg, the President's pollster.) She said, "There is a unifying principle here, which is to take the House back." Gradually, as the shock wore off, the Democrats began to see that their not being responsible for what the House did, and the fact that their legislative proposals wouldn't be adopted, offered opportunities for a new creativity. "It's like regrouping after Gettysburg," Miller said. "Some people want to go home. There are different degrees of shell shock settling in, and some can't adapt to the new role."

Though publicly the effort to attack Gingrich was headed by Bonior, Gephardt was completely aware of it but had to stand somewhat apart from it so that he could deal with Gingrich and Armey about day-to-day House business. But several Democrats said that they sensed absolutely no distance between Bonior and Gephardt on the question of taking Gingrich on. "Dick understands what's going on," one House Democrat said.

One House Democratic strategist said, "The theory is to jab him and jab him. He has an explosive temper. As controversial as the book has been, GOPAC has been at the heart of the issue. It comes up every time the Democrats meet." They prodded Gingrich to reveal all of GOPAC's contributors.

Though many Democrats were animated by their strong dislike of Gingrich, their belief that he had been mean and vindictive in his days in the minority, there was a larger purpose. George Miller said, "Newt is the nerve center and the energy source. Going after him is like trying to take out command and control." He went on, "Newt Gingrich is neither here nor there. He's the intellectual basis, the architect, and the moving force behind the things that will hurt the groups and people I represent." This was, of course, what Gingrich was out to do.

Though a few Democrats had been concerned about the attacks on Gingrich, fearing that this would alienate the public, which wanted Congress not to engage in bitter partisanship but to get things done, and would suggest that the Democrats had nothing positive to say, as new questions about Gingrich's dealings kept arising, their view changed. Some once reluctant Democrats decided that Gingrich's controversial arrangements were serious enough to warrant serious attention. Also, as legislation came to the House floor, the Democrats began to find ways to make their substantive points through the amendments they offered.

•

The Senate Democrats were still finding their footing under Tom Daschle, whose capacity for leadership several Democratic senators still questioned. But Daschle had won the race for minority leader precisely because a majority of his colleagues didn't want a strong leader. Daschle told them that he would be more inclusive than his predecessor, George Mitchell, who had kept a tight grip on the reins. It wasn't yet clear whether Daschle would prove tough enough for the coming battles. Daschle had also to win over many of those who had supported Chris Dodd in his try for the leadership, as well as Dodd himself. But, one Democratic senator said, the Democratic caucus was more focused on getting itself into some sort of working order than it was the last time the Democrats lost the Senate, which, he said, had taken three years. "Though we're not unified, there's a lot more interest in getting unified." He added, "Because Clinton isn't very popular, we know we have to figure things out for ourselves." A member of the Senate Democratic leadership said in mid-January, of the White House, "I'm spending a lot less time figuring out their strategy than in developing one on the Hill. Our situations are linked, but we're spending our time up here figuring out our way to handle the situation. It's an unusual team the President's collected down there. They seem not quite in synch with what they face right now. They face a big political challenge. You'd think he'd have the best minds around who'd offer things that are fresh and interesting. But the President and his staff still have not developed a coherent agenda. We've had two meetings there, and the second was a reflection of the first. We expected the President to say, 'We've put together a five-to-seven-part plan,' but it was another meeting of going around the room to hear ideas."

This senator also spoke to the political situation he found himself in: "This is not an easy time. It's not a case of being on a stage and playing to a stationary audience. You have Democrats who've become Republicans, Republicans who've become libertarians. There are two unsettling conditions out there: one is economic and the other is cultural. It's a very unsettling time politically."

Bob Dole, a highly effective Senate leader, a man very much respected within his own conference for his skills at working things out, was beset. Politics was changing, the Senate was changing—with the greatest change occurring on his side of the aisle. The understandings that used to hold the Senate together—in the absence of rules such as the House had, much of the Senate's business had to be conducted by unanimous consent—were vanishing. The days when Republicans would sit down with such Democrats as Henry Jackson or Edmund Muskie to work things out were gone. The Senate was becoming more like the House. William Cohen said, "The comity is gone. We used to never go into the state of another senator to campaign against him. Now it's routine." Members of the Senate used to socialize with each other—even across party lines—but with all the pressures to raise money, to get "back home," the long hours in session, and the breakdown in cooperativeness, there was little time for that now, even if there was the inclination.

A large number of people had thought that Trent Lott, who by temperament was more activist and partisan than Dole (though Dole had become plenty partisan in the last Congress), and closer to Gingrich—would make things difficult for Dole.

But some mutual friends of Dole and Lott told Dole that he need not worry about Lott—that he would be loyal, as he had been when he served as whip with Michel. They told Dole that Lott would actually do him good because he would keep the Senate conservatives from piling on him, and he would not play games when Dole was out campaigning. Many supposedly wise observers overlooked that it was in Lott's interest that Dole be a success—as majority leader and Presidential candidate—if he wished to succeed him. But the relationship became complicated as the year went on.

Dole's immediate and larger problem was Phil Gramm, of Texas, his chief Senate rival for the Republican nomination. Gramm wasn't subtle. During the Lott-Simpson contest for whip, Gramm said that this was the first round of the Presidential contest, that it would highlight the difference between himself and Dole. (Dole had close allies in the conference who didn't want to see him embarrassed, and two nonfreshman senators who were believed to have voted for Lott in the secret ballot were placed in purgatory.) A Republican senator said, "From the outset Gramm seemed to use opportunities to undermine Dole's influence or to stake out opportunities for himself." Gramm criticized the Clinton administration's efforts to help Mexico, which Dole supported. Gramm argued for forcing a Senate vote on including in the Balanced Budget Amendment a provision that required a three-fifths vote to raise taxes—which didn't have a prayer of passing, but could make Dole, who would have to vote for it, look weak if it failed. "Gramm kept egging it on," the senator said.

But Dole was not without his own weapons: he kept Gramm off the highly important and much desired Finance Committee.

The determined Gramm was a source of jokes within his own caucus. A Republican senator said, "With Phil Gramm running, you have to keep moving or Phil Gramm's footprints will be on your back. The joke is, Don't get in the no-man's-land between Phil Gramm and a camera."

Dole, unlike Gingrich, was no visionary. He also was no ideologue. His instincts had been moderate-conservative, but the nomination contest, and the changing chemistry of his caucus, were pushing him to the right. Dole was flinty and remote—he was known for holding things close to the chest, and confided in almost no one—but he had several loyal adherents in the Senate, who admired him for his ability. Dole was usually able to listen to the various wings of his party and work out something they could agree to. A Republican senator said, "This is where Dole's mastery comes in. You move a little bit this way and a little bit that and you hold it together. He's the only one who can do that." He added, "Dole's not one to spell out a vision of goals for America in the year 2002 but he moves on and he gets things done. He's like a shark: you have to keep moving or you die. He has no other interests. There's not a moment when he's in repose except when he's out on the balcony of his office getting sun and making phone calls."

Among the effects of the rightward trend of the Senate Republican caucus was the deliberate encirclement of some of the more moderate committee chairmen. The Budget Committee, under Pete Domenici, of New Mexico, a moderate-to-conservative who had supported a freeze in entitlements in 1985 and thereby earned the mistrust of some true conservatives, had since then been loaded up with conservatives. After the 1994 election, the moderates—Bob Packwood, of Oregon and chairman of the Finance Committee, Mark Hatfield, also of Oregon and chairman of the Appropriations Committee, Nancy Kassebaum, chairman of the Labor and Human Resources Committee, and John Chafee, of Rhode Island and chairman of the Environment and Public Works Committee—were looked on by Senate conservatives as not understanding the mandate, and so (not unlike what had happened in the House) task forces made up of people not on the committees were established on various subjects, to act as an outside force on key issues. Early in the year, a Senate aide said, "Clearly an effort is being made by Lott and the other conservatives to control these committees and the chairmen. That phenomenon permeates the Senate right now."

A conservative senator said of the task forces: "We wanted to show the committee chairmen that they wouldn't be able to sit and take their time and go through the regular process of getting geared up, which has always been fairly casual in the Senate."

Lott, a friendly man with a hyper temperament and a killer instinct, set a new style for a Senate whip. But even the kinetic Lott was a bit boggled at first by his new role. In his Russell Office Building office on an early January afternoon, he was trying to decide which of his office signs should say "Republican Whip" and which should say "Majority Whip." It was a choice that carried large meaning for him. He was learning that with his new eminence came invitations to embassy dinners and expectations that he would show up, and visits from foreign dignitaries. He was also getting his footing.

"Right now I'm showing Bob Dole what an active group can do," Lott said. "After a few weeks, he'll get addicted." He continued, "I'm an activist and I work hard. The whip has always kind of done what the leader let him do. But I feel I was elected to do the job and I'm going to do the job. I'm around all the time. I like to be in the legislative mix and I'm going to be there. I've got to show him that my intent is sincere."

Lott established a whip system that reached for deputy whips into the various wings and regions and age groups and classes, including the freshmen, represented in the Senate, and he put it to use as a full-time monitoring and informational system—keeping tabs on the concerns of the members, not just trying to get their votes when a bill was up. Lott said, "What I'm trying to do is encourage Republicans to think like a team rather than fifty-three independent contractors. It's important that you work it so that every time you win. I try to keep in touch with them constantly. By doing a whip check every week you check their temperature. Are they mad about something? Have they got heartburn on some amendment?"

But Dole, who had said almost nothing interesting for months—he was most at home with legislative talk—and whose Presidential candidacy was based on the thin ice of "inevitability," was facing a lot of problems.

5

THE NEW FEDERALISM

"We're in Charge, Let's Do It"

Newt Gingrich's desire to repeal the New Deal was blessed with fortuity: the election in November of enough Republican governors to constitute a majority of the statehouses, encompassing almost all of the major states. The Republican governors quickly became a new force in the land, and new stars in the firmament. Haley Barbour, the party chairman, was eager to show them off. Bob Dole, getting set to run for President, was eager to get their endorsement. For Gingrich, the governors represented an opportunity and a cover.

Shortly after the 1994 election, a barely noticed event was to have a profound impact on the debate in Washington over the future roles of the federal, state, and local governments, and a potentially historic effect on America's social welfare policy. The Republican governors, holding their annual conference, this time at Williamsburg, Virginia, hijacked the issue. Dole and Gingrich, the new congressional leaders, attended the Williamsburg conference.

The governors were quite pleased with themselves. Some of them—William Weld, of Massachusetts; John Engler, of Michigan; and Tommy Thompson, of Wisconsin—had won reelection by large margins. Moreover, Christine Todd Whitman, of New Jersey, elected in 1993, was gaining national attention for having carried out her promise to cut taxes by thirty percent. (One result of this, New Jersey Democratic Senator Bill Bradley charged, was to raise pressure on the property tax, "the cruelest tax of all.")

Gingrich had watched these races closely, and had campaigned with the conservative Engler, with whom he had formed close ties. Together, Engler and Gingrich had come up with the idea for GOPAC's providing audiotapes of Gingrich's campaign advice to candidates for state legislatures. The contributions and the tapes helped Gingrich build a nationwide network of supporters, many of whom now served in the House.

In an interview, Gingrich said, "The audiotape training program at GOPAC was invented by John Engler when he was the Senate majority leader in Michigan [from 1984 to 1990]. That's how far back we go. I was the keynote speaker in Wisconsin at a tribute [in 1989] to Tommy Thompson. I've known Weld pretty well. These are relationships that have been growing and developing and we now have a nationwide network. And so what you've got is this nationwide movement and electronic networking by computer and telephone and television increases that capability. And then we're all friends, I mean we all know each other."

Early in 1995, Dan Meyer, Gingrich's chief of staff, said, "People should look to Michigan, Wisconsin, and New Jersey to see what Newt's trying to do. He's basically following their script tactically. He's a student of what's happened at the state levels." Engler and Thompson had not only cut taxes but had initiated tough welfare reforms. Both states lowered welfare benefits and allowed fewer people to qualify for those benefits than before. Both governors claimed greater and more promising results for their innovations than the facts suggested. Some of the "progress" was the result of factors outside of welfare reform; in recent years both states had enjoyed an economic boom and relatively low population growth. Caseload reductions also resulted in part from restricting eligibility and benefits rather than placing people in jobs. Moreover, in the case of Michigan careful evaluations by outside experts showed that the reforms had little impact on the caseload.

Weld had cut taxes and in early 1995 proposed a very tough welfare reform—simply decreeing that welfare recipients go to work within sixty days—but his program, too, was short on giving people the capacity, through training, child care, and job creation, to go back to work. In fact, for all the talk of the states as "laboratories," as "innovative," not one state had yet implemented on any broad scale the kinds of changes the Republicans were now proposing.

But the facts were of less interest to key Republicans than the opportunity provided by the governors' request in Williamsburg that Congress turn the welfare program into block grants to the states (cutting federal costs and eliminating federal control) and end the concept of entitlement—the statutory requirement, under the Aid to Families with Dependent Children (A.F.D.C.) program, that all needy children whose families met state income tests would receive cash assistance. (The states' benefits varied widely. Under the existing system, Mississippi paid welfare recipients $120 a month for a family of three, while Connecticut paid such a family $680— a disparity much greater than any difference in the two states' economies. In Mississippi, the combined assistance of welfare and food stamps got people less than halfway to the poverty line.) The Republican congressional leaders readily agreed to the governors' request. The block grant concept would be a good deal for them: the governors would help them with their budget problem in exchange for control of the programs.

Engler was treated as a demigod in certain quarters on Capitol Hill, and his deportment suggested that he felt this was only right. In testifying before the Senate Budget Committee in early February, Engler, a portly man with an air of great certainty, attacked "a dizzying array of failed social programs that has destroyed families," and called for "getting rid of all the federal rules." He was listened to reverentially by the Republican senators.

Haley Barbour believed that the governors were to be showcased (thus Whitman had been drafted to give the Republican response to Clinton's State of the Union address). Barbour, the beefy, tough-minded former executive director of the Mississippi Republican Party, played a much larger role in the events of 1995 than was generally understood. Republican Senator William Cohen said early in the year, "Don't underestimate Barbour. He is a partner in this process." It was Barbour who often made things work between the sometimes incompatible House and Senate Republican leaders, who stepped in when he felt that the Republicans were getting "off-message," who lent the resources of the Republican Party to the purpose of getting the Contract enacted. He was an important strategist, at times proposing even the timing of the voting on certain issues. A Senate aide said early in the year, "Haley Barbour is spending most of his time with Gingrich and Armey and other key House figures. His sense is, the best way to get the revolution, the Republican agenda, is through the House and force it on the Senate, which he doesn't trust."

Barbour and Gingrich often noted that some of the governors—Engler especially—had at a certain point had low popular ratings (Engler was at nineteen percent in the fall of 1991) and then were swept back into office. (In 1994 Engler won sixty-two percent of the vote.) Barbour's view was that if the Republicans in Congress took tough measures early, they would, like the governors, end up in a strong position. Barbour said, "I think we'll go through the firestorm and emerge stronger. I really believe it. The leadership believes it. The freshmen believe it." (Later, Albert R. Hunt pointed out in the *Wall Street Journal* that Engler's now famously low rating was based on a private poll and a loaded question.)

There were other reasons why the Republican governors had newfound power. First, they were in a position to play a very big role in Presidential politics—especially the primaries, where their endorsement and their machinery could make the difference for a candidate in their state. Dole was quite and painfully aware of this. (John Sununu, the then-governor of New Hampshire, was of critical importance to Bush's winning that primary over Dole in 1988.) Second, their agenda nicely dovetailed Gingrich's—to smash the power of national groups that supported the "welfare state." In the view of Gingrich and like-minded Republicans, the large number of "categorical" programs that provided federal money for this or that activity had given rise not just to bureaucrats but also social workers and interest groups. For the Gingrich group, breaking the power of the political infrastructure of the welfare state was at least as important a factor as the issue of where the funds went. That infrastructure had to be destroyed because it didn't sustain anything they believed in, and because they saw it—with reason—as the epicenter of the resistance.

A third reason for the governors' power, and "most important," Barbour said, was that "the governors could be hugely helpful to them in getting across that this was the right thing to do." Barbour had been using the governors as vehicles of communication of Republican views—very successfully in his opinion.

After the Williamsburg meeting, the concept of block grants became Republican doctrine. Tony Blankley explained, "Newt was surprised that the governors were willing to accept more responsibility than we'd expected—that if they got sufficient block grants without micromanagement from Washington, they'd accept more responsibility and less funds. At a 7:30 A.M. breakfast meeting that extended for three hours on Tuesday, November 22, those conversations occurred between Dole and Gingrich and the governors. And so that triggered a reconsideration of what our welfare package would look like." He added, "We left Williamsburg feeling we had cut the Gordian knot on welfare, and we had."

Gingrich recalled, "At Williamsburg, people like Weld, Engler, Thompson, and Pete Wilson [the Republican governor of California] got up and said, 'You can do it. Be much bolder than you plan to be. Be much more aggressive than you plan to be. Take the hits and keep moving.' And out of that conference, I invited Engler to come and speak at our conference in December when we organized. And so the governors made us much bolder than we would have been without them."

The Contract had actually proposed to keep welfare as an entitlement program, but with tougher strings. It put little emphasis on block grants for the welfare program—treating them only as a possible fallback approach for an individual state. The block grant approach came to the fore, Gingrich recalled, "When we were in the meeting with the governors and they said to us, 'If you'll block-grant it and get the federal government out of the way, we don't need any more money.' And my ears perked up and I said, You literally would accept a flat line for five years if you were in charge? And they said yes. But they all agreed they had to have a real freedom to manage the programs. And I said, 'Fine. We're in charge, let's do it.' So it was at Williamsburg that we had the really big jump toward something which, after all, Reagan had talked about in both 1976 and 1982."

Gingrich explained that there was a direct connection at Williamsburg between welfare and his increasing inclination to go for a balanced budget in seven years: "That actually was the first big step toward thinking we could balance the budget. Because you would suddenly have a model for dramatically lower costs and for dramatic reform. See, we can't win this fight if we're just cheap. We can *easily* win this fight if we're transformational.

"And then the other factor was they emboldened me to think big and, frankly, if you think big, balancing the budget's the right level. It's the only fight which allows you to focus the country's attention on reshaping the entire federal government."

Gingrich had figured out that talking about "balancing the budget" was easier to rally people than saying "lower the deficit." He said, "People will take a much higher level of discomfort if the end result is a zero, that they are literally going to quit piling debt on their children. In other words, if we're going to pile fifty billion dollars a year onto the deficit, you'll take dramatically less discomfort than if I say we're going to *balance* the budget. You actually get more, dramatically more, I think, by going for zero."

The idea of turning programs over to the states in the form of block grants wasn't a new one, and its heritage wasn't entirely honorable. Richard Nixon had tried "revenue sharing" and Ronald Reagan had backed the "New Federalism," both of which meant in some form turning programs and the funding for them over to the states. But these efforts had mixed results. In the case of Nixon's experiment, boondoggles and cronyism, as well as ludicrous projects, were found. By 1995, the case that state control leads to more wisdom or honesty was yet to be proved. The rhetoric served in part to mask the motive. Tony Blankley said that turning more programs over to the states "has been one of the abiding dreams of the conservative movement since the 1960s. We've said it, but we never saw it happening until now." Speaking about the governors, he added, "We didn't know how open they were to much more dramatic action than we envisioned when we drafted our [Contract] bill in July." Blankley said, "After Williamsburg, everything else was detail."

The block grant concept had had more than a whiff of the old "states' rights" approach, turning on its head the idea that some programs needed to be run from the federal government because states couldn't be trusted to give all their citizens equitable or adequate treatment. There were reasons the programs had been made federal. Ending entitlement for welfare recipients would put to an end social welfare policy that had been in effect for sixty years. But in the New Deal, welfare had been intended as a support for widows, the disabled, and the aged, who weren't expected to go to work. By the 1980s and 1990s, those who were seeking help were mostly single mothers who were divorced, separated, or never married—and the vast majority of widows and married mothers were now working at least part-time outside the home. Whether all states could now be trusted to be equitable when, under the Republican proposal, they didn't have to be, and to give help to those who truly needed it was a matter of debate. In the past, some governors had followed patent racist politics. Now, several governors were playing suburban politics—favoring the suburban voters over those in the inner cities. This dovetailed neatly with national Republican politics. Moreover, there remained competition among states to induce industry to locate there by keeping taxes—and therefore state expenditures —low.

The argument over the relative roles of the federal government and the states was a worthy one to have, but, since partisan politicians were involved, it wasn't exactly conducted academically and the motives weren't always worthy. The great debate of 1995 could turn out to have been a missed opportunity. A number of institutes and individuals had weighed in on the subject over the years. Even Alice Rivlin had written a book about it, *Reviving the American Dream,* in 1992, in which she advocated turning certain kinds of federal activities over to the states—service programs, such as education and housing, but not income-maintenance programs, such as welfare. (President-elect Clinton's negative reaction to her book was a large factor in Rivlin's not being chosen O.M.B. director in the first place.)

When Clinton met with the National Governors Association in early 1993, he said that he wasn't going to forget what he had learned as governor about federal-state relations, and that he would be sympathetic to their requests for waivers so that they could experiment with welfare. He described himself as an "ardent devolutionist." Clinton liked to meet with the governors—he felt comfortable with them—and to talk their talk. But there was little structural devolution in Clinton's program for his first two years. With much difficulty, in 1994 his aides drew up a welfare reform plan—in his Presidential campaign, Clinton had promised to "end welfare as we know it"—but the subject took a back seat to health care reform. Clinton's proposal was unprecedentedly tough as Democratic proposals went, since it contained a provision for cutting off a welfare family if the parent refused to work without good cause, and gave states the option of not giving a family additional funds if a welfare recipient had additional children. Clinton's campaign proposal was to move people off welfare after two years, deliberately leaving vague the question of what happened next. People of varying views could read what they wanted to into it. (This was a pattern.) There had been a long struggle between Clinton's more centrist advisers (including White House aide Bruce Reed, formerly of the D.L.C., and Carol Rasco, the Domestic Policy Adviser and formerly an adviser to Clinton in Arkansas, and a few other officials) and his more liberal advisers (Health and Human Services Secretary Donna Shalala and several of her aides) over whether to impose strict limits on how long someone could stay on the rolls, or whether the law would be more flexible. Flexible—meaning that after two years recipients had to take a job, but if no private sector job was available and there weren't enough funds to create enough public jobs, people could continue to receive aid—won out. For the program to carry out Clinton's pledge to get people off welfare in two years, subsidized jobs, with newly created public service jobs as a last resort, would have to be provided, as well as training and day care—all of which was expensive. Therefore the ultimate Clinton bill wasn't as large or dramatic as some administration officials had first hoped. (The problem of cost had essentially kept the 1988 welfare reform program from moving large numbers of recipients into jobs. The result was that critics blamed the recipients for staying on the rolls.)

Some key House liberals had refused to sign onto Clinton's plan, and House Democratic leaders begged the administration to postpone introducing it, because they were struggling to win congressional approval of Clinton's health care proposal, because the Hispanic and Black Caucuses felt that the welfare proposal was racially targeted, and other liberals were squeamish about it. In 1995, Democrats would look back on it with nostalgia. In the meantime, the Clinton administration was running a backdoor welfare-reform program by granting waivers to governors who asked to be released from certain federal restrictions in order to try out new approaches. Not a single waiver was refused, even those that some of the President's political allies thought dimly of. By early 1995, the administration had granted twenty-three waivers, including ones to Engler and Thompson.

In 1994 Republicans, too, had introduced a welfare bill, with many co-sponsors, including Clay Shaw, Republican of Florida and in the 104th Congress the chairman of the Ways and Means Human Resources Subcommittee, with jurisdiction over welfare. The Republican bill was based on the same premises as the Clinton administration bill, and continued welfare as an entitlement. Like Clinton's, the Republican bill sought to get people off welfare in two years and provided funds for training and jobs. The 1994 Republican proposal offered an unseized opportunity for a compromise between the Republicans and Clinton.

Another force was also militating against a compromise in 1994, and turned out to become a big factor in the 1995 debate. Conservative Republican strategists, including William Kristol, the former chief of staff to Vice President Dan Quayle who had become a guru to Republicans, William Bennett, and Robert Rector, of the Heritage Foundation, said that the Republicans shouldn't push a variation on the Democrats' bill, but should change the terms of the debate to illegitimacy, and they urged a cutoff of funds to unwed mothers under eighteen.

As the 104th Congress gathered in 1995, the big issue in welfare reform was whether welfare would continue to be an entitlement, and whether the federal government would continue to put restrictions on how the funds could be used. These were the real issues lurking behind the "block grant" rhetoric. In several senses the debate wasn't on the level. Cutting spending for welfare—in order to spend the money for a tax cut, or whatever—wasn't the same thing as reforming welfare. Neither, necessarily, was turning it over to the states in order to break the power of the national lobbies. Block grants in themselves did nothing about getting people to work. And Clinton's generosity with waivers had allowed the states plenty of flexibility in drawing up their own plans. The battle cry of "turn the programs over to the states" overlooked this, as it did the idea that a reversion to the states could come with federal strings—of whatever philosophy. There was no real evidence that cutting off benefits lessened pregnancies. To the extent that anything worked in terms of getting people off welfare, it required money—for training, for day care, for subsidizing or even creating jobs. But in the new climate, even liberals didn't want to talk about spending *more* money for welfare.

Despite all the fuss, welfare constituted a tiny proportion of the federal budget: less than one percent. But in the previous four years the welfare rolls had risen dramatically, and were populated by increasing numbers of children born out of wedlock. (In recent months, the rolls had declined slightly.) Despite a widespread image, blacks made up less than half (forty percent) of the welfare population. But in recent years one out of three babies overall—and two out of three black babies—were born out of wedlock. For about half the nearly five million families on welfare, dependence was not a transitory thing, but lasted ten years or more, or until their children had grown up and they were no longer eligible. In some cases, a "family" was in its third generation of welfare recipients. The current program had almost no defenders, and the seeming futility of all efforts to brake the increase in children living in a single-parent household, especially those born out of wedlock, and to move recipients from welfare to work in any large numbers, plus the horror stories perpetuated by those trying to destroy the system, made welfare a highly emotional and political issue.

By 1995, the welfare debate had shifted sharply to the right. Gingrich, Bennett, and others had had some success in making illegitimacy the focal point of the debate. The Contract called for denying welfare permanently to single unwed mothers under eighteen and denying increased aid to parents on welfare who had another child, for cutting spending on welfare, and enacting "a tough two-year-and-out provision with work requirements to promote individual responsibility." That was the slightly spelled-out version; the *TV Guide* version said simply: "The government should encourage people to work, *not* to have children out of wedlock"—unarguable goals. Secretary Shalala claimed at a December press conference that under current circumstances the various Contract provisions for cutting off aid would throw five million children off the rolls, and Democrats took up the cry that innocent children were being made to pay for the sins of their parents.

Clinton passed up a number of opportunities to take a clear stand on the issue of entitlements—to demonstrate leadership on a subject he knew well. When the President failed to mention the subject in his State of the Union address, White House officials told inquirers that the President was holding back so that he could take the lead in putting together a compromise proposal at a conference on welfare that he was to convene in late January. The skepticism and worry on the part of those—within the administration and without—who felt that a vital principle was at stake was validated when at the conference the President didn't take a stand for entitlements.

The meeting, held at Blair House on the last Saturday in January and attended by a bipartisan group of Members of Congress and governors, seated at a large square table for five hours, yielded the kind of policy discussion that Clinton loved—but little else. An attempt by Carol Rasco to make a deal with the Republicans that would have turned the program into block grants was scotched by Shalala. (No one was sure whether Rasco had the President's at least implicit support.) Clinton told the assembled group that there were some vital interests to protect and that he didn't see how children could be protected under the Republican approach. He said that he had participated in the bipartisan welfare debate for twelve years and that the issue should be settled on a bipartisan basis, and that he would put forward his own ideas.

In early February, after negotiations among Gingrich and Engler and Shaw, the Republicans introduced their welfare bill. Engler's adviser on welfare, Gerald Miller, working with Ways and Means Committee aides, wrote the actual legislation. This was an unusually close collaboration. The House members got some strings (cutting off unwed mothers under eighteen, barring increases for recipients who had more children, and barring payments to resident aliens) and the governors got the block grants and weak work requirements—weaker, in fact, than under the existing law, and than in Clinton's bill—and a requirement that people be off the rolls after five years. Under the proposal, children born to a mother under eighteen would be barred from help throughout their childhood. The proposal also barred payments for children for whom paternity had not been established, even if the mother had cooperated fully in identifying and trying to locate the father.

As agreed at Williamsburg, in exchange for block grants the governors were to receive less money for welfare, and a fixed amount for five years. There was no effective guarantee of additional funds in the event a state experienced an economic downturn. It wasn't such a good deal for governors—but it was a while before several of them realized that. As it happened, Michigan and Wisconsin were the only two states that wouldn't have been hurt had there been such a block grant for the past five years.

Under the existing A.F.D.C. program, the federal government paid from fifty to eighty percent of a state's welfare costs, and if the caseloads grew, or there was a recession, the federal contribution grew as well. What the governors proposed, and the Republican leaders agreed to, was a radical change in the concept of the welfare program.

Moreover, unlike current law, states wouldn't be required to contribute funds of their own for welfare. The principle of entitlement was abandoned. The immediate victims would, of course, be actual and potential welfare recipients and their children. There was nothing to stop the states from lowering their welfare rolls by simply throwing people off the rolls, whether or not a job was available. Because the Republicans were committed to cutting spending on welfare, and openly acknowledged that they needed funds to pay for the tax cuts in the Contract and also to move toward a balanced budget, the Republican proposal provided no funds for job training or for creating jobs (the Contract had provided $10 billion). It required only that after two years, recipients (in graduated numbers, starting at four percent and rising to fifty percent in eight years) participate in "work activities," as defined by the states, which could mean as little as writing résumés. In the future, Congress could well cut the overall amount to go to the states for welfare. But getting free of federal restrictions was of more immediate interest to the governors.

The governors wanted the program to be turned over to them with no strings attached, but numerous Republican Members of Congress opposed that, either because they felt that they couldn't turn over the funds without accountability, or because they favored certain strings. Gingrich said later, "Part of it, frankly, was we got the governors and their staffs to come and see Shaw. I mean, once you get out of this baloney about doing everything at secondhand and you get a guy as talented as Weld or Engler or Thompson, give them the role, things happen."

A House leadership aide said, "Obviously these guys are closer to the electorates than people in Washington. They get in the same room and start reinforcing each other. That gives Newt and others examples to cite. We have moved very far from our original bill last year. Shaw's just trying to stay ahead of the train."

Despite their success at the hands of the Republican leaders in Washington, the governors remained unhappy about the fact that there were any federal strings attached to the block grants. The welfare reform bill revealed one of the Republican Party's contradictions: the tension between the desire for devolution and a desire for ideologically based micromanagement.

In light of the changing politics of welfare, and because he wanted to be able to sign a welfare bill—and also because of his innate caution—Clinton remained mum for quite a while on the subject of entitlements. Some of his own advisers—especially but not only Shalala—were upset that he didn't speak out on this key question. But a White House official said, "It's been clear to everybody from the outset that if the debate is defined as federal entitlement versus more power to the states, we can't win. It's too hard to explain. So we tried to change the focus of the debate, with some if not complete success, to one about work and kids." But they appeared to be changing the concept of entitlement, too.

Pollsters and other political advisers had warned their Democratic clients that "entitlement" wasn't a good word to use with regard to welfare, because it conjured up the picture that "shiftless" women who much of the public believed even had children because they would receive welfare, were "entitled" to something. A White House official said, "Communications people have said that 'entitlements' has become code for big government, and 'safety net' is what we threw at Reagan, and it worked." So the President started talking about preserving a "safety net" for children. Another White House aide said early in the year, "We're trying not to have the debate on this issue. It's virtually impossible to communicate. When people hear 'entitlement' they think it's the current system."

On February 10, Dick Gephardt, surrounded by more than a dozen other House Democrats, held a press conference to announce a Democratic welfare proposal. In order to win the support of as large a portion of the Democratic caucus as possible, Gephardt had to keep some issues (such as entitlement) vague: but he did go at what Democrats considered, or hoped, was the weakness in the Republicans' approach—that it didn't provide for getting people jobs. His proposal stipulated that welfare recipients begin training right away, immediately find a job, accept a public service job, or enter a training or job placement program. A few liberals considered the Gephardt "bill," consisting of only one page, so vague that they stayed away from the press conference.

Having surrendered the opportunity to define the argument in 1994,

Clinton didn't even reintroduce his bill in 1995. It wasn't just a case of the votes not being there. The White House rationale was that, as one aide put it, "Ultimately, this game will play out in the Senate, and there's a chance to do something bipartisan there." He added, "This gives us more flexibility to work something out." Implied, but unstated, was that a bill would do better if it didn't have Clinton's name attached to it. Also, there was the problem of finding the funds for the expansion of child care and for providing jobs that were in the original Clinton bill. It was assumed that the Republicans would pronounce the bill "dead on arrival" and therefore the payoff for introducing the bill wasn't high enough. But there were those in the administration who felt that they couldn't fight something with nothing. Clinton faced this kind of dilemma for much of the year.

In time, Clinton's desire to sign a welfare bill, and the pressures on him to stick with entitlement for welfare recipients, were to come into conflict.

Meanwhile, Gingrich, intent on, as he said on several occasions, replacing the New Deal with the New Federalism, was beginning to get his way. Few people were listening carefully, or realized the magnitude of what he was about.

6

THE CONTRACT MARCH
"The Constant Rat-a-Tat-Tat of Our Bills"

Out of Gingrich's strategic genius came the concept of rushing the Contract through the House, capitalizing on the political momentum coming out of the election, the Democrats' trauma, and the excitement of the opening of the new Republican Congress—and allowing little time for opposition to build. The strategy essentially worked, but the success came at a price.

The easiest issues came first: process matters on which there was no great dissent, and which also meant little to the lives of the citizenry. Yet almost everything the Republicans pushed, even the most neutral-sounding, had as its purpose the curbing of federal power. First came the Congressional Accountability Act—to have Congress governed by the same laws it imposed on the public—a proposal few Members of Congress dared vote against. Congress was already observing some of the laws, but the issue made for good politics. Still, in the name of separation of powers the Congress reserved enforcement to itself. Republicans saw the bill as the first of several steps to discourage the passage of new federal laws and to reconsider some already on the books. It was passed by the Senate on January 11 by a vote of 98–1 after Republican leaders pleaded with Democrats to stop pushing unrelated amendments (designed to embarrass Republicans by making them vote against such things as campaign finance reform and lobbying disclosure), and by the House by a unanimous vote on January 17. It was signed into law by the President on January 23, in an Oval Office ceremony, with the bipartisan leaders of Congress looking on.

Clinton, eager not to be left behind, said that the impetus of the bill should be used "to make much deeper changes in the culture of Washington that has too often disconnected it from ordinary Americans." Clinton, showing a new discipline, declined to answer press questions while he, as usual, signed the bill with his left hand, using multiple pens to be distributed to the leaders. Though the bill seemed to be an internal matter on Capitol Hill, it was—like many proposals enacted by the House in the name of the Contract—a move designed to appeal to the small business constituency of the Republican Party. In a press briefing, Gingrich said that Congress should experience "some of the inconveniences visited on small business."

In fact, Gingrich showed a testiness in that briefing that belied his early success, and was a sign of his new readiness to take on the press. Asked about Democratic calls that, like many businesses, Congress should not be able to put to personal use frequent flier mileage gained on business trips, Gingrich said that frequent flier policy was "pro-family," and that "despite your best effort to write a narrow, petty story," Congress was passing the Congressional Accountability bill in its third week—the earliest, he said, a bill had been sent to a President since 1933. Gingrich's decision to make his daily briefing open to television was a consequential one: it provided footage of his angry remarks and thus made it more likely that the television networks would run them. He was risking overexposure—his disapproval ratings had already been rising since the election—and repeated showings of his testiness and his know-it-all aspect.

The next item, putting limits on unfunded mandates—the spending obligations Congress imposed on state and local governments—was another concession to the governors (in this case of both parties). At Williamsburg, the Republican governors had insisted that if Congress was going to pass a Constitutional Amendment requiring a balanced budget, the states should be protected from having to spend even more for programs passed at the federal level. Further, they demanded passage of an unfunded mandates law as a predicate to their states' ratifying the Balanced Budget Amendment. Dick Armey said in an interview, "We felt that the governors had to have our assurance about unfunded mandates when it comes to the states ratifying the Balanced Budget Amendment." Some governors wanted protection from unfunded mandates to be written into the Constitutional Amendment requiring a balanced budget, but the Congressional leaders felt that adding that complexity might make the Amendment even more difficult to get through the Congress. The fallback position proposed by the Republican governors at Williamsburg was that Congress pass a limit on unfunded mandates before it took up the Balanced Budget Amendment.

But this innocuous-sounding legislation was part of the assault on federal programs, a way of curbing federal power, in this instance by making it more difficult to pass new laws, and making it harder to expand those already on the books. Together with the Balanced Budget Amendment, it would be a powerful brake on federal activity. Those two items, along with the movement toward block grants, would be a blow against many of the federal programs that had been established in the past thirty years. A Republican senator said of the unfunded mandates proposal, "Yes, part of the psychology involved is that it will end in fewer programs." Gingrich himself said at a press briefing that the unfunded mandates proposal was part of an effort to "reduce the size of the federal government, turn power over to the states." It was to be one of several attempts on the part of House Republicans to eviscerate the environmental laws, which would be particularly affected by this proposal.

Governors and mayors had for years pushed for legislation limiting unfunded mandates. For some, it was a matter of equity, but for many it was, like the proposal to put welfare into block grants, a way of releasing them from pressures to raise local taxes. Actually, the states were by far the net beneficiaries of federal largesse.

Dole, less inclined temperamentally and politically than Gingrich and his fellow revolutionaries to smash the welfare state, but with his own exigencies to please the Republican governors, had promised the Republican governors at Williamsburg that the unfunded mandates bill would be one of the first bills to be taken up by the Senate.

Though Dole had insisted to Republican senators during an organizing meeting in December that the Senate Republicans would have their own priorities and their own agenda, and wouldn't simply follow the House's lead, that wasn't how matters were turning out. The pressures on the Senate from within the party and its interest groups and constituencies to follow the House's lead became irresistible. So Dole was, with some resentment, taking up Gingrich's agenda, and Gingrich was suspicious that Dole, lacking enthusiasm for it, wouldn't push it hard enough. But neither man could let on publicly that they were anything but the best of comrades.

The unfunded mandates bill, prescribing special procedures, was so complex that few Members of Congress understood how it would work. Democrats, worried that the procedures were so cumbersome that they in themselves would be a bar to federal programs, complained that there had been no hearings on the measure in the House, and only one day of hearings in the Senate, followed by expedited procedures to bring the bill to the Senate floor.

During the Senate debate, Barbara Boxer, Democrat of California, brought to the floor a dizzyingly complex chart—nearly rivaling Pennsylvania Republican Arlen Specter's famous chart depicting the boggling structure that would have been set up under the Clintons' health care plan—

showing the steps that would have to be taken each time legislation requiring state spending came up. It wasn't clear to what extent the new law would apply to reauthorizations of existing laws, and thus make continuations of them more difficult. A Republican senator who voted for the bill said later, "I went down and voted party line because if I stopped and thought about the consequences—it really was a pig in a poke. Most people just decided to see no evil and hear no evil and vote for it. Some of that came from rushing to make sure we showed that in a Hundred Days we could make a difference."

Though Democrats were still reeling from the election, and knew that the bill would pass (it had bipartisan support), in each Chamber they began to show some signs of life, and stood in the way of easy passage of it. House Democratic leaders decided to point to the dangers the unfunded mandates proposal presented to environmental laws, in particular the Clean Air and Clean Water Acts. They attempted to make the case that the environmental laws, which included requirements that state and local governments deal with their own pollution, shouldn't be considered "unfunded mandates." A Democratic House leadership aide said, "We're trying to point out the implications and confusion. We try to figure out what would be the most natural and the most searing examples, and we decided on pollution in the West and South, on dumping, and on clean air and water. The bill is going to pass but we want to try to get the legislation tightened, and show what it really means." The newly engaged John Dingell argued that, "It is not too much to expect that states will clean up their mess without being paid by the federal government." Republicans responded by citing existing requirements that were both burdensome and seemingly absurd.

The House Democrats also tried to gum up the works by offering more than fifty amendments, several of them repetitive, throwing Republican leaders into a fright that they wouldn't make their hundred-day deadline. A leadership aide said, "We knew we were in trouble when 150 amendments were printed." The Republican leaders had, however, bought some insurance by planning to actually finish work on the Contract in fewer than a Hundred Days. (As the House consideration dragged on, Gingrich set aside the unfunded mandates bill to take up the Balanced Budget Amendment to the Constitution.)

Some Republican leaders began to regret early on that they had promised to bring up more legislation than the Democrats had under "open rules"—allowing an unlimited number of amendments—and this became an ongoing source of dispute among the leaders.

Because of the House's size, to prevent utter chaos, bills were normally brought to the House floor under a specific "rule," which stipulated how many and which amendments could be offered, and how much time would be allocated to the debate. The rules, which could have a tremendous effect on the outcome—by barring certain amendments—were set by the House Rules Committee, which in the last couple of decades was totally under the Speaker's control. In 1961, John F. Kennedy and Speaker Sam Rayburn wrested control of the Rules Committee from its then chairman, Howard W. Smith, of Virginia, a retrograde in many respects, including on civil rights. When the Republicans took over the Rules Committee in 1995 they rehung Smith's portrait in the place of honor. After a protest led by John Lewis, Democrat of Georgia and a hero of the civil rights movement, Smith's portrait was taken down.

In the Senate, Robert Byrd, the former majority leader and then chairman of the Appropriations Committee (now, of course, the ranking member), took charge. His intent was to slow down passage of the unfunded mandates bill in order to give the Democrats time to collect themselves and to build pressure against the Balanced Budget Amendment—his real target. Byrd said in debate, "I'm not concerned about a Contract with America." And, pulling a small copy of the Constitution from his jacket pocket, he said, "Here's my contract." Byrd, who had helped Dodd in his race for majority leader against Daschle, was also hazing Daschle, showing him and the world who knew the most about the Senate's rules. Byrd had done a similar thing to George Mitchell when Mitchell took over in 1989, but Mitchell took home the rule books and studied them for three weeks, and after that showed his command of Senate procedures.

At the same time, Byrd collected a small band of liberal Democrats who wanted to stop the Balanced Budget Amendment—which Daschle had supported in 1994. Dole, professing to be patient with Byrd, became increasingly less so as the debate on unfunded mandates threatened to go into a third week. A move by Dole to cut off debate by voting cloture failed on essentially a party-line vote (sixty votes are needed). But Dole recognized that the Democrats were imitating the Republicans of the last couple of years—when they had made liberal use of the filibuster.

According to one of Dole's close Senate allies, Dole never really liked Byrd, and as a strong-willed leader himself grew irritated with having to cope so often with Byrd's determination to dominate the Senate. (After the Senate passed the bill, Dole said, "If this was a warm-up, then we've got a lot of work ahead of us.")

Some senators became uneasy with all the pressures on the Senate to hurry up, to not fall too far behind the House in approving the Contract. Reporters regularly asked Dole if he could keep up with Gingrich's House. Senators took pride in belonging to "the deliberative body," and stood on their Constitutional prerogative to take care with measures that the House had enacted in response to "the passions of the moment." Senators quoted

George Washington's having said the Senate would be the saucer where the House's hot coffee would cool. In a speech on the Senate floor on January 12, William Cohen said, "A lot of people, especially in the press, are saying, Can the Senate measure up to the House? Will the Senate be able to pass the Contract with America on a fast track? If it is a race to the finish line in a Hundred Days, I think it is probably no contest. If it is a question of wise leadership, then, I think the conclusion could be quite different."

At the same time that Dole was trying to get the Senate to finish up on the unfunded mandates bill, off the floor he was busy trying to work out whether the Senate would approve the increasingly troubled Mexican bailout. Like Gingrich, he had made a commitment to help the White House on this knowing that it would be a serious problem. He had deputized Senator Robert Bennett, of Utah, to talk with House figures and knowledgeable outsiders. Now he thought that there was a growing possibility that the worst outcome would occur: that the bailout would be brought up for congressional approval and killed. The White House was coming to see it the same way. But Dole, feeling that the Clinton White House hadn't done its share and wishing to spread the blame, said, of the President, in an angry January 25 floor statement, "If he isn't going to help on his side of the aisle, we're not going to help on our side of the aisle." That same day, Gingrich made similar comments in his press briefing. The two had met and coordinated their statements.

Eventually, the Democrats gave way on unfunded mandates and the bill was passed by the Senate on January 27 by a vote of 86–10, and by the House on February 1 by a vote of 360–74. This provided Republicans with the argument—one that a by now exasperated Dole used frequently—that Democrats had held up action even on bills that they were *for*. The seventy-two-year-old Dole, preparing for his third and undoubtedly last Presidential candidacy, was trying to appear more relaxed, more philosophical than the sharp-edged and sometimes snappish candidate of the past. (Unfortunately, his advisers, trying to curb his snappishness, curbed also his acerbic and often quite funny humor.) Sometimes, this new persona seemed real enough, but one of Dole's closest Senate colleagues said that this would work until he was cornered. The strains of managing the Senate in a new partisan atmosphere, and maintaining supremacy over the Senate Republicans while at the same time running for the Presidency—against some other Senate Republicans—began to show early. Though he had tried (one could almost see the effort) to display patience while the Democrats held up action (for which House Republicans would blame him), his impatience began to get the better of him. And in a prelude to what Dole was to be in for all year, Phil Gramm, who was soon to declare his own Presidential candidacy, on February 14, said that the final unfunded mandates bill didn't go far enough.

In another bipartisan ceremony, the President signed the bill in the Rose Garden on March 22. By this time, however, relations between Clinton and the congressional Republicans had become ragged over numerous issues and Clinton was said by aides to be glad to have something else to sign. Aides said he felt he had to show the middle class that he could produce results for it. The White House was counting on the Republicans not being able to fulfill some of their Contract pledges—especially to both cut taxes and balance the budget—and on the Senate's stopping or ameliorating some of the more radical legislation passed by the House. This wasn't a very creative strategy.

In February and March, the House zipped through a stream of bills revising the crime bill passed in 1994 and making profound changes in regulatory policy and the legal system. This speed worried even some key Republicans. In a conversation in the House Dining Room on January 30, David Dreier, the Californian who had been involved in reorganizing the Congress, said, "The thing that has troubled me about the whole Hundred Days concept is that we're trying to do too much too quickly. We're going against the Founding Fathers. They wanted us to be deliberative." Dreier had been concerned about the Hundred Days concept when it was first discussed the previous fall, but he didn't weigh in because he didn't expect the Republicans to take over the House. Dreier had recently taken his concern to Bob Walker, telling Walker he wished that they had pledged to do these things in the first session rather than the first Hundred Days. Walker replied, "Dave, if we'd said first year instead of Hundred Days we'd still be debating your rules." By this time, Dreier had begun raising his concern in leadership meetings—suggesting that as Easter approached, they say that most of the Contract had been completed, that the rest of it would be by the end of the year, and that they blame the dilatory tactics of the Democrats for the fact that all of the Contract hadn't been passed. The leaders' response was that it was too soon to consider such a thing. Armey, who was in charge of moving the bills through the House, kept a computerized schedule—which changed frequently—and was determined to meet the original goal.

But there was on Capitol Hill a strong sense of overload, so many things going on at once that members found it hard to keep track. The House Republicans' reform abolishing proxy voting in committees meant that members had to be in more than one committee meeting, and perhaps also on the House floor, at the same time.

Part of Dreier's concern was that about fifty percent of the Contract had to move through the Judiciary Committee, which wouldn't have time to give the proposals careful consideration. In fact, some bills were given no hearings, and others were rushed through by the normally equanimous Henry Hyde, the Judiciary Committee chairman, who—indicating that he was acting at the leadership's behest—took to referring to himself as the "sub-chairman." The bills before the Judiciary Committee were often poorly drafted. Democrats discovered definitions applied to the wrong titles. A Republican senator said, "Our staff would call their staff and ask about something that was flimsy. The House staff replied, 'We missed that.' " In an interview in January, Hyde said, "We have two conflicting demands—being very open to amendments and trying to meet a very stringent timetable. Those are contradictory goals, a very hard compromise to fulfill. You end up making everyone unhappy."

But there was an important reason for the speed, as Blankley spelled out in an interview as the crime bills were rolling through the House. "The Democrats don't have a chance to organize a national opposition to any issue because they're coming too fast," Blankley said. "Look at what we did on health care or on lesser issues last year. Consider how long it takes to pull your coalitions together, identify your message, and start communicating with the public and the public to communicate with the members. It takes time to build up the pressure to oppose something. How in the world do you do that when a bill comes up on a Wednesday and is gone on a Thursday night? So the constant rat-a-tat-tat of our bills has put the Democrats in an extraordinarily difficult position where they can't marshal public support for opposition to any of our bills."

The 1994 crime bill, ultimately a Clinton victory, had to be undone by the Republicans as both parties vied for the image of being the tougher on crime, even though federal crimes constituted only about five percent of the problem.

Before he could bring the crime bills to the House floor, Gingrich had to negotiate his way past the pressures brought by the gun lobby, in particular the N.R.A., to repeal the ban on assault weapons during the Hundred Days. Dick Armey said that the leaders didn't want the debate on the crime bill "to deteriorate into a debate over guns." He added, "I was insistent on that." But Gingrich had to do some fancy maneuvering. (On August 1 the *Washington Post* disclosed a letter that Gingrich had written to the N.R.A. in January promising no gun control legislation during his Speakership.)

In a meeting at five o'clock on January 25 in room H 236, a conference room in Gingrich's complex, Gingrich, Armey, DeLay, and Bill McCollum, of Florida and chairman of the Judiciary Committee's Crime Subcommittee, held a tense meeting with four N.R.A. representatives. The N.R.A. representatives said that their membership was getting restive, and that the congressional leaders should understand that if they didn't do something the membership would "get rid of us and then they'll get rid of you." After a half hour, Gingrich said he hadn't realized the degree of alienation of the gun people (who had been so supportive in 1994)—which the N.R.A. said reached beyond their own organization. The N.R.A. representatives said that the Brady bill—the 1993 law imposing a five-day waiting period on the purchase of handguns—wasn't the problem. They wanted the 1994 assault weapons ban repealed. Gingrich vowed to find a remedy but said that there were other considerations: the completion of the Contract, the dangers of letting the crime bill go to the floor under a rule that allowed all sorts of amendments. As it was, the bill had been broken into parts so that amendments germane only to that part could be offered. This was a way of preventing the assault weapons ban from coming up at that point. Armey said later, "We have an agreement with the N.R.A.: Don't you put pressure on our crime bill, and we will take up the gun ban soon after the Contract."

The six crime bills went zooming through the House. Democrats offered amendments that were routinely defeated. Liberal Democrats expressed frustration that they received no help from the White House except for the President's threat to veto a bill that would end his program, enacted in 1994, to put an additional hundred thousand police on the streets, that he had made in his State of the Union speech. Late one night, the Democrats even offered an amendment that included the language of the Fourth Amendment (against illegal searches and seizures)—and the Republicans voted that down as well. Tom DeLay explained later, "It's our bill, it's not theirs. We have to run the floor."

The House approved a bill greatly widening the use of evidence improperly obtained, including in a search without a warrant. The other House-passed bills mandated that those convicted of a federal crime provide restitution to their victims (an easy shot that passed the House unanimously); substantially reduced the habeas corpus rights of prisoners on death row (Frank Luntz said that the death penalty was a huge favorite in his polling for the Contract, and House members cited poll figures in the floor debate); strengthened the laws for swift deportation of aliens who commit crimes (a popular notion, which passed 380–20); increased federal funds for prison construction and attached more strings to this aid (states that increased prison time for violent offenders would be favored, though the number of violent crimes was going down); put into a block grant Clinton's program of providing the hundred thousand more police, along with prevention programs passed in 1994 that the Republicans had labeled "pork."

These bills showed among other things, as the pending welfare proposal did, the House Republicans' vacillation between the principle of state and local control on some programs and applying strings to carry out their particular philosophy on certain issues. In an interview in February, Christopher Shays, a forty-nine-year-old moderate Republican from Connecticut, said, "One problem we have as a party is we have some conflicting interests and we want block granting and freedom for local and state governments when it fits into our agenda and we want restrictions when that fits our agenda. We make contradictory arguments." In the debate on the crime bill, Barney Frank, Democrat of Massachusetts and a patrolling presence on the House floor, said, "They will be federalists today and states' rights people Monday. And the only common thread is they want to undo what we did last year."

Democrats used anecdotal evidence to try to puncture the Republican front: they pointed out that under an earlier law that let local officials decide how to spend federal crime-prevention funds, a sheriff in Louisiana bought a tank. They also pointed out that Gingrich had been very critical of that law. An amendment by Charles Schumer, Democrat of New York, to prohibit use of federal funds for the purchase of tanks, airplanes, limousines, and yachts was defeated by a vote of 196–235.

In the midst of the debate on the crime bills, Patrick Griffin, in charge of White House legislative liaison, met one morning with the House Democratic caucus. A number of members, mostly liberals, expressed irritation that the President wasn't making a stand on some of the crime issues—in particular on habeas corpus and the exclusion rule. Griffin's response— that we're watching this and hope to make it better in the Senate—only irritated the members further. But the President had decided that he didn't want to take on habeas corpus or search and seizure. In 1994, Clinton, who believed in capital punishment and had carried it out as governor, backed limits on death row appeals. But the restrictions proposed by the Congress were extensive enough to cause some of Clinton's aides to think that he should veto the bill. On the other hand, a White House official said, the hundred thousand police "seemed like a clean one—a middle-class issue."

A House Democrat said later, "That afternoon we were to take up habeas corpus. Several members said the current tide of making these protections weaker would prevail, absent any indication that the White House gave a damn about it—that it would be difficult to go against the yea votes. There's a group of Democrats who feel these things are a bad idea and if they felt they would have help from the White House they would stand up against it, but if the White House is going to run and hide, why bother?"

Congressional Democrats were at the time agitated over several matters involving the White House. Many were dismayed that the Clinton staff, which was supposed to have shaped up, had bungled yet another nomination, this time the naming on February 2 of Dr. Henry Foster, an ob/gyn who preached against teen pregnancy, to be Surgeon General, replacing the controversial Joycelyn Elders. There quickly developed a number of problems with the Foster nomination, including the shifting number of abortions he said he had performed. Presidential aides, who knew that the Clinton White House had to put in a better performance than in its first two years—thus the nomination was rushed, because at that time there were several vacancies—were in shock. Because of past abandonments, Clinton aides knew that the President had to stick with this nomination. So they tried to turn things around, and they and their outriders said to one and all that now the President had the Republicans where he wanted them—in the midst of a debate over abortion. But the President's advisers, not to mention Democrats on Capitol Hill, weren't at all happy.

In late February, a Democratic senator said of the Dr. Foster nomination, "I found it a little surprising because I thought that Leon being there would prevent such things from happening. It just demonstrates a lack of care." He went on to say, "The more I see of the operation the more clear it becomes that it's pretty much all polling. They just poll the daylights out of everything from every angle. It inhibits good judgments and replaces using instincts. I've never been to the White House without hearing the staff and even the President talk about polls. Even the cross-tabs." (Cross-tabs are breakdowns into segments, which can tell one how, say, forty-year-old Hispanic women voted.) The senator said, "When you start talking cross-tabs you're into the fine points of polling."

The next set of bills, under the heading of "regulatory reform," went straight at the environmental and consumer protection and worker safety laws. Republicans capitalized on a widespread reaction against some regulatory excesses by offering proposals that went to the extreme in the other direction. In the process, it also repaid debts to some of the party's most generous backers. The Clinton administration—once again trying to keep up—reacted by taking actions of its own to streamline regulations, an exercise that had already begun in Gore's Reinventing Government project but, once again, appeared to be following the crowd.

The four regulatory reform bills passed by the House between February 23 and March 3 imposed a moratorium on new regulations for all of 1995, and retroactively to November 20; established a new method of "risk assessment" for regulations; required that regulations be subjected to a cost-benefit test; and applied a radical new approach in rewarding property owners whose property was seized by the federal government for environmental or other purposes. The latter proposal, concerning "takings," was the most emotionally packed issue. The proposal was backed in part by what had become almost a cult that insisted on a new interpretation of the Fifth Amendment's bar against the government's taking private property for public purposes "without just compensation," and also, strongly, by a coalition of Westerners and developers. An administration official said, "Some regulated industries, such as the chemical industry, saw it as a way of nullifying water and toxic waste regulations." The proposal would overturn sixty years of Supreme Court jurisprudence. Though fifteen Republican moderates had written to Charles Canady, of Florida and chairman of the House Judiciary Committee Subcommittee on the Constitution, complaining that the bill would establish a new entitlement, the bill passed by a vote of 277–148. A significant number of conservative Southern Democrats supported the regulatory bills.

The Democratic leadership did little on the regulatory bills except try to offer amendments that would embarrass the Republicans and could be used in TV spots. And they tried, in some cases, to get enough votes against a bill to suggest that a Presidential veto couldn't be overridden (which takes a two-thirds vote).

Gingrich had cleverly, and largely successfully, sought to avoid splitting the Republicans along environmental lines—rousing the Teddy Roosevelt Republicans to opposition—and stirring up the public, by casting the debate in terms of relief from regulatory burdens, rather than the attacks on environmental and health and safety protections that they were. Deliberately, the Republicans didn't use the word "environmental."

Ironically, the risk-assessment bill, and the cost-benefit bill, proposed in the name of constraining regulation, laid on extraordinarily complex new requirements. The legislation created *sixty* new opportunities for judicial review. Democrats argued that factors such as the value of human health were unquantifiable. Carol Browner, the head of the Environmental Protection Agency—the target of much of this legislation—cited the example of the EPA regulation twelve years earlier that ordered the removal of lead from gasoline on the grounds that it lowered children's IQ. "Under the House bill," Browner said, "we wouldn't have been able to make that decision. What's the dollar amount to put on IQ points lost?" On the House floor, Dingell asked, "What is the cost-benefit analysis that is going to determine the price of a healthy child?" He added, "What is going to determine what is a safe workplace, and what is this worth to American society?"

Republicans had a point in stressing the cumulative impact of numerous regulatory requirements on businesses, which might have to fill out multiple forms to satisfy government rules. But they were playing government by anecdote, reciting one apparently ridiculous ruling after another—a great many of them untrue. For good measure, the takings bill required that the funds for restitution to the aggrieved party would come out of the budget of the E.P.A.—another way of trying to cripple the agency's operations.

The moratorium bill was managed by freshman David McIntosh, of Indiana, who previously had headed Vice President Dan Quayle's Competitiveness Council, which had the mission of reducing regulations. Only one exemption to the regulatory freeze was granted—the House voted 383–34 to permit the duck hunting season to proceed. In the "debate," Richard Baker, Democrat of Louisiana, said, "If ducks were present tonight, they wouldn't be for this amendment."

Carol Browner tried to rouse the Clinton White House to action on the regulatory bills, but didn't get far. She wanted a strong Presidential speech on the subject, arguing, "Look, this is dynamite stuff." But the White House didn't want a repeat of the fight with Western interests over grazing and mining, and considered the regulatory bills back-burner issues, of no great interest to the public—until the House bills hit the front page of major newspapers. Eventually, on February 21, the President attacked the pending regulatory bills, saying "These are extreme proposals. They go too far." Administration officials used the word "extreme" a lot. Clinton didn't explicitly threaten a veto.

The Clinton White House had put a lot of thought into the matter of vetoes. White House officials said that they wanted to limit the number of veto threats made by Clinton, who was, after all, under pressure to "get things done." He couldn't look too negative. The veto strategy had several levels. In an interview, Leon Panetta said, "You can use the veto threat to get your opposition to challenge you and give you the veto you want—as opposed to try to get them to modify and improve their proposal. Or you can make a veto threat to see if you can force them to clean it up. Or there's the underlying rumble veto where staff members or Cabinet officers say that they'll recommend a veto to the President." George Stephanopoulos said, "In order of strength, there's 'strongly opposed,' 'simply unacceptable,' 'recommend a veto,' 'veto.' "

Gore, who was urging a more aggressive White House strategy, later called the Contract items "the most extreme and concerted assault on the environment in history." The President did indicate that he'd veto the regulatory moratorium, but Panetta let other officials know that Clinton would like to sign the risk-assessment and takings bills. And eventually, Clinton, in Florida on March 30, said, "There is a right way and a wrong way to relax regulations."

Proponents of the regulatory bills painted Democrats who opposed them as defenders of the status quo—a charge leveled at the Democrats in several contexts—and in some not without reason.

A House Democratic leader complained later that the administration didn't supply the requested information about details of cases where the pending regulation bills would cause problems. "It's hard to get the information," he said, adding, "Part of our problem is this stuff's been coming at us like out of a firehose. The administration's trying to figure out positions and by the time they decide, the debate is over."

The regulatory reform bills caused great discomfort to Republican moderates, some of whom not many weeks before had said privately that the Contract was a sham. Now they were in an ambivalent situation. On the one hand was their gratitude for being in the majority, and their desire to stay there; on the other were their consciences or their constituencies, or both. Some had to consider the possibility that if they bucked the party orthodoxy too often, they would be challenged by a conservative in the next primary. Even if the moderate had a good chance of winning, such a challenge was not an inconsiderable, or inexpensive, proposition. Some moderates, such as Shays, said that while they had signed the Contract, they hadn't signed up for the legislative proposals written in its name. Several moderates rationalized their support in the House for measures they disagreed with by saying that the Senate would change them. But, as Dole maneuvered for the Republican nomination, that was becoming less and less assured.

John Chafee, chairman of the Senate Environment and Public Works Committee, was disturbed by what the House was doing. "It has great appeal, but it's terrible legislation," he said in an interview. He added, "When all the artichoke leaves are peeled away, they are out for the Clean Air Act, the Clean Water Act, the Endangered Species Act; that is what they're gunning for. The truth of the matter is that some things have gone too far. The answer is to work this out one by one, not take a sledgehammer to it."

Sherwood Boehlert, a fifty-eight-year-old seventh-term Republican congressman from Utica, New York, a pleasant, friendly man, was one of the fifteen members who had written the letter protesting the takings bill. He voted against the risk-assessment bill and the moratorium. As he sat in the House Dining Room having lunch one day while the regulatory bills were moving through the House, he described the moderates' dilemma. At the week before's gathering of the Tuesday Lunch Bunch, he had expressed deep concern that in many instances a lot of moderates had been turning their backs on their natural allies, including the environmentalists, "on the theory that we didn't have to worry because the Senate will take care of it." Boehlert said, "I got a nod of agreement and that was about it. Maybe I added to the guilt factor of some of the moderates. I wanted them to think about after the Hundred Days." Boehlert added, "I have no doubt that we are in the majority today because of Newt Gingrich. People would ask why a Rockefeller Republican could support a conservative firebrand from Georgia. I'd say, He's brilliant, he's innovative, he's focused, he's disciplined. And there's another factor: I want to be in the majority. Some moderates are coming to grips with that."

In the first two months of the 104th Congress, Gingrich attended the Tuesday Lunch Bunch gatherings twice. He would walk in, take off his jacket, put down a yellow pad, and say, "All right. Talk to me." Boehlert said, "Gingrich is a master chess player. We moderates view him as our link to the leadership and we're comfortable working with him. Others in the leadership come to the table with their mind made up. He'll listen."

•

Over a period of four days, from March 7 through March 10, the House next passed three "legal reform" bills that, once again, while addressing some real problems, went to extremes to resolve them. The bills: attempted to reduce the number of "frivolous" lawsuits by adopting a version of "loser pays"; revamped civil litigation by curbing suits by investors against companies; and rewrote the rules governing product liability and malpractice suits in state (preempting state laws) and federal courts, by, among other things, capping punitive damages (at $250,000 or three times monetary damages, whichever was higher). Lobbyists for doctors and pharmaceutical companies won amendments adding their clients to the bills' protections. The bill to curb investors' suits—which sharply curbed their ability to sue and was criticized by Securities and Exchange Commission Chairman Arthur Levitt as providing an inadequate deterrent to financial fraud—passed by a wide bipartisan margin. The other two were subject to fierce debate as Democrats charged Republicans with favoring "the big guy" over "the little guy" and mocked them once again for being "federalists" on some issues, and seeking national standards on others. Republicans argued that, as Henry Hyde put it, "The uncertainty and unfairness of the present system discourages employers from investing capital, making better and more innovative products, and creating new jobs."

After a long argument within the administration, Attorney General Janet Reno and White House Counsel Abner Mikva (a former appellate court judge) wrote to Gingrich in early March, saying that the administration would strongly oppose legislation that would drastically change the existing product liability laws, and that the proposal was "a disturbing and unprecedented Federal encroachment on two hundred years of well-established state authority and responsibility." Mikva and Reno did not say that the President would veto the bill. The argument within the administration was over whether the administration should take the position that federal law should supersede state law on the legal reform issues. Mikva and Reno opposed a shift to federal control; others didn't want to make the fight with the Congress. A White House aide said in April, "We said there can be limited examples, but not an entire shift. That's where we are." He added, "It's still a little bit muddy."

Despite the White House position, Republicans managed to broaden the bill's reach through amendments bringing under their protection health care providers and health insurance companies, and products that had been approved by the Food and Drug Administration. The bazaar was open. There were more lobbyists outside the House Chamber than at any other time thus far in the year.

The National Association of Manufacturers, the Chamber of Commerce, and the National Federation of Independent Business backed the bill. The Wholesale Grocers Association was also in the coalition. Vin Weber explained, "Tort reform is largely for small business—N.F.I.B. is a real constituency that delivers votes, big business doesn't. It's a huge burning issue with small business, doctors, the A.M.A.; it's something you can actually raise a lot of money on. Gingrich is aware of that. It's nice and clean politically. The organized opposition comes from a group wholly in the Democratic camp—trial lawyers, Naderites. This is one case where campaign money does count."

The coalition behind legal reform ran misleading television ads asserting that Little League teams spent more on insurance than on bats and balls, and that the Girl Scouts were threatened by frivolous suits. (The trial lawyers also ran ads.) The coalition, with about three hundred members, agreed to press for all of the legal reform legislation, not just the part they were interested in—thus increasing their strength—and to form grassroots movements as well as take ads. The opposing group was made up of trial lawyers, consumer groups, and various advocacy groups that included Ralph Nader's Public Citizen, the National Women's Health Network, and Mothers Against Drunk Driving.

Gingrich had predicted that the tort reform issues would produce a bloody fight, with the trial lawyers, as usual, backing the Democrats. But it wasn't much of a contest. The bill passed by a vote of 265–161. House leadership aides spoke with Senate leadership aides about the Senate's taking up the product liability issue shortly after it passed the House; the House leaders wanted to capitalize quickly on the power of the coalition behind it. But that didn't work out—to Bob Dole's regret.

A White House aide said late that spring, "In retrospect it was hard to figure out how do we play in this completely changed environment. The Republicans put out rhetoric that they wanted to work together, but it became clear relatively fast that they wanted to pass the Contract come hell or high water. These guys were working on a fast track. The Democrats didn't have the resources and were making demands. We said we're not going to negotiate on these issues unless some Democrats are in the room. In the beginning, we tried to figure out how we could help Democrats. It became clear that the Republicans didn't want to deal with Democrats."

There had been negotiations on unfunded mandates and there were some quiet attempts to discuss regulatory reform with Tom DeLay, a major advocate, and his staff. But House Democrats raised objections to the White House talking with Republicans when Republicans weren't talking to them. They raised the question: What do you stand for? The administration tried to reassure the congressional Democrats that they wouldn't be left out. But the plain fact was that during this period there wasn't a lot for the Republicans and the White House to talk about.

Despite their success, the House leaders were running the risk of overinterpreting the Contract, and their mandate. For the time being, they were getting away with this, because things were moving so fast, and the Clinton White House blew such an uncertain trumpet, and it was all largely a blur to the public.

On February 22, the House Republicans celebrated the Fifty Days mark with press conferences and parties. A good bit had been accomplished. But given the pressures members were under and their substantial fatigue, Gingrich pledged that there would be no second Hundred Days.

Members were increasingly looking on the Hundred Days as boot camp: the strains had a kind of bonding effect, but the fatigue level was quite high and members were becoming snappish. Life was even harder on their staffs. In mid-February, Bill Paxon took over Head's restaurant, on Capitol Hill, for a party, but few of the exhausted Republicans turned up. "You've got to do your laundry sometime," a congresswoman said. Key members were finding it hard to get through to the frenetically busy Gingrich. And there was a sense that the hardest days—when budget cuts, the welfare and tax bills had to be considered—still lay ahead. By mid-February, Gingrich was growing concerned about moderate Republicans who were saying that this was not the time to cut taxes. The Republican leaders felt that they needed to remind the public that the Contract had pledged only to bring the issues to the floor for a vote—but they knew that, largely as a result of their own rhetoric, the public expected more.

Despite the celebrations, Gingrich and some of his colleagues were uneasy. A close ally said, "They're worried that they've taken on too much."

On the fiftieth day, Clinton journeyed to Capitol Hill to meet with the House Democratic caucus. The meeting with the President of the United States was held in a basement room, HC 6, with no windows. About 120 of the 204 House Democrats turned up. The members sat on folding chairs. (Blankley said that other spaces in the Capitol were occupied or not to be used for this sort of gathering.) The meeting began at about 10:00 A.M. Clinton said that there were issues where the administration would go along with the Republicans, others where it would differ—and that there would be more of those as time went on. He complained, as he had since the election, that his administration hadn't gotten credit for a lot of the things it had done. One Democrat said later, "It was like a public speech." Another said, "A good, competent performance, neither exhilarating nor depressing—a B, and a B is good at this point." At 10:40 A.M., while the President was answering the last question, about twenty members rose to be ready to leave as soon as he was finished. One Democratic member said later, "There was all this motion in the back. Why couldn't he leave

before everyone got tired? You lose your majesty and power and importance through incidents like that. When he makes a call, we want to be
intimidated by it." Another member said to a colleague at the end of the
meeting, "I wonder why he came."

On Monday, February 13, Gingrich, with a number of concerns on his
mind, held a scheduled retreat that went on for seven hours in room H 128
in the Capitol, known as the place where Sam Rayburn, the legendary
House Speaker, convened his "Board of Education"—a floating group that
met at the end of the day for bourbon and gossip. The room had typical
Capitol decor: a long mahogany table, rich blue carpeting, a large gilt-
edged mirror, and a chandelier. Attending the meeting were Gingrich,
Armey, DeLay, John Boehner, Dennis Hastert, of Illinois and the chief
deputy whip, Bob Walker, and Bill Paxon. By some accounts, the meeting
was "emotional." The two main problems, as Gingrich and the others saw
it, were that the Republican leaders weren't meshing well enough, and that
the public didn't realize how much the House had accomplished. The latter
point had a certain piquancy as well as a familiar ring. Walker said later,
"One topic was why people didn't know what we were getting done. We
came to the conclusion that everything was happening so fast that it was
hard to get across to the country what we're doing." Paxon said, "There
was a lot of blunt discussion about staying on message"—a familiar Clintonian term. "We didn't realize the enormity of getting out the word about
hundreds of legislative items in the Contract." Some of the problem was
attributed to a confusion of roles among the leadership.

DeLay came under criticism for not having a clear enough conception of
his own job; there was discussion about the sometimes overlapping activities of Armey and DeLay, and some questioning about how Gingrich saw
his role. There was discussion of the fact that the leaders' floor staffs on
occasion gave conflicting signals to the troops. Walker also said that the
committee chairmen had to be made to feel that they were part of the
leadership.

From one sentence in the *TV Guide*, the Contract grew a multipart bill
directing the President to take various steps on foreign policy. Some provisions were based on emotion and myth, and almost all of them interfered
with the President's authority to conduct foreign policy. It specifically ordered that the four Visegrad countries—Hungary, Poland, Slovakia, and
the Czech Republic—be admitted into NATO by January 10, 1999. (It did
not say what time of day.) The whole idea of admitting these countries into
NATO, and thus being responsible for their defense, had not been thought
through by either the administration, which favored the idea but on its own
timetable (a subject of internal dispute), or the Congress. The Republican

bill restricted the payment of U.N. dues until the U.S. had been reimbursed for multinational peacekeeping missions. It also prohibited U.S. forces from serving under U.N. commanders. The latter provision was based on the mythology that U.S. troops which came to grief in Somalia were serving under a U.N. commander. (But U.N. authority over the NATO authority had obviously produced a muddle.) Further, U.S. planes in Bosnia were under NATO command, and during Desert Storm an American commander made a field decision to put troops under a French commander. The bill also called for funding for S.D.I., or Star Wars. Some of the proposals were watered down in the Republican-controlled National Security Committee, and the date certain for the new countries entering NATO was removed.

On these foreign policy issues, as on certain others, Clinton Cabinet officers were out in front of the Clinton White House. Several officials felt that it was taking the President too long to shake off the November elections and become fully engaged in the issues before Congress—that the denial, anger, guru seeking, and séances at Camp David had gone on too long. Secretary of State Warren Christopher and Defense Secretary William Perry took it upon themselves to oppose some of the foreign policy provisions. In general, Cabinet officers didn't fear retribution from the White House—the President had enough problems without trying to discipline his Cabinet or replacing any more than he had to for ethics reasons, and anyway, it wasn't in his nature to discipline his lieutenants. Perry and Christopher began their offensive while still waiting for White House clearance. But before the bill came to the floor for a vote on February 15, the President threatened to veto it if it passed "in its current form."

The Democratic caucus decided that the S.D.I. provision was the most politically vulnerable. This decision arose out of Gephardt's system of committees and task forces to try to arrive at caucus-wide positions, unlikely as that had seemed at first. When National Security Adviser Anthony Lake and Christopher and a Defense official (Perry was traveling) appeared before the caucus on the morning of February 15, they gave solemn presentations about the peacekeeping and command-and-control issues. The elected politicians responded that that was all very well but they were going after S.D.I. The Democrats then decided to use six of the ten hours of debate on the bill on the subject of S.D.I. (The Republican leaders were now placing strict time limits on most bills. In fact, some key Democrats had concluded that their past taking advantage of open rules by offering a large number of amendments hadn't been useful: it had shown them as obstructive and unfocused. They conceded privately that the Republicans were now running the House the way Democrats had in the past—and would if they ever took over again.) And the Democrats stayed disciplined: various Democrats agreed to not take much time on their own amendments. The main Democratic amendment said that combat-readiness (a popular topic) and defense against short-range, "theater" ballistic missiles should have higher priority than deployment of S.D.I. This would enable members to vote for *some* missile defense, a less expensive system on which the Pentagon was already at work. The Democratic leaders arranged that the amendment would be offered by John Spratt, Democrat of South Carolina, a highly respected defense conservative. Using such people to present the Democrats' proposals was also part of Gephardt's new strategy. Conservative Democrats could try to enlist Republican support.

The Republican leadership, taken by surprise, lost their first major issue. The Spratt amendment carried 218–212, with twenty-four Republicans supporting it. Among them was John Kasich, of Ohio, forty-two, the chairman of the House Budget Committee, who had opposed S.D.I. before. Many of the Republican supporters of the amendment were moderates, such as Christopher Shays, who were upset that S.D.I. had somehow been appliquéd onto the Contract.

When the Republican leaders, holding a meeting in the Capitol on the budget issue, realized what had happened, Armey exchanged sharp words with Kasich. Armey said heatedly, "We lost that vote and you defeated it." Republican leaders considered trying to reverse the vote the next day, but decided that it would be too difficult. With their encouragement, Kasich did say the next day that he had made a mistake. But he didn't seem very contrite. An amendment to slightly water down the effect of the Spratt amendment had been agreed to, and the Republican leaders made much of that, but the fact remained that they had lost a significant vote.

7

MONEY RIVER

"We Know What We Want to Do and We Find the People to Help Us Do That"

───────────

For many years before they took over the House, Republicans watched Democrats turn incumbency into an assured source of campaign funds. They had seen a Democratic culture develop and predominate in the law firms and lobbying groups around Washington, and form with the Democratic Congress a mutual interest in maintaining the status quo. And, when, beginning in the 1980s, House Democratic political operatives showed remarkable prowess at extracting contributions from companies and business organizations that were more in tune ideologically with Republicans, the Republicans took careful notice. They came to believe—with some reason—that the two things that prevented them from taking over the House were the Democratic advantages in redistricting and fundraising.

In mid-October of 1994, a little over a couple of weeks before the election, Gingrich met with directors of political action committees (PACs) and warned them that they should begin backing Republicans. He was quoted as saying, "For anybody who's not on board now it's going to be the two coldest years in Washington." When the Republicans did take over the House they instituted a thorough, unforgiving effort to reap the financial rewards and build their own networks for passing legislation. The interconnection of money, access, politician, and legislation had been around for some time, but the newly victorious Republicans took it to new lengths. The audacity with which the Republicans went about this was stunning.

Ed Rollins, a longtime Republican strategist, said, "Republicans saw the Democrats' seven, eight, nine times money advantage and they started to categorize it, keeping score, and when they came to office, they said, 'Listen, the game has changed. If you want your client to get fair representation on tax and budget legislation, you do it our way.' "

The role that lobbyists played in writing the Republicans' legislation right on Capitol Hill was without precedent. The Democrats had their alliances with labor, elderly, children's rights, and environmental groups, and there was a sharing of ideas for bills and amendments. But sympathetic lobbyists had unparalleled access in the 104th Congress because the Republicans considered this the way to do business.

The Republican leaders—Gingrich, Armey, DeLay, Boehner—played a role in establishing this new network, and keeping their allies on the straight and narrow. When the National Taxpayers Union, a conservative group, and Friends of the Earth, a liberal environmental group, in January joined in calling for cuts in subsidies to mining, timber, and other interests, Armey sent out a "Dear Colleague" letter, saying, "It has been our concern that fiscally conservative groups have been serving as a front for the extreme environmental movement." In March, Armey, objecting to the direction of some corporate beneficence, wrote his colleagues, "I urge you to . . . challenge your contacts in the corporate world to change this disturbing pattern." But no one was as instrumental at defining the terms of the relationship between the new Republican House majority and the interest groups as Tom DeLay. DeLay wasn't out just to make the fruits of victory as bountiful as possible; he was out to change the very culture of Washington.

He was the major force behind the new regulatory reform bills. He led a business-backed assault on the federal bureaucracy. He had written the proposals on risk assessment and takings into the Contract and shepherded them through the House. DeLay, former owner of Albo Pest Control, in Houston, had become annoyed with regulations his company had to meet (he thought DDT shouldn't have been banned), and had made these issues his cause when he entered politics.

When the Republicans won the election, DeLay launched what he called "The K Street Strategy." As part of that strategy, when people from a lobbying or law firm wanted to meet with DeLay, they would be told to send a Republican. Otherwise, he wasn't interested. Some of DeLay's friends warned him that this was a bit blatant, but DeLay was unmoved. He had his own view of the world "downtown" from the Capitol. Chuckling as he described his K Street Strategy in an interview in July, DeLay said, "Well, it's very obvious that power is access and power is knowledge and the power of K Street was their knowledge of the Democrats. And they're trying to get that returned—they're telling their bosses, their constituencies, their clients, 'Don't help the Republicans.' They're working against us because their power is eliminated. We want more Republicans on K Street." He added, "Go through some of those firms and look at their structure. They've kept a Democratic structure and hired a few Republicans for the interim. The thing to do is go to their bosses and their clients and their constituents and say if they like what's going on here they'd better change their structures.

"It's the same thing with fund-raising," DeLay continued. "I sent a letter to the PACs that gave to Randy Tate's [representative from Washington State] opponent. I wrote them and asked them to contribute to Randy." DeLay continued, "The point is, to maintain this majority we've got to change the whole mind-set in this town."

A study by Common Cause showed that Tate was the seventh highest freshman recipient of PAC money in the first six months of 1995. David McIntosh, who had led the floor fights on some of the anti-regulatory bills, was tenth. McIntosh's staff director, Mildred Webber, had helped DeLay raise money for potential new members (including McIntosh) in 1994, and then managed DeLay's campaign for whip.

Actually, Washington had done more adjusting to the new powers than DeLay seemed to think. Many, if not most, law firms and lobbying groups had had Republican partners for some time. There had, after all, been Republican administrations for most of the recent years, and it never hurt to have contacts among important Republicans on Capitol Hill, whether or not they were in the majority. When the Republicans took over the House, many, if not most, of these firms added a Republican or two.

After the election, Republicans continued to keep watch on which lobbyists were donating to whom, and in some cases the Republican members themselves refused to see lobbyists whom they considered insufficiently loyal. Bill Paxon, the chairman of the National Republican Congressional Committee, distributed to Republican congressmen a compilation of contributions in 1994 by large PACs.

In seeking to overturn the environmental laws, after the election DeLay founded Project Relief, a coalition of more than three hundred business and other lobby groups as well as individuals that wanted regulations rolled back. DeLay met with some of its members almost weekly. Among them were representatives of the construction industry, the nonprescription drug industry, Bell South Corp., Federal Express, the Beer Institute, the Independent Insurance Agents of America, the National Restaurant Association, the Coalition of Energy Taxes, Boeing, and on and on. These groups did coordinated lobbying on the regulatory bills, and, of course, they had a lot of money behind them.

John Boehner, owner of a plastics-sales company, did his part by forming the Thursday Group, a collection of representatives of the National Federation of Independent Business, the National Association of Home Builders, the National Restaurant Association, and the U.S. Chamber of Commerce, plus ideological conservative groups such as the Christian Coalition, Americans for Tax Reform, and the Citizens for a Sound Economy. These organizations were in a position to wage expensive "grassroots" campaigns on behalf of items in the Contract, as well as lobby members. They were, Boehner said in an interview, the Republicans' "closest friends, people who had been with us year in and year out, through thick and thin. And they act as our eyes and ears on what's happening in the real world." Members of the Thursday group would form special superlobbies on individual legislative issues, such as "legal reform," and other issues as the year went on. The group met weekly in H 227, Gingrich's conference room—a large room with a long table and portraits of previous House Republican leaders, just down the hall from his office—where it was given a pep talk and "talking points."

As for the relationship with lobbyists, DeLay said, "You've got to understand, we are ideologues. We have an agenda. We have a philosophy. I want to repeal the Clean Air Act. No one came to me and said, 'Please repeal the Clean Air Act.' We say to the lobbyists, 'Help us.' We know what we want to do and we find the people to help us do that. We go to the lobbyists and say, 'Help us get this in the appropriations bill.' " (Putting policy directives in appropriations bills—especially regulatory policy—became a specialty of the House Republicans later in the year.) DeLay added, delicately, "There are some times we ask them to support us."

DeLay said, "Our friends are going to help us write legislation, the other side is trying to kill it. The environmental extremists helped write legislation. You don't think they wrote the Clean Air Act?"

The unusual role in legislating played by the interests in the 104th Congress kept on turning up. The *Washington Post* reported that a lobbyist for the energy and petrochemical industries wrote the first draft of the bill placing a moratorium on federal regulations, and that the bill was redrafted after lobbyists in Project Relief criticized it as too limited. The *Post* also reported that Project Relief lobbyists were given a Capitol office to use as a "war room" during the debate on the moratorium.

A bill to greatly weaken the Clean Water Act was, according to the *New York Times*, written by a task force of lobbyists representing regulated polluters working alongside congressional sponsors on the Transportation and Infrastructure Committee, "inserting one provision after another to satisfy industry groups like the Chemical Manufacturers Association, companies like International Paper, and organizations of the cities and states covered by the law." This was a change from past practice on the Clean

Water Act, which was praised in 1994 by Bud Shuster, of Pennsylvania, the then-ranking member of the Committee, as "completely fair" and involving the minority staff. (In 1995 Shuster said that press allegations of unusual industry involvement arose from the fact that "the national media is in the hip pocket of the environmental bureaucrats here in this town.")

And the *New York Times* reported that three attorneys from a law firm that lobbied on behalf of fifteen companies that would benefit from another bill to inhibit regulation actually conducted a briefing on the bill for the Senate Judiciary Committee staff. The firm's clients included the Edison Electric Institute, the utility industry's largest trade association, Philip Morris, and the chemical industry.

The Democratic Study Group charged that during a House committee writing of an anti-regulation bill, lawyer-lobbyists representing interested businesses were in the committee's majority staff offices writing material on the office computers, and the next day these lawyer-lobbyists sat next to the Republican chief counsel, whispering and passing notes to him as he responded to members' questions about the bill.

Pressed to define the difference between the way Republicans were doing things and how Democrats had done things, David Skaggs, chairman of the Democratic Study Group, said, "It's more than a nuanced or a subtle difference. There really has been a wholesale turning over of the legal responsibilities of members and staff. There's a big difference between that and telling the Sierra Club to take a shot at an amendment or us putting together a working group that helps vet an idea. There is some surface semblance. But having the paid employees of these groups sitting at the word processors up here and briefing members on what's in the bills and on the dais in committee meetings advising members is a whole new thing. There's not only consultation with, but delegation of discretion to. We were hired to make the call, not them."

Not surprisingly, following the 1994 election, the river of political money changed course. According to a Common Cause study of Federal Election Commission (F.E.C.) reports, in the first six months of 1995 Republican fund-raising committees received a sharp increase, more than doubling their intake of the year before, in "soft money." (Soft money was made up of legal contributions not covered by federal limits, and often involved contributions of $100,000 by individuals.) The amount contributed to the Democrats of course declined, and was only about half that received by the Republicans. The $20.1 million in soft money taken in by the Republicans in this period was an extraordinary amount of money for a nonelection year. Heavy among the donors were companies and individuals with interests before the new Congress; they included Philip Morris, the financial industry, and energy interests.

Some industries got smart shortly before the election. Late in the game, the six largest accounting firms made big contributions to members, most of them Republicans, who might be sympathetic to their desire for a limitation on their financial liability in securities fraud lawsuits. A provision to this effect was included in the securities fraud bill that passed the House.

In the first six months of 1995, GOPAC raised nearly $1.1 million—more than it received in all of 1994, the election year. Off-year receipts usually drop sharply.

According to figures collected by the Federal Election Commission, Republican House members received a total of $28.1 million over the period from January 1 to June 30 (more than double what they had received two years before); Democrats received $17.4 million (less than they received in 1993). The F.E.C. said that Republican freshmen were responsible for much of the increase in Republican funds.

A Common Cause study found that the "reform-minded" House freshmen raised $5 million during their first six months in office, about twenty percent more than the people whose seats they took raised during a comparable period in 1993. Common Cause also found that most of the newly elected freshmen received contributions immediately after the election from political action committees that hadn't contributed to them during their campaigns.

Citizen Action, a consumer group, reported that whereas before Labor Day of 1994 House Democrats had received sixty-one percent of all campaign contributions from corporate and other special interest PACs, in the five months following the election Republican House members received seventy-eight percent of such contributions.

Gingrich, asked about the role of the interest groups, was quoted in the *Wall Street Journal* as saying, "As long as it's out in the open, I have no problem."

8

FRESHMEN TROUBLE
"Their Knees Will Buckle"

Gingrich's first real crisis as the new leader of the House came over the Balanced Budget Amendment. This once hoary bit of conservative boilerplate now played a critical role in the Republicans' strategy. Supporters had narrowly failed in three efforts since 1990 to pass such an Amendment, but now the proposal had new import. Bill Kristol, one of the Republican Party's chief theologians, said in early February, "If the Balanced Budget Amendment goes down it creates a lot of problems with spending restraint." Kristol was most intent on this point, and seemed genuinely concerned. He went on, "The Balanced Budget hurts the Democratic Party for the next decade. It will force a number of budget-cuts-versus-tax-increase fights and that's good for us. The Balanced Budget Amendment issue will survive if it loses, but it would make a big difference to win it." Tony Blankley said, "Our objective isn't just to balance the budget, it's to transform the government. It's not just a green eyeshade proposal."

The fight over the Balanced Budget Amendment was quite intense because Democrats and Republicans saw it the same way: as an effective weapon for beating back or killing federal programs.

But the Clinton White House, which had ferociously and successfully fought a Balanced Budget Amendment in 1994, elected not to make the fight this time. A senior official said, "The President basically said, 'We're not going to fight it the way we did before.' First, we'd had close votes with the Democratic Congress and it would be a tough vote to win in this Congress. Second, the better approach would be to focus not on balancing the budget, but *how* they'd balance the budget and which constituencies would be hurt." The President said in the first meeting with the bipartisan leadership that he wasn't going to fight it as hard as before. One aide said later, "We're in a new hemisphere. We can't pick every fight." Another official said, "We could not have that be the only thing that defines him." The President's aides feared a Republican attack that said that Clinton opposed a balanced budget. Further, this aide said, "The party is split on the Amendment." But that hadn't stopped the White House the year before.

A leading House Democrat said, "If there was no chance of the President's being able to stop it, there was no point in getting involved in something that's hopeless. There were discussions back and forth about this: they did win the election and after the Republicans won in '81, the Reagan budget and tax bill went through. The Balanced Budget Amendment was the number one issue for the freshmen." Alice Rivlin gave strong testimony against the Amendment to the Senate Judiciary Committee, and she and Reich were known to be disappointed that the President didn't fight harder.

The White House settled for low-intensity warfare, working with the Hill Democrats on the one line of attack that united them: demanding that the Republicans reveal what cuts they would make to balance the budget. This was of course a debate ploy, since the Democrats knew full well that no such revelation would be forthcoming. Dick Armey had famously said on *Meet the Press,* in January, that the Republicans couldn't say how they would do it because "once Members of Congress know exactly, chapter and verse, the pain . . . to get to a balanced budget, their knees will buckle."

The House freshmen's intensity about the Balanced Budget Amendment caused Gingrich's crisis. They insisted not only on a Balanced Budget Amendment, but one that required a three-fifths vote in order to raise any kind of taxes. This version of the Amendment was sponsored by Joe Barton, a sixth-term member from Texas. Gingrich didn't believe that the votes were there for the three-fifths provision—not enough moderates or conservative Democrats would support it to provide the two-thirds vote (290) necessary to pass a Constitutional Amendment. Twenty to thirty moderates (including Nancy Johnson) were opposed to the three-fifths rule. (The opposition of moderates was one reason Gingrich attended a Tuesday Lunch Bunch gathering on February 14.)

According to a close ally, Gingrich didn't much care about the three-fifths provision. Armey told some members that he could live with requiring a Constitutional majority—an absolute majority, rather than just a majority of those present and voting—to raise taxes, and those he told didn't think he would be saying that if Gingrich didn't agree. Moreover, Gingrich and Armey knew that the three-fifths proposal would never pass the Senate and they wanted to send to the other side of the Capitol an Amendment that the Senate would approve.

But Gingrich couldn't afford an open split with the freshmen. (He tried to meet with them once a week to take their pulse and hear them out.) Having in their own minds inherited the earth, the freshmen demanded an Amendment with the three-fifths provision or no Amendment at all. When Gingrich told a press conference that he thought it would be difficult to pass an Amendment requiring a three-fifths majority for tax increases, the freshmen were enraged. Gingrich even took the precaution of phoning Rush Limbaugh to ask him not to take the freshmen's line, but Limbaugh didn't cooperate.

The goal of balancing the budget by 2002, now part of the proposed Amendment, had been reached in a rather happenstance way. When the Contract was being drawn up, Frank Luntz wanted to use the year 2000, telling the Republicans that it would be wonderful if when the illuminated ball in Times Square went down, signaling the new millennium, all parents in America would know that they weren't passing on more debt to their children. The members said, Wow!, Luntz recalled, but then the more budget-educated members said, We can't do it by 2000. So it became 2002.

The idea of putting an economic theory—by its nature a debatable one —in the Constitution was absurd and even reckless. It isn't conservative to fool around with the Constitution—especially to make a political point. To say as the Amendment did that it would take a three-fifths vote to have an unbalanced budget, as well as to raise taxes, was to invite minority rule. If tricks had to be employed to meet the required balance, as was likely, or the balance wasn't achieved because of political or economic realities, more public cynicism would result. Even some Republicans had misgivings. One leading Republican said, "Promising to balance the budget by 2002 is ridiculous. You can't know what will happen to the economy in the future. A one percent increase in unemployment reduces revenues by at least $50 billion. The public won't believe that the budget's not in balance because of a change in the economy, but will believe that we screwed up." According to the Congressional Budget Office, bringing the budget into balance by 2002 would require $1.2 trillion in budget cuts. Furthermore, Republicans had said that Social Security, defense spending, and interest on the debt would be exempted.

It was clear when the Republican leadership, the leadership staff, and the top committee staff members, on Friday morning, January 6, held their first weekly meeting that there would be trouble on the Balanced Budget Amendment. A leadership staff member said later, "Months ago when we were thrashing around with Armey about the number of days we'd need for each bill, the Balanced Budget Amendment seemed easy, it had been done before. At that point we knew we were running into trouble on the three-fifths for raising taxes." Even though it was, as the aide described, a "throwaway vote"—it was unlikely in the extreme that this Congress, anyway, would want to raise taxes—the vote count for the version of the Amendment including the three-fifths provision still fell short. So, the vote on the Balanced Budget Amendment, originally scheduled for January 19, was postponed a week. Other reasons were given, but the real one was that Gingrich couldn't get control of his troops. The freshmen were threatening to defeat the rule for debating the bill—thus defeating the bill itself —if the Barton version wasn't going to pass. Gingrich talked to Barton several times to try to calm him down.

Gingrich, Armey, and DeLay worked the freshmen hard. DeLay said, "We had thirty moderates who wouldn't take tax limitation in the Balanced Budget Amendment and twenty to thirty on the hard right who wouldn't take the Balanced Budget Amendment without the three-fifths requirement. We knew we were in trouble, and we had to make a leadership decision in mid-January that we might have to shift gears and back an alternative." The alternative was a straight Constitutional Amendment without the three-fifths provision, sponsored by Charles Stenholm, the conservative Democrat from Texas, and Dan Schaefer, a seventh-term Republican from Colorado. But the Barton people insisted that theirs be the only proposal allowed on the floor. DeLay said, "The first major issue, the crown of the Contract, could not go down. We had to pass a Balanced Budget Amendment." The leadership decided on a rule that would allow other proposals, and to work for Barton, but if it didn't prevail (as they expected), to shift their support to the simple Amendment. DeLay said, "On the last day before the vote we had a group of fifteen, twenty freshmen that were just refusing to cooperate. I had to show them the list of Democrats who would never vote for Barton. You could beat them up, you could shoot them in the streets, these people weren't going to vote for it. Finally, after a lot of discussions and meetings they began to understand."

To get some form of a Balanced Budget Amendment through the House, the leadership put together a coalition that included: the N.F.I.B., the Chamber of Commerce, the Americans for Tax Reform, the National Taxpayers' Union, the Christian Coalition, and the Family Research Council. Friendly talk radio hosts were asked to come to Washington, making it easier for members to join them in their broadcasts. Since the talk show hosts hadn't been accepted as legitimate members of the press gallery, the Republican leadership provided space for them. But the propagandizing got out of hand. Tony Blankley said later, "Some of our radio talk show friends wanted three-fifths or nothing. Rush was out there pounding away for three-fifths and nothing less." Armey said later, "It's always a problem in this business: you have to try to play the hand without overplaying the hand. In the case of Barton, we overplayed the hand."

In the floor debate, which began on Wednesday, January 25, Democrats argued that the Amendment would result in cuts in Social Security. But an amendment offered by Gephardt to take Social Security out of budget calculations, and a proposal, backed by the Clinton administration, calling for "truth-in-budgeting"—giving the specific details of how the budget would be balanced—were both defeated the next day.

For the debate, the freshmen were wearing large red and white buttons that said "3/5."

Gingrich, fearing that things were unraveling on the afternoon before the day of the voting, worked the floor and met with people one on one. In the early evening, in a meeting with some of the freshmen, Gingrich reached an agreement with John Shadegg, of Arizona, that the three-fifths proposal would be voted on again on April 15, 1996—tax day of the election year. The theory was that this would give the freshmen time to organize for that vote and to threaten electoral opposition to those who voted against it. But the main idea, of course, was to give the freshmen something so that they would calm down.

But Gingrich still wasn't sure that the backers of the Barton proposal would vote for the simpler alternative if theirs failed. He planned as a show of allegiance to make the closing speech on the Barton proposal. A final speech by a Speaker was a rare and important event. But in a phone call with Barton at about nine on Thursday morning, Gingrich tried to persuade him to support the Stenholm-Schaefer substitute if his own proposal failed. The conversation did not go well. Gingrich then told others that Barton wasn't going to help, so he wasn't going to help him by making the closing speech. At about ten, before the vote, Gingrich met with Barton. Barton was noncommittal. When the votes for the Barton version stopped at 253 —well short of the 290—the leaders knew that it wouldn't win. Right after the vote, Gingrich and Armey met in H 219, Armey's office, with Barton and some of his allies on how to persuade the freshmen to vote for Stenholm-Schaefer. It was decided that Barton and a freshman would go to a meeting of the freshmen.

The Stenholm-Schaefer proposal, the traditional Balanced Budget Amendment, carried and the Amendment was finally approved by the House on Thursday night by a vote of 300–132—with ten votes to spare.

On the House floor, a pleased and obviously relieved Gingrich pronounced the result "a bipartisan victory."

At a press conference the next day, Gingrich pulled from his jacket pocket the laminated copy of the *TV Guide* Contract that he always carried with him. Saying that a friend had given him a punch for making holes in the Contract as the items were approved, he proudly punched his first hole.

At the White House, just before a meeting on welfare, Clinton said, cryptically, "I'm glad they adopted the Stenholm amendment. . . . It makes the bill much better. I still believe that if it's going to be presented to the country, they ought to tell the country what's involved. There's a right to know here."

The glow of the triumph was somewhat dimmed that very afternoon when word spread on Capitol Hill that Armey, in an interview with radio reporters, had referred to Barney Frank, an avowed homosexual, as "Barney Fag." In an emotional speech on the House floor, Armey protested the airing of the tape and said that he had merely uttered "a stumbled word." Democrats leapt at the opportunity to embarrass the Republican leadership. But even some close to Armey thought that the "stumbled word" reflected backroom talk.

A Republican member close to the leadership said later, "We thought we had a cool spin on the three-fifths issue, but by Friday afternoon there was a generally down feeling about Armey's comment. It cast a pall. At the leadership meeting today Newt complimented us on our progress and said it was due to Armey. Yes, when you're marching with one foot in your mouth."

In mid-February, Sam Brownback, a freshman from Kansas, led a press conference of freshmen to announce that they wanted to eliminate four Cabinet departments—HUD, and the Departments of Commerce, Energy, and Education.

Brownback, a tall, serious man with wavy brown hair and a deep voice, came across as low-keyed and intelligent—not as a fire-breather. Thirty-eight, a former broadcaster, Brownback had worked in Washington as a White House Fellow, and by mid-February of 1995 had emerged as a leader of the freshmen.

"You have to look at the election," Brownback said in a conversation the day after the press conference. "Many of us ran a very aggressive, very ideological campaign. I ran a very conservative campaign, saying we should reduce the size of the federal government, reform the Congress, and return to the basic values that built this country. It wasn't an agenda designed for eastern Kansas—more price supports, more money for Kansas State University."

Brownback was one of the very few Republican challengers to not sign the Contract. "I didn't know how we would pay for the whole thing," he said. "I supported the tax cuts but nobody told me how we'd pay for them." Brownback said, "Most of my colleagues are very ideologically driven." When asked why, he said, "A number of us are the political children of Ronald Reagan. We came of political age under Ronald Reagan. We could say, This is someone I can believe in, he has a core set of principles.

"Last year's election was a populist election, much like the 1890s," Brownback continued. "The objects of anger then were banks and railroads. This time, big government was the target. It was too big and wouldn't listen. I'd go do an event and ask, What do you think we should do about the Congress? The answers: take a sledgehammer to it, build a moat around it. And that washed a number of us right into here. I won with sixty-six percent to thirty-four over a two-term former governor. I had never run for office before."

9

THE UPSTART

"Is This Really Written in Stone?"

John Kasich, the forty-two-year-old new chairman of the House Budget Committee, had big thoughts. Kasich, the son of a mailman, who since 1983 had represented a district in and near Columbus, Ohio, didn't think in conventional Washington terms, even conventional Republican terms. He didn't accept assumptions, even Republican assumptions, about why things had to be in the budget; he questioned virtually all of it. His attitude was a sort of innocence mixed with the courage to question the fixed ideas and protected preserves of his elders. Alice Rivlin described him as "fearless." Kasich, youthful-looking with short, cropped brown hair and blue eyes, was frequently described as "brash." While there was something to that, what many saw as brash was actually a strong motivation to reduce the deficit significantly, and to challenge assumptions previously unchallenged—and an enthusiasm about his job. Kasich's youthfulness and even exuberance—he was mercurial, and could become quite low when things weren't going right for him—contributed to the impression of brash but also to his ability to make himself a real force within the House. In 1994, as the ranking member of the Budget Committee, Kasich co-sponsored (with Tim Penny, a former Democrat from Minnesota) a deficit reduction package that wasn't quite thought through, but which the Clinton administration had had to fight hard and only narrowly defeated.

Now Kasich was developing as a force in the 104th Congress—reaching beyond the power that accrued naturally to a Budget Committee chairman.

He cultivated the freshmen (he attended their press conference about abolishing Cabinet departments), to whom he was a hero. Unlike his party's leaders, he had close friendships across the aisle—one of the strongest was with the very liberal Ron Dellums of California. (In June, Kasich and Dellums teamed up in an unsuccessful attempt to kill the B-2 bomber.) Later, he and Brownback joined up to form a group of about twenty members called the New Federalists, whose role was, Kasich said mischievously, "to maintain revolutionary zeal." The idea was to see that their elders—even Gingrich—didn't go slack on some spending issues or decide that it was too much trouble to abolish the Commerce Department.

Gingrich and Kasich were very close; Kasich, a bachelor, often dined with Gingrich. Still, when Kasich became Budget chairman in 1995, Gingrich placed Bob Walker on the committee as the second-ranking Republican, to keep an eye on him. Walker could be a useful liaison between Kasich and Gingrich. And Gingrich placed Dave Hobson, also of Ohio, on the committee as the representative from the Appropriations Committee and his own representative to the moderates. ("That was about making sure that we had everyone in the room," a Gingrich aide said.) Hobson also acted in a way as Kasich's keeper, the more mature man who often drove Kasich to or from work (and sometimes acted as a check on his more impulsive instincts). Thus, by having chosen Livingston as Appropriations Committee chairman, and surrounding his protégé Kasich with reliable allies, Gingrich had a tight grip on the whole funding process.

Gingrich sometimes felt that he had to discipline Kasich, and lost his temper with him. In an interview, Gingrich recalled that one night when the two men met in his office, he felt that Kasich needed some correction: "I was trying to get him to listen and he wasn't listening. And I mean he is absolutely one of the two or three most brilliant leaders we've got in the House and he was just off on a tear because he knew the budget and he'd thought it all through. I just screamed at him. It was he and I and then he brought in five of his members to explain to me why they shouldn't listen. And then I screamed at him in front of these five members." Kasich got the point.

Kasich shared some of the inclinations of his generation: early in the session he invited in a "motivational" expert who sought to loosen up the committee staff members by having them shoot Nerf balls at each other from plastic guns.

In a conversation in his office in the Longworth Building on opening day, Kasich expressed his understanding that he had a big job ahead of him. He had to find nearly $200 billion to pay for the tax cuts in the Contract (this would cover only the first five years' cost, and was to balloon to nearly $700 billion over ten years) and he had pledged that this would be done before the tax cuts were taken up by the House. Kasich had also been given the assignment by Gingrich of putting the deficit on a "glide path" toward balance by 2002. This was estimated to require about another $400 billion in the five-year budget plan. Kasich said, "It will be very difficult, because of 'the Zorro Principle'—death by one thousand cuts." He added, "People affected by a government program will be very vocal that the program be maintained—they'll organize in members' districts and say why that member must vote to continue the program. It's kind of like a gauntlet. You have to get people to open their minds to changing things." Kasich recognized that some of the harder work would come in trying to buck Republican-oriented groups, such as the agriculture and small business lobbies, and the "arts lobby." Kasich said, "We have a lot of rich Republicans. Support of the arts is thought of as a Democratic deal, but it's Republican." He added, "If any of these groups are the winners, then we are the losers. If we blink on any of them, we are the losers."

He said, "This is all definitely doable."

Inevitably, there were strains between Kasich and the other committee chairmen, who had programs to protect or wanted to make their own decisions, and didn't want this upstart to give them orders (through his budget).

Kasich continued, "These guys are in a culture where they learn how to spend, and now we come up to them—Newt and Armey and I—and say, 'You've got to pay $200 billion for this Contract and make a down payment on the balanced budget.' They say, 'What do you mean? This is the game plan?' You can't just shout and push. Part of what we've got to do is we've got to say to the committee chairmen, 'You've got to save X millions of dollars. To do that, you can cut the budget or think up some neat, cool stuff.' This is a cultural change for everybody."

In a conversation in late January, Kasich said, "I'm pretty upbeat. I think we'll get there because I'm beginning to see cultural change. The key is to show these folks they can fly."

One of the most historic policy decisions of 1995 was arrived at almost casually—or so it seemed. At a meeting on February 15, when Kasich was reviewing for the leadership where things stood on his effort to come up with a five-year plan to provide a "down payment" on a balanced budget, Gingrich hardened the goal to actually eliminating the deficit by 2002. Kasich, leery of this new assignment, asked, "Is this really written in stone?" Gingrich asked for a show of hands of those who thought the deficit should go to zero. All present raised their hands.

At his press briefing the following morning, Gingrich announced that when the House took up the budget, he would only allow floor consideration of plans that balanced the budget in seven years. "It was Newt way out there on his own," a leadership aide said. "The Senate had not bought into this yet. All he had was almost a flip vote in the House leadership the day before—it wasn't like there was a big deliberate discussion of the question—but he announced the policy publicly the next day so that nobody could backtrack from it."

By late February, Kasich was tired and discouraged. He was meeting resistance to making big cuts. He said, "There've been countless meetings with countless discussions. I try to let them know the enormity of the situation. I have my doubts about whether they're going to come through or not. I don't know yet."

Robert Livingston, the lanky representative from New Orleans, had an aristocratic bearing, but actually came from a modest background. He could speak in the soft tones of the Southern gentleman and often displayed a courtly manner, or, as became clear in the course of the year, he could switch to an arm-waving, shouting, old-style stump politician—with a real streak of toughness. A colleague said, "Livingston is a hard-nosed, tough guy. I said to Livingston yesterday, 'You've gotten this position because you're a son of a bitch.' " Having been given his post of House Appropriations Committee chairman by Gingrich, Livingston owed him much. At the same time the leadership took the unusual step of appointing freshmen to seven of the eleven vacant Republican committee seats. All this made Livingston less than a free man. The day before the Republicans gathered in Washington in December, Frank Luntz went to Livingston's office and grilled him on whether he was truly committed to the Contract and to substantially cutting back appropriations. The fifty-one-year-old Livingston assured the thirty-two-year-old Luntz that he would be committed and part of the team. When Livingston spoke to the Steering Committee, which made committee assignments, he told the members, "If you want cuts in NASA and public broadcasting, you need people who will stand up and do it."

Livingston himself was determined to make deep cuts in federal spending, including the "zeroing out" of several programs. In a conversation in January, he said, "I expect to zero out a lot of things before we're through." Early in the session there was some confusion as to the mechanisms to be followed for (1) making cuts, or rescissions, in money already appropriated for fiscal year 1995 in order to pay for some emergency funding (for military operations in Haiti and disaster relief for forty states, most of it for California) and to start to pay for the Contract; (2) providing the rest of the funds to pay for the Contract; and (3) starting on the "glide path" to a balanced budget. Kasich and Livingston had different ideas about how to proceed, and Livingston felt that Kasich tended to talk off the top of his head. Walker said, "John's strength is that he's so enthusiastic about what he does. You just have to make clear that what he's enthusiastic about are the team goals."

●

Kasich and Livingston went at each other virtually from the outset. Kasich wanted to specify which budget cuts should be made, whereas his committee's actual jurisdiction was to simply specify how much should be spent in the various categories of the budget. Making the actual cuts was Livingston's domain, and Livingston wanted no trespassing. Bill Archer, as chairman of the Ways and Means Committee, with jurisdiction over not only taxes, but also some entitlement programs, didn't want to be dictated to by Kasich. The chairmen of the various authorizing committees—the committees that write the laws and authorize the spending for such things as education and the Merchant Marine and agriculture programs—also didn't want Kasich dictating to them. But Kasich had doubts about these chairmen's capacity for being dispassionate about their own programs, just as he didn't trust the Appropriations subcommittees chairmen to not remain protective toward programs they had been protecting for years. And he feared that if he couldn't specify which cuts should be made, his colleagues might evade the hard choices and the House would end up with phony budget reductions.

Gingrich took personal charge of trying to reconcile his warring lieutenants, and beginning in mid-January, he held a series of meetings with Kasich, Livingston, and Archer. Some of the gatherings were ostensibly as social as they were about business—some of them were over dinner. Gingrich would ask the others what their problems were, what they needed —he would just let people talk. Other times, Gingrich would force a decision. Gingrich recalled the process in an interview as "getting the budget written in a collaborative way with all the authorizers and appropriators in the room yelling at each other so they all had something to do with it."

Kasich's devotion to all aspects of the Contract was suspect. Someone close to the leadership said, "Kasich is problematic on tax cuts. He said he'd oppose any tax cut unless a budget cut was already in place. They pulled him back from that—they don't want anyone to talk about not voting for a tax cut. He talks about not making the mistakes of the eighties, which infuriates Reaganites."

Gingrich paid detailed attention to the spending and budget issues because he knew that the legitimacy of the Contract would rest on its being paid for and that the large budget cuts to follow could define his vision of the federal government's role. He understood that the big cuts would be very difficult and (like Sergeant Stryker) he was shaping up his troops for the large and difficult assault.

Sometimes Gingrich addressed these issues on a member-by-member basis, but a lot also got decided at weekly meetings of a Budget Steering Group that Gingrich had established—consisting of Kasich, Livingston, and Archer, as well as Armey and Gingrich. The Budget Steering Group sometimes got into details such as how much to cut public broadcasting. According to a leadership aide, Gingrich would ask where the problems were and how they could develop a consensus to move forward. One person who attended these meetings described Kasich as "the bull in the china closet." He said, "Anytime there's a proposal, he tries to get as much as he can. He's very helpful to Newt except that Newt sometimes jumps on him when Kasich has been too relentless on somebody. Newt emphasizes that you have to do this in a way that doesn't destroy everybody. Newt says, Don't try to pound people, figure out a way to move them along." He continued, "This is his close circle on moving the budget stuff. Newt's trying to build a sense of determination within this circle. He talks a lot in big terms about the size of the task we're doing, and are we up to it and look at what we've already pulled off—isn't it amazing? As Kasich has learned to modulate himself, Newt barks at him less."

In the Budget Steering Group Livingston was instructed to find as much money as he could for the rescissions bill to pay for the emergencies and also to start paying for the Contract. Livingston was told to make some cuts in popular programs to test the public reaction. This led the House Republicans into their first, and costly, blunder.

In late January Gingrich met one evening in room H 227 with the chairmen of the authorizing committees and told them, "We have two challenges here." The short-term challenge, he said, was to finance the Contract, "And we have to focus on that intensely." Then he asked them to give him a longer-term view of ways to free up budget resources and form new kinds of relationships with the governors and others. An aide said, "He talks to them about how to work these things through with members of their committees and with the conference. Of his motto, 'Listen, learn, help, lead,' he says to the committee chairmen, we're now at the stage of listen, learn."

(Gingrich hardly ever used the Speaker's office just off the House floor, which showed in its sterility—not a scrap of paper on a desktop, which was often dusty. But the office was stocked with caffeine-free Diet Coke for those rare occasions when he did turn up. An aide explained, "Newt gets so wound up that he drinks caffeine-free Diet Coke in the office.")

The timetable for coming up with the cuts to pay for the Contract— originally promised for January—was slipping, and there began to be some sentiment among the House leaders that they shouldn't put forth their cuts until after Clinton offered his budget. The idea was to let the President make the hard choices first—but of course, by leaving out the important details, Clinton eluded their net.

At a tense meeting of the key budget figures at noon on February 1 in Room H 230—Gingrich's reception room, with a huge skull of a *Tyranno-*

saurus rex, lent by the Smithsonian, in a large glass case (Gingrich was an aficionado of dinosaurs)—Kasich argued that the proposed cuts to pay for the Contract would only have credibility if they were specific. Livingston argued that he needed flexibility, saying, "You cannot get out there and say what I'm going to do three months before I bring the bill to the floor. You lock me in and everyone opposed will throw wrenches into the gears." At this particular meeting, Gingrich handed out an article by Peter Drucker about Japanese management—emphasizing that managers shouldn't try to impose from the top.

In the end, Kasich's authority was limited so that Livingston's territory would be kept intact—but only if his committee did its job. Gingrich ruled that if the appropriators faltered, the Budget Committee would specify the cuts. A leadership aide said, "He'll go from there and deal with the spending chairmen, and nail it down with them, and then the conference."

A member involved in these dealings said, "Among the appropriators, and the others involved in this problem, the word was, If you don't do it, 'the kid' will. And everyone knew that 'the kid' was Newt's protégé and had his backing." Kasich's strong following among the freshmen added to his power.

The real problem was that no one knew to what degree public attitudes about spending had changed: though people told pollsters that they wanted the government smaller and spending reduced, and preferred deficit cutting over tax cutting, they still might object to cuts in programs that were to their own benefit.

Pete Domenici, Republican Senator from New Mexico and once again chairman of the Senate Budget Committee, was a serious man, just this side of solemn. Domenici, who had reddish brown hair, green eyes, and wore large glasses, often had a worried look, but that was because, having served as chairman of the committee when the Republicans last controlled the Senate, he understood the political realities of cutting the budget—which he once again was determined to do. (When in 1985 Domenici had guided the Senate toward cutting Social Security, the rug was pulled out by President Reagan and House Speaker Tip O'Neill.)

But Domenici wasn't much impressed by the Contract, didn't feel that this was the time to cut taxes, and wasn't interested in going through the contortions of passing an extra budget resolution just so the House Republicans could "pay for the Contract." His view was shared by Dole and Finance Committee Chairman Bob Packwood. Domenici was in fact irritated at Kasich for announcing on *Meet the Press* in December that there would be a separate and early piece of legislation to pay for the Contract. During a break in the program, Domenici complained to Kasich, "Why didn't I know?"

Domenici fretted about getting real change through the Senate, given that body's rules. In an interview early in the year he said, "There's no way the Senate can work the way the House does. So what troubles me is whether what they do and what we do will end up meshing in substance and in timing. We will not ingratiate ourselves with the public if we say we'll make fundamental change and don't make it, and don't achieve reform quickly. But as long as I've been here the Senate has more or less meandered through its work, partly because of our rules. There is a real tendency to be more accommodating to whoever is delaying things." Shaking his head slowly Domenici said, "The job of getting enough budget cuts —very difficult."

There were regular meetings between the House leaders and the chief money committee chairmen with their counterparts in the Senate—Dole, Lott, Domenici, and Hatfield. Haley Barbour was often at the meetings.

Despite Barbour's efforts, the relationship between the House and Senate leaders was less than great. Someone who dealt with both groups said, "The Senate looks at the House as a bunch of precocious extremists and the House looks at the Senate as fuddy-duddy tortoises. There isn't enough communication. The Lott-Gingrich relationship isn't enough. The Dole-Lott relationship is in transition. Dole and Gingrich don't like each other. The Gingrich people see themselves as far beyond Dole in intellectual leadership. The Dole people look on Newt and his ideas with disdain. There's generational difference, there's cultural difference, there's stylistic difference. Newt and Trent see eye-to-eye, but not Newt and Dole."

The first—and virtually simultaneous—actions in the House to cut back on spending caused an uproar unexpected by the leadership, one that threw them on the defensive for quite some time. The House Economic and Educational Opportunities Committee decided over February 22–23 to put the school lunch program, along with some other nutrition programs, into a block grant. At the same time, House Appropriations Committee subcommittees proposed rescissions that included cuts in education and job training, housing programs, home heating assistance for the poor, and public broadcasting. Funds for the President's pet program, national service, were also cut back. (Gingrich had questioned whether the Corporation for Public Broadcasting should receive any money at all.)

The Republicans' proposal to place the school lunch program in a block grant and to cut its funds—by not keeping up with inflation and rising school enrollment—gave the Democrats their first real political break. The school lunch program served the middle class as well as the poor, and thus had a strong following. The block grant proposal ended the guarantee that all eligible children would receive the food, and eliminated the mandatory nutrition standards—and was seized on by the Democrats as emblematic of Republican heartlessness.

The Economic and Educational Opportunities Committee's proposal also put the Women, Infants, and Children program (WIC), which provided assistance to poor pregnant women and preschool children—and was widely deemed successful—into the block grant with several other programs, placing its funding and its special standing at risk. William Goodling, chairman of the committee that voted these changes, had been a strong supporter of the school lunch program, and had been reluctant to make these changes, but was pressed by Gingrich. The changes were part of Gingrich's and other House leaders' effort to put about three hundred assistance programs (the large number was a consequence of Democrats' indiscriminateness) into a block grant—thus transferring authority to the states, undermining the power of the national welfare lobbies (as Gingrich desired), and saving money. At the same time, the Appropriations Committee cut funding for the WIC program.

The fact that the House Agriculture Committee balked at turning the food stamp program into a block grant gave the game away. It belied Republicans' insistence that nothing would be lost by turning these programs into block grants, that all that was going on was placing the programs "closer to the people." The food stamp program was of great importance to the committee's farming constituency, as well as to the Grocery Manufacturers of America, which lobbied to keep it intact. A few weeks later, on the evening of February 28, Governors Engler and Weld met in Gingrich's office with Gingrich and Pat Roberts, of Kansas and chairman of the Agriculture Committee, and Bill Emerson, of Missouri and chairman of the relevant Agriculture subcommittee, with Wisconsin Governor Thompson wired in by speakerphone. The governors wanted to reverse the food stamp decision. The outcome was ambiguous but basically favored the governors, giving the states the right to receive food stamps in a block grant once they had installed electronic protection against cheaters.

The White House was still of a divided mind over when and how much to attack Republican actions. But a number of people, including Democratic Party General Chairman Christopher Dodd and Gephardt, argued to a still somewhat hangdog Clinton—he hadn't got past the election yet—that making children the issue gave him the one unassailable constituency.

A White House adviser said in early March, "The President's anger ebbs and flows a lot. He's not happy, but has to get on with things to overcome given impressions of him. That takes a lot of work. It's easy to talk about the things you'll veto."

Still, the White House hesitated. Mrs. Clinton and Deputy Chief of Staff Harold Ickes, who was of a more liberal bent than some of his colleagues, and also more intense and decisive, were both inclined to take a more aggressive position against the Congress in general. Others in the White House were more inclined toward keeping Clinton's options open for negotiating a settlement on key issues, such as welfare and the budget.

But the school lunch program, with its middle-class as well as poor constituency, gave the White House an irresistible issue. Leon Panetta said later, "Frankly, it wasn't until they touched the school lunch program that we hit pay dirt in terms of the Contract." There was a similar "Eureka!" among Capitol Hill Democrats. A House Democratic leadership aide said, "You can't articulate to the public unfunded mandates and takings and the other junk, but you can articulate cutting food programs for children. Until now most of the issues were about process. This is real and affects people."

So, in a press briefing on February 22—the fiftieth day—after he had met with the House Democrats, Clinton denounced the cuts in nutrition programs, saying, "An old conservative adage used to be, If it ain't broke don't fix it." Of the changes in the nutrition programs, he said, "I do not agree with it. I don't think it's right." Clinton said, "We have no intention of abandoning the American people to unproved theories and extreme positions." Later that afternoon both Gephardt and Panetta made statements while brandishing a bottle of ketchup—a bit of a stretch trying to summon up a Reagan administration ruling that, for the purposes of the school lunch program, ketchup was a vegetable. The idea was attributed to George Stephanopoulos, who was in daily contact with aides to Gephardt.

The political problem for the Republicans was that the cuts and block grants gave life to one of their party's greatest liabilities—the charge that it was "mean," and "favored the rich." (The Democrats' albatross was "tax and spend.") While some of the cuts may have been reasonable, and got at duplications, the sum total was a blunder. Even some Republicans thought that the cuts should have been more widely spread. Business subsidies went virtually untouched. In all, the Appropriations Committee eliminated funding for—"zeroed out"—eighty programs, and Livingston made it clear that more were to be eliminated as the year went on and the regular appropriations bills were considered.

An agitated Frank Luntz said over lunch on Friday, February 24, "I'm angry. We blew the welfare question. Now we're on the side of taking food away from hungry children. We're on the side of Grinch and Scrooge, even though eighty percent of the American people think all these programs need some overhaul."

Others, including Bill Paxon, saw the "meanness" problem as well. An ally said, "But they're so deep into the schedule—getting things done—that they can't think about it." A House Republican leadership aide said, of the Democrats' assault, "We take it seriously. If we lose the public relations goal, we'll get killed. We have to do better."

Stung by the attacks, the Republicans argued that they weren't cutting the school lunch program, but were in fact increasing spending for it by 4.5 percent. The fact that this was a bogus argument didn't keep the Republicans from projecting great indignation about the accusations coming their way. First, there was no such figure, since the proposal didn't specify the spending levels within the block grant—that was the whole point of block grants—and in any event such a figure would not meet the additional costs resulting from inflation and a growing clientele. By normal budgeting, the "baseline" for the next year's allocation assumed the increase in inflation and growth in demand; anything below that was a "cut." This was the method of accounting that Gingrich and his allies were trying to break—so they could make deeper cuts and look less "mean."

Gingrich was furious at the reaction. But he also used his anger as a tactic. He had to undermine the authority of those—Democrats, the press, the "Washington establishment"—who were making the most effective point against the Republicans thus far. Clearly thrown by the Democrats' criticism of the cuts in the school lunch program, at a briefing on February 23 he said—demonstrating his facility for creating debate points, which sometimes tipped over into demagogy—that in focusing on block grants, the Democrats were protecting "the bureaucrats," while the Republicans, in proposing to give a tax credit of $500 per child, wanted the parents to have the money. These were, he said, "two very different views."

He kept up this line of argument for months, going ever deeper into attacks on the press. The point was not just to undermine its credibility with the public, but to intimidate it into ceasing to say that funds for school lunch—or other programs—had been cut, as opposed to saying that their rate of growth had been slowed. (Both facts were true.) His campaign met with some success. He talked about an "elite press . . . that is systematically dishonest." He said, of the school lunch controversy, "What we learned out of that is that liberals love their bureaucrats enough to exploit and frighten children."

But the Democrats kept up their attack, making much of the argument that some of the money saved by the cuts was to go to pay for the Republicans' tax cuts. Panetta said on *MacNeil/Lehrer,* "There is some sense of decency. . . . We ought not to be stepping on children . . . to move forward with tax cuts to the wealthiest in this country." He added, "I don't think people voted to have that happen."

Following the Appropriations subcommittees' cuts, Livingston, tired and defensive, conceded that with proposals to cut all of $17 billion now made —causing a storm—there was another $683 billion to go to pay for the full ten-year (estimated, these things are only guesses) cost of the tax cut and still more to get to a balanced budget. "It's doable, but it's not going to be pleasant," Livingston said.

•

Getting the rescissions bill through the House proved more difficult for Gingrich and the other Republican leaders than might have been expected and revealed the fissures in their coalition. Even before the bill was brought to the floor, Gingrich and Armey had to resolve a dispute between the anti-abortion forces and about forty moderates over a proposed anti-abortion amendment. Facing, according to Armey, the loss of the bill because of the moderates' revolt, on the night before the vote Gingrich persuaded Ernest Istook, of Oklahoma, the author of the anti-abortion amendment, to withdraw it. Sherwood Boehlert, the New York moderate, who attended the meeting, said, "Newt was open and listened to us. We said we thought there had been a commitment to not bring up abortion during the Contract. He said, 'Show me the numbers.' "

At the same time that the leaders were dealing with the abortion problem, Gingrich also faced a rebellion of a group of mostly freshmen who threatened to vote against the rescissions bill unless they were allowed a vote on a resolution to stop the use of funds from the Exchange Stabilization Fund to help Mexico. Clinton had turned to the fund to shore up the peso when it seemed unlikely that Congress would approve his original proposal for a bailout, which Gingrich had supported. (According to two House members, DeLay was stirring up the freshmen on this and other issues, nailing them down as his power base. DeLay said in an interview— grinning, as he often did when discussing his own mischief—"I would never do anything to pour cold water on revolutionaries.") Gingrich was most annoyed with the group, and felt that mob rule threatened.

Gingrich also had to work with a group of conservative Democrats whose votes were needed on the rescissions bill. He ostensibly mollified them by pledging that the funds in the rescissions bill not needed for natural disasters and other emergencies would not go toward the tax cut but would be put in a "lock box" and used for deficit reduction. Since the money was fungible, the concept of the "lock box" was meaningless, a fantasy for the convenience of the politicians. The irrepressible Kasich told reporters later, "Everybody knows that this is a big game on the 'lock box,' " adding, "It all comes out of the same pot."

Of the difficulties over the rescissions bill, Armey said later, somewhat philosophically, "When an unpopular bill comes along, there is the chance to say to yourself, 'Well, I can make the difference' "—and hold out support in exchange for some concession. Ostensible dissenters could be quite creative. Rescissions bills were particularly hard to pass because they cut spending already appropriated and counted on by a member's constituents or contributors.

The House leaders' management of the rescissions bill also left a number of Republicans unhappy. Chairmen of the authorizing committees felt that they hadn't been sufficiently consulted about the cuts. Numerous Republicans were angered by the fact that the rule for debate made it difficult for members to change the Appropriations Committee's work. Christopher Shays told Gingrich, "We're losing our moral authority to run this place." Shays, normally a strong Gingrich supporter, said later, "When people signed on to the Contract, a lot of them didn't like all ten items, but believed that they would be able to amend or vote against them. Newt said that when we win this place, we'll run it differently from the Democrats, we'll have open debate and a chance to amend. We did run this place differently in the first few days." But now, Shays said, "The idea that ideas win goes away."

Those liberals and moderates who did offer amendments were outmaneuvered by the Republican managers. The floor debate was unusually partisan and testy—a reflection of the mood established by Gingrich's and his fellow leaders' tough tactics—and by the Democrats' dislike of Gingrich and frustration at their own helplessness.

DeLay took the opportunity to offer an amendment to kill a pending regulation by the Occupational Safety and Health Administration (OSHA) on ergonomics (to avoid repetitive stress injuries), which passed by a vote of 254–168. (In June, OSHA dropped the pending regulation on ergonomics. The action was taken at the behest of the White House, which was trying to reach a compromise with the Congress, and was working from a list—supplied by McIntosh and DeLay—of most-disliked regulations.)

Just as the House was getting ready to vote on the rescissions bill, Kasich announced that the Budget Committee had found the nearly $200 billion in funds to pay for the first five years of the tax cut: the main "saving" was achieved by lowering the "caps" on what could be spent on domestic discretionary programs by $100 billion. Another $67 billion was to come out of the welfare and nutrition programs. The "savings" also included changes in the federal pension system that the committee of jurisdiction, Government Reform, had refused to approve. (The concept of lowering the spending caps was actually borrowed from Clinton's budget.) Other Clinton savings, including some minor ones in Medicare, were picked up as well. But the House Republicans put off until later consideration of substantial cuts in Medicare. Kasich said in an interview, "We don't want to do Medicare now. We'll do Medicare and Medicaid later. We can't get there without them." The House Republican leadership had in fact made a decision early on to not take up these touchy subjects during the Hundred Days.

Though, under the agreement reached among the money chairmen, Kasich was constrained from specifying what domestic programs would actually be cut, as an implied threat he put out a list of "illustrative examples." Livingston hadn't wanted Kasich to release the examples. Kasich announced—prematurely—that House Republicans had agreed to freeze defense spending.

The final vote, on March 16, on passing the rescissions bill—227–200, with six Republicans (including Boehlert) voting against it, and only six Democrats voting for it (some conservative Democrats were angered by a misunderstanding over the "lock box")—was narrow enough to throw a fright into the leadership and to reconfirm to Gingrich that as he moved into the more controversial parts of the Contract, his job would become increasingly difficult.

Clinton, who on the day of the House vote on the rescissions bill was staging a Reinventing Government event at a small print shop in Arlington, Virginia, was annoyed that he had to step on his own story by reacting to the House action. This actually represented progress: Clinton used to routinely, and without regard for the consequences, step on his own story. Clinton said the cuts would "cut too much of people, and not enough pork." But since this fell short of the veto threat that many had expected, Leon Panetta said to reporters while crossing the White House lawn that if the rescissions bill reached President Clinton's desk in its present form, "There's no question . . . that the President, in fact, would veto it." This was a hypothetical threat, because no one expected the House bill to be fully accepted by the Senate and end up on the President's desk. As it was, White House press secretary Mike McCurry said in an interview later, "We probably overplayed the President's response." He added, "The President is very leery of a full frontal attack on the Congress. He could look like a mad dog."

10

WELFARE CRISIS

"Boo if You Want to— Make Asses of Yourselves"

Gingrich was later to describe the House consideration of the welfare bill as *"the* crisis of the Hundred Days." He added, "We're winning on more of a shoestring than people realize."

The welfare reform bill, vessel of so many conflicting ideas and emotions and political exigencies, was a delicate problem for the Republicans, even as they seemed to be getting their way. The deal that had been made with the governors—to put the program into a block grant, end the entitlement, impose a few strings to satisfy members of Congress, and essentially finesse the subject of work requirements—kept crashing into walls.

Throughout the welfare debate, two opposing philosophies clashed. Generally speaking, Democrats believed that the solution, if there was one, lay in getting people on welfare trained to work and into jobs. Republicans believed that welfare provided incentives for poor people to not work and to have babies. In fact, at this point neither party was eager to be talking about expensive proposals to create jobs for welfare recipients. Though the existing system was considered a failure by both parties, the Republicans painted the Democrats as defenders of the status quo. The Republicans had three goals, which got confused: to "reform" the welfare program, to reduce the cost of welfare, and to send the program to the states.

The nature of the disagreement between the two parties—which was emotion-ridden, and heavily tinged by race, though no one said so aloud

—plus the bitterness that had already become the defining atmosphere in the House of Representatives, lent a particularly angry tone to the debate on welfare, starting in the Human Resources Subcommittee of the Ways and Means Committee.

In the subcommittee meetings, in a windowless room in the basement of the Rayburn Building—the meetings closely monitored by welfare rights lobbyists—there was a snarling atmosphere as the Republicans beat off Democratic amendments, which the Democrats, knowing they were out-gunned, were offering for the record. Working with officials of the Department of Health and Human Services, the Democrats made the Republicans reject amendments to, among other things, strengthen the "work require-ments," and require the states to provide child care for welfare recipients who went to work.

At the same time that the subcommittee Republicans were exercising their power, concern was growing among some moderate Republicans that the bill was unacceptably harsh. The leadership was faced with the possibility that the bill wouldn't even be approved by the full committee, despite its Republican majority. And so, Gingrich and his staff spent three days of tense negotiations among moderate Republicans, the committee Republican leadership, and the governors. The goal, a leadership aide said, was "What we could get out of committee. It boiled down to that."

Nancy Johnson, while concerned about several provisions, was particu-larly upset that while the bill killed any entitlement to benefits, the proposal didn't even require the states to maintain their existing level of effort. This wasn't something that the governors wanted. Other changes were made in order to get enough Republican support. The penalty of loss of benefits for an unwed mother under eighteen, which under the Contract was to last for life, was changed so that the benefits were restored when the mother turned eighteen. Johnson said, "It would have been a lifelong penalty for a teenage mistake." However, to assuage those, including the Christian Coalition, who saw illegitimacy as the heart of the problem, a new provi-sion was added to reward states that reduced the number of babies born out of wedlock. This hard-to-measure standard sent the bill careening into another wall, as anti-abortion forces, including the U.S. Catholic Bishops, objected that the illegitimacy bonus, and a provision for a "family cap" denying additional funds for children born to parents already on welfare, would encourage abortions. (A family cap had been put into effect in New Jersey, but a study released in April said that it had had no discernible impact on the number of babies born to people out of wedlock.)

The leadership struggled to ascertain just how many changes had to be made in order to get enough Republicans on the Ways and Means Commit-tee to vote to bring the bill to the floor without losing support elsewhere. A group of bipartisan women members had fought to have the bill include tough provisions for cracking down on "deadbeat dads," but got only part of what they sought. (This issue was one that the male-dominated culture on Capitol Hill had always had trouble coming to grips with.) The work requirements remained illusory. At first, the bill required only that twenty percent of the heads of welfare families be working, and it was vague on what constituted "work." After Democrats attacked the bill as "weak on work" and Robert Rector, of the conservative Heritage Foundation and a major adviser to Republicans on the subject, called the committee's work requirements "a major embarrassment," seemingly stricter work requirements were added: by 2003 half the single welfare recipients would have to be working—but it provided no funds for jobs or child care. Moreover, on the basis of historical precedent, the states weren't likely to spend to provide them. (Most of the states didn't meet the more modest work requirement in the 1988 welfare reform legislation.) The Congressional Budget Office released an official estimate that the states wouldn't be able to meet the work requirements before the fifty percent change in 2003 and the requirements wouldn't be effective because of the lack of resources.

The bill had some other remarkable provisions: one would let the states count throwing someone off welfare as the same thing as getting that person a job; another would allow a state to ignore all the work rules and still get at least ninety-five percent of its block grant money.

Meanwhile, frazzled Republicans who weren't on the Ways and Means Committee were just beginning to realize how radical a change was being proposed.

At lunch in the House Dining Room one day in early March, Marge Roukema, the moderate Republican from New Jersey, was bothered. Like a lot of her colleagues, she had been too busy on other matters to follow the welfare issue closely. And like a lot of them, she was feeling overloaded. But she had just come from a meeting of moderates, where she learned that the Republican welfare bill not only did away with entitlement, but was "open-ended at the state level." She said, "It doesn't require much of anything." She asked, of the governors who had shaped the bill, "Who are these governors? Are they all the governors? The end of welfare reform can't be that we let children go." Now she was uncertain as to whether she could support the bill. (She had voted against the takings bill, and the line-item veto. "Why would they want to give this power to Bill Clinton?") She planned to vote against term limits on the grounds that the change would lead to more corruption as Members of Congress, with an eye to their next means of employment, burnished their credentials with interest groups. She said, "I'm worried now that in making a deal to end entitlement we haven't thought through the consequences of turning it over to the states without requirements. We're giving the governors a blank check."

•

The bill fit perfectly into Gingrich's scheme to repeal the New Deal, smash the welfare state, and break the national power of the protectors of federal programs. It suited his purposes as well as those of the governors. It was also designed to save money.

In the course of the full Ways and Means Committee proceedings, in the large committee room in the Longworth Building, Jim McDermott, Democrat of Washington, stepped outside to talk for a few minutes. He said, "What's troublesome is not that changes are being made—none of us is willing to defend it all. But it's being done on the back of a galloping horse and without listening to anyone's arguments."

The new version of the welfare program, plus the proposals to put nutrition and other programs for the poor into block grants, were wrapped into one bill, HR 4, which the Republicans called a "welfare" bill, thus attaching the least popular name to programs—some of them popular—which had never been considered "welfare." Kasich counted the total savings—to be put toward the nearly $200 billion needed for the tax cut bill—at $67 billion. This made Republican protests ring hollow when they insisted that they weren't "cutting" the programs.

Gingrich's crisis occurred over getting enough votes for a rule to bring the welfare bill up on the House floor. (The bill also included the $200 billion in cuts to pay for the tax bill.) The House leadership, Gingrich said later, "was in a dangerous situation." In this instance, he said, if the rule failed he had no fallback plan. "When you start talking about losing the welfare rule," Gingrich said, "there was no natural coalition you could put together. Whatever you did would lose you other people. So it was potentially a very big muddle." At that point, Gingrich said, the leadership knew that it was going to lose on term limits. He added, "We were very worried that the sense of morale would break down."

The problem was that two different parts of the Republican constituency interpreted the provisions in two different ways—and Gingrich couldn't afford to lose either of them. The Catholic right-to-life movement, which saw some provisions as encouraging abortion, differed with the Baptist right-to-life movement, as reflected in the Christian Coalition, which sought those provisions in order to reduce illegitimacy. Gingrich argued that the alternative to rewarding states that reduced illegitimacy was to leave the current system intact. To try to assuage the bishops, the leaders allowed an amendment—the "diaper amendment"—to give out vouchers for baby paraphernalia such as diapers and formula and the like. Henry Hyde, a strong right-to-life supporter, was given an amendment that said that none of the federal funds under the bill could be used for "medical services," a vague term which, it was established in the debate, meant abortions. As it happened, the day before the vote on the rule, about a dozen Republican governors were in Washington and had lunch with Gingrich and Dole. Gingrich told them that he was in trouble on the welfare rule, and some of the governors canceled their afternoon events and went to lobby the House.

But some Catholics, including Hyde, weren't satisfied, and were set on voting against the rule. Some other Republicans, including Shays, were prepared to vote against the rule because it was particularly restrictive.

During the vote on the rule, on March 22, Gingrich and his chief of staff, Dan Meyer, worked the floor. Republicans looked anxious. There was a hush in the Chamber as members on both sides of the aisle watched the scoreboard. Fairly quickly, eight Republicans voted against the rule, putting it in jeopardy. The leadership had heard reports that no Democrats would vote for the rule. At this stage in a legislative fight, rumor and speculation carry almost the same weight as the careful whip counts. In the end, the 217–211 vote to adopt the rule was a narrow escape for the leadership. Three more votes against it would have sunk it. Fifteen Republicans, more than enough to defeat it, voted against it, but three Democrats voted for it. After the vote, leaders and staff still on the House floor asked what had happened—why they didn't get more Democrats. That afternoon, the meeting of the Speaker's Advisory Group—Armey, DeLay, Walker, Boehner, Paxon, Kasich, and chief deputy whip Hastert, as well as Gingrich —focused on the rule vote and how to make sure there were no defeats on the bill. Len Swinehart, Gingrich's chief lieutenant for working the floor, said later, "The vote on the rule really threw us for a loop. After the rule vote, everyone started working a little harder."

Haley Barbour and some pro-life governors, including Thompson, lobbied Hyde. The goal was to win back as many as possible of the fifteen Republican renegades on the rule—of which Hyde had been one.

Wearing "Save the Children" ties and scarves, the Democrats hammered away at the theme that the Republicans were proposing to "take food out of the mouths of children" to pay for their "tax cuts for the rich." Over and over, they charged that the Republican plan was "mean-spirited." The Republicans had handed them the issue by proposing to use the roughly $67 billion in savings in these programs to pay in part for the first five years of the tax cut. Despite their protestations on the floor and off, Republicans knew that the Democrats were making inroads with this point. The Democrats were learning something that the Republicans had perfected in recent years: the power of repetition of an uncomplicated point.

Bob Walker tried to define the bill for the Republicans by saying that "it is immoral to take money from decent, middle-class Americans who work for everything they have and give it to people who think they are owed the money for doing nothing."

The House debate on welfare was uglier than any in memory—Democrats (including John Lewis) invoked the specter of Hitler, while Republicans likened welfare recipients to animals—and House members knew that they had ventured into new territory. The last shreds of civility were gone. When Republicans booed Sam Gibbons, of Florida, as he described the bill as "mean," Gibbons shouted back, "Boo if you want to—make asses of yourselves." Even Armey, waving his arms, was trying to subdue the Republicans. The Republican leaders understood that it didn't much matter who was doing the shouting—that the entire spectacle looked bad to the American people. Ways and Means Committee chairman Archer, normally a most civil man, said that the emotional level of the debate was driven by "the dying throes of the federal welfare state." Archer had a point. This wasn't any old bill: it represented a fundamental shift in policy, and in authority.

The anger was also fed by the Republicans' use of muscle to control amendments. A few adjustments were allowed by the leadership in order to obtain enough votes for passage of the bill. Roukema was given an amendment providing for the revocation of driver's and other licenses from "deadbeat dads." Nancy Johnson was permitted to offer an amendment to add funds for child care. The Republican leaders were like old-time machine pols, handing out the goodies where they had to.

The Democrats, under Gephardt's prodding, set out to do the miraculous —find a Democratic alternative that the entire caucus could agree upon— and, to their own surprise, they pulled it off. Gephardt's seemingly fanciful goal of getting the House Democrats to act in unison came to pass. In large part this reflected the Democrats' understanding of their new reality. Robert Matsui, of California, a liberal on the Ways and Means Committee, said, "We've really moved to the right. It's astonishing how right we've moved." As in the case of S.D.I., Gephardt saw to it that the proposal was formulated around that of a conservative Democrat. In this instance, Nathan Deal, a second-term Democrat from Georgia, who had been working on the welfare issue, was tapped. Deal was reluctant to take the lead in offering the alternative, but House Democratic leaders persuaded him to do it. Building on the work of a task force of liberals and conservatives, a lot of shuttle diplomacy among the conservatives, the Black Caucus, and the Hispanic Caucus went on. Matsui and Charles Rangel, who represented Harlem, went to Gephardt to seek reassurance, since they were sticking their necks out for a proposal they found unsatisfactory, that conservative Democrats would in the end vote for the Deal proposal. Conservative Democrats— who had established their own group, called The Coalition, of twenty-three members—said that they would vote for the Deal proposal only if the liberals did. At a Democratic caucus on the morning of March 15, a lot of skeptical questions were raised about the Deal proposal. Liberals were bothered by the provision that no one could stay on welfare for more than four years, but they were attracted by the fact that the proposal kept welfare as an entitlement. To them, that was the core issue. But a Democratic leadership aide said, "We'll be talking about children and work and not use the word 'entitlement'—not if we can help it."

The Deal proposal stressed work, requiring that welfare recipients join a work program right away. Thus were the Democrats trying to get to the "right" of the Republicans.

Barbara Kennelly, a pragmatic liberal from Connecticut (her father, John Bailey, was a chairman of the Democratic National Committee from 1960 to 1968), said, "The Deal bill is probably something we never would have considered a year ago, but times change. The cutoff after four years bothers some, but at least it's an entitlement. Everyone's knocking themselves out to give a little." Kennelly added, "Maybe one reason we're in the minority is that we all wanted it our own way." A number of Democrats, Kennelly among them, were retroactively angry with Clinton for not having pushed welfare reform in 1994 and saddling them instead with a hapless health care proposal. Of the challenges now before them, Kennelly said, "It would be very hard to do it right, because to have a good welfare program you have to invest a lot up front—in schooling, training, day care. I feel that there is a formula that given enough funds could work. Whether you could do that in this day I don't know."

Gephardt also arranged for a liberal alternative to be offered: this would give the conservative Democrats something to vote against—and the liberals something to vote for (that was sure to go down to defeat) before voting for the more conservative alternative. Then, Democrats who voted for the Deal substitute could vote against the Republican bill—without being vulnerable to the charge of having voted against "welfare reform." These are the kinds of maneuvers a congressional leader has to arrange in order to protect his flock.

The administration quietly got behind the Deal proposal. It was seeking to avoid a situation, like that concerning several other elements of the Contract, where a large number of Democrats voted with the Republicans. A White House aide said, "We couldn't let that happen on welfare reform, because that would make a veto threat hollow. It would be harder for us to show flaws in a House Republican bill if one-third of our party was for it."

During the floor maneuvering, however, the Democrats had some internal confusion over whether to vote for amendments that would make the Republican bill better, on the grounds that it would pass and they should get what they could, or let the bill that passed be as objectionable as possible. This was a dilemma they were to face often. The word that reached Democrats on the floor on this matter was confused.

The vote on the Deal substitute showed great party discipline on both sides—uncommon Democratic unity. It was rejected by a vote of 205–228, all Democrats voting for it and all but one Republican against it.

(It was a big blow to the Democrats, and made Gephardt's job harder, when Deal announced two weeks later that he was switching parties. This would make it more difficult to get liberals to agree to conservative Democrats' proposals. But Deal's move was a precursor of switches by other Southern Democrats. The South—or at least the white South—was becoming increasingly Republican, the split between blacks and white Republicans becoming sharper all the time. Deal was the only white Democrat in the House from Georgia. A Democratic leadership aide said, "Ultimately, it gets down to carrying your district." In 1992 only thirty-five percent of Deal's district voted for Clinton.)

While the President's voice stayed muffled on the subject of welfare entitlement, the face his advisers put on the subject was that they wanted the dust to settle, that the governors would come to realize that they were getting themselves into a bad deal.

Clinton did decide to make a big issue of the "deadbeat dads," but while this was a popular subject, it wasn't at the core of the welfare issue in Congress. He talked about it in one of his Saturday radio addresses, and in a speech. It was a way of trying to keep Clinton "in the game," if only on the perimeter.

Gingrich felt confident enough, on the basis of reports from his lieutenants, that the Deal substitute would be defeated to keep a speaking engagement in New York on Thursday evening. During his dinner speech, an aide handed him a note saying that only one Republican vote had been lost on the Deal substitute.

But Gingrich knew he wasn't home free, and returned to Washington the next morning so that he could be on the floor on Friday to lobby on the final votes. Earlier in the week, the leadership had thought that twenty to thirty Democrats, or even more, would vote for the bill—that they wouldn't vote against "welfare reform"—but the Deal proposal gave the Democrats cover for voting against the Republicans' bill.

Gingrich's role was to turn people who were prepared to vote "wrong." He was the only one who could do that: people who wouldn't listen to Armey or DeLay or a committee chairman or other members would listen to him. Hyde helped by announcing earlier that he would support the final bill. Gingrich worked on Roukema. The Republican leadership was fearful about what the Democrats would propose, in their motion to recommit the bill to the House (sitting as a Committee of the Whole when it works on amendments) with instructions to change the bill in a certain way—a prerogative of the opposition that can be used mischievously and cause trouble. It was worried that the Democrats would move that the provision for rewarding states that lowered illegitimacy rates be struck from the bill. Such a motion, backed by Democrats and winning support from pro-life Republicans who opposed the provision, might have carried. But the Democrats didn't offer it: their strategy at this point was to not try to "improve" Republican bills. The recommittal motion instead specified that the savings should go to deficit reduction, and not to tax reduction, and it failed—but not by a wide margin. Mike Oxley, of Ohio, who was in the chair, had been instructed by the leadership to bring down the gavel quickly to end the voting, so that the Democrats wouldn't have time to persuade some on their side to switch. Officially, roll calls were to last only fifteen minutes, but over the years had taken longer if it served the majority's purposes, and Gingrich had ruled that they could take only seventeen minutes. The final vote for passage of the bill was 224–199; nine Democrats voted for it and five Republicans against. Johnson and Roukema voted for it. Gingrich had prevailed, but he and his allies knew that it was a costly victory.

In March, Governor Tommy Thompson, realizing that the bargain wasn't such a great one, told the Senate Finance Committee that while he still supported block grants he thought they should be allowed to rise in relation to inflation, or in case of an economic downturn. And Engler himself told a Senate committee that there should be a "rainy-day fund." (The House bill contained a modest amount for loans which had to be repaid with interest.)

Since the President wanted to be able to sign a welfare reform bill, it was left to Panetta to comment on the House-passed bill, which included the cuts in nutrition programs. Panetta, careful not to suggest that the President was against welfare reform or that he would veto the bill, said, "It's really like parents taking their kids' lunch money so they can have a night on the town." Panetta did say that the President strongly opposed the House-passed bill, and would work with the Senate for a better one.

Clinton on occasion did give some clues—very obscure ones—that he might in the end insist on entitlement, by another name. He or Panetta sometimes used the words "safety net" to convey the idea. This question was developing as one of the key tests of Clinton. If he abandoned the principle of entitlement in the interest of signing a bill, it would be testimony to the charge that he had no core. In a speech to the National Association of Counties, meeting in Washington in early March, Clinton attacked the Republican welfare bill as "too tough on children and too weak on work," and criticized some aspects of it—but said not a word about "entitlement" or even "safety net." Nor did he make any veto threat. Though his advisers weren't entirely united, it was understood around the

White House that it wasn't a good idea for the President to veto a welfare reform bill. The "tough on children" was a safe refuge and, aides explained, could be interpreted as meaning that entitlement should be preserved. It could also be interpreted as meaning that it wouldn't. The idea, a Clinton adviser said, was to get across that "we have to provide protection for children, without losing the notion that states often know what they're doing." Yet in a meeting with a group of columnists in the Oval Office that afternoon, Clinton, when asked, did say that entitlement should be preserved. But this wasn't something he was willing to say publicly—or fight for.

By now, it seemed, everyone was being cute. The Republicans were pretending to be "reforming" a program they were trying to destroy. The President was dodging the most important issue and dealing in word games, while his aides encouraged people to think whatever they wanted to think were his intentions.

At the same time, Gingrich was determined that whatever emerged from the Congress would end welfare as an entitlement program and turn it over to the states. He said later, "The governors will not accept the reform if it remains an entitlement, because then they can't manage it. The whole game has been that these entitlements just rise automatically. And one of the core debates that is gradually emerging is whether or not financial reality matters, or whether you simply say, 'I want it that way, don't tell me about money.' That's a very big question."

11

DOLE'S DIFFICULTIES

"We Don't Have the Will in This Body"

As the Senate took up the Balanced Budget Amendment in early February, both the majority leader and the minority leader were having problems.

The Republican race for the Presidential nomination was having a wider impact on—and was causing deeper splits in—the Republican conference than was generally understood at the time. The caucus was split into a Dole camp and a Gramm camp. Richard Lugar and Arlen Specter were eyeing the nomination as well, but the Dole-Gramm race, with the impatience and cocksureness of the eleven Senate freshmen mixed in, was defining the Republican conference. Though Republican Whip Trent Lott seemed loyal to Dole as his majority leader and made himself helpful to him, some Dole supporters in the Senate believed that out of public view Lott supported Gramm for the nomination. A Republican senator close to the leadership said, "Lott actively supports Gramm, but doesn't admit it publicly—it's all behind the scenes. Lott and Gramm are very close personal friends and political allies." This senator continued, "At the Houston convention in '92, Gramm yielded time and the microphone to Lott on two occasions to introduce candidates to the Senate. I am confident that even then they were planning for Trent to enter the leadership." He added, "Even with Trent's public neutrality, he's going to see that the right wing will have a chance to show what they want to do. Trent votes with them on a lot of things. You'll see a split between Lott and Dole."

Dole had to juggle being out on the trail and trying to run the Senate—and make sure that he wasn't usurped. A Republican Senate ally of Dole's said, "The last thing Dole wants to do is to be out there in the cold and have Trent take over. If it were Alan Simpson it would be a different story. Obviously, Simpson doesn't want a higher position; if you have someone below you who wants a higher position you get nervous. When Dole has to spend more time on the campaign trail, he would feel that Simpson was doing his bidding. If it were Trent he'd have to worry that he would be responding to other forces."

Dole's taking a number of new positions aimed at obtaining the support of the right, including the Christian Coalition, was not without risk. The strategy was to win the nomination and then tack to the center—a strategy reportedly based on advice from the late Richard Nixon. The right was further right, and more insistent, than it was in Nixon's day. And Dole's conversion on such issues as affirmative action and taxes—moving to the right on both—reinforced questions about what this masterly legislative tactician really stood for. His denunciation, on May 31, of Hollywood and record executives for violence in movies and rap lyrics was a clear play for the "values" constituency—including the Christian right, which vetted his speech—and was a success from his point of view, even though it came without prologue, and didn't seem to come from inside him. (He was also treading ground already trod; Bill Bennett was angry with Dole for stealing his punch line by singling out Time-Warner, Bennett's chosen foe.) Dole considered the speech "a thousand-strike," according to one adviser, and repeated the comment of a prominent journalist that with that speech he had sewn up the nomination.

Republican senators who supported Dole—a group of ten that included three committee chairmen and two members of the leadership—met for breakfast in Dole's office every Tuesday morning with members of Dole's campaign and Senate staffs. (Dole didn't attend.) Sometimes there were errands for some members of the group to run: to urge some eminence in their state to announce for Dole, to act as an emissary to a certain group. This group was instructed to keep the rest of the Republican senators, as a Dole adviser described it, "in tune with Gingrich." The adviser added, "They have to recognize that popping off against Gingrich doesn't help Dole."

Dole had attracted the support of a number of Senate Republican moderates who sometimes caused him problems on his rightward course. Gramm's support within the Senate was much weaker, and reflected his outsider status and his abrasive style.

Over the years, several would-be Presidents had found that inside support was insufficient to carry the country.

•

The Senate Republican freshmen had banded together and met weekly, and brought pressure on the leadership to pass the House's agenda without much delay. Like their House counterparts, the Senate freshman class was the most activist since the Watergate class of 1974. But there was a big difference: the Watergate class sought dispersion and decentralization of power, while the class of 1994 sought to strengthen the power of the leader, so as to enforce ideological unity. Among the ringleaders in the Senate were Jon Kyl, of Arizona, and Rick Santorum, of Pennsylvania. Santorum, not one of the Senate's deep thinkers, irritated some of his seniors through his omnipresence. One of them said, "He's busy, busy, busy. He hangs around in the cloakroom and kibitzes conversations between the majority leader and the minority leader. Anytime anybody is trying to work things out, there he is."

Many of the freshmen, and some of the sophomores, were impatient with Dole's leadership. They found it unimaginative and visionless. They felt that there was no focus, no message, and not much leadership. One freshman said, "You express the usual caveats about who else could be leader, and all of us have respect for Dole, but we're from a different generation in politics, and it became apparent to everyone in the conference that we really don't have an agenda. The House has its Contract with America, and our leaders didn't have a plan." He also complained that too often the Republican leaders—but he really meant Dole—"hold things too close to their chests."

Connie Mack encouraged the freshmen and also took up their cause—as did Lott and Dan Coats, of Indiana. John McCain, of Arizona, who was Gramm's national campaign chairman, also took up the freshman cause and used what opportunities came along to show—without suggesting so directly, of course—that Dole was a wishy-washy leader.

Dole, according to a senator close to him, was annoyed by those mini-insurrections, but tried not to show it publicly.

Gingrich also made mischief in the Senate. In an interview he said, of his own freshmen, "When they get to feeling bad, we'll send them over to sit and talk with the younger senators and they can all compare notes about how frustrated they are. And that'll increase the pressure on the Senate." He continued, "There's eleven freshmen combined with the fifteen or so C.O.S. [Conservative Opportunity Society] members who now serve in the Senate and give us a pretty big bloc over there. All the activists and all the grassroots pressures that helped us in the House are all going to come to bear in the Senate."

Tom Daschle still hadn't established himself as the Democratic leader. The Democrats liked the mild Daschle well enough, and some of the Dodd supporters were coming around, but Daschle had yet to become someone his party deferred to, much less feared. Also, his flock knew that he wasn't yet making much of a public impression, and wondered whether, given his low-key aspect, he would ever be able to do that. Now, facing the Balanced Budget Amendment, his situation was extra-complicated. Daschle himself had supported the Amendment in the past, while most of his caucus opposed it. And now Robert Byrd had assumed the floor leadership against the Amendment.

At the same time, liberal interest groups banded together, and worked in an unlikely coalition with Byrd, to slow things down in the Senate in order to gain time to stir up local grassroots opposition to the Amendment in states with Democratic senators who had supported it before. Among those in the coalition were the American Federation of State, County, and Municipal Employees, church groups, the Leadership Conference on Civil Rights, Common Cause, the Children's Defense Fund, the American Association of Retired Persons, and Bob Greenstein, of the Center for Budget and Priorities. These groups particularly wanted to head off Republicans' ability to claim, if the Amendment passed, that every budget cut was being made in the name of the Constitution.

At a long meeting in early February, Daschle told the group that he was undecided. Other members of the Democratic leadership who had also voted for the Amendment the year before were Minority Whip Wendell Ford, of Kentucky, Harry Reid, of Nevada and co-chair of the Policy Committee, and Byron Dorgan, of North Dakota, a member of the committee. Opponents of the Amendment thought that if Daschle committed to opposing it, he would then feel that he had to be on the winning side, and that Dorgan and Reid owed him their leadership roles. Also uncertain was the vote of Kent Conrad, also of North Dakota, who had voted against the Balanced Budget Amendment in 1994. Dorgan, fifty-two, and Conrad, forty-six, were both serious men, Conrad having a teacher-like mien. (Conrad had served as Assistant State Tax Commissioner in North Dakota when Dorgan served as Tax Commissioner.) Dorgan, Conrad, and Daschle were close friends and the North Dakotans had strongly supported Daschle's candidacy for majority leader. The North Dakotans were holding out, saying they were uncertain how they would vote. To what extent these little dances represent real indecision or are designed to suggest an agony that is not really there—as a way of getting attention, or winning a concession, or trying to persuade the other side that it is being taken very seriously—only the individual politician knows, and he or she may not know, either.

A proposal offered by Daschle on February 3 to require the Amendment's sponsors to say where cuts would be made to reach a balanced budget—the "right to know" amendment—was more a clever move than a serious proposal (House Democrats tried a similar gambit), but for Daschle it had the effect of uniting the Democratic caucus for the time being. Daschle, in an interview later, said that at that point he hadn't made up his mind on the Balanced Budget Amendment itself. A number of Democratic senators who opposed the Amendment went to talk to Daschle about it. But he didn't really have a choice. Had he supported the Amendment, he would have been in an untenable position within his caucus.

Robert Byrd made eloquent statements against the Amendment in both the private Democratic conclaves and on the Senate floor. A Democratic senator said, "Byrd was the prime influencer against it because he made very strong and obviously deeply heartfelt statements about the Constitution and what we were doing to it." On other issues, Byrd could be as boring as the next senator—going on at great length and invoking ancient Greek history and even embarrassingly talking about his dog Billy (and pulling out the dog's picture). But like some other politicians, when an issue arose that he felt very strongly about, he went to an unaccustomed level of eloquence and germaneness.

Byrd, using placards on which were printed certain provisions of the amendment (C-SPAN had led to the use of props and sometimes the Senate floor resembled an unregulated highway), argued that the Amendment wasn't really workable—that it would rely on unreliable estimates—that its definitions were hazy. But his strongest arguments were against putting that sort of thing in the Constitution. He described the Amendment as one that would "burst at their seams the very pillars on which this Constitutional system rests: the separation of powers and checks and balances."

The Republicans had formed a "rapid response team," made up of ten Senators who met in Dole's conference room every morning at nine for about an hour, to coordinate speakers and themes for the day. A major responsibility was to respond to Byrd. One day the team fielded Rick Santorum. The opponents could not have appeared more different. Byrd, seventy-seven, white-haired, wearing a gray suit and a black sweater vest, looked like a solon of old, a throwback. Santorum, thirty-six, with thick black hair and a toothy smile, was a product of the TV age. And he was no match for Byrd, who tore his arguments apart, and left Santorum appearing to gulp for air. The following week the large and portly Robert Smith, of New Hampshire, was sent out to do battle with Byrd, and ended in throwing his arms in the air.

Paul Sarbanes, Democrat of Maryland, also made strong arguments against the Amendment. He maintained that the exception that in the event of an issue of national security the Amendment could be waived by a vote of an absolute majority of both chambers might not be a sufficient protection. He pointed out that when Franklin Delano Roosevelt in the summer of 1941 asked for a one-year extension of the draft, it passed the House by a one-vote margin—203–202.

•

The Republicans, led by Orrin Hatch, chairman of the Judiciary Committee, were working hard to line up the votes. It soon appeared that all the Republicans except Mark Hatfield, of Oregon, would support the Amendment. Nancy Kassebaum, of Kansas, had opposed the Amendment in 1994 and would have preferred to do so again, but felt that she couldn't cause serious problems for her fellow Kansan Dole.

Hatch's problem was that he needed the votes of fourteen Democrats (if Hatfield stayed opposed), but that any concession he might offer to get Democratic votes caused some in his own caucus to threaten to oppose the resolution. Further, Hatch and Dole were reluctant to make changes in the House-passed proposal: they wanted (as did Gingrich) to avoid a House-Senate conference and further votes or any risk that the Amendment could get derailed.

Haley Barbour played an active role in trying to get the Amendment through the Senate. The Republican National Committee sent out faxes to the several hundred radio talk show hosts, and it ran ads in ten states where Democratic senators were considered undecided—which the senators didn't appreciate very much and which in some cases backfired. Senators don't want to appear to have succumbed to an ad. Barbour himself called on Hatfield, and encouraged Oregon state legislators to come to Washington to try to persuade him to vote for the Amendment. Though Hatfield, chairman of the Senate Appropriations Committee, was known as a "deficit hawk," he had principled objections to the Amendment. He argued that passing the Amendment was postponing the inevitable decisions that had to be made, and that it "trivialized" the Constitution. Hatfield believed it was "obnoxious" to say that the Constitution could be suspended by a three-fifths vote. He said, "To give Congress the authority to suspend *anything* in the Constitution is wrong." He was put off by comments that the Amendment was needed to give the Republicans "political cover" for the hard decisions to come. Hatch sent the teleminister Robert Schuller to try to persuade Hatfield. In his visit to Hatfield, Schuller held up a calendar picturing his Crystal Cathedral, saying it was debt-free, financed by members before it was opened. Schuller told Hatfield, "That's how the government should run." Later, Hatfield told Hatch, "Orrin, it didn't work." Hatch said that he had Billy Graham lined up. Hatfield replied, "He won't come to do that, Orrin."

In a speech on the Senate floor on January 30, Daschle let it be known that he would oppose the Amendment. (The next morning, Gingrich, at a meeting of the Governors Conference, in Washington, expressed disappointment with Daschle's switch and said that no matter what happened, the House would proceed as if the Amendment had been adopted, and would seek a balanced budget by 2002.) In the Senate, Democrats sponsored amendments to specify that the Social Security trust fund, which was in surplus, would not be used to balance the budget. But Daschle couldn't use that issue as the reason for now opposing the Amendment because there had been no change in this policy since he supported the Amendment the year before. The Social Security issue was a useful one for the Democrats. One Democratic senator said, "It has a constituency out there that can mobilize phone calls, and all of a sudden there's people providing a balance to the talk show hosts." To argue, as some Democrats did, that the Amendment would result in "raiding" or "looting" the Social Security trust fund was a bit of a stretch—what they really meant was that as long as the fund was being used to pay for other government expenses, it wasn't safe. Under the current system, the government borrowed from the trust fund to finance other operations. But, at least theoretically, the funds had to be repaid. But the issue wasn't entirely fraudulent, as some charged, saying that the Social Security trust fund was already counted to offset some of the deficit—and that to now argue that it shouldn't be was hypocritical. But to count it in computations that said that the budget was in balance—as would happen under the Amendment—would also be hypocritical.

The forthcoming election appeared to play a role in some senators' votes —as did the fact that the 1994 election was past. Democratic Senators Joseph Biden, of Delaware, and Tom Harkin, of Iowa, both of whom had opposed the Amendment in 1994 and were up for reelection in 1996, now supported it. This bothered a number of their Democratic colleagues. On the other side, some senators who had supported the Amendment in 1994, when they were up for reelection, now opposed it, or were leaning against it. (Dorgan had supported it as a candidate in 1992.)

In the Senate debate Bingaman made a point that struck several Democrats: he argued that, with the House having adopted a rule on opening day that income tax rates could only be raised by a three-fifths vote, working people were being set up for other taxes. After a while, the mood in the Senate shifted, and defeat of the Amendment, which had seemed unlikely at the outset, now seemed possible. The stakes for both sides were immense: Democrats increasingly saw the Amendment as part of the Republicans' agenda of cutting deeply or killing federal programs; Republican senators saw it not only as giving them leverage for making such cuts but also as a test of their leader. If the Senate failed to do what the House had, condemnation from Republican constituencies would be forthcoming, and Dole's effectiveness would be questioned.

In the days leading up to the vote, the White House tried to head off a Republican victory. The President became more active and other officials worked with Byrd on "talking points"; when it seemed that it might actually be possible to defeat the Amendment, the White House worked with Byrd on the vote. The administration compiled a state-by-state analysis of the effect of the Amendment—though there was no real way to know—and warned senators of its likely effect on various programs (even though that couldn't be known). On the Friday before the scheduled final vote, National Economic Council Chairman Laura Tyson, Secretary of the Treasury Robert Rubin, O.M.B. Director Alice Rivlin, and White House Counsel Abner Mikva held a press conference—essentially aimed at the North Dakotans—saying that the Amendment offered no protection in case of an economic downturn. That night, the President called Dorgan, and on Saturday he devoted his radio address to the subject, saying that a balanced budget was bad economics in a recession. He warned that if the Amendment passed, budget decisions could ultimately be made by federal judges instead of elected representatives.

According to a unanimous consent agreement between Dole and the Democrats, reached after one cloture vote failed but a second seemed likely to succeed, final voting on amendments and then passage were set for Tuesday the twenty-eighth—four weeks after the debate began. The debate had gone on for thirty-one days, longer than on any subject since the civil rights debates of the mid-sixties. Dole was in a very tight spot. He had to get the Amendment through the Senate but if he made concessions in order to do that he could come under criticism for that, too—and in fact he did. Another Republican said, "There were objections to those trying to work something out that the goalpost kept being moved." The proponents needed three more votes.

On the afternoon before the scheduled voting, Phil Gramm objected to the fact that Hatch (who was very close to Dole) was negotiating with Sam Nunn, Democrat from Georgia, over a Nunn amendment to prohibit the courts from enforcing the Balanced Budget Amendment. Nunn argued that the courts shouldn't be making budget decisions, including decisions to raise taxes. Gramm said that there should be no deal with Nunn unless he brought two other undecided Democrats with him. But Dole insisted that the Republicans make a deal with Nunn, and the amendment was accepted on the morning of the twenty-eighth, and Nunn said he would vote for the Balanced Budget Amendment. According to some Constitutional scholars this was an unprecedented restriction on the courts. (Some said the Amendment would overturn *Marbury v. Madison,* which nearly two centuries ago established the principle of judicial review.) Trent Lott explained later that when the leadership saw that eight Republicans supported a similar amendment, "We realized we had to do something about it."

The Republicans had been working that morning on getting John

Breaux, Democrat of Louisiana and a centrist, to commit to support the Amendment, but Breaux was waiting for Nunn. With Nunn's announcement, Breaux said that he would support the Amendment. That left the Republicans one vote short. At the Republicans' Tuesday policy lunch, the discussion centered on the possible availability of Dorgan's or Conrad's vote. That morning, Dorgan had made a speech in which he said that unless a change was made to protect the Social Security trust fund, he would vote against the Amendment. Conrad also made a speech laying out his conditions, which included the protection of Social Security and suspension of the Amendment in case of an economic downturn.

Clinton's February budget had handed the Republicans an argument, and several of them pointed out that his budget proposal had deficits of $200 billion "as far as the eye can see." Therefore, they said, a Balanced Budget Amendment was needed. But the Republicans couldn't accept Dorgan's proposal to not count surplus Social Security funds in the budget, because that would have added roughly another $260 billion to the total deficit—which, when added to the $1.2 trillion needed to balance the budget, made reaching that goal all the more difficult. That left Conrad, Wendell Ford, and Hatfield. Ford had promised the other Democratic leaders that his wouldn't be the sixty-seventh vote for the Amendment.

But despite the pressures from Dole, Hatch, and Haley Barbour, Hatfield gave no sign of budging. Hatfield's objection was on principle, and hard as that is for some politicians to understand, there was no way he could change his position. Hatfield, a former professor, was an early and steady opponent of the Vietnam War. He didn't mind sticking out. Nonetheless, Hatfield said in a conversation outside the Senate Chamber on the day of the voting that Dole had spent a lot of time with him that day, and other senators were pressing. He said that the Oregon legislators, sent over by Barbour, were "nonthreatening." Hatfield said with a small smile, "I'm staying right where I am. I arrived there with conviction and I'm not moving."

In mid-afternoon, also off the Senate floor, Trent Lott leaned in fatigue against a sea-green dumpster and said that the Republican whips were making sure that all Republican senators understood they were to vote to kill all of the amendments Democrats were offering. Then he showed a letter from Gingrich saying that he would agree to a provision in the legislation spelling out how the Amendment should be carried out—the "enabling legislation"—that would say that Social Security shouldn't be counted in reaching a balanced budget. Gingrich had agreed to the letter that morning. Some Democrats questioned whether an ordinary statute could supersede a Constitutional Amendment, and they also knew that a statute could easily be repealed, or overlooked.

Shortly after six, Thad Cochran, the other Mississippian and chairman of the Republican conference, paused to talk in the reception room off the Senate floor. Cochran, white-thatched and soft-spoken, was of a different temperament from the hyper Lott. Cochran was a Dole man. The reception room, very ornate, was furnished with large red leather sofas and armchairs with gold trim. The word among the Republicans, Cochran said, was that Conrad and Dole—with Gingrich's concurrence—were very close to resolving some statutory language saying that the Social Security trust fund would be counted until 2012, or perhaps 2010, and that the only thing that remained to be worked out was the choreography. Domenici had approached Conrad in the Democratic cloakroom and offered a proposal to stop using the trust fund in 2012. By offering to stop counting the trust fund as of 2010 or 2012, the Republicans were simply offering to merely require what was going to happen anyway, when the baby boomers retired and surpluses no longer existed.

Domenici returned a little later and offered to move the date back to 2008. Conrad called a member of his staff to ask how much of the trust fund would be used up by then and after he was told that $1.3 trillion of Social Security surpluses would have been by that time, Conrad went to where Domenici was seated on the Senate floor, sat down next to him, and told him that that wasn't acceptable.

There ensued one of the strangest scenes ever beheld in the Senate Chamber. Seated on the Republican side of the aisle, Domenici and Conrad began discussing a Domenici formula that would allow the use, starting in fiscal 1997, of ninety percent of the surpluses for that year, then eighty percent in the second, and seventy percent—ratcheting down by ten percent a year the amount of the Social Security surplus that could be used, until they were using none of the funds. This, too, confirmed for the Democrats that the Republicans envisioned using Social Security funds to balance the budget. Gradually a mass of Republican senators, plus Paul Simon, of Illinois—who supported the Balanced Budget Amendment—formed around Domenici and Conrad. Domenici could be seen making notes on a piece of paper. On the other side of the aisle Democratic senators looked on, appalled. Dorgan kept a clear distance.

As the mass around Conrad grew, Dole finished his closing speech—decrying "scare tactics" and saying, with passion, and some anger, "We're trying to protect these programs . . . the debt threatens every program." Dole said, "If there was any message last November. . . . And different people heard different messages; some didn't hear any message at all, and some are here, and some will be voting. We need help, we don't have the will in this body. I hear speeches at night when I can't sleep." When Dole concluded he suggested the absence of a quorum, in order to gain time. Dole then joined the group around Conrad and Domenici, which had now grown to about ten senators. Aware that they were creating a spectacle—

the galleries were packed for the big moment of the final vote, and several House members, mostly freshmen, were gathered in the back of the Chamber—Dole suggested that the group remove itself to the Republican cloakroom, behind the Chamber.

In the cloakroom, Domenici explained to Conrad how a balanced budget could be reached without using Social Security. Conrad recalled later, "They told me they could do the concept of a formula for saving an increasing amount of the trust fund year by year, and they said we could do it by statute. We'd been having that discussion for days. Simon had suggested it. I said in the cloakroom, 'What you guys don't get is that Byron and I come from financial backgrounds. We don't believe you should raid trust funds to pay down debt.' I said, 'I'm not a lawyer.' I said, 'I would have to have Constitutional experts review whether what you're saying would work.' "

With matters in this state of uncertainty, while those in the Senate Chamber wondered what on earth was going on in the cloakroom, Conrad told the Republicans that he was also concerned about economic downturns. Hatch replied that they couldn't do anything about that. At that point, Bill Cohen muttered, "How many bottom lines are there?"

Daschle, troubled that Conrad was a captive and outnumbered in the Republican cloakroom, and feeling that he should be extricated, went there and said that he needed to talk with Conrad, urgently. Daschle was trying to provide Conrad with a time-out. Conrad was known as someone who gnawed on things. As Daschle led Conrad into the Democratic cloakroom, Lott followed them right in—another strange sight—so Daschle took Conrad to his leadership office where they were joined at a dining table by Dorgan and John Hilley, Daschle's chief counsel and former staff director of the Budget Committee. Daschle and Dorgan, concerned, told Conrad that he hadn't looked so great out there on the Senate floor. According to Conrad, Daschle asked him where his negotiations with the Republicans stood, and when Conrad replied that they were still talking about protecting Social Security through a statute, Hilley commented that that discussion had been going on for several days and that the Democrats' legal counsel had said that that wouldn't work. When Conrad told the others about the pending "ten percent solution," Daschle replied that that didn't work, that it wasn't right to let the Republicans use the other ninety percent, and eighty percent. Besides, they were offering to do this through a statute, which would be superseded by a Constitutional Amendment. At that point, Daschle asked Conrad, "Do you want to go ahead and vote?" Conrad replied, "We'd might as well."

Daschle said later, of Conrad and Dorgan, "Those are probably my two closest friends in the Senate. I have reason to talk to them outside my role as minority leader." Daschle added, "I have a developing sense of my role as leader, especially on Constitutional issues, especially on a large issue of principle. It wasn't my role to try to persuade people. I discussed it with several senators, but in those discussions, I told them, 'This is my view,' but didn't say, 'You've got to do it.' Senators don't like to be told what they've got to do. That may have been more persuasive." This was a very different view from that of Lyndon Johnson—who it was hard to imagine would have tolerated Conrad's behavior, or even let it get to that point.

Dorgan reentered the Chamber at 7:25 and went over to the Republican side and told Dole, "We may as well go ahead and vote." The galleries could see Dole's face fall and other Republicans look stricken. As Conrad returned to the Democratic side, Gramm, carrying a chart, chased after him to the forward right corner of the Chamber and tried some persuasion of his own. What Gramm did simply isn't done, but a lot of what preceded it was pretty strange, too, and a little unnerving. It was as if they were chasing the Constitution around on the Senate floor.

There were audible gasps when Dole suddenly called for a recess until 10:00 A.M. the next day. The agreement had been for a vote that day and it was a serious matter to break a unanimous consent agreement. Byrd demanded an explanation. Dole said, "We think we still have a chance to resolve this, to get sixty-seven votes or more. If we fail we fail." Hatch looked exhausted, and didn't think that postponing the vote was a good idea. Several senators seemed in shock. A Democratic senator said later, "In a democratic society you have to be able and prepared to lose. It's in a dictatorial society that the leader never loses." Byrd, taking the floor, called the breaking of the agreement "a travesty," and said, "We see the sad spectacle of senators on the other side trying to go over until tomorrow in order to get another vote for this Amendment. . . . It boils down to an *insatiable, insatiable* desire to get a vote for victory. We are tampering with the Constitution of the United States!" He said, "This is no place for deal-making, backroom huddles. . . . This has every appearance of a sleazy, tawdry effort to win a victory at the cost of amending the Constitution of the United States." These were rare words in the Senate Chamber, but it was a rare situation.

An angry Dole replied, "We don't take the Constitution lightly." He said that Byrd's charge was "out of bounds." The rest of the Senate was dead quiet, senators in their chairs, paying close attention and recognizing that the institution could be nearing a breakdown, or the beginning of long-lasting resentments. Dole, getting more worked up, said, "I think the sad spectacle is that we may lose this vote. . . . What are the American people to think. . . . They sent us a loud and clear message last November."

On a voice vote on whether to adjourn for the night, the Republicans quietly said aye, the Democrats no. Conrad, sitting at his desk like a chastened schoolboy, said no. At 7:41 P.M., a shaken Senate adjourned.

·

While the dealings with Conrad were going on in the Senate on Tuesday evening, Gingrich and some of his staff, meeting with the governors about food stamps, were becoming concerned about the reports they were getting from the other side of the Capitol. At one point, John Kasich and Dan Meyer, Gingrich's chief of staff, went over to the Senate side, to find out what was being negotiated. Meyer said later, "It was our feeling that people in the House who had voted for the Balanced Budget Amendment shouldn't be put through another vote on it." The whole rigmarole with the freshmen would have to be gone through again. Meyer recalled, "Somebody said they were throwing the cat back on our porch—to not have it die on their porch, but have it die on ours."

At the White House residence that night, Clinton was having some people from Arkansas in to watch a University of Arkansas basketball game. Panetta and Patrick Griffin, head of legislative liaison, were in touch by phone with Daschle. Panetta and Griffin went to the residence and told the President what was happening, and that the advice from the Hill was that he should stay out of the matter at that point, so as not to raise the ante for him or for the Democrats. (Nor did anyone think his voice would carry weight.)

When Dorgan and Conrad held a press conference on Wednesday morning —stating their objections to the Amendment—most people thought that they were saying that they wouldn't support it, but Conrad, at least, was still undecided. During the press conference, Conrad received a note that Domenici wanted to talk to him. That afternoon the two North Dakotans and three other Democrats—Feinstein, Reid, and Ford—met with a Constitutional law expert from the Congressional Research Service of the Library of Congress, who told them that a statute couldn't overcome a Constitutional provision. This group, plus Ernest Hollings, but minus Conrad, sent a letter to Dole saying that if he put protection of the Social Security trust fund in the Constitutional Amendment they'd be prepared to support it. Conrad said that he didn't sign the letter because it didn't say anything about a provision for protection in case of an economic emergency.

Dorgan and Conrad had succeeded in highlighting the Social Security issue—the safest political ground for opposing the Amendment. Other Democratic senators had tried to do this through offering amendments, but they couldn't get enough attention to the matter. This episode did show that just as the Founding Fathers intended, a thinly populated prairie state had as much power in the Senate as a large, populous one. North Dakota counted for as much as New York or California. And the Senate was acting as a saucer to cool the House's hot coffee.

•

When the Senate convened at 10:00 A.M. on Wednesday morning, Dole looked tired; there were dark circles under his eyes. He said that Republicans had made several suggestions about protecting Social Security, "but it's never quite enough, never quite enough." Dole said, "The American people don't care when we vote. This is no time for retreat." He warned that if the Amendment didn't carry on the next vote, he would file a motion to reconsider and "leave it out there a year. Let us see what happens." He added, "I think sometime about next September"—that is, shortly before the elections—"might be appropriate to reconsider this whole issue."

At the lunch that day of the Senate Republican Steering Committee, a relatively conservative group, with about forty senators present and seated at a large square table, the subject was whether to continue negotiations with Conrad. One senator said later, "There was a resounding no." Also at that lunch, a freshman brought up the idea of sanctioning Hatfield, and the idea was almost immediately rejected. It was more important, the senators agreed, to focus attention on the Democrats.

The battle of the press conferences and faxes was on. Republicans were giving the radio talk shows another day to stir up support for the Amendment. Dole phoned Rush Limbaugh. On his program that day, Limbaugh said, Let Clinton win it if he wants, and he suggested a new bumper sticker, "Win one for the zipper." New York Republican Al D'Amato said that Clinton should be ashamed of himself for "thwarting the will of the American people." Gingrich, in his press briefing, said that Daschle and Feinstein "lied to their states to get reelected." According to a CBS/*New York Times* poll, eighty percent of the public supported the Balanced Budget Amendment, but only thirty percent supported it if it meant cutting Social Security.

A great deal of pressure was put on Hatfield before the final vote. George Bush called him the night before. Close to a dozen colleagues went to see him or called him at home. Business groups called him. Shortly before the vote on Thursday, March 2, four or five other senators met with him. About an hour before the vote, Hatfield received a call from Elizabeth Dole, and, just before the final vote, Bob Dole visited him in his office for about twenty minutes. Dole made a strong case about the dire impact that failure to pass the Amendment would have on the Republican Party and its leadership. Hatfield offered, "Under those circumstances, I'll resign." Dole said he couldn't accept that. Then Hatfield, in his office in the Appropriations Committee rooms in the Capitol, watched Dole's closing statement on television and walked upstairs and voted "no."

The senators stayed in their seats during the vote, which happened only on momentous occasions, rising when their names were called. At the end of the reading of the names, Gramm dramatically burst through the doors to the Chamber and cast the last "aye" vote. At that point, the vote was 66–34, one short of the number needed, but Dole changed his vote to no, so that he could move to reconsider the vote at another time. He looked bleak and shaken. Despite efforts on the part of his aides and allies to paint a positive picture of his leadership on the issue—they said that he had delivered ninety-eight percent of the Republicans, more than had ever before voted for the Amendment—they all knew that this was not a good moment for him.

At a press conference afterward, Dole said that Clinton "has abdicated his responsibility and has taken on eighty percent of the American people." Republicans attacked the "Somersault Six"—Daschle, Dorgan, Ford, Feinstein, Bingaman, and Hollings—for changing their position on the Amendment from 1994.

At a White House briefing, Clinton, trying not to look too pleased, pointed out that the Republicans still hadn't presented their budget. This didn't seem to be a very strong point (Clinton's budget had gone nowhere), but administration officials pressed it for some time.

That morning, on the Senate floor, Dole said, "I am excited about the prospect of taking this case to the American people." With some bitterness, he referred to "the obituaries" about him, saying that they were premature.

At a press conference that morning, Gramm announced that he and Armey would try to write the Balanced Budget Amendment as a statute. Hatch, a Dole man, said, "It's a nice try by a Presidential candidate, but it does not wash."

Because of Dole's plight, the announcement that Ben Nighthorse Campbell, of Colorado, would switch from the Democratic to the Republican side was moved up from the following Tuesday to Friday, the day after Dole's defeat on the Balanced Budget Amendment. This made the Senate party lineup 54–36. (Campbell, a rancher, jewelry-maker, and motorcycle rider, had been discontented with political life for a long time, and at that point wasn't happy with the local Democratic Party, or with Bill Clinton.) At the press conference announcing the switch, Dole looked overjoyed. Now there was an up ending to what had been a very down week. (Politicians were very conscious of the weekend talk shows.) At the press conference, Hatch, like Campbell, wore a bolo tie.

Over the weekend, there was increasing talk from some Republicans that Hatfield should be stripped of his committee chairmanship. The movement was led by Santorum and Mack, but it got some public encouragement from Lott, who said in a television interview that Hatfield's vote "exhibited an awful lot of arrogance." This threatened to throw the Senate Republican conference into deeper turmoil—but it had been coming for some time.

Right after the 1994 election, some of the younger Republicans began to talk about stripping both Hatfield and Chafee of their chairmanships because they didn't share the views of most of the caucus, or of the electorate in November. (This was of course the intent of the staggered terms prescribed by the Constitution.)

A moderate Republican senator said, "Mark Hatfield is respected by the older members for having strong beliefs. The freshmen are not in a position to question Mark's character. They're questioning someone who has been here nearly thirty years. They have to earn their spurs before they act like Cromwell."

After a Senate Republican leadership meeting on Tuesday, March 7, Mack told reporters that, "Yes, people should vote their conscience, but Hatfield was in a leadership position and the Balanced Budget Amendment is the keystone of the Republican Party." At the regular Tuesday Republican conference lunch that day, in the Mansfield Room, just off the Senate floor, Mack and Santorum pressed for a special gathering of the Senate Republicans to decide Hatfield's fate. By custom, the special conference had to be called, but several senators, including some very conservative ones, such as Don Nickles, of Oklahoma, made it clear that they thought this was a very poor idea. It threatened the entire seniority system and could set off a civil war within the Republican conference.

Thad Cochran, the conference chairman, to get it over with, announced a special meeting of the conference for the next day. Cochran publicly made the point that not in this century had a senator been denied the chairmanship of or membership in a committee because of a vote. In an interview Cochran said, "Everyone realizes that you may have a reason to disagree with a conference and if that reason is consistent with your conscience you should vote that way. We were elected to represent our constituents, and that decision is up to them. We weren't elected to represent the Republican conference. In a case like this a respected person has voted one way instead of another, and that doesn't justify punishing him."

Dole was known to be quite angry with Hatfield—there had been tension between the two men for years—but more than one Republican senator said that Dole didn't want to punish Hatfield, because he might need his vote at any time, and Hatfield really might resign.

In the specially convened conference meeting (also in the Mansfield Room) on Wednesday, the solons sat in folding chairs arranged in rows. Hatfield sat in the back of the room. Only two senators—Mack and Santorum—said that Hatfield should be stripped of his chairmanship.

Conservatives Larry Craig, of Idaho, and Lauch Faircloth, of North Carolina (a Jesse Helms protégé), were critical of Hatfield's vote. Slade Gorton, of Washington, said that Hatfield had cast the wrong vote but he supported Hatfield's retaining his chairmanship. Domenici, Hatch, and Alan Simpson also supported Hatfield. It was clear that Hatfield wasn't going to be punished, but the meeting was an opportunity for airing frustrations. The freshmen—in particular Jon Kyl, of Arizona, and Fred Thompson, of Tennessee—argued that the seniority system should be changed. A group was appointed to propose changes to Dole. One Republican senator said afterward, "It wasn't a great moment for the Republican Party. We were focusing on the vote we lost rather than on the Democrats who changed their vote. We put on a spectacle."

Hatfield hadn't gone unarmed into the meeting, which he later described sardonically as "the inquisition." The by-all-appearances gentle senator was prepared to fight. He had taken a count and found eight senators ready to strip him of his chairmanship. And he had found that according to Senate rules, it was the full Senate that confirmed chairmanships. He had lined up three Democrats (one was Robert Byrd) who said that they would argue on his behalf if the issue did come to the Senate floor. Hatfield said later, "If the vote had been close, or had there been a majority against me, I was ready to call for public hearings and a Senate vote. I wasn't going to bow down to political retribution without a fight."

Following the meeting, Hatfield approached the mob of reporters gathered outside the Mansfield Room and said, smiling, "I'm Chairman Mark Hatfield." He said that he had listened carefully to the feelings of the freshmen and that he had led "a few rebel causes" in his day. Graciously, he said, "When they look at the House they feel frustrated. I regret very much that it should reflect on the leadership. I want to commend Senator Dole on his leadership."

Dole said, "I got hurt by this more than Hatfield, so I feel fairly strongly about this."

12

LIMITS

"You Had to Maximize the Fear"

Because of the defeat of the Balanced Budget Amendment in the Senate, Republican Chairman Haley Barbour suggested to the House leaders that they put off a vote on term limits for two weeks, so as not to have two major defeats close together. Everyone knew that the House wouldn't adopt a term limits measure, so the challenge was to make the best of it. The publicly stated reason for the delay was that it was to allow more time for the outside groups supporting term limits to whip up support.

The Judiciary Committees of both Chambers had approved a Constitutional Amendment limiting terms to twelve years—two terms for senators and six terms for representatives. Except on the part of the freshmen, there was little enthusiasm for term limits among Senate Republicans. Judiciary Committee Chairman Hatch opposed the idea—as did his House counterpart, Henry Hyde. Key members of the House leadership—Boehner and DeLay—opposed the idea, and Gingrich was known by his close allies to be none too enthusiastic about it. But Gingrich had no choice but to appear to be all for it. (Boehner later switched his position, saying that term limits was "a bad idea whose time has come"—a meaningless expression used by many politicians who have to explain a supposed change of heart.) Senate leaders decided not to bring the proposal to the floor until the House had voted; if it failed in the House there was no point in putting senators through a vote on the issue.

The term limits idea, strongly backed by some grassroots groups, was part of a movement to hogtie and flail—and delegitimize—the Congress. It went in precisely the wrong direction. Limiting the number of terms would remove the possibility that some members would develop expertise in an area, and be able to contribute real knowledge to a discussion or to the legislating on a given issue. And it would strengthen the unelected staff and the lobbyists—who would have even more knowledge than the members than some staff already did. It could make members all the more dependent on interest groups, which might offer employment when time was up. Length of service wasn't the problem; the problem lay in the need for the legislators to raise large sums of money to stay in politics. The 1994 election showed that the voters were capable of imposing their own term limits. In fact, half the House members had been serving only since 1990. The issue was often described as one that divided Members of Congress generationally, and while there was some truth to that—longtime incumbents didn't think poorly of themselves and many wanted to stay on the job—it also divided members along philosophical and attitudinal lines. Most of the House freshmen had run on term limits in the anti-government climate of November 1994.

The delay notwithstanding, the failure of the Balanced Budget Amendment in the Senate put more pressure on the House leaders to pass a measure that no one thought would pass. Armey said later that about 200 of the needed 290 votes for a Constitutional Amendment were in hand on the basis of conviction, and "the rest we had to get on fear." Armey continued, "You had to maximize the fear. The way you maximize the fear is you limit the number of votes, limit the ability to vote for a safe haven [an alternate proposal] and say 'I voted for . . .' "

On Thursday night, March 13, the leadership negotiated with the most fervid supporters of term limits, and reached a tentative agreement that there would be only two votes on the issue. "I was on cloud nine," Armey said. But when the strong backers of the Amendment checked with the groups behind it the deal fell through, because they wanted a vote on another alternative—letting the states set term limits—that they thought would have the best chance of passing. So, on Friday afternoon and stretching into the late evening, Armey met with representatives of the groups—which included the Christian Coalition and the American Conservative Union—and other strong backers, in Gingrich's office. Gingrich could be there only part of the time because he had to meet with the key budget figures to discuss the "lock box" for the rescissions bill. An agreement was reached to allow three votes. Armey said, "The cat's in the bag and the bag is closed tight."

The House debate on term limits, on March 29, was fairly desultory, since the outcome was known. Sherwood Boehlert spoke strongly against term limits, saying that an "arrogant clique of people in the shadow of the Capitol are proposing to overturn what the Founding Fathers set out." When Hyde, one of the last of the great orators in the Congress, was about to speak, a large number of members came to the floor to observe. The rotund, white-haired Hyde was a principled, cheerful conservative, and he plunged headlong into the term limits debate. "I just cannot be an accessory to the dumbing-down of democracy," Hyde cried. He argued that expertise and experience were essential and irreplaceable. "You do not get them out of the phone book," he said. When he finished, he was given a standing ovation and John Dingell crossed the aisle to shake his hand. Dingell sponsored a sly proposal that would have made the Amendment retroactive, but this of course was rejected, by more than two to one.

To show his bona fides (if not what he really thought) Gingrich closed the debate, and launched a new strategy of blaming the forthcoming defeat on the Democrats. "I have frankly been surprised by our friends on the left," Gingrich said. On the final roll call vote the Amendment was defeated 227–204, sixty-one votes short. Gingrich, now in the chair, announced, "The joint resolution is not passed."

Following his defeat on the Balanced Budget Amendment, it was all the more important to Dole to pass *something*. The matter at hand, the line-item veto, which would give the President the authority to veto sections of an appropriations bill rather than being forced to accept or veto the entire bill, should have been easy. The House had already passed it by a large bipartisan vote, and President Clinton had repeatedly stated that this was something on which he and the Congress could reach agreement.

House leaders had been keen on passing a line-item veto bill on February 6, Ronald Reagan's eighty-fourth birthday. Reagan had been a fervent supporter of a line-item veto and the idea had become Republican orthodoxy—even to the point of apparently wanting to give significant new power to a Democratic President. But the Republicans didn't think that there would be a Democratic President for long. And the Republicans chose to try to accomplish this through a statute rather than a Constitutional Amendment, which would require a more lengthy process. The result was to actually give the President less power than a Constitutional Amendment would.

The bill passed by the House on February 6 did require a two-thirds vote of the House and the Senate to override the President. In effect, it sanctioned minority rule.

After the bill reached the Senate, Dole ran into a problem. There was a serious dispute within his ranks over how strong the President's powers should be. The dispute, which went on for weeks, was between John

McCain, of Arizona, who favored the House-passed bill, and Pete Domenici, who wanted to give the President less power. The majority of the Senate Republicans favored McCain's approach, but Domenici, as chairman of the Budget Committee, was not without influence. Eventually, Dole instructed his staff to sit down with the staffs of the relevant senators and work something out. A Dole aide said, "The biggest issue was to get people to sit down and talk. On the face of it there were irreconcilable differences, and there was concern that if we took Domenici's approach, we would lose in the Senate."

In the meantime Dole, blame-shifting, taunted Clinton to speak up in strong support of the legislation. Clinton's response was to say that he wanted the "strongest possible" legislation and his aides said that he was "working very hard" on the bill.

The result of the deliberations among Senate Republicans was an absurd decision that each item in the thirteen appropriations bills would be treated as a separate bill. It was estimated that, under this approach, the appropriations bills of the year before would have amounted to 9,625 mini-bills. Byrd, who was once again conducting a talkathon, made fun of the idea, referring to these new items as *billettes*—dragging out the word for full effect. "This is Tomfoolery," Byrd railed, and he pointed out that the Constitution, in specifying the President's veto power, referred to "every bill," and "it." Byrd said, "If it's two thousand little *'its,'* how is he going to sign *'it'?*" The compromise proposal required a two-thirds vote to overturn a veto, as McCain sought, but it also contained, for Domenici, a "sunset" provision which would have the new law expire in the year 2000, giving Congress an opportunity to evaluate how well it was working. Several senators complained privately that it wasn't clear how the bill would work at all.

The bill was passed by the Senate on March 23 by a vote of 69–29. Then Dole and Gingrich began to wonder whether they really wanted to give Clinton this new authority.

13

THE CROWN JEWEL

"We'd Rather Parents Have the Money Than Bureaucrats"

The pressures against tax cuts had grown to the point, and paying for them was proving so troublesome, that in early March even Gingrich considered cutting back on the tax cuts pending in the House. Members, including an insistent Kasich, reported strong sentiment at town meetings in their districts for reducing the deficit before cutting taxes. Polls were reflecting this sentiment as well. But no one could be sure whether public sentiment for deficit reduction had so taken root that people were ready to accept cuts in programs that affected them, whether they really did prefer deficit reductions over tax cuts—or whether, as numerous skeptics believed, they were saying what they thought was the proper thing to say.

Gingrich concluded that the House Republicans shouldn't backtrack on their Contract commitments during the Hundred Days. Besides, the $500-per-child tax credit was *the* major commitment to the social conservatives, and the Christian Coalition, which had pledged to spend a million dollars on lobbying for the Contract, and wasn't getting any other matter of real importance to it—such as school prayer or an anti-abortion measure—during the Hundred Days. It let the leadership know that a retreat on the tax cut "wouldn't be looked on kindly," according to a leadership aide.

Besides, Gingrich understood that whatever the House did, the Senate was sure to modify. Armey had made this point strongly. Also, Armey said, to reduce the proposed tax cut then would be a confession of weakness. Gingrich's lieutenants started instructing House Republicans that the Senate was going to be rougher terrain for tax cuts than the House, so they should stick with the leadership's proposals.

By late March, in fact, the House Republican leaders were becoming quite agitated about the Senate. The House leaders didn't criticize Dole publicly; the frustration was couched publicly in such terms as, The House acts quickly but the Senate is a deliberative body. And there was some understanding on the part of the House people that, bad as things were, Dole was trying to get things done. But a House leadership aide said, "We're having trouble with our Senate brethren. They're sending over bills that aren't worth diddly." The immediate cause of distress was the Senate's version of the House-passed moratorium on regulations: in place of the House's year-long freeze on new regulations, the Senate-passed bill would require that any regulation with an expected economic impact of $100 million be sent to Congress, which would have forty-five days to reject it. In a meeting on the afternoon of Monday, March 28, in room H 227, of Gingrich, Armey, and DeLay and two representatives of the freshman class, the leaders exploded in a cascade of Senate bashing. The Senate lacked the guts to make fundamental changes, it was said. The Senate was extremely weak on regulatory reform, it was charged. DeLay was especially angry over the Senate's modification of the regulatory freeze. There was anger at Domenici and at Packwood, who were balking at cutting taxes. It was charged that "millionaire" senators were selling them out. (Neither Domenici nor Packwood was anything close to a millionaire.) Gingrich, who got pretty worked up himself, said he'd be damned if he would let the Senate dictate to the House after the House had done so much work. Some expressed anger that House Republicans had had to cast some tough votes, especially on the rescissions bill—cutting subsidies for low-income housing, and summer jobs—and now the Senate might restore some of these things. Gingrich vowed to appoint conferees—representatives of the House in House-Senate negotiations on the final version of a bill—"who will never give in."

The congressional Democrats, and Clinton, were putting the Republicans on the defensive by defining their tax cut proposals as "for the rich." The charge had some basis, because the Republicans' proposal would grant the $500 credit to couples earning up to $200,000 (whereas Clinton's proposal would cut off such credits at $75,000). Moreover, the tax credit wouldn't be available to millions of families who didn't earn enough money to qualify for tax credits. Further, it reduced taxes on capital gains; removed the alternative minimum tax on corporations that otherwise had so many deductions that they would owe no taxes (a major reform in the 1986 Tax Reform Act); and repealed the 1993 tax increase on high-income Social Security beneficiaries. Democrats charged that the top one percent income earners would get twenty percent of the benefits.

•

Gingrich hadn't had much time to savor his victory on welfare reform. Now the tax bill, the last major Contract item, was in trouble. By the beginning of the last week in March, Gingrich and the other Republican leaders believed that they didn't have the votes to pass the bill, which was scheduled to be brought up the first week in April, just before a planned three-week House recess to recover from the Hundred Days and to proselytize the home folks about how much had been accomplished.

Two groups of Republicans—each made up largely of moderates—were demanding changes in the bill. A group of about forty, led by Mike Castle, of Delaware, and Fred Upton, of Michigan, backed a provision stating that the tax cuts couldn't go into effect until the C.B.O. certified that Congress had approved a budget plan that would eliminate the deficit by 2002, and then only in stages. Castle, a former governor of Delaware, told reporters that many members were skeptical that Republicans could cut taxes and balance the budget and that his proposal would help them "to get out of an awkward situation." Sherwood Boehlert was one of those moderates who felt that tax cuts should wait. He said, "I'm very uncomfortable with having tax cuts now when we're cutting off funds for programs that have proven they work."

Another group of a hundred and two Republicans—nearly half the caucus—backed a proposal to lower the income limit on those who could receive the $500 tax credits to $95,000, rather than the $200,000 in the bill. This group, headed by Greg Ganske, a freshman from Iowa, signed a letter to Gingrich to this effect. Gingrich did succeed in talking Ganske out of holding a press conference about the letter.

A Republican close to the leadership said, "They're in a very difficult position. A significant scaleback on anything amounts to the hard-core base of the party to an abdication of the Contract. The tax cut is the core of the Contract. It matters a great deal to the Christian Coalition and to Jack Kemp and the supply-siders as well as assorted other conservatives. If you don't produce on either term limits or tax cuts you take a hard knock. Newt understands he has to produce on a tax cut or he has a serious problem."

There were philosophical as well as political reasons why cutting back on the tax cuts—especially accepting the lower ceiling—was very hazardous for the Republicans. If the Republican Party said that it would target tax cuts by income group, conservatives would rebel, saying that Republican tax policy shouldn't proceed according to "class warfare." The idea that the tax code should produce greater equity in society was the province of the Democrats. Republicans argued that lower taxes increased growth. For Republicans to start talking equity was to be playing on Democratic terms.

Some schisms within the House Republican conference also came into play on the tax bill as the exhausted members stumbled toward the end of the Hundred Days. There was a growing concern about the freshmen. A senior Republican said, "A large number of moderates, and some other senior members, are afraid that you have an extraordinarily arrogant group in the freshman class—that there's no other way but their way. It's taking a toll. Their lack of sophistication is a big problem. They don't realize that you have to form a majority. They're applying a litmus test to people with far more experience."

The original tax cut proposal for the Contract had no income cap at all, and that was how Dick Armey liked it. In fact, he preferred a flat tax, but felt that this was too much to try to achieve during the Hundred Days. He later introduced a flat tax proposal, various versions of which were gaining adherents among Republicans. Dole tried to preempt the subject by announcing, along with Gingrich, on April 3 that Kemp would head a commission to study the question. This neutralized Kemp for the time being, and got the pressure off Dole to declare himself on the subject. But putting Kemp in charge of the commission was actually a fallback for Dole, who had wanted Dan Quayle and former Defense Secretary Dick Cheney and Kemp to endorse his candidacy, but they declined. But Dole also needed to take control of the tax issue, and needed Kemp to not endorse anyone else. (Vin Weber, who signed on as "co-chair" to the Dole campaign on April 25—this should have been a clear sign that Gingrich wasn't going to run for the Presidency—had, as one of his assignments from the Dole camp, keeping Kemp under control. Weber was also expected to be helpful on the Gingrich front. A Dole adviser said, "It's better for Vin to say something to Newt than Joe Gaylord.")

When the Contract was being drawn up, Armey had argued that to put any cap on the tax cut was to "play into the hands of class warfare." Armey said in an interview later, "Oh Lord, oh mercy, yes. It started out with no cap." But budgetary considerations prevailed, and the $200,000 cap was set. From then on, Armey said, "We had a commitment to our constituency groups to cap it at $200,000." He listed the Christian Coalition, the Family Research Council, the American Family Association, Americans for Tax Reform, Concerned Women for America. The latter group, headed by Beverly LaHaye, was, Armey said, the largest conservative women's advocacy group in America.

But the most important group was the Christian Coalition. While this essentially middle-class movement might not seem one that would be terribly concerned about families earning from $100,000 to $200,000, it had a lot of contributors in that income range, and it was the people in that range, a Republican analyst said, "who do a lot of the work for the Republican Party. They knock on the doors, turn up at the caucuses. To turn our back on them would be risky." A lot of the Christian Coalition members who attended Republican Conventions were upper-middle-class.

Armey's strong view that the cap not be lowered was shared by DeLay, whose freshman constituency was heavily identified with the Christian Coalition, and by Paxon, who as chairman of the National Republican Congressional Committee had his own debts and expectations.

Another fissure also turned up in the intraparty arguments over the tax bill. As Armey described it, "Conservatives felt that incrementally—here, there, and along the line—the moderates got too much deference. So we had one of those what I call 'Popeye moments'—'Okay, I won't take this anymore.' So they said, 'On this issue, we're going to test the relative standing of the conservatives and moderates.' " Armey continued, "When people feel they've been taken for granted, attitudes harden. Newt is very, very good at listening to tones. It was like term limits: those who are opposed are relatively passive about the issue. Those for them are passionate about it. So the issue is bigger than the polling data. Newt is very good at hearing that."

To push their point, conservative House Republicans (rising to about sixty-five in number) created their own group—the Conservative Action Team, called CATs—forming yet another splinter in the House, and another source of pressure on Gingrich.

On Tuesday, March 28, Gingrich said publicly that the tax bill was in trouble. The following night, in room H 227, the leadership met with advocates of the two proposals to put limits on the tax cut—along with Kasich and Jim Nussle, who served on the Ways and Means Committee and spoke for Archer. The object was to convince both groups that the leadership, and Gingrich in particular, was very serious about deficit reduction. As evidence, he described the arduous meetings of Kasich and Livingston and Archer. The meeting went on until 11:30.

On March 30, Bill Kristol put out a fax making the political argument clearly enough. "In mid-1996," he wrote, "campaigning for larger House and Senate majorities and for the White House, Republicans must be able to tell voters that: a Democratic Congress and President raised your taxes in 1993; a Republican Congress cut your taxes in 1995."

In the end, the Castle-Upton group got meaningless language, saying that before the tax cuts could be implemented Congress would have to have passed a budget that put the deficit on the path to zero. The Ganske group, which wanted to lower the income cap, got nothing.

When the agreement with the Castle-Upton group was announced on April 3, Gingrich said, "One incentive we have is that if we don't pass this, we're not going home."

For all his ostensible worrying about the status of the tax bill, Gingrich was a better psychologist than many others. Barring serious mishandling, certain issues are destined to win congressional approval—treaties, trade agreements—because in the end not enough people are willing to bring humiliation on the President who backs them. In this case, the psychological pressures against voting down the last item in the Contract, on the eve of a recess—of undermining their leader at such a moment, on the bill he had called the "crown jewel" of the Contract—were very large. However members rationalized it—they'll fix it in the Senate, you don't want to defeat the last item on the Contract, I voted for alternative X, I want to keep the process alive—they would find a way to not defeat their leader at this point. And they wouldn't want to be responsible for a downbeat ending to the Hundred Days.

But members aren't necessarily aware of these motivations, and the leadership has to make sure that nothing goes awry.

On April 4, the day before the scheduled vote, Gingrich, on the House floor, said to one of his lieutenants, "I haven't felt right about this vote for the past two weeks." A worrisomely large number of Republicans were withholding their votes on the rule. About a dozen Republicans with many federal workers in their districts said they wouldn't vote for it because of a provision raising federal employees' contributions to their pensions that had been put in the second part of the bill—which contained the remaining budget cuts to pay for the cost (estimated at $200 billion) of the first five years of the tax cuts. The pension provision was added by the leadership in the Rules Committee—an uncommon but not unheard of maneuver. (Gerald Solomon, of New York, the Rules Committee chairman, said that he didn't expect the pension provision to become law—that it was just a way of plugging a hole in deficit reduction.) A few Republicans were threatening to withhold their vote on the rule because the income cap for the $500 tax credit hadn't been lowered. A couple of Republican members told the leadership that they preferred to vote no, but would vote yes if their vote was needed—a common practice. Roukema's position was unknown—"She's always out there," a somewhat exasperated leadership aide said. Gingrich himself talked to Shays and to Steve Gunderson, of Wisconsin and also a moderate. Armey said, "I don't consider any issue settled until the cat's in the bag and the cat's in the bag when we get 218 votes." (Armey was also fond of saying, "The cat's not in the bag until the cat's in the bag.")

On the night before the vote, Shays went to Gingrich and told him that many moderates were upset that the proposal to put the cap at $95,000 hadn't even been debated in the conference, even though nearly half the conference was for it. Gingrich was most understanding, and said that that had been a subject of hot debate among the leaders, and conveyed to Shays that he had been for airing the issue but Armey and DeLay had come down hard against that. Gingrich even said that if the Republicans had to lose on the rule in order to learn a lesson, so be it—that the upcoming struggle on balancing the budget would be far more difficult than anything they had done so far. But, Gingrich added, he hoped that the leadership didn't need the kind of message that would be sent by defeat of the rule. He also conveyed to Shays that he felt the leadership had made other mistakes, which had to be avoided in the future given the difficulties that lay ahead.

Asked later in an interview if some of the complained-about rough handling of committees and certain segments of the conference might not have been necessary in order to get what he wanted done during the Hundred Days, Gingrich replied quickly, "That's Armey's defense." He added, "The thing is, it worked." He went on to say, "But I think you can't sustain that. I really believe in the moral of listen, learn, help, and lead. And I think it's always to your advantage to let people get it out of their system, and if you tailor a bill not just transactionally, but through a cybernetic feedback loop, you get smarter. And the more people who help make you smarter, the smarter you get." As for the tax bill, Gingrich said, "I think we got very tired and we decided that opening the door to that discussion would tear us apart and so we just backed off and decided we'd try to win by effective persuasion. But I think we shortchanged a lot of our members. You don't want to win in a way that you bruise people so badly. Victories ought to be won in such a way that people want to win more of them, not in such a way that they resent it. And this one was not good. It was not the right way to do it."

This was a Gingrich characteristic. He would concede a mistake in something he *had done* (or, in this case, someone else had)—after there was nothing to be done about it. It was a disarming technique. It helped hold people in the process he ran, and got them to forgive him, even admire his apparent candor. That way, said a colleague, "He can do what he wants, and also convince his critics that they've gotten through to him. It's a fairly easy tactic to say, 'Gee, you guys are right—we won't make that mistake again.' And then you can go on to the next fight."

Republicans who had supported the Ganske proposal for a $95,000 cap on the tax cut were understood to still be unhappy, as were those with large numbers of federal workers in their district. On the day of the vote, the word was that some Democrats would support the rule, but Republican vote counters never relied on this kind of information on the grounds that the Democratic leaders might succeed in turning those votes around. Gingrich said later, "We thought there probably were some Democratic votes for the rule, but we don't count that way. We think on a rule vote we should always be able to win on our side because it's too dangerous."

The lobbies had been at work. Active alongside the Christian Coalition was the coalition of small and big business and conservative family groups that Boehner had put together.

The Republican leadership's floor aides were sufficiently concerned that the Democrats might offer a recommittal motion—with instructions to lower the cap to $95,000, and perhaps to also knock out the provision on pensions—that might succeed that they were studying precedents for lodging a point of order against such a move.

Gingrich approached Roukema on the House floor that morning and asked if he would have her support on the rule. Roukema, a strong supporter of lowering the cap on the tax credits, replied—referring to her vote for the welfare bill—"Newt, I gave at the office." Also that morning, DeLay called her during a committee meeting, and she gave him the same reply. In an interview at lunchtime, Roukema said, "It's nonsense, their holding our feet to the fire on this"—the cap on the tax credit—"they should have given it to us." Roukema planned to vote against the rule early and then leave the floor, so that if the rule failed, it wouldn't be her vote that "brought it down"—though votes, like money, were fungible.

But there was another uncertainty: some members told the leadership they would vote for the rule but not passage of the bill.

There was a keyed-upness on the House floor on Wednesday afternoon, April 5. Not only was there to be voting on the "crown jewel" of the Contract, but there was also the sense that school was about to let out. At long last, the grueling Hundred Days were nearly over. (Actually, it was declared that they would end on day ninety-three, Friday, April 7.) That morning, the Ringling Brothers circus appeared on the Capitol grounds, with elephants and clowns and all—and Gingrich and Dole getting into the pictures—and virtually no one failed to make the obvious joke about the metaphor presented by the clowns. It was a sunny, clear day, one that Gingrich declared "an historic moment." Radio talk show hosts were invited to broadcast live from the balcony off of Gingrich's office suite. What happened on the House floor that day would shape the analyses of the Hundred Days and define what Gingrich could say in a planned televised address on Friday night. (Gingrich's reception room had been cleared of all but a desk, so that he could start rehearsing.)

During the vote on the rule, which took place at 2:00 P.M., most members (but not Roukema) stayed around to see what happened. DeLay was still collaring people on the floor. Several freshmen and sophomores clustered around the leadership table. As time for the voting was about to run out, the votes for the rule were 217—one short. Then a bloc of Republicans who had been withholding their vote went with the leadership. When the ayes reached 221, a clear margin of victory, with twenty-one seconds to go, Republicans cheered and tossed pieces of paper into the air. The final tally was held until the hotheaded Robert Dornan, of California, the sole Presidential candidate in the House, rushed in, to cheers, and voted, making the vote on the rule 228–204. Nine Democrats, most of them from the South and the Sunbelt—several of them thinking about bolting the party altogether—voted for the rule. When the Democrats tried to make a point of order against the federal pensions provision, arguing that it constituted a tax increase, Gingrich and Walker, two old pros at gumming up the works, watched carefully. But now they were in charge, and had the power to dismiss such intrusions.

The debate on the tax bill illustrated the deep differences between the two parties, the Democrats charging that the combination of tax cuts and spending cuts bill wasn't "fair," and Republicans arguing that it was better to give money to families than to the federal government. Dingell argued, using a well-trod metaphor, "This is a Robin Hood-in-reverse proposal." The class warfare inherent in the debate was Gephardt's meat; he persisted in this line of attack even as other Democrats abandoned it, having decided in the Reagan years, and again in 1994, that it didn't work.

Gephardt's substitute proposal contained no family tax credit (though, like Clinton, he had proposed one in December), but gave tax deductions for college education, and closed a loophole through which wealthy individuals could evade taxes by renouncing their citizenship (an issue that had recently become controversial). A week earlier, Gephardt, in the face of the deficit-cutting climate, had cut his own tax cut in half.

Gephardt said, "It is not too late for us to come together tonight on this tax plan, to stand for the middle class. . . . It is not too late to say to America, We stand for that young struggling family, and the privileged can take care of themselves."

Archer said, facetiously, that it "seems strange to me that the gentleman is the leader of the Democrat Party in the House of Representatives, and yet has not chosen to offer the President's own tax proposal." The President's proposal seemed not to exist. DeLay said that the Democrats "want to confiscate the income of the American family to pay for their failed welfare state." For Bonior, who represented a blue-collar district in Michigan, class warfare came naturally; it was in his bones. (Bonior had prominently opposed the NAFTA treaty.) Bonior said, "We have heard Republicans talk about renewing American civilization. We have heard our Speaker talk about renewing American civilization. But they do not seem to understand that you cannot renew American civilization by taking Big Bird from a five-year-old, school lunch from a ten-year-old, summer jobs from a fifteen-year-old, school loans from a twenty-year-old, in order to pay for a tax cut for the privileged few in our society." Bonior went on,

"Do you realize that since we began working on this Contract, we have met for nearly a hundred days, we have cast about two hundred and fifty votes, we have not adopted one amendment that deals with income, one amendment that deals with health care, one amendment that deals with education, one amendment that deals with job training? Not one." The Democrats rose to cheer. Armey rebutted Gephardt and Bonior by saying, "Starting today, relief is on the way . . . relief for the families, relief for the elderly, relief for the small business entrepreneur and relief for savers and relief for investors." Eighty-four Democrats voted against Gephardt's substitute, leading to a final vote of 119–313—a big defeat. Some Democrats voted against it because it didn't have a family tax cut, and some voted against it because it had any tax cut all. Afterward, David Skaggs said that he and others voted against Gephardt's proposal because they didn't think they should be making tax cuts at all at that time. "It was a more clean political statement on our part that we should deal first with deficit reduction," he said.

Rubbing it in, Archer said that given the vote on Gephardt's substitute, he wasn't going to take the trouble of raising a point of order against Gephardt's motion to recommit, which did put the income cap for the child credit at $60,000 and barred tax cuts from going into effect until a budget plan with specific numbers showing that it was leading to balance in 2002 had been adopted, made the increase in costs of federal pensions applicable only to Members of Congress, and closed the loophole for citizenship renouncers—a grab-bag designed to get votes but with no clean philosophy behind it. When the Republican leaders learned that Gephardt's motion wasn't simply a straight reduction in the cap, they relaxed. And the Republican moderates weren't in a mood to upend Gingrich at that point. They had a big stake in his success and they also knew, one leadership aide said, that anyone who did vote to undermine the leadership on this issue might be stripped of a committee chairmanship—or face a primary opponent. (Later in the year, an e-mail document slipped out which reported Gingrich's threats, in a meeting in September, against recalcitrant members of the Agriculture Committee: they would be knocked out of the line of succession for chairman, or would be removed from the committee, and would lose their chairmanships of other committees.)

Gephardt seemed to have misjudged the situation, even blundered, but he was in a bind. Shays had gone to him and said that if he offered a proposal simply to lower the cap to $95,000, about fifty Republicans would vote for it. But the prevailing view in the Democratic caucus at that particular point was that the budget cuts being proposed in order to pay for the tax cuts should be applied instead to deficit reduction. A Democratic leadership aide said, "The message from our caucus was, Scale down the tax cut." On the other hand, the Democrats didn't want to offer a substitute proposal that didn't have a single tax cut in it: that would have provided

Republicans with excellent material for TV ads. The Democratic leaders also felt that the fact that the Republican leaders didn't oblige 102 members of their own caucus who were seeking a cap, and didn't provide an effective (if there was such a thing) brake on the tax cuts until it was clear the deficit was going to be substantially reduced, gave Democrats understandable reasons for voting against the bill without having supported an alternative.

There was also another factor: the Democratic leaders didn't want to aid the Republicans by adopting a "fairer" tax bill. A Democratic leadership aide said, "We weren't interested in helping them out."

But the heart of the matter was that the Democrats had failed to come up with an alternative vision. They were reduced to opposing what the Republicans were doing—making themselves vulnerable to Gingrich's charges that they were the forces of the status quo, the protectors of the welfare state. They had in fact dug in to protect many of the things that were under assault by the Republicans, figuring that they should try to at least keep structures intact and fight another day for more funding. The fact that the assault was everywhere had Gingrich's intended result of dividing and confusing, weakening the Democrats' ability to fight back. They offered no coherent response to the onslaught.

Gingrich closed the debate. As if in prayer, Gingrich was somewhat eloquent and gracious. He said, "I want to thank everyone on both sides of the aisle." He continued, "I find standing here tonight a truly historic and the same time a truly personal experience." Unable to resist the dig at Clinton's economic program, and the opportunity to draw the contrast between the two parties, Gingrich said, "Two years ago we voted by a one-vote margin to raise taxes. . . . The country said it wasn't okay to raise taxes, that government was too big, it spends too much and it needs to be brought under control." He held up his laminated Contract, and summed up the accomplishments of the Hundred Days.

Urging a vote against Gephardt's motion, and employing a characteristic formulation, Gingrich said, "We'd rather parents have the money than bureaucrats." Speaking calmly and clearly, Gingrich said, "Ask yourself: in your constituents' lives, will not a little less money for the federal government and a little more money for those families be a good thing? And is that not what this Congress was elected to do?" When he concluded, Republicans stood and cheered him, with reason. Only one Republican—Ganske—voted with Gephardt, and thirty-seven Democrats voted against his motion.

On the final vote on the tax-cut bill, cheers went up when the tally reached 218 for it. At the end of the vote, Gingrich, now in the chair, announced the final count as 246–188. Only eleven Republicans opposed the tax cut bill, and twenty-seven Democrats supported it.

Afterward, Sherwood Boehlert, having, like a number of other moderates, faced yet another dilemma, said that despite his support of the $95,000 cap, he had voted for the rule and for passage of the bill, "because I wanted Gingrich and the leadership to succeed." He added, "I pray for the Senate, but I really think it will take care of the $95,000."

While the debate was still going on in the House, Clinton said, "I do not believe it is wise to have a tax cut of this magnitude . . . with the deficit we've got."

There was one important piece of business to get done in the Senate before it could leave for the much-anticipated spring break—the Senate was to take two weeks off, the House three. The "upper body" had yet to pass its version of the rescissions bill. Deciding on the composition of budget cuts of roughly $16 billion fractured both parties. After the Democrats threatened to filibuster, Dole and Daschle, working with Leon Panetta, late on the night of April 5 came to an agreement on what should be in the bill. Some funds were restored for education, summer jobs, national service, and job training.

The White House involvement came after a large argument within the administration over strategy: whether to negotiate to fix the bill or let Congress send the President one he would veto. Those arguing for a veto, on principle, were Tyson and Reich. On the other side were Panetta and Rivlin, arguing that they should fix the bill, rather than be seen as against deficit reduction. They argued that this would be a disastrous first veto. Clinton sided with the latter group and signed off on the deal that Panetta had negotiated.

After the deal was struck, some people said that this was a hopeful example of how compromises could be reached—at least with the less "revolutionary" Senate Republicans. Dole had acted more like the congressional leader of before than the trapped and flailing Presidential candidate. (Dole was to announce his candidacy the coming Monday.) The bill contained spending on emergency assistance and debt forgiveness to Jordan. Dole had inserted the debt forgiveness, which Clinton had promised Jordan, in order to make it harder for the President to veto the bill. Daschle and Clinton had shown that they could be pragmatic. But on Thursday, April 6, rebellion broke out in both parties' caucuses. Conservative Republicans, especially the freshmen, felt Dole had given away too much. Liberal Democrats balked at Daschle's deal, while the more pragmatic Democrats, including Chris Dodd, defended Daschle. But Daschle couldn't sell his deal to his caucus. When it appeared—on the eve of the desperately longed for recess—that the Democrats would filibuster by amendment, and a cloture attempt by Dole failed, Dole and Daschle made another deal. It restored funds for education reform, Head Start, child nutrition, and a few other programs.

In the Senate Chamber that evening, some Democrats tried to get further changes, while John McCain spoke on behalf of the freshmen (and probably Gramm), saying that he hoped there would be no more compromises of this sort. Able legislator that he was, Dole incorporated the latest changes in a large en bloc amendment—joking at one point that it contained "a couple of changes in the Constitution"—and in the end the Senate voted 99–0 to pass a $16 billion rescissions bill, and to get out of there.

The skirmishing over the rescissions bill was the Spanish Civil War of the budget battle to come.

14

NEWT UNCHAINED

"We're Beginning to Break Through"

Going into the celebrations of the Hundred Days, Gingrich could rightly claim success. He had done a remarkable thing, and demonstrated that he was a leader. He set a goal, motivated his troops, even galvanized them, and met the goal. Whatever one thought of the substance of his achievements, he had set the agenda for the House, the Senate, and the nation. Of course, the ten items in the Contract were chosen for the ease with which the new House leaders thought they could be passed (with the exception of term limits), and Gingrich's leadership style was a combination of inspiration and brutality—as most effective leadership is.

But there were some clouds over his success: the fact that the public had increasing doubts about Gingrich, and the real possibility that he had overinterpreted the mandate of November 1994. Further, as Gingrich was quite aware, the Leviathan task of passing a budget that would leave no deficit by 2002 was yet before him. At the same time, polls showed that the public still knew little about the Contract. Gingrich's poll ratings had continued to decline—a matter that troubled him, as did Frank Luntz's blunt warning that he himself could jeopardize the reelection of Republican members. On April 7 an NBC/*Wall Street Journal* poll said that only 27 percent of those surveyed viewed him positively, while 39 percent viewed him negatively. His friends told him that he was overexposed, and for some time they had been urging him to tone down his rhetoric. Conversely, Clinton's ratings had improved somewhat, reaching 46 percent approval to 44 percent disapproval, and the Congress itself had risen in the public's estimation to a record 42 percent. However, an ABC/*Washington Post* poll indicated that most people didn't think the Congress had accomplished much. And the "meanness" issue was still a problem—the obvious anxiousness of Republicans to dismiss it gave away that it was a problem. Just after the Hundred Days, Frank Luntz told a seminar that the Republicans now had an eight-point deficit with the middle class, whereas at the beginning of Congress Democrats and Republicans had been even.

Other outside Republicans felt that their House brethren had been overly confident since the election day in November about the level of public support for what they set out to do. One said, "The mandate wasn't that large and wasn't that clear."

Though Gingrich claimed that this had been the most productive period since Franklin Roosevelt's Hundred Days, it fell substantially short of the amount of legislation that was fully enacted in the early thirties—albeit a time of a real national emergency. By this point in Gingrich's reign only two Contract items—restricting unfunded mandates and requiring Congress to comply with the laws it imposed on others—had been signed into law. But by any other measurement, Gingrich's Hundred Days—which actually ended on day ninety-three—had been productive. A real beginning had been made on effectively repealing much of the social legislation of the mid-sixties, and even some of the ground rules established by the New Deal. The Congress had given itself the assignment of balancing the budget within a few years.

Gingrich was reveling in the attention he was getting at the Hundred Days' end, and made a large number of television appearances extolling his achievements, leading up to a remarkable nationwide address on April 7. At times in these interviews he would seek to minimize his role, but his modesty had an obvious false note. He would say that he had played only a small role in running the House, that the real credit was due Armey, that his own role was to think big thoughts while Armey ran the House—while in fact Gingrich had often been involved in the minutiae. In this period, Gingrich was showing more than a touch of megalomania. This was revealed particularly in an extraordinary document put together largely by Gingrich himself to serve as a briefing book for Republican members on how to talk about the impending large cuts in the budget. A Gingrich aide said, "He wanted to make sure that the members could go home for the Easter recess and talk during the recess about the budget in a positive way." The August 1982 recess—in the midst of a deep recession, and following a Reagan budget compromise that angered conservatives—had been "a disaster," the aide said. And Gingrich, he said, had been giving a lot of thought about how to avoid that. Moreover, Republicans had come back from the previous weekend saying that the Democrats' attacks on them for being "mean" to children were getting through.

In early March, Gingrich began to scrub large parts of his schedule in order to spend hours at a time thinking the paper through and typing it on his computer at a stand-up desk. The document was in effect the world according to Newt, a compendium of thoughts, nostrums, doctrine, dogma, slippery assumptions, and half-baked ideas to explain how he thought the entire federal government should be transformed. "This is Newt unchained," a friend of Gingrich's said. "He's had GOPAC and a course on renewing American civilization, and now he has a majority of the House. Everyone is to be proselytizing on behalf of Newt. It's holistic. It's hard to make limited government into something positive because it involves ending things, so he romanticizes." As the Hundred Days' end approached, Gingrich briefed every Republican member, in small groups, and their senior staff on his document. He was still using language as a mechanism of control.

Inevitably the Tofflers' and Gingrich's theories about the information age weighed heavily in his document. (Bill Bennett and Jack Kemp disdained Gingrich's Toffler/Third Wave talk, which they thought tipped into futurism and mysticism.) In the document, Gingrich said that if the government had undergone the same rate of improvement as the productivity of the computer chip over ten years, the federal government today would be providing the same level of services and programs with only four employees, at a total budget of $100,000. Gingrich was a true visionary, but sometimes he produced vision run amok. The document was full of poll-driven buzz words: "opportunity," "safe," "prosperous," "children." He was now trying to indoctrinate Republican members with some of the sayings on his GOPAC tape. In the budget document he was saying that society could be perfected and that a very large role in that would be played by a balanced budget. Gingrich was deadly serious about this approach to getting through the politics of balancing the budget.

The goal of the paper, he said in an interview later, was "to lay out a common doctrine. I've tried to inculcate in every single subcommittee an attitude and a way of thinking about government that is brand-new." He went through some of his prior efforts that few had thought made sense—taking on Jim Wright, fighting Bush's tax increase, saying in 1994 that the Republicans "could win control of the Congress and that the Contract would work." He continued, "So when we do a briefing now, people have a certain bias. They think it's real."

At a rally in front of the Capitol on Friday morning, April 7, Gingrich began, "Well, as I was saying last September . . ." He continued, "We are celebrating the act of keeping our word." The rally was thinly attended— Republicans were exhausted and trying to clear out of Washington.

•

A lot of effort went into Gingrich's nationally televised prime-time address that night (of the large commercial networks, only CBS ran it). No Speaker had ever done such a thing. His advisers opted for a scripted speech rather than a more spontaneous presentation, for fear he would use undocumented "facts," and wander. Kenneth Duberstein, who had worked in the Reagan White House and was now a prominent lobbyist and adviser to Republicans, was brought in to help Gingrich; a speechwriter was brought in; so was Michael Deaver, who had brilliantly staged Reagan; and Robert Teeter, a Republican pollster, to talk over issues with him.

For his speech, Gingrich was perched (his jacket tugging at the button; Gingrich was sensitive about his weight) on a desk in front of a window with a flag beside him, and he delivered the speech with command—looking more Presidential than the President often did. The speech was full of optimism (none of his anger showed) as he talked about some of his familiar themes—"a new partnership with the American people," reducing "bureaucratic micromanagement from Washington," and "opportunities created by the new information society." In talking, as he often did, about technological change, he ridiculed the government, as he often did, by holding up a microchip and a vacuum tube and saying that the Federal Aviation Administration's rules were "so complicated and so wasteful that they have not been able in seven years to figure out how to replace the vacuum tube with this [chip]. This is a microchip that has the computing power of three million vacuum tubes." Gingrich held up the vacuum tube on many occasions (and Gore used it as one of his Reinventing Government examples), but in reality vacuum tubes were used on only two hundred out of fifteen thousand facilities (the tubes cost $10, as opposed to $15,000 per chip, and, though slower, they worked). He gave his familiar diagnosis of the ills of society and restated his belief that government and money weren't the answer. And he began his public proselytizing on the balanced budget. (He also argued once again that funds for school lunches had been increased, not cut—a charge which clearly still rankled.) As he neared his close, Gingrich said, "This remains a country of unparalleled possibilities. We as a people have the natural ability to respond to change. That is what we do best when the government is not in the way." He ended, "And we promise to begin a new partnership so that together we and the American people can give our children and our country a new birth of freedom." It was an effective speech.

In an interview during the recess, I asked Gingrich how well he thought he was doing in the test he had laid out for himself on opening day—whether there would be a whole new debate on new terms—and he replied, "I think we're about a third of the way there. We have made it possible to discuss things which were literally undiscussable just six months ago. So in that sense, we're beginning to break through." Gingrich continued, "Some things are frankly going to help us." He was referring to a recent report of the trustees of Medicare that the trust fund would run out of money in 2002. This was a new point for Gingrich. He added, "But when the moral burden has shifted so that the people who refuse to change Medicare explain how they're going to pay for it over the next fifteen years, then we've begun to really change everything."

Though Gingrich professed not even to think about his ethics problems, he could get quite worked up about his Democratic tormentors. He said, "You've got a bunch of bitter and vicious, mean-spirited people who capriciously lie, and I get tired of it occasionally. But it's psychological, it's not intellectual." Referring to one charge recently made against him—without apparent foundation—"Gephardt, who I think had disgraced—and you can quote me as saying this—exercised no discipline in his party. They got up on the floor of the House and they said things that were patently, factually false, and they said them for four days. And if I thought about it, I'd frankly get bitter and angry. I refuse to think about it."

Asked what he thought was the reason behind the Democrats' charges, Gingrich replied, "It's about hatred and hysteria. I think they believe that I am the architect of their defeat and I think they are enraged and I think that they're in tremendous agony because it's the first time in their career they've not been in the majority. I think it's driving them nuts. And I think they're behaving in ways that are more psychological than political. But I'm not their therapist, so it's not my problem."

Gingrich added, "Their problem is that the world they're defending is gone."

By contrast to Gingrich's Hundred Days speech, the response by Daschle and Gephardt, hokily delivered from a schoolroom in northern Virginia, seemed negative and carping. They, too, went over familiar ground. They veered between saying "We should work together" and attacking Gingrich: Daschle said, "Many of Speaker Gingrich's ideas are so extreme . . . and wrong" that Senate Republicans oppose them. Daschle also said, "Powerful interest groups' lobbyists are actually sitting in the committee room, writing" the Republicans' legislative proposals. Gephardt said, "We will work with the Republicans wherever we can. But we cannot agree to policies that hurt the middle class and working families who need someone to stand up and fight for them."

That morning Dole had crossed the Capitol to address the House Republicans, gathered on the House floor. When Dole told his House audience that he now had the one additional vote needed for Senate passage of the Balanced Budget Amendment he received a standing ovation. He also told Gingrich privately that he had the vote.

Dole didn't actually have the additional vote at that point, but he had a secret target he was working on—Bob Kerrey, Democratic senator from Nebraska, who had dropped some hints through Alan Simpson that he might be available. However, if Dole did come up with that needed vote, John Breaux was prepared to switch from support to opposition. Though this would seemingly be hard to explain, Breaux was prepared to say that now that he saw the impact that balancing the budget by 2002 would have he had changed his mind. James Exon, who was retiring from the Senate, let it be known that he would switch his vote to "no" if need be. (Kerrey later sent word to Dole that he wasn't available.)

As the Hundred Days period neared the end, Clinton was still speaking muffled thoughts in muffled tones. He had had opportunities to seize the microphone, but his voice didn't get through. He was essentially irrelevant on Capitol Hill; what proposals he had made were ignored. Some observers attributed his behavior to a deliberate, clever, "rope-a-dope" strategy, but that wasn't the case. In fact, the President's advisers considered themselves to have conducted a strategy of "counterpunching"—Stephanopoulos's term. Clinton was still thrown by the election and uncertain about how to proceed, still confused by the cross-pressures to stand on principle and to get results. It was for this reason that on the one hand he would issue veto threats (sometimes at unlikely contingencies), and on the other also say, "I was not elected to produce a pile of vetoes"—a Morris-Curry line. He couldn't, as several suggested, "be Harry Truman," because he wasn't Harry Truman; Truman's snappy, scrappy approach wasn't in Clinton's nature, and he already had a problem with authenticity. Many Democrats were demoralized by or even disdainful of his passivity. But everyone also understood that the major tests—on the budget, and on welfare—were still ahead. Capitol Hill Democrats were actually schizoid about having the President involved in the legislative fights, not sure that he was a help to them.

A meeting on April 6 between the President and a group of Democratic representatives from the Southwest (a series of meetings with regional groups was planned) descended into a very hostile encounter, with the President, according to several reports, "screaming" at the members. Several of the members criticized the President for apparently not planning to veto a bill extending tax breaks on health insurance for the self-employed that also contained a huge tax break ($63 million) for Rupert Murdoch and a provision letting some very wealthy people renounce their citizenship so that they didn't have to pay taxes. Some had signed a letter to Clinton asking that he veto the bill. (A hundred and thirty-nine Democrats—more than half the caucus—had signed the letter.) The major consideration within the White House was that vetoing a bill extending a tax break for the self-employed might be interpreted as consenting to a tax increase.

The House members also told Clinton that he should be less passive and reactive. The members themselves weren't in a particularly good mood, it being an early morning meeting after the House had stayed in session late to pass the tax bill, and the President's mood wasn't at all good when he heard what the members had to say—as it often wasn't when he was criticized. Lloyd Doggett, a liberal from Texas, told the President that people didn't think he stood for things. The President blew. "That's a lot of shit," he shouted. He said that twenty former House members had lost in 1994 because of the gun lobby, and he had stood up to it. He said that he stood up to things all the time. With that, a couple of members tried to ease matters with jokes, but the President wasn't amused. After the members left, Clinton was still seething.

The management of the White House had improved somewhat—this was due mainly to Erskine Bowles, a South Carolina businessman and friend of Clinton's who was the first to get the role of Deputy Chief of Staff for management right. (Bowles planned to leave in the fall, for family reasons.) But there were still numerous meetings that were called suddenly and ran long and many changes of signals. These things in themselves wouldn't have been of great consequence if Clinton had had a clear sense of where he wanted to go. But he was still struggling for definition of his Presidency. Despite pledges to Panetta by the President, the Vice President, and the First Lady when he was offered the job of Chief of Staff, Panetta was never really empowered to run the White House. The Clinton Presidency still suffered from the lack of an overarching concept and the White House from no overall guidance and direction. Clinton had numerous advisers, in and out of the White House, and a cacophony of voices coming at him. For some people, this enhances their performance; for Clinton, it underlined his own indecision and lack of clear purpose on all but a few matters. More than in his first year or so as President, Clinton seemed to lack sure instincts. And he still lacked discipline, jumping from subject to subject and theme to theme. (This was also a failure on the part of his staff.) A top staff member said in April, "It's never going to be entirely clear where the President should be. This is a tough period. The President wants to be in the center of political action, but how do you do that without being trapped in the legislative maw?"

At the same time that preparations were underway for the President's own appearance marking the end of the Hundred Days, Clinton did some things that his staff described as "quintessentially Presidential": within a week he made a one-day swing to Haiti, and met at the White House with British Prime Minister John Major and Egyptian President Hosni Mubarak. McCurry said, "We're enjoying the commanding heights of a Presidency. Only a President can get to that level." Other Clinton advisers wondered about the efficacy of stressing foreign policy when he might be keeping the focus on the Congress and his objections to what it was doing. Sometimes it seemed that Clinton couldn't win. Actually, Clinton was still paying only fitful attention to foreign policy, which didn't engage his mind as domestic policy did. There was debate within the White House over how much time Clinton should devote to foreign travel. He would go to Russia for VE Day, it was decided, and the emphasis would be on commemorating the twenty-seven million Russians who died in the Second World War rather than on his meeting with the increasingly erratic and controversial Boris Yeltsin. Clinton hankered to go to Ireland as well, given his intervention between the British and the Irish Republican Army, through allowing Sinn Fein leader Gerry Adams visas to come to America—even to attend St. Patrick's Day celebrations at the White House. Still pending was whether the IRA would make good on its pledge to begin disarming. Others concluded, rightly, that it was too early for the President to take a victory lap in Ireland.

The plan was for the President to give a major speech, defining his own position on the day that the Republicans celebrated the end of the Hundred Days. He would have a good venue in the annual convention of the American Society of Newspaper Editors meeting in Dallas, on Friday, April 7. The White House settled on the theme of education—a subject on which he could draw a clear line between himself and the Republicans. In his travels, Clinton had found that he got a positive response when he talked about education, which he had long seen as the key to opportunity and economic growth. (This should not have been news, but some White House aides talked of it as such.) Moreover, the subject polled well, and was a major program on which Clinton could be united with the congressional Democrats. A month of Presidential events on the subject of education was to follow the speech to the A.S.N.E.

This unimaginative idea—Clinton had talked about education a lot, and the Hundred Days celebrations called for a more pointed response by Clinton—horrified Morris and Curry, who first saw the speech on the Wednesday before it was to be given. For months, the two men had discussed the fact that at some point Clinton had to give a speech that was a full-blown response to the Republican jihad, and as the Dallas event approached that seemed to them the right moment. In a meeting on Wednesday night (Gore was there), the President decided to go with the Morris-Curry approach. So at the last minute (literally overnight) and again unbeknownst to almost anyone else, Morris and Curry drafted a new speech; and Morris—not the White House staff—figured the strategy of which bills the President should threaten to veto. They felt, as Curry put it later, "Look, it's 1964 and the Beatles are playing at Shea Stadium. You don't give a concert across town. You try to get on the program. You have to get ahead of the issue and talk directly to the national debate." The completed new speech was handed to Panetta and Stephanopoulos on Thursday. Many staff members were surprised to learn only at the last minute that the speech wasn't about education. "Never a dull moment," a staff member said later.

The Hundred Days speech in Dallas was thus a critical moment in the Clinton Presidency. Clinton moved away from the advice of almost all of his own staff and made a big decision about a defining speech. Reinforced by his newest set of advisers, he was starting to get a sense of where he wanted to go. But would this last? Or was it simply yet another zig?

Clinton's Dallas speech was only partially effective, because he tried to cover a great deal of ground and it was quite listy, and in the end legislative. Clinton ad-libbed a fair amount of the speech—as Morris was encouraging him to do in order to find his own voice and gain confidence. Morris said later that Clinton winged two-thirds of the Dallas speech. Clinton did make some strong points about what he had accomplished in his first two years and what he still hoped to accomplish—a minimum wage increase, new tax breaks for education, incremental changes in health care coverage. He also called for political reform—lobbying and campaign financing—but all through his Presidency he had spoken of these subjects only sporadically (another concession to the Democratic leaders). There had been a running argument among the President's advisers about whether he should talk more than he did about the fact that the economy had improved—several thought this a strong political point—but the President and some advisers worried that doing so might make him seem insensitive (Bush-like) toward those substantial numbers whose economic lot had not improved. In the Dallas speech the President hewed to the latter argument. He said, again, "I was not elected President to pile up a stack of vetoes," and he added, "I was elected President to change the direction of America." He described himself as in "the dynamic center," which was a hard concept to grasp— or get excited about. But Clinton (with the help of Morris) was working toward a new definition of his Presidency.

Stressing his eagerness to get things done, Clinton said, "Good-faith compromising, negotiating our differences, actually listening to one an- other for a change, these are the currency of a healthy democracy." (McCurry said that these remarks were in part aimed at Dole, who was about to enter the Presidential race. McCurry said, "It was timed directly for Dole's announcement. Does Dole want to be majority leader or Presidential candidate? The President was telling him, 'We can get a lot done together, or we can offer the voters gridlock.' ") Clinton attacked the House-passed welfare bill as "weak on work and tough on kids"; he attacked the House- passed tax bill as "a fantasy" that wasn't "going to happen." He listed some government programs that shouldn't be cut (education, immunization, school lunch, and other nutrition programs). He said that the House-passed legal reform bills, repeal of the commitment to add a hundred thousand new police, or repeal of the assault weapons ban weren't acceptable.

The speech's transformation, and the number of White House staff people who knew that something unusual had happened, meant that the presence of Morris, who until then had been kept under wraps, had to be made public. His role had been kept quiet so as to not provoke questions about what this meant for Stan Greenberg, who had polled for Clinton in 1992 and thereafter, or for James Carville, his flamboyant political adviser who had essentially been in charge of the 1992 campaign—or about whether the President, under the influence of a new Svengali, was once more trying to change his identity. Those few White House aides who had known of Morris's presence referred to him among themselves as "Charlie" —a code name that Morris had invented to keep others in the White House from knowing who the President was talking to on the phone.

Any new approach that the staff members hadn't been aware of was ascribed to "Charlie." Panetta would say, "Charlie has suggested . . ." Shortly after the Dallas speech, a White House aide said, "Charlie has been very influential in the past month." He added, emphatically, "Charlie has *never* been in a White House meeting." (On Clinton's behalf the Democratic National Committee had also signed up the polling firm Penn & Schoen.)

After the Dallas speech, Panetta went to the President to argue that there had to be some process for integrating the latest new outside adviser with the rest of the White House. Laura Tyson, who had replaced Rubin as head of the National Economic Council after Rubin replaced Bentsen as Treasury Secretary, made the same argument to Gore and Erskine Bowles.

Bill Curry, forty-three, slightly chunky with wavy blond hair and a lack of solemnity, who had formally joined the White House staff in early February, was often the transmitter to the others of Morris's ideas. McCurry said, "Curry implements Morris's plans." This wasn't easy, because certain staff members, in particular Panetta, Ickes, and Stephanopoulos, resented Morris's meddling and took it out on Curry, whom they saw—with good reason —as Morris's agent. Panetta virtually wouldn't speak to Curry for weeks.

To bring at least some more order to the situation, at Panetta's behest the President took to holding a weekly evening meeting in the residence, on Wednesdays or Thursdays, with Morris and Panetta, Gore, Bowles, Ickes, Robert Squier (a political consultant who was close to Gore), and Jack Quinn (Gore's chief of staff). Mrs. Clinton, whose role in policy decisions was played down though no less important than before, was said to attend only on occasion. It was as if a separate cell was making key political and policy decisions. (One staff member remarked that Clinton had brought his failed health care concept of "managed competition" into the

White House.) It wasn't unusual for a President to have competing views within a White House—Franklin Roosevelt and John Kennedy certainly did—but to have separate cells was unusual.

Following a campaign swing through Texas and California, Clinton took advantage of the fact that the Congress was on a long recess and held the second prime-time press conference of his Presidency. Seeking a headline, and hoping to forestall the Republicans from putting the welfare bill in the huge end-of-session measure that would encompass major parts of the new budget (the reconciliation bill), thus making it harder to deal with as a separate item, Clinton called on Congress to have a welfare bill on his desk by the Fourth of July. He knew there was no possibility of that, but hoped he could thus make the Republicans seem dilatory on welfare reform. Many of the questions were about the agenda of the Republican Congress. The President's delivery was clear and crisp, he was obviously well prepared. Unfortunately, when he was asked if he was concerned about his voice being heard, since Republicans seemed to be dominating the political debate, Clinton replied, "The President is relevant here"—a line that journalists made much of, and that Republicans took pleasure in mocking.

The next day, the Alfred P. Murrah Building, housing more than five hundred federal workers in Oklahoma City, was blown up.

15

OKLAHOMA CITY

"This Is Not a Matter of Partisan Politics"

The White House got word of the explosion of the federal office building in Oklahoma City a little after 10:00 A.M., from CNN. McCurry gave Clinton the word just as he was about to begin a photo op in the Oval Office with Turkish Prime Minister Tansu Ciller. Following the Oval Office session, the President and the Prime Minister adjourned to the Cabinet Room for more discussions. Panetta, who had just spoken with Attorney General Janet Reno, handed the President a note telling him that Reno had dispatched the F.B.I. to Oklahoma City. At noon, the President, Deputies Chief of Staff Erskine Bowles and Harold Ickes; Deputy Attorney General Jamie Gorelick; James Lee Witt, director of the Federal Emergency Management Agency; White House Counsel Abner Mikva; Deputy National Security Adviser Sandy Berger; Cabinet secretary Kitty Higgins; Stephanopoulos; Mark Gearan; and McCurry gathered in Panetta's office. The purpose was to assess, amidst numerous rumors, what the situation actually was (there was concern that there might be a second bomb, there were reports that the phone system was down in the federal office building in Boston), and whether and when the President would make a public statement. Someone —no one seemed to recall who—suggested that the situation was sufficiently uncertain that the President shouldn't make a statement, but have Reno do so instead. Gearan and Stephanopoulos visibly blanched; they had lived through the aftermath of the F.B.I. assault on the Waco compound of Branch Davidians—two years ago to the day—and the fierce criticism of

Clinton for seeming to hide out and not making a statement until the next day, whereas Reno (knowing exactly what she was doing) was all over television outlets, taking responsibility. Stephanopoulos said, "We've been here before."

Panetta proposed that the President make a statement as late in the day as possible, with the benefit of as much information as possible, before the broadcast networks aired their news programs. An adviser said later, "Everyone agreed that the President had to be firm, brief, and avoid speculation." The meeting was somber; some of the President's Secret Service agents knew some of the agents who had been in the Oklahoma City building. At 4:30 P.M., the President and some of his advisers met in the Situation Room, usually used for international crises, in the basement of the West Wing, where Panetta had organized an interagency task force, to participate in a teleconference with other government officials and to get the most up-to-date information. Much of the federal building had been blown away and it was clear that the death toll would be terrible, a horror compounded by the fact that the bomb had destroyed the building's day-care center. (The final toll was 167 dead.) One problem was how to deal with the speculation that the perpetrators were Middle Eastern. Clinton felt that it was important to warn people not to jump to conclusions.

The President's statement, at 5:30 P.M., was firm—as firm as Clinton could be. He would never come across as firm as Reagan (at his most Eastwoodian) did. Nonetheless, he handled the situation well, meeting one of the primary requirements of a President. The question was whether people would now listen to him. He vowed to bring to justice the "evil cowards" responsible for the explosion. (Clinton added the word "evil" to his prepared remarks.) He said, "I will not allow the people of this country to be intimidated. Let there be no room for doubt: we will find the people who did this. When we do, justice will be swift, certain and severe."

On Friday, after Timothy McVeigh—who had been picked up by an Oklahoma policeman on the afternoon of the bombing for driving without a license plate and carrying a concealed weapon, and was already in a county jail and was about to be released when prison officials noticed his resemblance to a drawing of "John Doe No. 1," one of the two men being sought—was arrested for the bombing, the decision was made at the White House to let Reno announce the arrest, as the Justice Department had suggested. Clinton would follow with a press briefing. False reports that "John Doe No. 2" was being closed in on made it appear that law enforcement officers were cracking the case with lightning speed. As it became apparent that McVeigh was perhaps tied into the militia movement in Michigan, a consideration at the White House was how to talk about that and not imperil a fair trial.

The nation began to get an education about the militia movement, paramilitary organizations in various states that trained with weapons and had strong and sometimes paranoid feelings against the federal government. The fact that a building in the "heartland" of America had been selected, perhaps to make the point that no place was safe, had the result of angering people all the more. That innocent federal workers (all at their jobs by 9:02 A.M., when the bomb went off)—and many of their children—had been murdered for simply doing their job cast a special pall over the event, and put "bureaucrats" in a new light.

Mrs. Clinton was credited with the idea of turning the President's Saturday radio address into a televised appearance of the President and Mrs. Clinton before a group of federal workers' children seated on the Oval Office carpet. (The idea actually came from Maggie Williams, Mrs. Clinton's Chief of Staff, and Stephanopoulos.) Both Clintons spoke to the children sensitively. But they were nearing a line; White House aides said that how many appearances the President should make had been carefully considered, that they knew it was important that they try not to do anything that appeared to be for political purposes—in itself a political calculation. The Clintons' planting of a dogwood tree on Sunday in the South Lawn of the White House, in memory of the victims—as suggested by one of the children—as they prepared to fly to Oklahoma City seemed to draw them closer to the line. A White House aide said to a media figure, "They were born to do this."

Clinton's powerful and moving speech at the memorial service on Sunday afternoon arose from the fact that Clinton was at his best as a quasi-preacher (just as his speech November 13, 1993, to black ministers in Memphis was one of his very best as President). His Oklahoma City comments were moving and brief, again showing sensitivity on Clinton's part. "The anger you feel is valid, but you must not allow yourselves to be consumed by it," the President said. "The hurt you feel must not be allowed to turn into hate, but instead to the search for justice." He added, "Those who trouble their own house will inherit the wind." And he started on a theme that was to become more prominent in the ensuing days: "When there is talk of hatred, let us stand up and talk against it. When there is talk of violence, let us stand up and talk against it."

But the White House couldn't leave it at that, and booked the President that night on *60 Minutes*—one of the highest rated programs on television —to talk about his proposals for new laws to counter terrorism. One had the sense of White House aides saying "and then . . . and then." (The last time the President appeared on this program he and his wife spoke to the nation about allegations of his philandering.) Clinton was now very close to the line. This was a preemptive move to show that he was in charge and was tough on terrorism. No one would get to his right on this. Among his proposals, to be added to his earlier proposals to counter foreign-bred terrorism, were expediting deportation of illegal immigrants charged with breaking U.S. laws (though no foreigners were implicated in the Oklahoma bombing), and giving the F.B.I. broader authority to investigate and conduct wiretaps. In his comments on *60 Minutes,* Clinton addressed the fact that many militia members felt that the botched raid at Waco, which ended in the deaths of at least seventy-five Branch Davidians, and an attack on a white separatist, Randy Weaver, in Idaho—one that was authorized by the F.B.I. because earlier a U.S. marshal was killed while attempting to arrest Weaver—by the Bureau of Alcohol, Tobacco and Firearms that had ended in the killing of Weaver's wife and their fourteen-year-old son, were parts of a plot by the federal government and should be avenged. The President said, "I cannot believe that any serious, patriotic American believes that the conduct of those people at Waco justifies the kind of outrageous behavior we've seen at Oklahoma City, or the kind of inflammatory rhetoric that we're hearing all across the country today. It's wrong."

Clinton's proposals were the result of a sorting out at the White House of proposals from the F.B.I., the Justice Department, and Members of Congress. White House aides said an effort was made to not tread on civil liberties, but in many eyes that effort wasn't entirely successful. The Justice Department proposals were said to be more restrained than those of the F.B.I. Whenever an event occurred that might justify stronger government actions, law enforcement officers pushed for long-desired tools. And ever since the F.B.I. came under strong criticism for its infiltration of groups opposing the Vietnam War, black militant organizations, and the Ku Klux Klan, the guidelines on their potential actions were restrictive, and the F.B.I. claimed that those guidelines had been interpreted so as to inhibit legitimate action. Therefore, some of the proposals were for broader use of powers than the F.B.I. already had, and some were to broaden those powers—fewer constraints on wiretapping and infiltration of "hate groups" and access to such records as hotel and telephone bills. The President also proposed adding a thousand new federal agents to the F.B.I. A White House official said that if F.B.I. infiltrators were put into every militia it would be back to the bad old days; that the government couldn't surveil a militia if it was obeying the law, but could if the group was collecting guns illegally and advocating violation of laws.

As the President dominated the response to the Oklahoma City bombing, his rivals were struggling for their footing. Some made missteps. Shortly after the bombing Phil Gramm and Bob Dole advocated retaliation against whatever foreign government had perpetrated the act. (It turned out that the alleged perpetrators had been based in Kansas.) In the early hours of Sunday morning, Gingrich and his wife made a middle-of-the-night inspection of the Murrah Building. Later that day, when he was asked by a reporter if his anti-bureaucrat rhetoric had contributed to the attitude that led to the bombing, he responded angrily, "That's grotesque. I think that's very offensive on your part. I can't believe you would say that. It is grotesque to suggest that anybody in this country who raises legitimate questions about the size and scope of the federal government has any implication in this."

In a speech in Minneapolis on Monday, April 24, the President gave his muted opponents an opening—and they seized it. In strong, well-stated remarks, Clinton denounced "the purveyors of hatred and division," and said that those who "spread hate" must be stood up to by others. But then he said, referring to "some of the things that are regularly said over the airwaves," that "they leave the impression that, by their very words, violence is acceptable. . . . It is time we all stood up and spoke against that kind of reckless speech and behavior." (Ex–Watergate felon G. Gordon Liddy advised listeners on how to shoot B.A.T.F. agents and said that he used handmade drawings of the Clintons for target practice.) Even some political observers friendly toward the Clinton administration felt that the President's Minneapolis speech was inopportune, giving the appearance that he was trying to take political advantage of the situation by charging that right-wing radio talk shows had been poisoning the atmosphere, encouraging hatred of the federal government. White House aides said that Clinton's remarks were consistent with those he had made in his State of the Union address about "our civil life." Because he hadn't kept up the theme, his Minnesota speech appeared to be rooted only in the moment.

Rush Limbaugh said, "Make no mistake about it: liberals intend to use this tragedy for their own political gain." Phil Gramm said that the President was on "thin ice" and Dole said that "You don't make politics out of people's misery." A horrible and pointless argument over moral equivalency began. Aides said that Clinton saw earlier than others that Waco would be used as a diversion, if not an excuse, for Oklahoma City, and sure enough, some political figures, including Gingrich, began to call for hearings on Waco—and then on the assault on Weaver's cabin in Ruby Ridge. In an appearance on *Meet the Press* on May 7, Gingrich spoke sympathetically about strong anti-government feelings in parts of the West —against federal agents, the federal government, and Washington, D.C. The debate soon enveloped the N.R.A., which had encouraged fear of the federal government and had referred to B.A.T.F. agents in a recent fund-raising letter as "jack-booted government thugs" and described federal agents "wearing Nazi bucket helmets and black storm trooper uniforms to attack law-abiding citizens." Republican congressional leaders decided to postpone the effort to repeal the ban on assault weapons.

Though several White House aides felt that the President had made a mistake in his Minneapolis speech, they had no choice but to put his comments in as good a light as possible—compounding the problem. Since Clinton didn't want to appear that he was backing off, in Iowa the next day he said, "This is not a matter of partisan politics," and added that "reckless speech . . . should be spoken against whether it comes from the left or the right." This lame attempt to retroactively spread the blame suggested that the President himself thought he had misspoken. (A White House adviser said that "airwaves" wasn't in the prepared text of the President's speech.)

In any event, the President's rhetoric was toned down after the Minneapolis speech.

In the course of this period, Clinton was considering an Oval Office address, but even within the White House that was seen as an overreach.

Clinton utilized various opportunities in the ensuing days to talk about Oklahoma City—including at the usually jovial White House Correspondents Dinner on Saturday, April 29, and a commencement address at Michigan State on May 5, where he attacked the militias. Some of his political advisers had counseled against this, arguing that the militias had significant blue-collar support. (The President also used the occasion of the trip to single out Liddy—as opposed, presumably, to Limbaugh—in an interview with the *Detroit Free Press*. "I cannot defend some of the things that Gordon Liddy has said," Clinton said.)

And some Clinton aides thought the President went too far when, on Friday, May 19, in an obvious stunt he demanded that the N.R.A. give to an organization helping families of police officers who died in the line of duty the money raised through the controversial letter.

Clinton and his aides felt that his handling of the Oklahoma tragedy had helped him politically. His approval ratings in most polls shot up; the majority of people said they felt that he had acted like a leader. People working in the White House called friends to point out the positive poll ratings.

At a meeting of the bipartisan leadership with the President, at the White House on Wednesday, April 26, the talk was of the need for a united response to the bombing. Those present—who included Dole, Gingrich, Gephardt, Bonior, and Oklahoma's two senators, Republicans Don Nickles and James Inhofe, and key figures on congressional Judiciary Committees, plus various government officials and White House aides—received reports on the situation from the F.B.I. and FEMA. There was now little hope that more people would be found alive. Nickles suggested that officials wait before deciding whether to replace the Murrah Building on the same site, and whether it should be low-rise or high-rise. Clinton praised the idea and suggested that the Oklahomans caucus and get back to him.

Gingrich said little in the meeting, but he did talk about the need to follow through on a bipartisan basis and to make it clear that others who might be thinking of taking such a violent step would be deterred. Orrin Hatch suggested that limits on habeas corpus should be added to the proposed legislation (they were); Joseph Biden, the former chairman of the Senate Judiciary Committee, expressed misgivings. (Despite all the talk about co-operation, the President's legislative proposals inevitably invited other proposals and divisions of opinion—and some bipartisan misgivings.)

While the meeting was still going on, Gingrich went out on the White House lawn to give an interview to Wolf Blitzer, of CNN. "This is a very unique chance for us to set a new tone for this city and for the country," Gingrich said. He spoke approvingly of the bipartisan meeting, calling it "a very sober meeting," and adding, "I've been in meetings now with four Presidents and I would say this one was different."

Though Gingrich tried to project harmony, and a number of people were hopeful that indeed Oklahoma City had changed the climate in Washington to a less contentious and partisan one, the cynical but realistic Tony Blankley had a different take on the situation. In a conversation not long after the White House meeting, Blankley said, "My instinct is that this will not be a significant moment—that the mood will pass."

Gingrich was effective in his May 7 *Meet the Press* appearance—level and calm. Gingrich knew how to modulate his tone, and he and his staff were aware of the varying effects he could have. Blankley said, "He can make the same point about an opponent in a bemused way, in a concerned way, in a disappointed way, or in an angry way. And the angry way is often less effective than any of the others."

(Gingrich used the Easter recess to off-load some political freight. He and his advisers decided to drop his daily televised briefings. Blankley said that the problem was the "flamboyance" of some reporters, but the real reason was that a number of Gingrich's friends thought that he had been seriously overexposed, and too often came off in a negative light. His numerous appearances weren't doing his poll ratings any good. On April 30, he also resigned from his chairmanship of GOPAC, which had become a big political burden because of the ethics charges.)

From the time Gingrich became Speaker, friends had urged him to tone down his rhetoric, and now in the wake of the bombing they stressed the point some more. Gingrich did tone down somewhat—for a while. But so as not to look as if he were backing off, he continued to refer, disparagingly, to "bureaucrats."

White House aides said that when Clinton saw that he was getting through to the public—including in a place that had been as politically alien to him as Oklahoma—he gained new, or long-lost, self-confidence. As White

House aides saw it, the Oklahoma bombing gave Clinton an opportunity to talk about and take the lead on subjects on which he had been at a disadvantage, and he could now look Presidential. Mike McCurry said, "The debate in America is shifting out of economic policy and to moral values and what kind of society we are. The Republicans have had strong, resonant statements on that and the Democrats have fallen short. This gives Clinton an opportunity to talk about civil discourse and social values. Oklahoma has been a great opportunity to do that. Clinton is struck by the power of these themes."

Leon Panetta said, "He's feeling much more confident about his ability to get across to the American people." He continued, "These events gave him the sense that people were looking to him for that kind of leadership —particularly in a place like Oklahoma—that people were responding to him. It meant that he could reestablish ties with people from that area of the country."

Another White House aide said, "In Oklahoma, we just hit"—he snapped his fingers.

One aide said, "It's very possible that the audience for this is huge. The people who are going to decide the next election are moderates. We tried all year to say we're the mainstream and they're the extreme—now we can show that. Until this tragedy the Republicans felt comfortable pandering to the militia types in their rhetoric." He added, "The question is how you get people to change their minds about the country. The other part is getting them to see *him* differently."

A sad postscript to Oklahoma City was the closing of Pennsylvania Avenue in front of the White House. There had been two attempts to scale the White House fence—the attempts were successful, but the intruders were stopped before they could do any real harm. The closing had been considered for some time—the Secret Service had been advocating it—and the idea gained strength even before Oklahoma City, as a result of other attempted assaults on the White House. The Oklahoma City bombing clinched the argument for shutting down to traffic the most famous stretch of land in Washington. The barricades went up overnight, reminding some of the secret, overnight erecting of the Berlin Wall.

16

THE BUDGET
"How Do We Get in This Thing?"

Gingrich had always understood that the struggle over the budget would be the most important—and the most perilous—stage in the revolution. The dry figures that Congress and the President would clash over would define the role of government. The budget reached into every recess of the government; it set policy in thousands of areas. The budget battle was where most of the political differences would be settled. The Hundred Days were just the prelude.

Starting in late February, Dole and Gingrich began a series of meetings, the first one in Dole's office, to discuss the timing and the substance of the fiscal 1996 budget. Aware that the Republicans' proposals would be controversial, the two leaders decided that the House and Senate versions would move forward simultaneously, to protect each Chamber's party from having to take the flak alone. The goal was to finish the budget resolution, setting the contours of the final budget, by Memorial Day. They were not to finish until just before the July 4 recess.

Pete Domenici, dubious about the idea of trying to actually balance the budget by 2002, for some time after the election ascribed the House Republican leaders' setting that goal to their unfamiliarity with the arithmetic and set his own goal of making "a down payment" on a balanced budget. At an evening meeting in February, Domenici was taken aback by comments by both House and Senate leaders about their intention of not just winning approval of a Balanced Budget Amendment but of also actually balancing the budget. "I thought we were talking about a down payment," Domenici said. He felt that some important decisions had been made that he hadn't been party to. But he said that if the others were serious about that goal he'd start working on it. By the time the Balanced Budget Amendment failed in the Senate by one vote, Domenici knew that the Republicans were now so far out on a limb on balancing the budget—and on responding to Democratic taunts that they couldn't do it—that he would have to try to do so. He then briefed about forty Republican senators on what would be involved.

Domenici told his Republican colleagues that he didn't intend to include tax cuts—which many of them favored, and which had already been passed by the House.

On the House side, Kasich was having problems of his own. He and Gingrich worried that Domenici wouldn't try for zero deficit by 2002, thus leaving the House exposed. Gingrich felt that he would have to persuade Domenici. Kasich was deeply worried about the size of the Medicare cuts that would be necessary, and at one point rejected his staff's proposal on that. Gingrich said in a speech on April 28 that actual changes in the Medicare program would be considered apart from the budget process (so as to buy time, and also keep the subject from sinking the budget). The Medicare trustees' report that the fund would run out in 2002 was another stroke of fortuity for Gingrich, since balancing the budget, plus cutting taxes, would require steep cuts in Medicare.

Still burnt by the school lunch episode, in the spring Gingrich launched a major crusade to persuade the press to refer not to "cuts" in Medicare but to "slowing the rate of growth" of the program. Blankley summoned reporters one by one to lecture them on this point. Gingrich and his people were aware that polls showed that when people were asked about cutting Medicare in order to balance the budget, they were opposed twenty-five percent to seventy percent; but when they were asked about cutting Medicare so as to save the trust fund, they were in favor seventy percent to twenty-five percent. Kasich and Barbour also tried to enforce the new vocabulary.

On the basis of the R.N.C.'s constant polling on Congress, Haley Barbour warned the House leaders that Medicare was being equated with Social Security. "Haley said," Chris Shays recalled, " 'You're going to get "school lunched" on Medicare and you're going to get killed. Start talking about the trustees' report.' So we started talking about the trustees' report." (Similar reports had been issued regularly, and temporary fixes were made.)

Having taken on the budget as his personal project, Gingrich involved himself in seeing to it that the Budget Committee drafted a plan that the

House would pass. He met with about thirty-eight Republicans from rural areas who were upset that proposed cuts in agriculture programs were too great, and mollified them by adding a stipulation in the budget that the subject would be reexamined if land values declined steeply. Gingrich had more than these members' votes in mind; he didn't want a repetition of 1948, when rural America decided that Republicans were uncaring about them and a large number of Republicans were turned out of the Congress.

Gingrich said in an interview that he talked to the Republican conference "all the time" about what they had to do to stay in the majority. He pointed out that no Republican House majority had won reelection since 1926.

For the budget, Gingrich also met with Dan Burton, of Indiana, the leader of the new conservative group CATs, who sought assurance that they would be able to offer floor amendments to strike certain funding. Gingrich assured him.

Kasich involved all of the Republican Budget Committee members, plus Democrat Mike Parker, of Mississippi, in a line-by-line review of the budget. The hypothesis was that if the goal was to balance the budget by 2002, some radical things would have to be done. Kasich also had to balance the rural representatives off with city representatives; the rural representatives wanted the city folks to give up as much as they had. Kasich had to keep the chairmen of the authorizing committees from blowing up over his committee's working proposals. He wasn't totally successful; in a meeting with the leadership, Floyd Spence, chairman of the National Security Committee, accused Kasich, who was seeking a freeze on defense expenditures, of cavorting with the enemy (presumably Ron Dellums and other Democrats) and undermining America. Spence and Livingston won out over Kasich on defense expenditures.

Shortly before Kasich's committee finished its work, the House Republicans, on Friday, May 5, went off to a retreat in Leesburg, Virginia. Senate Republicans "retreated" at the Library of Congress from 8:30 A.M. to 2:30 P.M. on the same day. The senators discussed among other things how to take the partisanship out of the Medicare debate. The House Democrats retreated to Piney Point, Maryland, at the Harry Lindeburg Training School, which provided training for seafarers.

Senate Democrats went to a conference center in Williamsburg from Friday until Sunday.

Kasich hated the Leesburg retreat. Other Republicans weren't crazy about it, staying as they were in what they regarded as cells at a place called Xerox Document University, or X.D.U., a training center for Xerox employees. (Some members bought T-shirts with X.D.U. on them.) Retreats of both parties used to be paid for by lobbyists, who then attended, but now that this approach had fallen into deserved disrepute the members had to pay their own way. Some of the Leesburg conference was taken up by Gingrich's encouraging his troops about the budget, telling them, "We've got to charge ahead." Governors Engler and Weld put in an appearance—Engler to tell of his miraculous political recovery after he cut programs.

Gingrich also produced the Prime Minister of New Zealand, James Bolger, to talk about "downsizing." Gingrich had had a conversation with him about his country's efforts to downsize its post office and was impressed.

The attendees were broken into five sub-groups, each—Clinton-style—run by a facilitator. In all five groups members expressed doubts about Gingrich's theories about the Third Wave. In their reports to the group at large, they had some bad news for Gingrich. First, the Democrats' school lunch attack was still working. Second, nobody understood or could "relate to" his Toffler talk. One member said later, "To many Members of Congress it's sort of amorphous. Newt was given a bad time but he joked about it."

At the request of a number of the members, and after some grumbling that they wanted the details, Kasich gave a rundown of his nearly completed budget. This went well enough, though problems did arise about agriculture cuts and reductions in the cost-of-living adjustments (COLAs) for civil service pensions. Adjustments were made in these, and also as a result of Leesburg the reduction in Medicare under consideration was scaled back. Cuts in veterans' benefits were also reduced, and a proposal for vouchers for veterans' medical care was dropped.

What Kasich hated about Leesburg was an effort by Armey and Thomas Bliley, chairman of the Commerce Committee, to get him to back off from specifying in his budget report anything beyond the numbers for Medicare. He was not to get into policy. Kasich had planned to issue suggestions of how to reach those numbers. Armey handed Kasich a piece of paper with suggested broad, vague language. Kasich, enraged, saw this as another effort to keep his budget as general as possible, and as an affront. Gingrich, who was at this meeting, said nothing. Kasich then called together the members of the Budget Committee, who became indignant on his behalf. Gingrich then apologized to Kasich, saying, "We screwed up." The problem was resolved in Kasich's favor but he remained unhappy over the incident.

Also at Leesburg, pollster Linda DiVall advised the Republicans on how to talk about Medicare: don't use the word "cut" in the same sentence with Medicare, talk about "preserving" it, or "saving" it. Gingrich had already accepted this advice, as he did her suggestion that it should be stated that people already in the Medicare program should be able to stay in it, but would be given "more options." Now the troops were being drilled at Leesburg.

By early May, both Dole and Gingrich were calling for Clinton to join in forming a bipartisan commission to deal with reducing the cost of Medicare —and thus lighten the burden on themselves—but Clinton (as they must have expected) wasn't interested in helping them out. All the same, Gingrich, in television appearances, talked about painless ways to reduce the growth of Medicare costs—and stressed (as pollster DiVall had advised) increased "options."

At Piney Point the House Democrats heard from pollsters and fretted some more over what to do about the dearth of Democratic-leaning talk show hosts. They also got advice from some experts about how to handle their own appearances on talk shows. They decided that their issues would be Social Security, Medicare, and education/children. This wasn't much of a "vision of the future"—which Gephardt had said they would develop by spring. After the conference, Gephardt said that Democrats would "fight Medicare cuts made for the purpose of getting a tax cut for a privileged few."

Like his counterpart, Domenici worked with other committee chairmen and with Dole, or a Dole representative. He had to deal with the increasing number of conservatives that Dole had put on his committee, and in the Senate as a whole with a bloc of moderates, as well as the radical freshmen. The tax cut issue was particularly difficult: most of the freshmen and others —including Phil Gramm (who, like Dole, had been more associated in the past with deficit reduction)—favored the House-passed tax cut, but a majority of the Senate Republicans (Domenici included) preferred deficit reduction and didn't want any tax cut at all. Domenici was close to Dole and wanted to help him win the nomination but was having problems. Another Republican senator said, "Pete wants to stay close to Dole, but it's increasingly difficult to get cues from Dole. Dole is hard to predict. Managers of bills don't know what he's up to."

Domenici also had to juggle the home-state concerns of committee members—himself included. He handled this by asking the senators to state their specific objections and then propose what should be cut instead. Domenici himself wanted to save two large federal nuclear weapons laboratories in his state. Charles Grassley, of Iowa, was the most successful, getting major relief from cuts in agriculture programs. (The money was found in education programs instead.) Richard Lugar, of Indiana, also running for the Presidency, had hoped that far deeper cuts in agriculture would be made. Water projects in states of Republican committee members and other powerful figures, such as Appropriations Chairman Mark Hatfield and Finance Committee Chairman Bob Packwood, were saved.

When Domenici's committee had all but finished its work, others felt that the public wasn't yet ready for large cuts in Medicare, and Gramm was demanding tax cuts, so final action was put off for a week while Republicans worked on persuading the public, and Domenici worked on the tax problem. His solution was to say that if there was a dividend from balancing the budget—as expected—it would be put toward tax cuts.

In the end, Domenici put out a budget that he didn't completely agree with but thought he could get fixed in the appropriations process. (He was a member of the Appropriations Committee.) Associates said that Domenici didn't agree with some of the cuts in education programs.

Domenici had by now grown more comfortable with the idea of balancing the budget, and in fact told his committee, "This has been exhilarating for me." James Exon, the ranking Democrat, said, "I don't agree with everything, but I've never seen anyone with the courage to do what you've done."

Both committees' proposed budgets charted a radical reduction in the size and role of the federal government. They both sought to reduce federal spending by about a trillion dollars over seven years. Both provided for fewer agencies and programs, and cut spending for discretionary domestic programs—a category that covered education and training and nutrition and infrastructure and scientific research—by one-third. If they went too far in certain categories, they asked questions that hadn't been asked for too long.

The major difference between the two committees' proposals, offered— as planned—within a day of each other, on May 9 and 10, was that the House Budget Committee plan incorporated the $353 billion in tax cuts (over seven years, the new timetable for reaching a balanced budget) passed by the House earlier, and therefore had to make more spending cuts. The Senate budget permitted the use of the $170 billion "dividend" that was supposed to result from balancing the budget, and only if it was independently certified that the budget was indeed on the way to balance. This was a blow to Gramm, but Gramm's supporters believed that he could prevail with an amendment on the Senate floor.

Both committees reduced the Earned Income Tax Credit for the working poor—in effect raising their taxes. This program, which had long enjoyed bipartisan backing, supplemented the wages of those trying to work their way out of poverty. The idea was to encourage people to work their way off welfare—presumably something Republicans favored.

The Senate budget proposed to eliminate a hundred federal programs; the House committee, more than 280 programs. The Senate committee proposed to get rid of the Commerce Department, while the House committee proposed to eliminate Commerce, Education, and Energy. Both committees turned Medicaid into a block grant and cut its funding, and both made steep cuts in Medicare (the Senate committee, $256 billion; the House committee, $288 billion), substantially reducing the rate of growth (the House by about half; the Senate by about one-third). The Senate committee froze defense spending at the same level that Clinton had proposed (which constituted a cut); the House committee increased Clinton's Pentagon budget by $67 billion over seven years. Both made heavy cuts in education and training programs. (Kasich pointed out that there were 163 job training programs. The administration had proposed consolidating them, but the legislation hadn't been passed by the Congress.)

Both committees proposed elimination of Clinton's national service program and made cuts in his innovative program of providing direct government loans for college education, which lowered the costs to the students. The Senate committee reduced funds for Clinton's Goals 2000, which was to encourage schools to reach higher standards; the House committee abolished it. (The House committee also cut in half George Bush's pet "Points of Light" program.)

The committees proposed either a curb or elimination of federal funding for the Corporation for Public Broadcasting. The House committee eliminated funding for the National Endowment for the Arts and the National Endowment for the Humanities and the Senate committee cut their funding by fifty percent. The House committee called for cuts of $25 billion in "corporate welfare"; the Senate committee called for no such cuts. But the House committee's proposed cuts weren't a sure bet in the House, either; Archer, along with his fellow Ways and Means Committee Republicans a dutiful protector of corporate interests, said that he didn't think he could come up with more than $12.5 billion in cuts in corporate subsidies. (Kasich believed that a fight with Archer would add to his own credibility.)

Both committees relied on optimistic economic assumptions to reach their goals, Kasich's committee going the further in this.

House passage of the budget, on May 17, wasn't in question. Gingrich had ironed out the problems that had arisen over the committee's proposals (agriculture, civil service) and had suggested that any remaining dissatisfied Republican member see him in his office. Only one did. At a press conference on the day the House was to take up the budget, Gingrich referred to "primal screaming by the Democrats at the end of their way of big government spending, big taxes."

Although the votes to pass the resolution in the House seemed assured, Gingrich had concerns. He said later, "You worry about, Will the public pressure grow in such a way that you can't win? Will the members get confused and decide that maybe they can't really do it? What will happen in the Senate, which is a much harder institution than the House and where you have less of a revolution underway? The Senate is still growing into the revolution. So you're sort of aware of a lot of different factors that are going on simultaneously."

The Republican leaders had trapped the Democrats by requiring that any alternative budget proposed on the floor be balanced. The Democratic leaders had no interest in proposing a balanced budget, which would require cuts distasteful to them and mute their attacks on the Republican budget. So Gephardt was driven to offering a proposal he didn't support, a modified version of the Domenici budget, sponsored by Charles Stenholm. Gingrich had great fun pointing out that the Democrats were "so bereft of ideas" that they were offering the Senate *Republican* proposal. A number of Democrats were discomfited. Though the leadership didn't actually push the Stenholm alternative, David Skaggs said, "I think it recognizes fundamentally that many of us were unhappy with a Democratic vacuum."

Though there were several possible targets for the Democrats in the debate—a change in the cost-of-living formula that would have the effect of lowering entitlement payments, including Social Security; the funny business in the economic assumptions—the Democrats concentrated their fire on the Medicare cuts.

To emphasize their point, Democrats brought to the House floor large photographs of elderly constituents, and spoke of the potential effect on them of the budget cuts. This hokey demonstration (and further erosion of parliamentary dignity) was shortly aped by Republicans, who produced large photographs of children. Their poll-driven message was that they were seeking a secure future for the nation's children. (Kasich said later he had no idea who the cherubs were whose photograph he held up.)

Though the outcome was foreseen, each side was making points in the larger battle for public opinion. Republicans, clearly on the defensive about Medicare cuts, again and again repeated the formulation, "Only in Washington is an increase called a cut."

The "Democratic substitute" was clobbered on a vote of 100–325. More Democrats voted against it than for it. The emptiness of their party's position was there in plain sight.

In the closing speech, Kasich, one of the most articulate members of the House, said, "The twenty-first century is about the power of the individual, not the power of the bureaucracy," which "in some respects takes away the incentives for the individual to fly." He said, "It's my dream for everybody to fly in America." By now the House Chamber was nearly full. Turning to the Democrats, Kasich said, "We're going to do this now. We are going to put the pendulum back and we have our vision for emphasizing the individual. That doesn't mean the government does not have a role." As he closed, he received a standing ovation. The House Republicans were proud of their new star, who had brought them to a new place. So had Gingrich, who then took the chair. On the roll call vote the Republican budget won the necessary 219 votes with three minutes to go. Cheers erupted. When Gingrich announced the final vote, 238–193, there were more cheers.

Despite this victory, there clearly wouldn't be enough votes to override a veto of a reconciliation bill that closely reflected the House budget.

At a press conference the following day, Gingrich said somberly, "This is the beginning of six months of hard work and not the end of a process."

When the Senate took up its budget the following day, the only significant question was what would happen on taxes—how this latest embodiment of the Republican nomination contest would play out. Now Dole, despite his closeness to Domenici, had to find a way to get the Senate on record as definitely in favor of tax cuts rather than make them contingent on a balanced budget, as the Senate Budget Committee had—without giving Gramm a victory.

So Dole, as was his custom, initiated some backroom meetings. When Gramm learned that these talks were taking place, he told *his* allies that he didn't want them talking to Dole until he had his opportunity to offer his tax cut amendment. Dan Coats—a sophomore from Indiana who, like Gramm, favored the House-passed tax cut—obliged. But then the vote on Gramm's amendment was an embarrassing 31–69. A full twenty-three Republican senators voted against Gramm. They included all of Dole's allies, and the vote constituted a rallying-around of Domenici as well as Dole. A Republican senator said, "Domenici works day and night on the budget. He will come over to us individually and say, 'Look, I need some support over here.' He means that in two ways: he wants us to continue to voice our opposition to going too far in the direction of the House, and he wants our support when he comes back with a conference resolution." Had Gramm's amendment by any chance carried, it would have undone the coalition needed to pass the resolution in the Senate, not only because of the number of Republican senators who wanted no tax cut at all, but also because it would have required far deeper spending cuts. A Gramm strategist had said that offering the large tax cut was a "big" opportunity for Gramm, and it was suggested that Gramm could "win by losing" by proposing things that earned the gratitude of activists. But his loss was greater than his supporters had expected.

Dole, thinking ahead (at least, as far as the Republican Convention), voted with Gramm. As for those who voted against Gramm, Thad Cochran, of Mississippi, a Dole ally, said, "Some were probably influenced by Presidential politics. They know Gramm's running for President, trying to posture and get himself positioned to campaign against Dole on this issue. And those of us who are for Dole are sensitive to that. Some of us were influenced to some degree by that consideration. But we don't want to admit it. We want to talk about the fact that we voted against the amendment only on its merits." He added, "But there were strong reasons on the merits. I thought the amendment was inappropriate. It would unravel a coalition needed to pass the resolution."

Once Gramm's amendment went down to defeat, Dole resumed his meetings, in the President's Room off the Senate floor, to find a solution. Joining him were Domenici, Packwood, Coats, and Rod Grams, a freshman from Minnesota who had run on the issue of a tax cut and felt vehemently that the Senate should vote for one. The meeting became quite heated. Dole, addressing Coats, said, "If you'd given us time to work this out, instead of waiting until the Gramm amendment was voted on, we could have had this decided. You guys are blaming me for not getting this done, but you walked away from the table."

Overnight, Dole and Grams worked out an amendment that changed the Budget Committee's wording from "may" enact a tax cut if the budget was in balance to "shall." The amendment was adopted the next day, Thursday, by a vote of 54–45. Lott said afterward, "There are a few Republicans in the Senate who don't want a tax cut; unfortunately, some are in very key positions. Under pressure from Dole and me and a circular movement—you surround them and keep up the discussion—we got the Grams amendment. There will not be a budget conference report that doesn't have tax cuts."

To try to embarrass the Republicans, the Democrats offered fifty-seven amendments. Many proposed restoring funds for such things as Medicare, Medicaid, and education, rather than using the money for tax cuts. An amendment that would have shifted to education some of the anticipated "dividend" nearly passed. But the Democrats' large number of proposals blurred the point they were making.

The Democrats used charts and posters for the benefit of the C-SPAN audience. One poster showed a fat little man with a top hat and a walking stick, ostensibly the "wealthy" who would benefit from the tax cut. Republican freshman Rick Santorum had had a poster placed on the floor giving the number of days the Senate had been discussing the budget, without any serious plan from the President. In a new low for decorum and respect for the Presidency, the poster said, "Where's Bill?" This made even some of Santorum's fellow Republicans uneasy. (Early in the proceedings, Domenici had brought up Clinton's February budget to show its lack of support, and it was rejected 99–0; the Democrats didn't want to get caught up in that game.)

At 6:10 P.M. on Thursday, May 25, the Senate adopted the budget resolution by a vote of 57–42. Three Democrats—Charles Robb, of Virginia, Bob Kerrey, of Nebraska, and Sam Nunn, of Georgia—voted for it. The Republicans had a long way to go, but the Senate had followed the House, which had followed Gingrich's lead, in paving the way for something that hadn't been expected five months earlier.

•

The argument within the administration over whether the President should veto the final rescissions bill lasted for over a month. It would be his first veto, and those who opposed it argued that his first one shouldn't be of a bill that reduced the deficit. Others argued that he should veto it on principle because it cut education and training funds too much while allowing new spending on highways and courthouses. The final bill nearly doubled the Senate's cuts in education and made substantially larger cuts in the national service program.

Dick Morris had argued early on that the President shouldn't veto a deficit reduction bill, but came to believe, as did others, that it was important for the President to show flint in his dealings with the Congress. Clinton, who wanted to veto the bill, to use it as a model, told his advisers, "I have to show them I can do it, and how to negotiate with me." In the end, the view prevailed that it was time for the President to show decisiveness against the Congress, and on the morning of May 17, the day after House and Senate negotiators completed their conference on the rescissions bill—the day the House was voting on the budget resolution—there appeared a deliberate leak in the *Washington Post* saying that the President would veto the bill.

Bob Livingston, standing outside the House Chamber, was livid. "The President just knocked the hell out of what we're doing today by saying he'd veto the rescissions bill. There's $10 billion net savings in fiscal '95 in there. So step one is already thwarted by the President." Livingston pointed out that the rescissions bill contained aid to Jordan and help for Oklahoma City, as well as disaster relief for California, Texas, and Louisiana. At a press conference later that day (featuring representatives of Boehner's coalition of interests behind the Republicans' budget resolution), Gingrich called the President's action "a tawdry manipulation of the process," and "shameful." Gingrich threw such a fit that the deliberation behind it was evident. (Tony Blankley said in an interview, "We are only heated in our rhetoric when it is useful to be heated.")

Announcing his veto that day, Clinton said, "A bill that cuts education to put pork in is the wrong way to balance the budget." The presence of the "pork" in the bill made it "a great opportunity," Mike McCurry said, for emphasizing the differences between congressional Republicans and the President.

Clinton actually sought to change only $1.5 billion of the $16.4 billion rescissions bill. Edward Kennedy, who had rounded up enough senators to guarantee that a veto wouldn't be overridden, argued, along with Chris Dodd, that the President shouldn't juxtapose education with "pork"; they said that that cluttered the message, that the President should simply say, "They are trying to take away your kids' college education."

There ensued a back-and-forth between the White House and major

Republican figures in the appropriations process—the Republicans saying that the White House hadn't given them proper warning, and White House officials saying that they had. It appeared that the Hill figures were more in the right about the etiquette of vetoing, but this was no big thing.

Also unhappy was Robert Byrd, who as the ranking member of the Senate Appropriations Committee had been a negotiator, and had signed the conference report, along with nine other Senate Democrats—several of whom now felt that they had been blindsided by the White House. (All of the House Democratic negotiators had refused to sign the report.)

There followed a period of public posturing on both sides, Gingrich darkly warning of a "train wreck" in the coming fall—a temporary shutting down of government agencies because the President and the Congress were in a stalemate over the budget and appropriations bills—because of "highly chaotic" White House pressure on the appropriations process. Livingston, referring to the fact that Clinton had signed bills authorizing appropriations for the projects, said, "the pork" was "*his* courthouses." But, because of the nearly $10 billion in savings in the bill, the Republicans wanted to reach agreement with the White House.

When Clinton, trying to resolve the problem, called Trent Lott rather than Dole, Republicans speculated that this was the work of Morris. Dole was said to be displeased. The Republican speculation was correct: the past relationship between Morris and Lott was indeed a factor. Though both Morris and Lott said they no longer had a professional relationship, they kept in touch—"We occasionally talk," Morris said in an interview a little later. A back channel to Lott could be a valuable thing. Clinton and Dole (who wanted Clinton's job) had had a prickly relationship all year. Neither seemed to know how to talk to the other. At the same time, Morris spoke highly of Lott to Clinton, telling him that Lott was someone he could work with, get things done—that Lott knew how to cut a deal. The Clinton-Lott-Gingrich-Morris (Lott had some influence over Gingrich) channel turned out to be critical to getting a settlement on the rescissions bill—and it turned to bigger things after that.

So Clinton, despite his earlier vows, did get involved in the details of the negotiations. On the evening of May 23 he also called Gingrich and Livingston, who had met to take his call. According to Livingston, Clinton wanted to increase funds for education, and said that he had strong reservations about a provision backed by industry and supported by members from the Northwest—including Hatfield—to expedite timber-salvage sales on federal lands. Environmentalists were opposed. (That same evening, Clinton was meeting with some environmentalists.) Clinton told Gingrich and Livingston that he would call back at 10:30 P.M. When he hadn't by 11:15 P.M., Livingston went home. In the interim, a man had climbed the back fence of the White House, and was subdued by gunshots by the Secret Service.

Livingston described the political exigencies of both sides as he saw them. "The President needs to show strength, obviously, if he's going to get reelected, and the best way he can assert a strong personality is by vetoing," Livingston said. "I think that plays heavily into what he's doing now with the rescissions bill. And on our side, we just may want to pin him down on some of his convictions, to test him and see whether or not he flinches. Politics runs on both sides of the aisle and on both ends of Pennsylvania Avenue."

Three weeks later, sitting in his office on a Friday afternoon, Livingston, tired and just getting over a bad cold, his lanky frame settled into a large burgundy leather chair, expressed his frustration at dealing with the White House on the rescissions bill. "Nobody down there can make a decision, nobody," he said. Sometimes, in his agitation, his voice went up an octave, until it rose to a squeak. "Anytime you get a decision, they change their minds. You can't get anybody to agree on anything in this White House. There's always another detail that they want to talk about."

After five weeks of on-and-off negotiations, in late June, the Republicans and the White House reached an agreement on the rescissions bill. It contained about $700 million more for education, training, child care, and the environment, but it also contained the provision for timber cutting (for a slightly shorter period), and left in some of the "pork." Some key Republicans, including Gingrich, concluded from this that when the bigger budget issues came around, Clinton was likely to blink first. But the White House got what it wanted most—more money for education and training, while the Republicans got a substantial start on deficit reduction.

The House accepted the compromise on June 29, but in the Senate, much to the fury of Dole, Democrats Carol Moseley-Braun, of Illinois, and Paul Wellstone, of Minnesota, objecting to reductions in the Low Income Home Energy Assistance Program (LIHEAP) and cuts in education and job training, waged a filibuster on the eve of the July 4 recess. Finally, on July 20, Dole let the two holdouts have votes on their issues, and after both amendments failed, the bill was passed by the Senate and sent to the President, who signed it into law on July 27. This had been a lot of goings-on—seven and a half weeks of back-and-forth—over a relatively piddling amount of money. The question was whether it was a harbinger for the fall.

Meanwhile, the Clinton White House had been going through intense and extensive debate over what should be the President's approach to the Republican budget. This could be a fateful decision, affecting what happened on some of the biggest issues of the year. Not long after Clinton sent his first, and politically irrelevant, budget to Congress, within the White House the issue became when—not whether—the President should move from his position of simply attacking the Republican plan to entering into negotiations on it. The other argument was over what form a new initiative should take—whether Clinton should offer a new budget.

When Clinton had begun to discuss with Morris his Hundred Days speech to be given in Dallas on April 7, he mused over the idea of offering a balanced budget himself. A speech offering a balanced budget was briefly considered for the President's appearance before the A.S.N.E. But Clinton wasn't ready yet.

In meetings with his staff in April, Clinton began asking questions that suggested he was uncomfortable with simply being on the attack against the Republican budget. He would ask, "Are we sure we're in the right position?" Or, "When do we get into this?" Or, "How do we get in this thing?"

The attacks, by the President and his aides and by Democrats on Capitol Hill, were designed to reach the public about what was in the Republicans' proposal and to stir a reaction against them—and give the President leverage in negotiations. Having earlier accused the Republicans, with some success, of cutting school lunches "to pay for tax cuts for the wealthy," Democrats were now accusing them of cutting Medicare for the same purpose. The tax cuts were thus charged against programs more than once, which didn't seem to embarrass White House aides at all. An official said, "You can pick and choose how they're paying for it. The point is, it becomes a very good arguing point."

Though Clinton believed that the Republicans' proposals made unacceptable trade-offs, and were worthy of attack, a Presidential adviser said, "In his gut, he just didn't like being there." Another White House official said at about that time, "He wants to get into it, for two reasons. One is to have some significant impact on the policy as it develops in legislation, and two is that he feels 'I don't want to politically give them any ground' " —which the Republicans could claim because Clinton didn't have a real budget.

Though he joined in the public attacks, the President was ambivalent about them, at times suggesting to aides that they should be toned down. But in a meeting with congressional leaders as late as mid-May Clinton stressed that it was important that they continue to "educate" the public about the proposed Medicare cuts for at least a few more weeks. He said that he didn't think it was necessary that the Democrats offer an alternative.

For some time, Clinton thought that the Republicans would come to him for help on Medicare, and they could then start dealing. Mike McCurry said, "The President's instinct is to 'smoke them out.' But the purpose of smoking them out is to talk with them." But when Gingrich and Dole on May 2 called on the President to join in discussions with them—to give them some cover on Medicare cuts—most White House aides thought it was too early to talk. The Republicans' position needed to be softened up more. But the Republicans' charge that Clinton was being only negative, and was, as Dole put it several times, "AWOL," or "absent without leadership," was beginning to hurt, and Clinton became increasingly worried that it would stick. One White House official said, "The President felt there was a connection between the facts that his budget wasn't in balance and his political situation was seen as irrelevant."

The President's concern over his own situation came up in meetings on strategy for dealing with the Congress on the budget issue. In mid-April, the National Economic Council budget group developed a memorandum for the President about tactics and negotiating strategy for dealing with the Republican budget resolution. The consensus of the group was that the President shouldn't engage until after the resolution had been finally approved. The question of presenting a balanced budget wasn't addressed.

In a meeting on April 21 with the budget group about the memo, the President said, in effect, "I'm the President; I have to lead; I can't be in the position of just attacking." To this group, at least, this was a new kind of talk from Clinton. After that, he began to ask his advisers whether he should submit a new budget. "Do you think it's a good thing?" he would ask.

At another strategy meeting between Clinton and his economic advisers a week later, the possible offering of a balanced budget was discussed.

Meanwhile, in the meetings in the residence at night and in phone conversations, Morris argued that Clinton shouldn't surrender the high ground of being a deficit-cutter that he had gained in 1993. Politically, Morris told him, this was the route to winning the Perot voters in 1996, a group that could decide the election. Morris urged Clinton to "show some leadership" by offering a plan of his own. Al Gore was making similar arguments.

Though Gore has been portrayed as an early supporter of the President's making a new offering, he initially started out on the other side. In a meeting with Clinton and advisers in April, Gore said that the Republicans should have an opportunity to "have a rendezvous with reality." He said this in other White House meetings as well. Gore argued that the Republicans should be allowed more time to define themselves and to confront their own difficulties. Gore wasn't of the view until about mid-May that the President should offer a new budget—his view shifted after the Republicans had shown that they could cobble together a budget resolution despite their tough self-assignment—something that Gore, like some others, had thought they couldn't do. By that time, Gore was allied on this issue with Morris, Curry, Don Baer, and Jack Quinn, his chief of staff. Gore had separate conversations with Morris. Gore argued that as a matter of both Presidential stature and credibility, Clinton should offer a new budget.

Also, Gore argued—and Clinton understood this—Clinton had to have an answer when the public asked, What is *your* plan for reducing the deficit?

Morris and Curry proceeded in the belief not only that the main thing that had gone wrong in Clinton's first two years was that he had formed an alliance with the Democratic congressional leaders, but also that too many Clinton advisers—Panetta and Stephanopoulos in particular—were still having the same discussions with House Democrats as if they were still in the majority, that they were all still in denial. They thought that both Stephanopoulos and Panetta, a former congressman, were too inclined to view matters through a congressional lens.

Those who opposed the President's going ahead with a new budget at that time—especially Panetta and Stephanopoulos—felt that those who were advising him to do so (with the exception of Gore), as one put it, "didn't have a clue what it meant. They had no Hill experience and didn't know the budget."

A key goal of Morris's strategy of moving Clinton to the center was to force the Republicans out of the mainstream. Therefore, they shouldn't be given an opening on fiscal issues. Morris was particularly keen on forcing Republicans out of the mainstream on social issues, and he was very involved in the confrontational strategy against Japan on trade, which, a White House aide pointed out, "has almost become a social issue." (Morris pushed for bombastic statements about Japan in Presidential utterances, not always with success.)

But Panetta and Stephanopoulos were strongly opposed to doing anything anytime soon to relieve the Republicans of the burden of following through on their Contract promises—which, they and other Democrats were sure, couldn't be fulfilled. (The Contract had said nothing about cutting Medicare.) They were vehemently opposed to interrupting the strategy of attacking the Republicans' proposals to cut Medicare—even though one and all knew that at some point Clinton was going to have to acquiesce in some Medicare cuts. Stephanopoulos, probably the most hard-line on this issue, felt that the President shouldn't step in before the Republicans said "uncle." Stephanopoulos said, "It's agreed that slowing the rate of growth of Medicare is necessary, but not on their terms—not to pay for a tax cut, not simply to allow them to follow a wrong-headed budget balance, and not in isolation from the rest of the health care system. They have to pay the price for getting us to help." Stephanopoulos continued, "They know they can't meet their goals; that's why they're trying to rope us in." He was in part guided by an unhappy memory. He said, "They're right in the place that we were in August 1993, when we had to do the painful things on our own. [Clinton's economic program had faced solid Republican opposition.] Eventually we have to be there, but the question is when and the price they have to pay to get our cooperation." Stephanopoulos also worried that a sudden turnabout by Clinton would signal weakness. Panetta said in an interview later, "I was opposed to backing off the strategy we had worked out with the Hill."

As for other advisers, Tyson thought that the President should wait, that he was defining himself through the attacks on the Republican budget, but that at some point, probably in the summer, the White House would have to engage with the Congress. Tyson sent the President a newsletter by Kevin Phillips, the iconoclastic Republican commentator, which indicated that the strategy of attacking the Republicans' budget was working.

Alice Rivlin had been saying for a while that the Clinton White House needed to think through its "endgame." She felt that it was in an embarrassing position for having said that the way to get its February budget in balance was through Medicare cuts to be made in the context of a health care plan, without producing a health care plan. Rivlin was unhappy about defending a budget that didn't have more deficit reduction. There was also a growing concern among some officials that at some point the President would decide that it was time to propose a health care plan, and then there would be a rush job to come up with one. The President had already said that any new plan would be incremental—as many officials had argued in vain that the original Clinton plan should have been. To avoid a last-minute rush, in April, on the QT, Rivlin, Tyson, Shalala, and Carol Rasco began to meet on Saturdays in Rivlin's office to work out a health care proposal. If anyone asked what they were doing, they would respond, "Oh, just having a ladies' lunch and talking about clothes." (Ira Magaziner wasn't invited, but he did sit in on some larger meetings later.)

Donna Shalala argued strongly that the President shouldn't offer a new budget for a couple of months. She had spent hours testifying before congressional committees on Medicare and felt that the Republicans were increasingly on the defensive. Furthermore, she had been assured that the administration wouldn't change its position. She wanted to wait until the appropriations and reconciliation bills had been passed, sometime in the fall, on the ground that not until then, when there were real cuts, would the American people have a clear idea of what the Republicans were doing. Believing that the President was responding to editorials questioning his leadership, but that the public didn't care, Shalala sent a memo to the President saying that he should stop reading the clips.

In larger meetings, Stephanopoulos, Panetta, and Harold Ickes were joined in opposition by Rahm Emanuel, a White House aide who handled some political matters. (Gore and Stephanopoulos had had several differences in the course of the Clinton Presidency, which at times became shouting matches. An underlying source of tension within the White House was Stephanopoulos's closeness to Gephardt, potentially Gore's strongest rival for a future Democratic nomination, but the two men also had different approaches to politics and different temperaments.)

But if, as Morris sought, Clinton through offering his new budget and through other moves was essentially presenting himself as the Independent candidate for 1996, a big question was how the Democratic base would take this. In one staff meeting, Curry, urging that there be no delay, said that the Democratic constituency groups were "dormant, they're depressed —I can't get them to come out to dinner." (Panetta expressly didn't invite Curry to a set of meetings with Tyson, Reich, and others, to draw up a new budget, unless the President expressly invited him.)

One problem was that Congress was slipping further and further behind the statutory timetable for writing its budget. This meant that if Clinton held off offering a new budget and offering to talk until Republicans had a budget, he would have to go on all the longer being on the attack— without a plan of his own. And the attacks on the Republican budget, stressing Medicare, seemed, like the Democratic campaign in 1994, another reenactment of stale Democratic politics. Some White House aides justified the attacking without offering an alternative by pointing out that that was what the Republicans had done for the past two years, most notably on health care. But the big difference, others replied, was that one was a congressional party and the other a President, and a President had to function in a different sphere: the longer the President held out the less he looked like a leader.

When the President traveled to Russia during the second week of May, Panetta was left in charge of the administration's response to the Republicans. Panetta argued that the Republicans' proposal to scale back the Earned Income Tax Credit "represents a tax increase on twelve million working families earning less than twenty-seven thousand dollars." Panetta, Rivlin, and Tyson held a briefing in which they sharply criticized the Republican budget, and the President was perturbed by the harshness of the attack. On Air Force One, he asked Rubin if he didn't think they had to offer a budget that was in balance in ten years. Upon their return, Rubin told colleagues that the President wanted to proceed with a balanced budget. Most of the President's advisers believed that he made up his mind between late April and early May to go in a new direction. A participant in the process said, "Dick Morris and Al Gore, in that order, made that happen."

There was something different about the President's decision-making in this instance from what had often gone before. Having been persuaded by a couple of advisers, and his own instincts, Clinton wasn't frozen by deep division among his advisers—in this case, the opposition of almost all of his staff. This time, he made up his mind and overrode most of his staff. He heard them out, invited their arguments against his decision as a way of testing what he wanted to do. Sometimes in an Oval Office meeting when Panetta or Ickes or Stephanopoulos would make a reasoned if insistent argument against his going ahead with a new budget, Clinton would say, "You're wrong," or, "I don't agree with that." He said to his staff, "I have to have something to offer, rather than be seen as standing on the sidelines." He argued that while the Democrats in Congress could do that, he couldn't.

At a meeting in the Cabinet Room in mid-May, Gore, sitting opposite the President, said, "I know you're in a different place from your advisers, I know you're in a different paradigm."

Morris maintained in an interview later that Clinton had always wanted to propose a balanced budget, but was stymied by his "bureaucracy" and that the only reason it took him so long to present one was that Clinton had to do the work on a new budget himself. "His bureaucracy couldn't do it for him," Morris said. But these claims didn't square with other evidence: that in drawing up the first budget, after the election, both Clintons felt he had been underappreciated for lowering the deficit and so why bother; that Alice Rivlin, the budget director, was the strongest deficit-reduction "hawk" in Clinton's entourage and was unhappy, though a trouper, about the first budget; that the President's advisers, working very hard, drew up a budget once it was clear what he wanted to do. No serious work on a new budget could begin before the President decided he wanted one—for fear of leaks.

Morris explained later that Clinton "needed a place to stand in order to move the earth. He couldn't criticize Republican cuts without a balanced budget of his own." Then, expressing a thought strikingly like the one that had led Gingrich to push for an actual balanced budget, Morris said, "The only idea that was big enough to compete with Medicare cuts and education cuts was to balance the budget." Like Gingrich, Morris was looking for something that would lift the debate above the details. "He had to demonstrate to the people and the press and to himself that you didn't need to do what the Republicans were doing to balance the budget," Morris said, adding, "Clinton fit the carpet to the room."

Though Panetta was strongly in favor of the President's waiting longer before offering a new budget, he was also concerned that a "train wreck" would make everyone look bad. In early May, he said, "They're carrying some big torches up there. We're saying, 'Put down your torches.' " Asked why the administration shouldn't just let the Republicans have their "train wreck," Panetta replied, "It's bad for everybody. It's bad for Congress *and* the President. You don't win. The best thing is to try to resolve these issues before you get there. If the government shuts down, people don't differentiate about whose fault it is."

White House officials had the contours of a "grand compromise" in mind: the Republicans would cut back on the tax cuts, and restore funds for education, and the two sides would agree to slowing down Medicare—but not cut as much as the Republicans proposed—in the context of reforms in the health care system. A White House official said that it was essential to make cuts in Medicare in the context of health care reform because then, "politically you can't criticize it." Panetta sent clear signals about the nature of the "grand compromise," but the Republicans, for all their calling on the White House to enter discussions, weren't really ready for that—they wanted to be in a stronger position—and didn't actually think that the President would ever want to talk. This was one of many misreadings that each side made of the other.

The President and others considered a nine-year path to balance—figuring ten years would look like a cute reach for a decade—but Clinton decided to go for ten years (explaining that the cuts in a nine-year plan would be too harsh), knowing that he would probably have to compromise at the end on a shorter timetable. He also knew, according to a close adviser, that he would have to compromise with the Republicans on taxes, including a capital gains cut. But the only way the White House could come up with an acceptable balanced budget in even ten years—with a Medicare cut substantially lower than the Republicans'—was by using more comfortable economic assumptions from the O.M.B. rather than those of the Congressional Budget Office (which the President had pledged in his 1993 State of the Union speech he would go by). White House officials knew that this would not be without political cost, but decided that it was a risk worth taking.

The alternative was to find $200 billion more in cuts. A White House aide said, "We needed to be for balance, but those who were pushing hardest for balance were undervaluing how important Medicare was, and those worrying about timing were overvaluing the importance of Medicare." It was also decided to ask for $25 billion in "corporate welfare," the same amount as in Kasich's budget, since there were those who would term such cuts "tax increases." (This was why the administration hadn't proposed cuts in corporate welfare in the first place.)

The Clinton White House had ardently fought against the concept of a balanced budget the year before. Not long before that, the idea had been the province of very conservative Republicans. But the ground had shifted so much that by proposing a balanced budget, Clinton was now entering the mainstream. An unhappy but resigned White House aide said, "To argue against balance, we would have had to start a year ago to say balance is not the issue." Panetta said later, "We had always assumed that when we negotiated we would end up with a balanced budget." He had told his colleagues that they would have to develop a balanced budget at some point, to have available for negotiations with the Republicans.

In mid-May, Panetta gave a hint of White House movement by saying, on *Face the Nation,* that he agreed with the idea of taking the budget to balance, but the Republicans' target year of 2002 was "arbitrary." He said, "You don't let the date set policy. Policy should set the date."

But around the beginning of June, Panetta was sufficiently worried that the President was about to commit a large error that he called on two Cabinet officers to try to persuade Clinton not to go ahead with offering a new budget. Panetta told them that the Hill Democrats were following the White House's strategy and now the White House would be abandoning them; that the strategy was working; that a new budget plan was far from ready; and that the pain required to balance the budget in ten years was so great that it was going to eliminate the differences between "us and them," and the constituencies that backed Clinton would feel that he was just marginally different from the Republicans. Robert Rubin, the Treasury Secretary, was always for fiscal restraint, but he had doubts about the President's timing. There seemed no logic to it.

Another high administration official described Panetta as "beside himself." This same person described Stephanopoulos as "distraught." A Cabinet official said, "George couldn't believe that this was happening."

Stephanopoulos and Pat Griffin, the White House legislative liaison, asked Labor Secretary Reich to try to talk his friend the President out of going ahead with a new budget anytime soon. In March, Reich had privately urged the President that if he felt compelled to respond to the movement toward a balanced budget in Congress he not only should delay such a response, but also consider the idea of moving to a capital budget, in which investments in future productivity aren't counted as current expenditures. Reich tried to convince Clinton—he had been trying for some time—that this would be consistent with his "investment" strategy (investing in education and training and infrastructure) and would be easy to explain to the public. As Reich explained it, "It's about spending for a European vacation or for your child's college education" or "business borrows for expensive machinery if there is likely to be a healthy return on investment." But Clinton had tried in vain, if sporadically, for two years to get across the "investment" idea, and felt there had been little return for his efforts.

Reich had also argued strenuously that the President should speak out strongly against the Balanced Budget Amendment and warned in an Oval

Office meeting that if it passed, "You will be presiding over a debacle in economic and social policy." He argued that a balanced budget was bad economics and bad social policy.

Reich said in an interview in July, "There is at any time in Washington a policy contest going on. But the bigger question is whose debate it is, who is framing the debate. The great contest of the next eighteen months is, Do you want large or small government, do you want a balanced budget? Those are Republican questions. The Democrats and the President must frame a different debate, which is how do you raise incomes and reignite upward mobility."

When Mrs. Clinton sat in on some of the meetings about the President's submitting a new budget, she said little. This was one of several ways in which her operating style within the White House had undergone some subtle changes. But, as was often the case, she was protective of her husband, asking what effect such a move would have on the Democratic Party's constituent groups, and trying to make sure that the backup work for the President's new budget was sufficient. (At the same time, aides played down her role.)

Whereas before, in meetings in the Roosevelt Room, she would sit at the center of the table, across from her husband, she now sat somewhat down the side from there. In an Oval Office meeting, she would now sit behind other officials. But no one doubted that she continued to play a powerful role on policy, political, and personnel decisions of importance to her husband. Her instincts were if anything increasingly pragmatic. People who went to her for help in persuading her husband to take a firmer stand on the welfare issue, particularly as it pertained to children, found her unresponsive. People who went to ask for her help in holding off a new budget (more than one Cabinet officer did) found her "sympathetic" but noncommittal. "Have you spoken to the President?" she would ask. In pursuing a less overt role in policy and seeking to soften the edges, she seemed at times to be floundering, reaching this way and that. In late June, it was announced that she would write a weekly syndicated column. A friend described her as "dispirited." This friend said, "She hasn't had a good time. He's had a good time."

But she remained one of the President's three most influential advisers —the others being Gore and, by spring of 1995, Morris.

Having made up his mind to offer a budget, Clinton was eager to get on with it. He asked his staff, "Don't I have to do this sooner rather than later?" Clinton had in mind getting into Republicans' negotiations on their budget resolution, which were to begin in June. Morris and Curry were also impatient. But Clinton's budget aides, who were working extraordinary hours, kept saying that the new budget wasn't ready, and that the President shouldn't claim that he had a plan until he had one. His political aides, having lost the big battle, wanted him to wait at least until the Republicans were finished with their conference on the budget resolution, giving the President something specific to go against.

But Clinton was champing to make a prime-time address from the Oval Office on his new budget. Mike McCurry told Clinton that he was only going to be able to do this once and he had better have some backup. In an interview in early May, McCurry said, "The President has a sense of the endgame. We keep trying to get him to resist the temptation to make his moves toward the endgame." These efforts notwithstanding, the President blurted to New Hampshire Public Radio on May 19 that he was going to have a new budget which would be in balance in ten years. (The interview wasn't released by the White House, but aides who had been in the Oval Office when Clinton made these comments understood right away that this was going to present a problem.) Clinton also said in the interview that he wanted to review the "actual budget the Republicans finally agree on" before he offered his own. These remarks set off a tempest among Republicans.

Aides tried to analyze why Clinton had made these comments, but the most likely explanation was that he just felt like saying it. One aide said, "He thought he was just talking to New Hampshire," in which case Clinton hadn't yet completely absorbed the fact that a President couldn't confine his remarks to one group or one state—a problem that was to recur. When, on Tuesday, May 23, the President was being prepared for Rose Garden remarks that would march back from the New Hampshire comments, the statement offered by Morris virtually committed the President to a new budget. The President's ultimate comments were less committal. An aide encountered in the White House sighed and said, "It's going to be a long year."

On the evening of Memorial Day, several top aides, plus the Vice President, came back from their abbreviated holiday weekends to discuss when they could be ready to offer a budget. The President wanted to know how soon the new proposal could be drawn up in a form that he could present. Subsequent events—an uproar over the President's remarks about a new use of U.S. troops in Bosnia, and the celebrations (led by Clinton at a White House lunch and at a Pentagon ceremony) of the rescue of Air Force Captain Scott O'Grady after five days in Serbian-held territory in Bosnia— were said by some White House aides to have gotten in the way of an Oval Office address on the budget, but the plain fact was that the budget wasn't ready. The President was hell-bent for going ahead. He had made one of the most important decisions thus far of his Presidency.

•

On May 16, the House passed a bill that dramatically reduced the reach of the Clean Water Act of 1972—widely regarded as the most successful of the environmental laws. By some estimates, the bill would remove half the nation's wetlands from federal protection, making them available for developers, agriculture, and industry. Transportation and Infrastructure Committee Chairman Bud Shuster, of Pennsylvania, said that the bill was necessary so as to remove control of the nation's water protection laws from "environmental extremists."

This time, a troubled Sherwood Boehlert led over thirty moderate Republicans in opposition to the bill. "This is a terrible bill," Boehlert said, but it passed by a vote of 240–185. Boehlert and others took comfort in the fact that there weren't enough favorable votes to override a veto.

In the wake of the bill's passage, Clinton made his most effective performance thus far to demonstrate opposition to a congressional action. Morris and Curry had been arguing that the White House was "giving away" the environmental issue by not aggressively confronting the Republicans on their efforts to weaken the laws. Other White House aides still believed that the environmental issue wasn't all that important politically, that it wasn't a "cutting" issue.

Teddy Roosevelt–like, Clinton appeared in a picturesque setting at Pierce Mill, in Rock Creek Park, with a clear view of the running stream behind him. He said that he would veto the House-passed bill and accused the House of colluding with industry to produce a "Dirty Water Act." There should have been more events like that.

17

NEWT SOARS, DOLE MANEUVERS

"Let's Shake Hands Right Here in Front of Everybody"

Through another bit of verbal carelessness, Clinton stumbled into a "town meeting" with Gingrich in New Hampshire. Both were scheduled to be in the state on the second weekend in June, and when Clinton allowed that he would like to take Gingrich around to places in the state he had visited as a candidate in 1992 and engage him in a joint discussion with some citizens, Gingrich, who rarely missed a spotlight, jumped. Though some Presidential advisers had deep misgivings about Clinton's sharing the stage with Gingrich, it did guarantee more press coverage than Clinton alone would have received.

The fact that Gingrich was going to New Hampshire at all inevitably heightened speculation that he might yet enter the Presidential race. But Gingrich was actually after other things: remaining the definer of Republican positions for as long as possible—until the race itself if he could, and even into the Republican Presidency that might follow Clinton's first and only term—and selling his book, which was about to be published. A close associate of Gingrich's said, "He's dragging it along as far as he can. He wants the Republicans to run on his agenda." Gingrich himself said in New Hampshire, "I'm trying to shape the entire language and ideas of the 1996 campaign."

Gingrich was soaring. "He's untethered," a close associate said. "There's no one who'll say no to Newt now. Joe Gaylord won't stand up to him." He was receiving more attention than any other political figure in the country, President included, and he was about to make big money. (In a response to a warning from the House Ethics Committee, Gingrich said that he would pay his own expenses for his twenty-five-city book tour. Friends had advised him that a book tour was a poor idea.) He also said that he would donate the royalties from the books he sold at signings to a program, Earning by Learning, which he helped start, that paid children to read. Gingrich was very proud of that program, and talked about it a lot. (The *Wall Street Journal* later revealed that almost half the donations to the project, from business and trade associations as well as Gingrich's speaking fees from such groups and others, went to a part-time staff member in Gingrich's office who was writing Gingrich's official biography.) He estimated that the signings would bring in about $100,000—a tiny portion of the $4.5 million he hoped to earn from the book, *To Renew America*. (The novel, *1945*, was published at about the same time—the trashiness of it slightly reduced after early excerpts produced much snickering. There was still a "pouting sex kitten" but now she wasn't "athwart" anyone.)

Gingrich still did not intend to run for President in 1996. He needed more time to put personal problems behind him, and to build something resembling a campaign organization. But according to a close adviser, Gingrich did plan to run in 2000: the eight-year term limit on his Speakership would be about to run out, and he would have wrung about all he could from the Congress. In a recent conversation with Phil Gramm, Gingrich had said that he would run only if Dole's candidacy collapsed because of some physical ailment. Gramm was reportedly not pleased to hear this. The close adviser said that Gingrich didn't want Gramm to be President. Dole, however, was more likely to let Gingrich set the agenda.

In any event, Gingrich's political standing in the country wasn't the sort of thing on which successful Presidential candidacies are built. An NBC/ *Wall Street Journal* poll, released on June 8, showed Clinton trouncing Gingrich in a Presidential matchup (55–28); when Republicans were asked if they would like to see Gingrich seek the nomination, 21 percent said yes and 64 percent said no.

From the outset there was a false air to the encounter between Gingrich and Clinton in the backyard of a senior citizens complex in Claremont, the site originally picked for a Clinton event. On a sunny afternoon, a forest of green trees behind them, the nation's two preeminent political figures sat on tall stools, and in this most unusual situation came off as a couple of guys with white hair, in blue suits, chewing the fat. The wonks were showing off. People could well forget that there were big issues at stake. Both men strove for amicability. Gingrich, wearing his cherubic face and nice-guy demeanor, also played to the audience by referring more than once to having spoken that day with his mother and his mother-in-law about Medicare.

Gingrich made some not-very-funny jokes about New Hampshire's moose and donuts, and he laughed a little too hard and loudly at Clinton's not-wildly-funny jokes.

When Clinton said that the rate of increase in Medicare and Medicaid costs had to be reduced—"We agree on that"—a delighted Gingrich, with perhaps unconscious condescension, asked the audience to applaud the President of the United States. When they got a question about political reform, Gingrich proposed a "blue ribbon commission," which Clinton said he accepted "in a heartbeat." Gingrich, who had little interest in reforming the campaign finance or lobbying laws—and Clinton hadn't seriously pursued campaign finance reform in his first two years—said, "Let's shake hands right here in front of everybody," and the two men shook hands. (This was followed in subsequent weeks by Clinton's apparent efforts to lure Gingrich into establishing such a commission—knowing that Gingrich, dependent on the new flows of money in his party's direction, wouldn't be eager, which turned out to be the case.)

They mutually complained about the press, and Clinton seemed envious when he said that sometimes it takes a "fairly extreme statement" to break through Washington's static and that Gingrich could "break through like nobody I've seen in a long time."

A few differences—on the role of the U.N., on the minimum wage, and on Clinton's national service program—were aired, but their supposed fundamental differences weren't. Clinton did take the opportunity of making the closing remarks to raise some of the "big issues": about the role of the federal government, about the importance of reducing the budget deficit "as opposed to dealing with . . . the needs of our people for more investment in education and training."

The tone of the event matched the public desire, as reflected in polls, for "civility" in politics. It was seized upon by idealists and cynics alike. The two men's labored camaraderie was fake and misleading, and in a sense said all the rest of it's a game, we're just kidding. It was a faux event.

Following the weekend, Gingrich was on a high. He had got more than he had counted on out of the New Hampshire trip. He had been put on a Presidential level. He felt that though the time to run for the Presidency hadn't come, he had done the right thing for 2000. But Gingrich wouldn't want to totally let go, as long as the speculation helped him—and helped him sell his book. (Within two weeks the book was on the best-seller lists.) In an appearance on the *Charlie Rose* show, on July 6 Gingrich said that if there continued to be speculation that he would run for President, "More people will read the book . . . it doesn't cost me anything to not say no."

But Gingrich remained tempted, more inclined to run than Joe Gaylord, for one, wanted him to be. Gaylord thought that the timing wasn't right: that Gingrich, for all the coverage of him, was still a stranger to the party's

rank and file, that the new Republican advantage hadn't yet been ce-
mented. Gingrich's beginning to say later that if Dole's candidacy collapsed
and Colin Powell didn't run, he might, not only kept the speculation use-
fully alive but fit Gingrich's thinking that campaigns went on too long,
anyway—so he still had time to get in.

In mid-June, Bob Dole had another problem to work out. Earlier in the
year, he had said that he wasn't certain he would allow the nomination of
Dr. Henry Foster as Surgeon General to come to a vote in the Senate. Phil
Gramm had then one-upped him by saying that if Foster's nomination was
brought to the floor he would filibuster against it. Yet for Dole to keep
Foster from even coming to a vote was an untenable position: it looked
mean, and it would be an extreme act. But he couldn't allow Gramm to
grab the limelight. So the master tactician came up with a plan: as soon as
he thought he had the votes, he would let the nomination come up and
move at once to cut off the filibuster before it happened, showing that
there weren't enough votes to end a filibuster—thus depriving Gramm of
his opportunity and Clinton his nominee. He would have two votes on the
filibuster, on consecutive days, depriving the Democrats an opportunity to
peel away Republicans.

Some Republican senators were perturbed because they felt that Foster
should be voted on on the merits. Some, such as also-candidate Arlen
Specter, supported the nomination, which both Clinton and the far right
had turned into the issue of abortion. (Specter was pro-choice.) Dr. Foster's
having given varying accounts at first of how many abortions he had performed allowed some opponents to cast the issue as one of "credibility."
One Republican senator said, "It's an abortion issue which is defined as a
candor issue."

After being heavily coached in Sunday afternoon training sessions by
White House aides and allies, Foster had made a successful appearance
before the Labor and Human Resources Committee. He showed himself to
be a decent, compassionate man, who had done important work trying to
lower teen pregnancy among poor blacks. But there was a legitimate question of whether, through a combination of White House blundering and
his own naïveté and his having become a pawn in the larger abortion issue,
he could have the moral authority that a Surgeon General, whose role was
essentially that of a preacher, should.

Dole wanted more than the forty-one votes needed to block a cloture
move, so as to protect any Republican senator from accusations of casting
the vote that killed the Foster nomination. When he had forty-three votes,
he scheduled the roll calls to begin two days later.

On Tuesday, June 20, the day before the first of the cloture votes, at the regular Republican Policy Committee luncheon, Dole made a personal appeal. He had enough votes, but was making sure they were nailed down. "This is a matter of leadership," he said. "We have to stick together on this thing." He added, "The White House has been playing politics. The guy hasn't been forthright. We should get it over with this week."

Trent Lott had been carefully counting the votes. Lott prided himself on his vote-counting prowess. He said, "I look into their eyes. I went to each member at least twice. I watch their eyes, I watch their body language. Until they look me in the eye and say, 'Yes, I'm with you, you can count on me,' I don't put them down as with us." In the case of the Foster vote, Lott said, "I said, 'Look at me now. I'm not talking to you as Trent Lott or as the whip, I'm speaking for the leader when I say this is the plan and this is what we want you to do.' "

On the first vote, June 21, on the nonfilibuster filibuster, the Senate voted 57–43 to cut it off—three votes short of the 60 needed.

Clinton, trying to establish his own leadership, said somewhat heatedly, "A small minority [of senators] are using the nomination to dictate a litmus test to the rest of America."

The vote on the second roll call, on June 22, was the same as on the first.

Yet, following his victory, Dole made a strangely sour speech to the Senate. "Facts can be stubborn things," Dole said, referring to past Democratic efforts to deny Presidential nominations. "They are rarely noted by the media, not often used in this Chamber," he said, "but they show that we have a double standard and it is alive and well. . . . We hear all the hand-wringing over there [the Democratic side] and all the talk about Presidential politics on this side and nothing about Presidential politics downtown. This is not about Presidential politics."

After the voting on Dr. Foster, there was a great deal of speculation, Washington-style, about its implications. There was speculation that Clinton had helped himself, and Dole had hurt himself, by their respective positions on abortion in relation to the Foster case. Poll data received at the White House showed Clinton to be doing very well in this respect. (This may have had something to do with Foster's being almost constantly at Clinton's side when Clinton was in Arkansas the following weekend.) A Dole supporter said, "I don't think the Foster issue will be a general election problem for Dole. And it's hard to overstate what it did for the nomination fight. It undercut the conservative challenge of his being both the Senate leader and a candidate. It also deprived Gramm of his time in the sun." Dole's legislative prowess was widely admired in Washington.

But of course this had nothing to do with leading the country.

18

BUDGET REDUX

"If It's Not Right, It's My Call"

Minority Leaders Tom Daschle and Dick Gephardt were growing increasingly concerned that the President was going to short-circuit their strategy of attacking the Republicans on Medicare by offering his own budget. Panetta had been warning them that the President felt that he needed to offer a new budget, and soon. A same-party congressional leader has a lot of sources of information about what's going on in the administration, and both leaders knew that virtually the entire White House staff was against the President's putting forth his own budget anytime soon, and that Panetta and Stephanopoulos were particularly upset.

Daschle and Gephardt each had lunch with the President in late May, and tried to convince him to stay on his present course. Clinton said that at some point he needed a budget, a blueprint to work from, if he was going to end up in negotiations with the Republicans. He said he was worried about the possibility of a "train wreck."

Gephardt argued that there were a lot of people "out there" who hadn't yet received the information about the Republicans' proposals, that they didn't tune in, and that it takes an extraordinary effort to get through, and more time was needed.

Other leading congressional Democrats met with Clinton in late May and said that they needed more time to soften up the Republicans. (One said at that time, "I think the President being the policy wonk that he is really feels uncomfortable not going forward full speed ahead and offering his serious budget.") Clinton's D.L.C. colleagues in the Senate (Chuck Robb, of Virginia, Joseph Lieberman, of Connecticut, the current chairman, and John Breaux, the past chairman) advised the President that he should agree to talk to the Republicans, but not offer his own budget, lest it become the issue.

Gephardt and Daschle had been sharing their concerns and after his lunch with the President, Gephardt called Panetta and suggested that the two leaders meet together with the President. We understand where he is, Gephardt told a sympathetic Panetta, and he understands where we are, and we need more time to get our point across. (Gephardt told Panetta that the President should follow the example of the Mel Gibson figure in the movie *Braveheart*—William Wallace, the leader of the Scottish rebels who sought independence from England. Wallace's battle strategy was to wait until the enemy was vulnerable and then strike.) On Thursday afternoon, June 8, Daschle and Gephardt met with the President in the Oval Office. They urged him to wait until later in the summer or the early fall. Daschle told the President that he felt more strongly about this than about any other matter he had discussed with him. Gephardt told the President, "You have to show patience."

The two leaders left the meeting aware that the President wanted to go ahead soon, but under the impression that he hadn't made a decision as to when he would move, and that they would talk again. On the following Monday, Gephardt phoned Panetta and asked the status of the matter and was told that no decision had been made and that he would be informed when one was. At about nine-thirty the next morning, June 13, Gephardt learned from a report by Wolf Blitzer, on CNN, that the President would announce a new budget that evening.

One reason for the White House's secrecy was that Clinton and Gore felt, not without reason, that once Members of Congress were briefed the story would be out and the ensuing controversy would overtake the President's speech—and the networks would turn him down on the ground that he wasn't making news. They were willing to take the risk of ruffling congressional feathers. (In an unusual move, and as a sign of the importance he attached to what he wanted to do, Clinton had Gore call the networks to ask for the time. And, ironically, that's how the story got out.) The President wanted to reach as wide an audience as he could with his statement that he favored a balanced budget. Thus Panetta went along with misleading his old colleagues. Later that morning, Griffin phoned aides to Daschle and Gephardt to tell them that the President would be making a speech that night, and asked if they thought a meeting that day was a good idea. They said that it was too late for that, that there was nothing left to talk about. Later that day, the President and Gephardt traded calls (Gephardt was at a daughter's graduation) but never spoke directly.

•

At a Cabinet meeting at five that afternoon, Clinton said that the President of the United States had the responsibility of being in the discussion, and that "the ticket to admission to American politics is a balanced budget." To some of his Cabinet officers, he seemed more confident and determined than they had seen him in a long time. Clinton told them that he believed that he was doing the right thing, and, "If it's not right, it's my call."

In his unusually brief (five minutes) Oval Office address on Tuesday night—which ran on all the broadcast networks and CNN—the President, seated stiffly at his desk, hands clasped in front of him, said right off that he proposed to balance the budget by cutting $1.1 trillion over ten years, and wouldn't raise taxes. He said that his five priorities were to not cut education, to control health care costs, to "cut taxes for the middle class and not the wealthy," to "cut welfare but save enough to protect children and move able-bodied people from welfare to work," and to not "put the brakes on so fast that we risk our economic prosperity." He continued, "This can be a turning point for us." He said that Medicare could be cut without cutting benefits. "This debate must go beyond partisanship," Clinton said, knowing that it wouldn't. In an allusion to the positive public reaction to his polite encounter with Gingrich the previous weekend, Clinton said, of the budget debate, "We ought to approach it in the same spirit of openness and civility [as] when the Speaker and I talked in New Hampshire last Sunday," and that both sides should "forget about who gets the political advantage."

Dole, in his response, getting in the latest groove, made a friendly reference—"As I told the President when we spoke earlier this evening"—that this was "a moment of powerful potential." But, being in quest of nomination, Dole also attacked Democratic philosophy and reminded the audience that Clinton's first budget had been defeated in the Senate 99–0.

The documents that had been released to the press by the White House that afternoon weren't very detailed. In essence, Clinton proposed to cut most discretionary domestic programs by twenty-five percent, less than the pending Republican budget resolutions, and to exempt education, training, and science research. His health care proposal, far less sweeping than his original one, consisted of insurance reforms and (as before) a dependence on "managed care" to cut costs. His Medicare cut (about $125 billion) was more than $100 billion less than in the Republican proposals ($256 billion by the Senate, $288 billion by the House), and assumed that there needed to be no increases in premiums or other changes for beneficiaries. (But only by relying on the more optimistic economic projections of the Office of Management and Budget could the administration keep its Medicare figure that low.) The President made no actual proposal for changing Medicare—nor was he going to. That way, it was thought, the heat could stay on the Republicans, who would have to present a real proposal for the reconciliation bill in the fall. By preserving his middle-class tax cut, first proposed in the post-election panic, Clinton put more pressure on domestic programs. Like the Republicans' plans, Clinton's also assumed $170 billion in savings as a result of balancing the budget.

Clinton had already said that he wouldn't cut agriculture programs as deeply as the Republicans were proposing to do. (At a National Rural Conference in Ames, Iowa, in late May, he had pledged to protect a pork research project at Iowa State University.)

The expressions of anger at the President's speech in the House Democratic caucus and message group meeting the next morning, and some public statements by House Democrats, went further and were more disrespectful of the Presidency than any in memory by members of the same party. The White House sent Stephanopoulos, Griffin, and Alice Rivlin to the caucus. Rivlin, who tried to explain the economic theory behind the new approach, was virtually hooted at. The Democrats' anger was fed by the sneaky way the matter had been handled and also, as it happened, by the Clinton-Gingrich get-together in New Hampshire the previous Sunday. A Democratic leadership aide said, "The worst thing for House Democrats was the Sunday event with Gingrich. They feel that Gingrich is under a dark ethics cloud. He'd thrown dirt at Democrats for years, and there he was being treated like he's Mother Teresa." But there were substantive objections as well, especially the fact that Clinton himself was proposing a tax cut and cutting Medicare to balance the budget—the very thing the Democrats had been accusing the Republicans of (at a different level). A Democratic aide said, "A lot of times in Washington, people complain about the timing when they're really upset about the substance." Numerous Democrats believed there was no substantive point in going for a balanced budget. The Democrats had been making an issue of the fact that the size of the tax cut under discussion among the Republicans was about the same size as the Medicare cut. "You can use Medicare and the tax cut for literally almost every group," a House Democrat said. In the caucus meeting on Wednesday morning, Rosa DeLauro, a leader of the message group, said that she felt "betrayed."

A White House aide said, "They were replaying ketchup in their heads. That worked. And people here agreed." He added, "Everyone felt that that period succeeded. And they wanted to have the same opportunity on Medicare."

The House Democrats felt that they had found the issue that would help them retain their seats and even augment their ranks in 1996.

•

On Capitol Hill the same day, Panetta met with Gingrich, Dole, Domenici, and Kasich. Panetta, speaking as a former Budget Committee chairman himself, told the group, "In the end, you're going to have to move toward us on education, Medicare, Medicaid, and the tax cut—it's that simple."

Gingrich remarked that they could probably agree to eight years to balance the budget, rather than the Republicans' seven or the President's ten.

Domenici remarked, "Newt, don't start negotiating here."

Matters were made worse on Capitol Hill by comments by an unnamed "administration official" that the new budget was a "declaration of independence" from the congressional Democrats, adding, "They did not get us elected; sticking with them has caused us some of our biggest problems." The President's move fit Morris's theory of "triangulation": that Clinton should distinguish his differences with both Democratic and Republican policies.

George Miller, co-chairman of the House Democratic Policy Group, said, "We've known since the election that the President would have to do what's good for the President, and the Democrats in Congress would have to do what's good for them. But you ought to try to give the other party leaders some heads up." Miller said, "I think Clinton *wanted* a pretty sound chorus of Democratic anger." Some House Democrats cited a recent poll by the *Los Angeles Times* that indicated that their message about Medicare/ taxes was beginning to get through. They felt that they had been following White House strategy—one that helped them as well—and suddenly the President cut them off at the knees. They decided to, as one member put it, "ignore the President's proposal and keep doing what we're doing."

David Skaggs, one of the less agitated Democrats, said, "The timing was odd; there is no presenting reason to do this right now. The soonest occasion would be when the Republicans couldn't reach a budget resolution agreement or had reached one—an external event to which he could say, I'm stepping in now. This was a *deus ex machina* action with no apparent reason. One of the reasons people feel betrayed is they had taken the cue from the White House to beat up on Republicans on Medicare every day. They thought they were being good soldiers and suddenly the rationale wasn't there."

Black members were already upset with Clinton's having pledged a review of affirmative action; Hispanics were already angry over Clinton's appearing to play to the growing national antipathy to immigrants. A Democratic member said that he had never heard such talk about a President by members of his own party. "People just trash him as if he's nothing." Referring to a recent Clinton television appearance, the member said, "Here he comes off Oklahoma and looks more like a President than ever, very Presidential and moving. Then he goes on *Larry King Live* and does a Brando imitation. I don't know why he needs to do that. He's the President of the United States."

The anger of certain important Democrats could spell trouble for the President later. Charles Rangel was furious. David Obey, of Wisconsin, the ranking Democrat on the House Budget Committee, a man quick to anger and slow to forget and by now many times provoked, said to the press: "I think most of us learned some time ago, if you don't like the President's position on a particular issue, you simply need to wait a few weeks. If you can follow this White House on the budget, you are a whole lot smarter than I am."

The outburst was stronger than the White House expected, and some officials worried that the reaction would affect their dealing with the Congress all year.

Some senior administration officials expressed their unhappiness privately. Referring to the Republicans, one said, "They were squirming. We made them squirm. And then suddenly, we were doing what they were doing." Some thought that the thing could have been done without blowing up the Democratic Party—and continued to believe that it should have been done later.

Gingrich, wheeling through Capitol hallways as he returned to his office after delivering a speech on medical technology innovations (mentioning Pitt the Younger and Adam Smith and the Tofflers) to a forum convened in the basement by the Progress & Freedom Foundation, had a very satisfied look. After all, Clinton in his Oval Office speech the night before had just come over onto his territory. Further, Clinton was now providing cover on Medicare. To boot, the Democrats were now deeply split. (One Gingrich adviser was less delighted, because Clinton had taken from them the argument that the Republicans were for a balanced budget and the Democrats weren't. "We were always able to fall back on that when we were criticized for 'cuts,' " the adviser said.)

"I think it's helpful," Gingrich said with a slightly wicked smile, adding, "It changes the whole model of the debate." He continued, "He agrees that the budget needs balancing, he agrees that Medicare needs change, he agrees there should be tax cuts, he agrees domestic spending should be restrained, he agrees defense has been cut deeply enough. I mean, the President has now conceded that on those major issues we're right. Now we're arguing detail, and I think that's an enormous step."

Gingrich and Dole, who met three times in the course of the day after the President's speech, issued a statement welcoming the President's new approach. Republican leaders speculated that the deep division between the White House and the House Democrats could help the Republicans win more of their tax cuts and spending cuts. In one strategy meeting, Gingrich said, "Anything is possible with Clinton." He added, "You can't assume anything with Clinton. Just because he doesn't propose something doesn't mean he won't accept it in the end."

(Just as Gingrich told people that Clinton was so unpredictable that he could never tell what he was going to do, Clinton told people that he never knew which Gingrich personality he would encounter—"his Jekyll or his Hyde.")

The Saturday, June 17, papers carried stories saying that the President's new budget would run a $200 billion deficit on into the future. This was the same deficit amount as projected by his first budget of the year. Republicans were soon criticizing his second one on these grounds.

But because the Republicans, after first welcoming the President's concession, effectively dismissed Clinton's budget out of hand, both Clinton and the Capitol Hill Democrats avoided some of the damage that the Democrats had anticipated. Since his new budget wasn't taken seriously, either, the Democrats and the President had more time to attack the Republicans for seeking to cut Medicare "to pay for tax cuts for the wealthy."

Clinton, who at times reminded people that he was capable of the long view (that characteristic helped elect him in the first place), turned out to be right that he needed a specific counterproposal on the budget in order to have legitimacy when he criticized the Republican proposal. His interest and those of the congressional Democrats inevitably diverged. They had different exigencies.

The battle within the White House left its scars. For the first time, there were distinct factions, suspicious of each other and even plotting against each other. "Welcome to Beirut on the Potomac," one White House aide said not long afterward. One camp consisted of Morris, Curry, Don Baer, and Jack Quinn, plus Doug Schoen, of the Penn & Schoen polling group Morris had brought in—who kept in close communication with each other. Gore was often in sympathy with this group. The other consisted of Panetta, Stephanopoulos, Ickes, and some more junior members of the staff. The issue was only in part ideology. Though the Morris group was intent on moving Clinton to the center and keeping him there, and the other group tended to reflect more traditional Democratic politics, the philosophical demarcation lines weren't so clear. It wasn't as if the Clinton White House was clearly divided between liberal Democrats and the D.L.C. As one official put it, "Morris is a gyroscope, with no given set of beliefs." Morale was low among those not in the Morris-Curry camp—because they had lost power, or because they didn't know what was going on, or both. It wasn't just that some of them had lost a big struggle over the budget, but also that aides would work hard on a policy, or a speech, only to see it torn up at the last moment, or disappear into a black hole. One aide said of Morris, "It's not that he's not clever, but it's what he does with people's work." Curry was still treated badly by White House aides of longer standing. Though his title was Counselor to the President, Panetta didn't include him in the regular 7:30 A.M. meetings of top Presidential advisers. Other aides didn't understand why he had suddenly landed in their midst. This turmoil was, of course, the fault of the President, who should have set his staff straight. Aides felt that just as the White House was beginning to work better, a new spanner had been thrown into the works. Not everyone disagreed with everything Morris proposed—he and Curry had some good ideas. The problem was the new unpredictability, and the worry that Clinton would seem even more unrooted—and the resentment of a power shift.

Some observers saw a danger in having a man without an anchor become the chief adviser to a President without an anchor. Inside the White House, the question was which Bill Clinton would be offered to the electorate in 1996. The Morris camp argued that by guiding Clinton back to the center, and away from the demands of the congressional Democratic Party, they had shown him the way to the place where he was most comfortable. According to this argument, Clinton did have a core but had been lured away from it by his advisers and the Democratic powers-that-were on Capitol Hill. Someone with a strong core shouldn't be very lurable. If Clinton was back to where he was most comfortable, that should be apparent in his demeanor as well as his actions as the year went on.

The Senate-House conference on the budget resolution took three and a half weeks, largely because of the difference between the two houses over taxes, and to a lesser extent, over defense. Clinton's new budget was a nonfactor. The problem was that the pressures on Dole were different from those on Gingrich, and the conferees representing the two houses were pulled in different directions.

The two sticking points were the tax cuts and defense. Twelve moderate Republican senators wrote to Dole saying that tax cuts shouldn't be considered until it was clear that the budget was on its way to balance, as certified by the C.B.O., while most House Republicans were insisting on a sizable tax cut without delay. (There was a great deal of such letter writing in the 104th Congress, leading one Republican congressman to remark, "I wonder when we're going to get around to governance.")

Dick Armey struck the position that the final tax cuts had to amount to $300 billion, a figure he knew wouldn't be reached, but one that he hoped would buttress the House negotiators' position. After some time, Gingrich said that $250 billion would suit him. (A leadership aide said, "If we're debating between $250 and $300 billion we're in happy hunting ground.") Archer became impatient with Domenici's lectures (as Archer saw them) on why the tax cuts had to be limited to the dividend that would come from balancing the budget. Domenici, the experienced legislator with twenty-one Senate years behind him, tried to be patient with Kasich, who, he felt, was learning.

On Wednesday, June 21, after the conference had reached its third week, Gingrich, Dole, and Haley Barbour met in Dole's office. Barbour was worried that if the negotiations weren't completed before the July 4 recess things could begin to unravel. The conferees agreed easily to in essence split the difference on Medicare, calling for cuts of $270 billion. And they had agreed on abolishing only the Commerce Department; Domenici had strongly opposed abolishing Education and Energy as well.

Domenici had proposed the day before that the Senate was willing to split the difference on the increase in defense spending and that the most that the tax cut could be was about $228 billion. (Domenici asked Gingrich to meet with three senators who had problems with even splitting the difference on defense; Gingrich said that he would.) Armey, who attended the meeting, spoke at length about the importance of a larger tax cut. Gingrich said that he would have real problems taking back to the House a tax cut below $250 billion. At that point, Dole, who felt that the time had come to reach an agreement, leaned over to Gingrich and suggested that the two of them and Barbour get together and work it out.

In the course of these discussions, Gingrich more than once suggested doing something-or-other in the early years and that they could worry about the later years "after we get President Dole in the White House." Dole would simply nod, treating it not as a friendly jest but as sensible planning.

Dole seemed to feel that it was very important that he, himself, deliver the votes on the budget. When other senators or even staff members suggested that they would have a real problem getting people to agree on this or that, Dole reacted as if he didn't like any suggestion that he couldn't personally deliver the votes. He would say, "Look, you know [X] will be there, and so will the others." One participant in the conference said, "He needed a certain kind of budget that, as a Presidential candidate, would give Phil Gramm no footholds." Dole couldn't let it appear that the Senate moderates could tie his hands. The participant said, "He took the thing that Gramm was trying to beat him up on—that he's just a deal-maker—and turned it into his greatest strength. He was saying, 'Yeah, I'm a deal-maker. I'm the deal-maker who can deliver a budget, I'm the deal-maker who can stop Henry Foster.' "

In the meeting of Gingrich, Dole, and Barbour, Gingrich noted that he had publicly suggested tax cuts of $250 billion, and said that "every billion

I go below it I get extra heat." (The CATs group had been warning Gingrich against going below $250 billion.) Then Gingrich added, "I do not believe I can go below $245 billion. If I go below that it starts to become a huge problem on our side."

Barbour then intervened, saying, "Look, Bob, can we agree on $245 billion? Can we close the deal?" But the matter remained unsettled, as both sides tested the waters.

On the next day, Thursday, when the Senate conferees still weren't prepared to offer the House enough in the way of tax cuts, Sheila Burke, Dole's chief of staff, called Dole, who was on the floor (dealing with the Foster nomination), and asked him to come back to the meeting. Dole told the House conferees that what they were offering the Senate wasn't sufficient, and he asked Burke to go see Dan Meyer, Gingrich's chief of staff. She managed to get some more funds for education, to mollify moderates William Cohen and Olympia Snowe (also Republican of Maine), and for agriculture, to mollify Charles Grassley.

Burke called Dole and suggested that he meet her in Meyer's office—Dole and Gingrich could get to each other's suites through a back passage, avoiding public hallways—and Meyer called Gingrich and asked that he join them. The Senate side was now proposing a split in defense, and a tax cut of $240 billion. Gingrich said, "Look, I can't tell you that I'll have a revolt in the House over defense—it's very bitter for me to have to accept this number—but I can't go lower on taxes." Dole left to meet in his office with Domenici, where he told Domenici, "We've got to do $245 billion on taxes and a little on defense and they'll give us back some agriculture and some education." The senators returned to Meyer's office and said, "We have a deal." (The smallish office was now filled with so many people—the Republican leaders and their chiefs of staff, Meyer's assistant, committee aides, press aides, and the like—that it took on the aspect of the stateroom in the Marx Brothers' *A Night at the Opera*.) The hope was to announce the agreement in time for the news broadcast that night. Kasich had left for the airport, to go to Ohio, but called Gingrich, and when he learned of the pending deal, returned to the Capitol. He wasn't happy about all of its details.

Domenici won the point that the tax cuts couldn't be considered until congressional committees working on the final reconciliation bill produced legislation that the Congressional Budget Office certified would put the budget on the path to balance. Because of the resistance the House tax cuts would meet among several Senate Republicans, Dole had been careful to keep the conferees from stating how the tax cuts would be applied, saying that that would be up to the Finance Committee. Dole said that he would have trouble sustaining the $200,000 cap on a family's income for receiving the child tax credit. "That made a huge difference in getting the moderates to go along," one conference attendee said. "They weren't faced with policy yet." There was much commentary at the time that Dole had lost out to Gingrich in the conference, but in fact Dole, his Presidential ambitions in mind, wanted a conference result that was closer to the House position.

Gingrich was satisfied with the results. He said in an interview, "Remember that we started in January with the Senate, which didn't believe in a balanced budget goal, didn't believe in seven years, didn't believe in tax cuts, and didn't believe defense should be increased—other than that we were very close."

But the proximateness of $270 billion in Medicare cuts and $245 billion in tax cuts was going to cause Gingrich problems.

19

BOSNIA

"Is This Administration Policy Now?"

The fall of Srebrenica on July 11 signaled the collapse of United States and U.N. strategy for Bosnia. The six so-called safe areas, designated in May of 1993 by a U.N. resolution, hadn't been guaranteed any real protection. Later that month, to head off proposals by other countries that the U.S. join in international protection of these areas, Secretary of State Warren Christopher had succeeded in getting an agreement—solemnly signed in a State Department proceeding—that the allies would protect those areas, with the U.S. promising to help from the air if the United Nations Protection Force, or UNPROFOR, got in trouble.

When Srebrenica came close to being overrun by Serb forces in the spring of 1993, pictures of the fighting had exerted a strong emotional pull on the public, and had led President Clinton to vow to take strong new action. Its actual fall, a little over two years later, produced harrowing pictures of Muslim women being herded into buses, and draft-age men being led away to an unknown fate (later determined to have been a massacre, one of several)—"ethnic cleansing" before our very eyes. U.S. policy making was in even more disarray than usual. The U.N. role had come to a dead end. The "Contact Group" of countries that was supposed to find a diplomatic settlement was moribund. The relationship between Secretary of State Warren Christopher and National Security Adviser Anthony Lake was still not a good one, replete as it was with mistrust and unilateral maneuvering, and this had substantive effects on U.S. policy making.

The President had once again checked out on the question of Bosnia —and on foreign policy in general—unless paying attention to it was inescapable. Yet some high foreign policy officials had the increasingly sickening sense that Bosnia could destroy Clinton's Presidency. Clinton eventually came to understand this as well.

If the United States had to honor Clinton's pledge, made in 1993 without a great deal of thought, to assist in a withdrawal of the UNPROFOR troops, the likelihood of casualties was very strong. One official said, "If he gets caught in a Desert One [Jimmy Carter's failed effort to rescue hostages held in Iran], he can't survive it."

There were within the administration a few voices that said that since UNPROFOR wasn't tenable for much longer, the administration should go ahead with letting the forces withdraw and "get it over with." (This would avoid having the withdrawal take place too close to the 1996 election, and would clear the way for greater arming of the Bosnian Muslims.)

In the view of some officials, the administration's Bosnia policy was a horror—a foreign policy horror, of course, but also a domestic political horror. They volunteered that though they had inherited a bad situation— the Bush administration had taken a pass—they had made it worse. They did this, the thinking went, by talking about the problem in a way that suggested that the U.S. could do more than it was willing to, and by using inflated rhetoric. They had said that the Bosnian Serb attack on Muslim-held areas in Bosnia was an affront to the U.S.'s national interest, but, this thinking went, if it was an affront to our national interest, officials should have been willing to put a half million troops in Bosnia. But they hadn't been and weren't going to—the assumption, a valid one, being that the public would be strongly opposed.

Bosnian policy had been characterized by ad hockery. This tendency, plus the lack of harmony among the policymakers, plus Clinton's inattention, led to serious embarrassment, and more strain within the alliance, when in the late spring of 1995 the Bosnian Serbs launched newly aggressive strikes against the safe areas.

On Sunday, May 28, with Sarajevo (one of the six) coming under fierce shelling from heavy Serb weapons, the chief policymakers met at the White House. In what had appeared at the time a triumph, the U.S. and its allies had in February 1994, under threat of bombing, forced the Serbs to put their heavy weapons under U.N. protection, rather than remove them from the area. Now they were being used by the Serbs. Sarajevo was enduring the worst fighting in fifteen months, leaving many dead and wounded. On the previous Thursday, Serb shelling killed at least seventy-one people in front of a crowded café in Tuzla, another "safe area." The U.N. "peacekeeping" mission appeared to be close to collapse, its authority nil.

The U.S.-backed policy of trying to get Slobodan Milosevic, the leader of

"Greater Serbia" and a perpetrator of the agony of Bosnia, to curb the Bosnian Serbs in exchange for a lifting of U.N.-imposed economic sanctions was getting nowhere. (A senior policymaker said, "Nobody likes that policy, but no one knows what else to do.") The allies were split over how lenient to be toward the man who had whipped Serb nationalism into war fever four years ago.

After the NATO air strikes on May 26 and 27 on bunkers in an ammunition depot in the Bosnian Serb headquarters, Pale—which had been strongly urged on reluctant U.N. officials by the United States—resulted in the Serbs taking nearly four hundred U.N. peacekeeping troops as hostages, the administration was deeply embarrassed. Some U.S. officials said they had assumed that U.N. officers would take steps to protect their troops from being taken hostage; others admitted that they had miscalculated the Bosnian Serbs' reaction to the bombing. (The Serbs had taken hostages before.) The purpose of the U.S. pressure, which had gone on for two weeks, to conduct the air strikes was to shore up the credibility of the U.N. peacekeeping effort. The resulting debacle came at a time when the Republican Congress was being particularly aggressive in trying to redirect foreign policy.

The purpose of the Sunday White House meeting of the foreign policy "Principals" was to figure out what to do. They considered contingency plans for rescuing trapped U.N. soldiers. The last thing that the administration wanted was a withdrawal of the U.N. forces, which could lead to casualties as well as embarrassment. The officials discussed whether they shouldn't be willing to help move UNPROFOR troops that were in untenable positions. The theory was that since the U.S. had a commitment to help the allies if they were in dire straits, and to help them withdraw if it came to that, mightn't it make sense to help them in ways that could keep them from having to withdraw? The administration had also made a commitment to police a peace agreement.

On Tuesday, May 30, McCurry, briefing reporters, said that the U.S. might broaden the circumstances under which it would use ground forces to help peacekeepers, to include protecting a "reconfiguration" of those troops as well as an outright "extraction" of them.

The story set off cries of outrage on Capitol Hill, and speculation that the U.S. might get itself into a land war in Bosnia. The speculation was fed further by the dispatch of 2,200 Marines on ships to the Adriatic, a maneuver that administration officials described as "purely . . . a precautionary measure." It would seem that using U.S. troops on the ground to move peacekeepers around was fraught. But the administration was now in a corner of its own making. (At the same time on Tuesday, May 30, the allies, meeting in The Hague to discuss the expansion of the U.N. force in Bosnia and giving it heavier equipment, agreed to establish a "rapid reaction force," whose main responsibility was to aid U.N. forces that got in trouble.)

Tony Lake, who had been out of town over the weekend, felt that in light of all the press and other attention to the possibility of a changed policy on Bosnia, the President should provide some explanation of the new policy in a speech he was to give to the U.S. Air Force Academy, in Colorado Springs, on Wednesday, May 31. Warren Christopher, who at the time was at the meeting in The Hague, felt strongly that the President shouldn't say anything. He believed that too much had been said already that suggested an increasing likelihood of the use of U.S. ground troops in Bosnia, that there was no point in stating a new policy which hadn't come into effect and might not be called for. Christopher called Lake and Tom Donilon, the Assistant Secretary for Public Affairs and Christopher's chief of staff, called McCurry. Lake felt that if the President didn't speak out amidst all the speculation, he would seem evasive.

The President's statement, which was changed only slightly as a result of the phone calls, said, "I believe we should be prepared to assist NATO if it decides to meet a request from the United Nations troops for help in a withdrawal or a reconfiguration and a strengthening of its forces." He added, "We have received no such request for any such assistance, and we have made no such decision." Lake himself told the press that the issue remained "up in the air."

The reaction on Capitol Hill was predictably strong. Dole said that using U.S. forces and equipment to help the U.N. force regroup "is nothing more than a policy of reinforcing failure." Dole was still championing the lifting of the arms embargo against the Muslims, and threatening to bring a resolution to the Senate floor imminently. (The Clinton administration was strongly opposed, on the ground that it would cause the U.N. forces to pull out, and lead to a wider war.) Clinton received almost no support on Capitol Hill. But Gingrich gave a muted response, saying, "We should wait to see what's happening." He added that Washington should not ignore pleas from "our allies of half a century . . . but at the same time we don't want to go and get involved."

In his Saturday radio address, Clinton narrowed the conditions under which United States forces would help UNPROFOR troops. He now said that the U.S. forces would be used only if UNPROFOR troops "become stranded," or "if a U.N. unit needs an emergency extraction." (This made the second time in ten days that the President had to take back something he had said publicly; the other was his premature announcement about a new budget.) After the radio talk, McCurry said that the U.S. would not become "a taxi service." A close adviser of the President said later that

Clinton regretted having made the statement at Colorado Springs. Another, being more to the point, said that the President was furious, that "he felt he had been mousetrapped," and that this episode deepened his lack of confidence in his foreign policy advisers (which had been an on-and-off thing for nearly two years). A President shouldn't be, or feel, "mousetrapped" by his own aides. Clinton's lack of involvement had caught up with him.

But Clinton's radio talk left questions as to what the new policy was. Christopher associates said that it was his influence that caused the President to modify the commitment in his Saturday radio address.

At the end of the week, McCurry, as an able press secretary should, tried to limit the damage. He explained that the purpose of Clinton's comments to the Air Force Academy in Colorado Springs was to convince the countries contributing UNPROFOR troops to keep them in Bosnia, saying, "We think that in the end [UNPROFOR] is one of the few pieces of leverage left to try to get them to agree to a diplomatic solution." He said, "There was a concern that the Europeans would throw in the towel."

Compounding the confusion, Defense Secretary William Perry, in Paris, said that relocation of peacekeepers was still "theoretically possible."

There were recriminations within the administration. Christopher supporters, in and out of the State Department, charged that Lake had abused his access to the President in overruling the Secretary of State, and that he hadn't understood the new policy. Matters weren't helped by the fact that neither Christopher nor the Deputy Secretary, Strobe Talbott, was invited to a briefing of the President on Friday night, June 2, by Perry and Chairman of the Joint Chiefs of Staff John Shalikashvili on the eve of their trip to Paris to meet with defense ministers and military chiefs of countries that had sent peacekeepers to Bosnia. When Talbott learned of the meeting, he phoned Lake, who told him that it was simply a military briefing. Christopher, who landed at Andrews Air Force Base about a half hour before the meeting, returned to his office and fumed. A subsequent photograph in the New York Times, showing Leon Panetta at the meeting, but not the Secretary of State, set off an internal explosion.

Lake later explained and apologized to the Principals who had not been invited—Christopher, U.N. Ambassador Madeleine Albright, C.I.A. Director John Deutch—and told them that the judgment had been that there shouldn't be an appearance of another Bosnia crisis meeting. He thought that this little session put an end to the matter. But it didn't. Christopher allies and outriders were still talking about these events—putting Lake in a bad light—weeks later.

A senior administration official said that this set of events was "more than an anecdote, because from that point on the Bosnia policy went into free fall." He continued, "Dole came on stronger than ever. The administration lost the sense of momentum it had had since Oklahoma City. The Presidency seemed confused. The allies were appalled."

In hearings before the Senate Armed Services Committee the following week, John McCain said that bombing an ammunition dump "smacks so much of the failed strategy of Vietnam that it gives me nightmares." Perry and General Shalikashvili offered differing explanations of what the new policy was. Sam Nunn had to pursue a long line of questioning in order to extract what the new policy was. John Glenn, Democrat of Ohio, asked Perry, "Is your statement this morning cleared by the White House?" And, "Is this administration policy now?"

On Thursday, June 8, Gingrich gave an angry speech to the International Republicans Institute, saying that the U.N. rules of engagement in Bosnia are "utterly by any standard insane, crazy." He said, "of the elite media," that it "doesn't want to cover" the fact that "the Soviet Empire is gone." He said that the end of the Soviet Empire "is a good thing," adding, "I know for some people in the administration it was a heartbreaker." He said, "For seventy years the American left was systematically wrong. . . . The Clinton administration is staffed with people whose historic record about the role of force, the nature of freedom, the structure of the world, is just wrong. And it's like hiring as a school bus driver someone who has had thirty-seven wrecks." He added, "It's dangerous first of all, because your enemies watch. When you are weak and confused on Bosnia, the North Koreans are watching. . . . You're never engaged in foreign policy on one topic."

On the same day as Gingrich's speech, the House voted 318–99 to lift the arms embargo. Lee Hamilton, Democrat of Indiana and the former chairman of the House International Relations Committee (formerly Foreign Affairs), who opposed lifting the embargo, said later, "The administration didn't work very hard on it." He explained the large vote for lifting the embargo: "By far, the dominant factor was frustration about Bosnia and the administration's handling of it. This was a way of expressing frustration and it's a relatively cost-free vote for an American politician. It has strong surface appeal, and there's not really any negative to voting for it. I never had any doubt about how the vote would go."

The lifting of the arms embargo was part of a foreign aid bill that slashed the aid program (about one percent of the budget) by two billion dollars over the next two years, and imposed numerous changes in foreign policy. Among the areas covered were abortion (restoring restrictions on aid for international family planning programs) and policy toward Cuba, China, North Korea, Ireland, and refugees from Indochina. The bill also folded the Agency for International Development, the United States Information

Agency, and the Arms Control and Disarmament Agency into the State Department. (The administration fought the latter provision even though Christopher had earlier sought that very change, only to be overruled by Gore.)

The overall direction of the bill was a clear sign that House International Relations Committee Chairman Benjamin Gilman, a moderate from New York, wasn't following his own inclinations.

Worried that the votes for passage were too "soft," and seeking to provide cover for Republicans—especially the freshmen—for voting for foreign aid, which most had opposed and some had run against, just before the Memorial Day recess, the House leaders suddenly put off further consideration of the legislation.

On June 7, Henry Hyde's move to repeal the War Powers Act, which (at least ostensibly) curbed an administration's authority to wage war without the consent of Congress, was defeated, even though Gingrich took to the House floor to make the final speech defending the proposal. Gingrich was furious that the administration hadn't supported the Hyde proposal even though he thought he had secured a commitment that it would do so.

Clinton had said in a Rose Garden appearance on May 23 that he would veto the House bill. He said, "Taken together, these constraints represent nothing less than a frontal assault on the authority of the President to conduct the foreign policy of the United States." McCurry, summoning one of the administration's lines of attack on the Republicans, underlined Clinton's veto threat, saying that the bill "takes us . . . towards isolationism." But the House ignored the President and adopted the most intrusive legislation on foreign policy in history, of which the lifting of the arms embargo was a part.

After Srebrenica fell, and with Zepa and Gorazde, and other safe areas, in jeopardy, Clinton foreign policy officials gathered again to figure out what to do. Jacques Chirac, the new French President, had proposed an attempt to retake Srebrenica militarily. This proposal didn't appeal to Clinton administration officials (or even the French military, or the British). With his first proposal going nowhere, Chirac then said he wanted to send a thousand additional French troops to Gorazde and requested that U.S. helicopters ferry them in. This posed a new crisis for the administration. Several high officials believed that the proposal didn't make sense—that posting another thousand troops wasn't enough to save the town, and that sending in helicopters would be too risky—but didn't want to appear to give Chirac the brush-off. Chirac, adding a new and bold voice to the dithering allied policy making on Bosnia, compared the current situation to appeasement of Hitler by Britain and France before the Second World War.

At a two-hour meeting of the foreign policy Principals (the President didn't attend) on Friday, July 14, the question of how to respond to Chirac was hashed over. The officials didn't know whether Chirac was being sincere or cynical—knowing that others wouldn't agree with his proposals, he could say that he had tried to turn things around in Bosnia, but since the allies wouldn't back him up the UNPROFOR forces should be withdrawn. Some thought that he might be being both.

Now the President decided to become engaged, because of Chirac's statements and requests; of the harrowing pictures on television of refugees from Srebrenica; and because of the challenge to his policy on Capitol Hill. Morris had spoken to him about the dangers Bosnia posed to his reelection.

The principals decided on July 14 that, though they didn't agree with Chirac's proposals, it was important to take a stand at Gorazde—because a number of British troops were stationed nearby, because the Bosnian government wanted such a stand to be taken, and because this particular "safe area" was a sizable town, whereas Zepa, which stood between Srebrenica and Gorazde, was but a series of small villages.

The Principals generally agreed that the proper response to the situation was to protect Gorazde through air strikes, this time (as opposed to nearly a year earlier when Gorazde was "defended" by a couple of "pinprick" bombings) with serious bombing, which would include targets beyond Gorazde. Officials had in mind taking out Bosnian Serb air defenses and other military targets, including infrastructure. If carried out, this would be a far greater attack than NATO had launched in Bosnia to date. Since the administration officials felt that if they dismissed Chirac's proposals they would be playing into his hands, General Shalikashvili was dispatched to London to meet with allied defense ministers and to ask questions about Chirac's proposal.

At the London meeting Shalikashvili proposed the bombing alternative, the French continued to push for adding a thousand troops to the defense of Gorazde, and the British argued against changing the situation—and the American proposal went nowhere.

Some officials became apprehensive that there would be no agreement and that the result could be the collapse of the NATO alliance. At the end of the following week, amid agonizing negotiations in London with the allies, with Christopher and Perry in attendance, and numerous calls between Clinton and Chirac and British Prime Minister John Major, the United States won an agreement of sorts on its bombing proposal. The agreement that was reached—to threaten the Bosnian Serbs that if they attacked Gorazde, they would be met with heavy bombing—left a large number of questions, and clouded any sense of an administration triumph (though it was trumpeted as one). The administration still had to work its way toward the desired end to the "dual-key" arrangement by which any NATO attacks had to be approved (and often weren't) by top U.N. officials. The U.S. had agreed to this arrangement under pressure from the British and French, and now U.N. officials showed scant interest in giving up this authority. There remained questions about the circumstances under which an air attack would be launched, and whether other "safe areas," including Sarajevo, would come under the same protection.

While the allies discussed how to implement the new policy and whether to expand it to other "safe areas," the Bosnian Serbs fired on Bihac, and continued their assault on Zepa (which fell on July 25) and the shelling of Sarajevo.

The administration's optimism that it could get rid of the "dual-key" arrangement was shaken on July 27 when Britain and France insisted on maintaining it (as did U.N. Secretary General Boutros Boutros-Ghali). The British and French attitude suggested that they were less than enthusiastic about the U.S.'s policy of heavy bombing attacks. Once again the administration was exposed as having claimed more of an agreement than had been there, and more of a plan than existed. Officials were upset by the failure to shake the U.N.

At Clinton's specific request, Dole had put off Senate debate on his resolution calling for a lifting of the arms embargo. Clinton had appealed to Dole on the ground that the allies were having very sensitive talks in London.

But after the London meeting, Dole was critical of its results: "The conferees wrote off Srebrenica and Zepa, vowed to protect Gorazde at some point, that point not being clear, and declined to respond to the dramatically worsening situation in Bihac and Sarajevo." So, on July 25, the Senate debated Dole's resolution. Dole had revised the resolution, which was co-sponsored by Joseph Lieberman, from the one he had offered the year before, to allow for an UNPROFOR pullout *before* the embargo was lifted, and to give the President twelve weeks to act on a request by the Bosnian government that UNPROFOR withdraw before lifting the embargo.

The Senate debate was emotional; senators sensed they were taking no small step in flatly reversing a major foreign-policy tenet of the administration. This was the strongest such action since the Vietnam War. It wasn't something that would be lightly done to any President, but now Clinton's standing was so low, and his policy on Bosnia had been so erratic, that the Senate didn't balk at overruling him—by a vote of 69–29. Though it was said that some Democrats would change their position if it came to a vote to override a Presidential veto, this was still a substantial rebuff. Despite the administration's strong efforts, including a visit to the Hill by Christopher, twenty-one Democrats voted for the resolution. Five Republicans voted against it.

In the debate, Dole said, "This is not about politics," and he added, "This is about life and death for a little country."

After a great expenditure of effort on the administration's part, the U.N.

on August 1 did agree to leave the decisions about bombing to the commanders in the field, and to include the other remaining "safe areas" in its ultimatum. (The Pentagon had been less eager: institutionally it was more leery of military involvement than its counterparts, but wanted more "robust"—a foreign policy makers' cliché—action if there was military intervention.) The administration's calculated risk in not discouraging a Croat offensive that began on August 4 against Serb-dominated territory in Croatia (figuring that a successful Croat attack could change the equation) paid off at least in the short term.

At the same time, foreign policy officials held meetings, some with a newly involved President, to work out a new negotiating position to present to the relevant parties in the former Yugoslavia, and to the Western allies and Russia. Clinton now recognized the danger to his Presidency posed by Bosnia. The swift Croatian victory—with the Serbs suffering a stinging defeat—gave the administration the opening it had hoped for, and Lake went off with a new negotiating plan. The plan—offering the Muslims fifty-one percent of Bosnian territory and the Serbs and Croats the rest (Serbs then controlled about seventy percent), in a unitary state, coupled with a threat to lift the arms embargo and of bombing Serb-held areas if the Serbs didn't agree, and offering to end the economic sanctions on Serbia proper if Milosevic recognized an "independent" Bosnia—was actually a variation on some earlier proposals, but administration officials hoped that the parties would realize that the bombing threat was more credible this time. They let it be known that the President's emissary didn't simply ask the Europeans to go along (as Christopher had in May of 1993 only to meet with humiliation) but was more insistent. Some officials were pained by the charge—and their own knowledge—that the settlement in effect rewarded "ethnic cleansing," but they knew no other way to end the war, without making it bloodier.

Christopher objected to Lake's heading the delegation to talk to the allies and the Russians about new negotiations—so Peter Tarnoff, Undersecretary of State for Political Affairs, was sent along.

The President's decision to get more involved, one official said, had a lot to do with the more confrontational Congress. An adviser said, "He was about to lose control of foreign policy on a fundamental issue." He added, "The passage of the Dole bill made the President and others more aware of the political danger, that Congress could do real damage to American foreign policy, and of the problems presented by Presidential politics—meaning Dole. The fall of Srebrenica sent ten to fifteen senators across the line. Britain and France set up the rapid reaction force. The administration knew it had to get back on the offensive. The President was trapped between the groundswell of congressional anger and a bad situation in Bosnia."

•

On August 11, Clinton vetoed the measure lifting the arms embargo. Dole agreed to put off the override vote until after the August recess because of the delicate and highly important negotiations going on.

The tragic deaths of three U.S. officials on the peace-making mission to Bosnia, led by Assistant Secretary of State for European and Canadian Affairs Richard Holbrooke, the follow-on to the Lake mission, on August 19 on a dangerous road leading into Sarajevo, wiped out a whole layer of expertise on Bosnia. The tragic accident was symbolic of the U.S.'s weak position in the area: the Serbs had closed the airport, and wouldn't guarantee safe passage on a better road, so the mission had to, or the administration thought it had to, acquiesce in taking what was called the most dangerous road in Europe.

Gorazde was shelled in mid-August, but NATO didn't respond. Despite signs to the contrary, officials insisted that the peace plan didn't give Gorazde, an isolated enclave in eastern Bosnia surrounded by Serbs, over to the Serbs. The military was more willing than the diplomats to give up Gorazde, the protection of which would require a higher level of U.S. involvement, and greater risk. Later in the month most of the peacekeepers pulled out of the Gorazde area—so as not to leave them vulnerable to being taken hostage—with assurances that it could be defended by airpower.

In Washington, traumatized officials regrouped to resume the peace mission, under Holbrooke. They had lost friends as well as valued colleagues. The reconstituted mission went off on Sunday, August 27. Holbrooke said that if the Bosnian Serbs resisted a solution, they could face heavy bombing, or a withdrawal assisted by NATO (European countries didn't want their forces to go through another Bosnian winter) and a lifting of the arms embargo. Holbrooke had strong feelings about Bosnia: he would have taken a more aggressive position a lot earlier, and he was frustrated by the lack of response from the West to a series of Serb atrocities, and by the Clinton administration's irresolution. He publicly had called the West's response to Bosnia "the greatest collective failure since the 1930s." Holbrooke, fifty-four, had taken part in the Paris peace talks to end the Vietnam War, was one of the smartest people in the foreign policy enclave, and now he had an opportunity to make major history. Though he could be abrasive—as he knew well (he joked about it, which suggested more mental health than that of a lot of other people in Washington)—he also had a brilliant mind, and he was energetic and dogged. Besides, abrasive was probably just what the Bosnia negotiations needed. Whereas not long before he might have slunk away in frustration, he was now the most visible figure of the Clinton administration, and his views counted for much.

When the horrible shelling of Sarajevo, killing thirty-seven and wounding eighty people, occurred on Monday, August 28—the day Holbrooke was to commence peace talks in Paris—the administration and the allies faced a new dilemma. The Bosnian Serbs had just said that they were willing to deal—which might or might not have meant anything. But to not respond to the shelling, peace talks or no, would have been to abandon the London-agreement pledge to meet an attack on a safe area with heavy retaliation, and would leave the administration, as well as its allies, with no credibility at all. Besides, it was thought, a strong retaliation might in fact spur the talks on. And now the allies could proceed without needing the approval of the U.N. civilian authorities. The administration having pushed hard to unburden itself of the dual-key arrangement, it was important to test out the new one.

But there were few doubters within the administration after the shells hit Sarajevo. Retaliation, it was thought, would give credibility to the threat part of the peace initiative. Though there were some in the administration who were troubled by the possible negative effect on the peace talks of retaliation, Holbrooke himself called from Paris to urge the administration to strike back hard. Also, Alija Izetbegovic, the President of the Bosnian Muslims, and Foreign Minister Muhamed Sacirbey made it a condition for meeting with Holbrooke in Paris that the allies would retaliate.

The President, vacationing in Wyoming, agreed that the strikes should go forward, but he had signed off on air strikes in advance if there was an act of violence that called for retaliation. (Clinton had been frustrated since the embarrassing "pinprick" bombing.) The bombing began, wave after wave, on August 30. By September 7, the bombing, plus the situation on the ground and negotiations in Geneva, led to a tentative outline of a Bosnian peace agreement.

Thanks to ethnic cleansing, the map of the former Bosnia-Herzegovina had been redrawn into fairly clear-cut Muslim, Serb, and Croat territories. The easy victory of the Croats over the Serbs had changed the military dynamic. And Serbian President Slobodan Milosevic wanted the sanctions off his country and figured it was time to deal. His taking charge, giving the Bosnian Serb leaders the cold shoulder, exactly fit the administration's plans.

Holbrooke continued his shuttle, pressing for a peace agreement. In mid-September the Bosnian Serbs agreed to pull back their heavy weapons from around Sarajevo and NATO suspended the bombing campaign, while stressing that they could quickly start again. Now, as the possibility of peace loomed the President was faced with the problem of having to make good on his promise to station 25,000 troops on the ground in Bosnia to help keep that peace.

Still, it was an obviously pleased and relieved Clinton who on October 5 was able to announce a cease-fire in Bosnia, with peace talks, and then a peace conference—in Paris—to follow.

The week before, he had presided over a White House signing of a follow-on agreement between Israel and the Palestine Liberation Organization (this time, joined by King Hussein, of Jordan, and Egyptian President Hosni Mubarak) to the one signed on the South Lawn in September 1993. The follow-up agreement had taken longer than expected, and this signing was more pro forma than the last, but the White House was no less happy.

In fact, the President and his aides couldn't resist a series of background briefings (the President met with a group of columnists for two hours) praising their prowess on foreign policy. This would have been better left undone: for one thing, it's better to let the public discover these things than to try to pound the message into them; for another, they could have been setting themselves up.

20

THE REAL REVOLUTION
"It's Piled High with Our Agenda"

In large part out of necessity, the House Republicans sought to implement their program through the spending bills for every department and agency of the federal government. Policies that there either wasn't time for (or there possibly weren't the votes for) passing as regular legislation were put into the appropriations bills—to a fare-thee-well. It was a way of getting around the regular processes of holding hearings and "marking up" a bill, subcommittee reporting it to committee, committee getting a rule and taking it to the floor. If the Gingrich Republicans couldn't get something done in one place, they did it somewhere else. Because appropriations bills must eventually be passed, putting a policy in the form of a rider on a spending bill could have a better shot than trying to get it enacted the regular way. The Republicans understood this, and, as in so many instances in the 104th Congress, carried it to new lengths. Gingrich considered this the real revolution.

Under the firm, but hidden, hand of the House leadership, the appropriations bills were loaded up with policy. This covered everything from abortion to regulatory policy, plus some longtime ideological passions of the Republican right. Tom DeLay said in an interview in mid-July, "We've known from the beginning that appropriations would have to carry much of the load of what has to be done." As a member of the Appropriations Committee himself, DeLay was the enforcer for the leadership.

As an example, DeLay pointed proudly to "my bill"—the bill produced by the Appropriations Subcommittee, on which he sat, on the Veterans' Affairs, the Department of Housing and Urban Development, and Independent Agencies, which would be coming before the House shortly. It included several DeLay hobbyhorses: it cut funding for the Environmental Protection Agency by a third and its funds for enforcement by nearly half, and contained seventeen riders prohibiting enforcement of both pending and *existing* E.P.A. policies. "It's piled high with our agenda," DeLay said, adding with a grin, "Half the markup was about spending and the other half was about policy and legislation." Carol Browner, the administrator of the E.P.A., said in an interview, "Taken together, this is a concerted, orchestrated effort to shut us down."

The riders would also, among other things, undo policies affecting pesticides, toxic waste, and emissions from oil refineries. One rider would bar the E.P.A. from spending any money on enforcing wetlands laws. The riders also included DeLay's proposal to block enforcement of emissions tests required by the Clean Air Act as applied by the E.P.A. One of the bill's riders contained, almost *verbatim,* sections and key phrases in a position paper of the Cement Kiln Recycling Coalition, a group of cement companies who used hazardous waste as a fuel to operate their kilns, objecting to an E.P.A. regulation that would tighten the standards for emissions from their cement kilns. The bill also barred HUD from enforcing the Fair Housing Act, which protected minorities against discrimination by insurance companies as well as by mortgage lenders.

Every rider put on an appropriations bill was cleared through Armey's office. Armey sought to keep the peace between the relevant Appropriations subcommittee chairman and authorizing committee chairman, whose jurisdiction was being invaded. He also sought implementation of the program.

At the top of the command structure, as usual, was Gingrich. Though he often asserted that he didn't get involved in the details of running the House, he was very involved in the appropriations process, because that's where the agenda was. Gingrich met with every Appropriations subcommittee chairman before a bill was drawn up. (Sometimes Armey sat in.) A Gingrich aide said, "He wants to make sure that they are aware of leadership concerns and concerns of the conference." He sought to make sure that spending reductions were made in line with the budget resolution, he resolved disputes, he untied legislative knots, and he put his considerable weight behind certain spending priorities. With his interest in science, he saw to it that NASA took only a minor cut, much smaller than it would have otherwise, and he protected funds for scientific research. (But programs for generic technology research—programs that, unlike the space program, had no strong local constituency—were cut drastically.) He also pushed for more spending on veterans than the Appropriations Committee had planned.

But all didn't go smoothly. The budget resolution was theory; the appropriations bills were the real thing. It was harder for members to rationalize that the Senate would fix it, that it would be fixed in conference. Further, to Gingrich's annoyance, the House Republicans began to split into factions more than they had all year. Armey said in late July, "You have two groups who look at things as they come out of the Appropriations Committee. The right says, 'You're not going far enough.' The left says, 'You're going too fast.' And they're starting to face off on the rules for debate." The first crisis occurred on July 12, when freshmen and other conservatives joined with Democrats to defeat the rule for debate on a bill that would have phased out the National Endowment for the Arts over three years. The freshmen had the most leverage on a rule vote, since almost all Democrats opposed a rule on a bill, whereas several Democrats might support the bill itself. After some post-midnight mediating by Gingrich and Armey, a compromise was struck whereby the agency would be abolished after two years. Following this, a leadership aide said, "Things started to snowball." The freshmen were joined in these battles by many sophomores, plus some senior conservatives (the CATs).

The following week, the leadership faced a crisis over the legal services program, a longtime conservative bugaboo. (It was established during the Nixon administration.) Freshmen and their allies wanted to eliminate the program, but Harold Rogers, of Kentucky and chairman of the pertinent Appropriations subcommittee, along with other Republicans on the subcommittee, didn't. Armey said, "You can have a hundred Republicans who will vote with the Democrats to defeat the rule on legal services and forty Republicans who say if you go that far right *we'll* defeat the rule."

Armey met with conservatives on Tuesday, and on Wednesday night from eight until midnight he met with both those who wanted to kill the program and those who wanted to protect it. The latter included some members of the Judiciary Committee, which had authorized the program. The resolution was that the program would be cut by forty percent in the first year and phased out over two years.

The Republicans were confronted by some realities of politics and human nature. The Members of Congress who served on various committees and subcommittees tended to take a proprietary interest in the programs under their jurisdiction. They might even have tried to get on a certain committee for the purpose of protecting a certain program, or segment of the economy. This was true of even some conservative Republicans. It was especially true of Appropriations subcommittees. Armey said, "If they have a constituent interest back home, they try to get on the committee to protect that interest." He added, "For one thing, we're just learning—we're learning how to sail a ship to the right that has been built to sail to the left."

The Republicans, especially the freshmen, were learning that it was easier to start programs and to build them up than to eliminate them. Armey told a group of freshmen, "We've got a hundred ways to skin a cat and no way to kill it." A case in point was the Commerce Department—the one Cabinet department that both the House and the Senate agreed in the budget resolution should be killed. Getting this done was of particular interest to the freshmen, with the enthusiastic backing of John Kasich.

But the Appropriations Subcommittee with jurisdiction over the Commerce Department didn't want to kill it. Ten other House committees with jurisdiction over the Commerce Department also weren't interested in standing by while the Appropriations Subcommittee killed it (even if it wanted to). (At the same time, Commerce Secretary Ron Brown was rallying the department's business allies to call on their friends in Congress to keep it alive.) Sam Brownback said, "It's very instructive: the process was all built to build, and then when you want to get rid of something, it's built to protect." The freshmen were getting instruction in, and were frustrated by, the iron triangle—the mutual protection group consisting of the agency, the congressional committees with jurisdiction over it, and the lobbies who seek things from it and make political contributions to members of the pertinent committee. "We're facing reality," Brownback said. The freshmen threatened to vote against passage of the appropriations bill covering the Commerce Department, and had enough votes to kill it.

Armey said, "When you're building up government, it's easy. The hardest thing to do in Congress is cut spending—it's as hard for Republicans as for Democrats."

On July 25, Gingrich sent a letter to William Clinger, of Pennsylvania, the chairman of the Committee on Government Reform, nudging him to report out of his committee a bill to kill the Commerce Department, to be included in the big reconciliation bill in the fall. Armey handed Clinger the letter on the House floor. The freshmen considered this a satisfactory outcome for the time being.

Several agencies which helped the economy of a certain region were singled out by the House Budget Committee for abolition but survived the appropriations process: the Tennessee Valley Authority (T.V.A.), the Appalachian Regional Commission, and the Economic Development Administration.

The riders placed on the appropriations bills in 1995—a violation of House rules prohibiting legislating in an appropriations bill unless specific exceptions were made—did everything from deal with a member's parochial concern to make sweeping changes in policy. In some cases, spending cuts themselves made policy. One Appropriations subcommittee doubled the proposed size of the cut for the National Labor Relations Board; it had issued an injunction of which a Republican sophomore disapproved. The subcommittee with jurisdiction over Health and Human Services adopted amendments that placed restrictions on federal embryo research and that abolished the family planning program. These were in part payback to the Christian right groups that had been patient during the Hundred Days. The subcommittee also stopped a new OSHA regulation tightening fall-protection rules that was opposed by the home-builders lobby (the sponsor of the amendment, freshman Mark Neumann, of Wisconsin, had been a homebuilder), and barred OSHA—again—from developing regulations to protect workers from repetitive stress injuries. OSHA's enforcement budget was cut by one-third. An agency that helped enforce the Endangered Species Act was abolished.

A rider to prohibit the Agriculture Department from implementing new meat inspection rules received sufficient bad notices in the press—it would have barred regulations to test for *E. coli*, and the public could readily recognize its effect (there were television stories about children who had died from the disease)—that the Appropriations Agriculture Subcommittee backed off.

One bill simply abolished the President's Council of Economic Advisers, whose role was to provide dispassionate economic analysis—and also to help an administration pursue its economic policies. One Republican suggested that the White House subscribe to the *Kiplinger Letter* instead. (Removal of the agency would save $3.4 million over seven years, but the amendment wasn't about saving funds.) One bill barred further funds for the Mexican stabilization—this and the C.E.A. elimination were among the riders passed by the House. (The House in July, with the Mexican economy still in trouble and its political situation shaky, voted to halt disbursement of the rest of the bailout package.)

The loading on of policy riders became so extensive that Livingston finally blew. On July 13, Livingston said, "The more we get sidetracked on policy issues, not fiscal issues, the harder it is to get legislation to the President's desk." He added, "Policy issues probably don't belong in appropriations bills." Livingston tracked down Gingrich at the Reagan Library, where he was speaking, to complain that one bill, for the Departments of Labor, Health and Human Services, and Education, was becoming perilously overloaded. But Gingrich had other imperatives. In an interview, Livingston said, "I balked at saddling appropriations bills with amendments that became instead of the tail on the dog the dog itself." Gingrich was displeased with Livingston's attitude.

•

It was a chastened Livingston who presided over an Appropriations Committee meeting ten days later, when it gathered at 4:00 P.M. in room 2360 in the Rayburn Building, a large cream-colored room with blue drapes, to consider the Labor-H.H.S.-Education bill. The nearly fifty-six committee members sat at an E-shaped table, with numerous lobbyists (mainly for social causes) lined up outside for seats. The proposition facing the committee was an amendment by Ernest Istook, Republican of Oklahoma, and strongly backed by David McIntosh (who though not on the committee was present) and ardently championed by Armey and Gingrich. It embodied a long-standing conservative purpose to "defund the left"—though no one in the Appropriations Committee room used those terms—by prohibiting private groups that received federal funds from lobbying.

The proposal also covered federally funded agencies and programs—such as legal services, the Corporation for Public Broadcasting, the National Endowments for the Arts and for Humanities—that the Republicans felt promoted the liberal cause. And the federal government had for years used nonprofit organizations to administer some educational and social programs, which the right also felt helped the left. Vin Weber said, "It's central to the Republican revolution to rid themselves of something they perceive as taxpayer-financed agents of the left—or at least not fund them. Over the years the restrictions on the nonprofit groups' use of federal funds for lobbying were tightened, but this didn't go far enough for the right." The breadth of the effort to break the power of the left (such as remained) was exemplified by efforts on Armey's part to dissuade corporations from making contributions to liberal organizations. In April, Armey wrote to various C.E.O.'s urging them to not contribute to "public policy advocacy groups" or groups "that support expansion of the welfare state." Some public policy groups did see a drop in their contributions.

The rider on "defunding the left," Livingston said later, "had such import that the leadership determined we should take it." Among the affected groups would be the A.A.R.P., environmental groups, the American Bar Association, the Red Cross. It also covered, for the first time, public interest litigation, such as civil rights suits. It imposed new limits not just on lobbying at the federal level, but also of state and local governments. It covered all forms of political advocacy, including attempts to influence public opinion. The new attempt to tighten the rules further allowed these groups to spend only five percent of their nongovernment money, no matter its source, for lobbying, and called forth a bill with sweeping implications—and one that would require a large amount of bureaucratic oversight.

The atmosphere in the committee room, though civil, was tense. A far-reaching proposal, with large and to some extent unknown implications, was being rammed through on an appropriations bill. Even John Porter of

Illinois, the chairman of the Labor, Health and Human Services and Education Subcommittee, a moderate, was perturbed. "I'd like to bring this back to reality," the white-haired, quiet-spoken congressman said in the meeting. "Last I heard, this is the Appropriations Committee." He pointed out that the amendment now before it was actually "a freestanding piece of legislation." He continued, "We can't pass these kinds of measures in appropriations bills," adding, "I believe that this bill is already overloaded."

Livingston, standing at a podium, gavel in hand, said that "the Chair is very sympathetic" to Porter's argument. He said the committee had already "added things to the bill that, frankly, exceed the purpose of 'appropriations bills.' " He added, "However, early in the year the leadership put into motion a process" whereby if the authorizing and appropriating committees agreed, legislation would be added to appropriations bills. The bothered but now docile Livingston said, "It has been a leadership decision to move ahead with this initiative."

Democrats, to make a point, moved to expand the proposal to cover government contractors. They knew they wouldn't prevail. David Obey told the committee, "If we're going to apply it, we should apply it to the big boys"—he mentioned companies like Lockheed Martin Corp., which he said take "full-page ads," and "the so-called think tanks" that point to defense "threats"—"not just the groups Mr. Istook doesn't like." Obey said that Catholic Charities had written to say that it opposed the proposal. Democrats pointed out that the committee was "considering" a thirteen-page bill in the form of an amendment.

DeLay, arriving late, said, "This is just the way that we're going to have to do business this year." He added, "Unfortunately, this committee is going to carry most of the load."

On the Democratic side, David Skaggs stood, jacket off, wearing suspenders, and made a quietly impassioned statement charging that the amendment had Constitutional as well as practical failings. The amendment, he said, "is designed and intended to intimidate recipients of federal grants, and associates of such recipients, from exercising their Constitutional rights, and to free expression of political views, and to petition their government." He argued, "It is styled as if its only purpose were the modest one of keeping federal dollars from being used to lobby the federal government. In fact, the amendment would have much greater reach—using the long arm of the federal government to fundamentally restructure the ability of universities, research organizations, nonprofits, and their employees and suppliers to communicate with policymakers and to participate in the political life of America." He pointed out that the amendment not only prohibited the use of federal grants funds for political advocacy, but that it also prohibited "any grant to an entity which has exceeded something called a 'political advocacy threshold' for any of the preceding five years."

Therefore, he argued, "The amendment would restrict political expression using even the grantee's *private* resources and even for years in which no *federal grant* was involved."

Skaggs said, "This makes the McCarthy era . . . look like child's play. . . . We should be ashamed of it."

When he finished, the Democrats applauded.

DeLay, smiling, said, "When you can't answer the arguments you throw up a smoke screen." He said that the Istook amendment was actually "my amendment." Of course, the Democrats' amendment to cover federal contractors was defeated, and the Istook proposal was adopted. Two Republicans—Porter and Ralph Regula, of Ohio—voted "no."

The Republicans' goal of actually killing, "zeroing out," certain programs and agencies—such as the National Endowment for the Arts (N.E.A.), the National Endowment for the Humanities (N.E.H.), the Corporation for Public Broadcasting (C.P.B.) ("privatize" it by removing its federal funding)— was meeting with more resistance than they had anticipated. Getting rid of such programs was meant to be an important symbol of the new regime.

But though these and other programs were being dealt big cuts—forcing layoffs of nearly half the staff of some—that they weren't being killed outright was a disappointment to the Republican leadership and most of the freshmen. And the freshmen had reason to question whether the programs would actually be ended in the time periods set by the Congress. The legislation providing funds for them covered only the next fiscal year; future sessions of Congress would not be bound by any agreement to kill the programs by a given year. An amendment offered in the House by Cliff Stearns, a conservative Republican, to assure that the N.E.A. would die after two years was rejected 227–179. Stearns said, "I'm afraid that it will not be shut down," adding, "I don't think there's the will to do it."

DeLay said in an interview that the problem was, "We don't have 218 hard-right votes. It may be the vast majority of the party, 190 out of 232 [the party lineup at that time], wants to do those things but another forty to fifty don't."

The Republicans also found out—as Kasich had suggested earlier—that there was within their own party a powerful, even if not especially large, constituency for these programs. The constituency that sustained the N.E.A., one member of the leadership explained, "are the richest people in America." He added, "They're country-club Republicans who wanted to be loved by the beautiful people. They're the richest people on the contributor list, and that affects the vote count."

Armey said, of the constituency for public broadcasting, "A lot of members want when they go home to go on a college campus and be adored, and also by all the museum people and the people who put together the charity ball—a lot of Members of Congress think it's nifty stuff to go to the charity ball and have their picture in the paper."

Armey conceded that the Democratic attack on the Republicans for trying to "kill" Big Bird and Barney had been successful. What the Republicans had overlooked in their zeal to end culture programs that they felt gave aid and comfort to the enemy was that public broadcasting had a constituency of communicative people, many of them community leaders and not all of them liberals. Gingrich, who in early March began backtracking on his attacks on public broadcasting (he appeared on the Atlanta outlet and contributed $2,000), said in July that he wished he hadn't talked about killing public broadcasting, but had instead talked about getting it privately financed. (A move on the House floor in early August to eliminate the funding for the third year was rejected, with several conservatives, including some freshmen, voting against the move.)

By late July, it was apparent that the Republican leadership may have gone too far, even for the House, in carrying out its crusade through the appropriations bills. The bills to fund Veterans' Affairs and Housing and Urban Development and other agencies and covering Labor, H.H.S., and Education, and several small agencies, were in trouble. In both cases, moderate Republicans in sufficient number to kill these bills (if the Democrats opposed them) were bothered by what they saw happening.

Sherwood Boehlert, the moderate from New York, was now ready to go into open rebellion. He was particularly troubled by the one-third cut in the E.P.A.'s budget and the seventeen riders. In late July, Boehlert said in an interview, "I think the Republican Party could be the majority party for a generation to come unless we blow it. We have to soften our edges. If we turn our back on the environment, we're making a major miscalculation, because by overwhelming numbers the American people are concerned about the air we breathe and the water we drink."

Just the day before, the Tuesday Lunch Bunch had discussed the two most controversial appropriations bills and decided to draw the line on the Labor-H.H.S.-Education bill: to make it clear to the leadership that their concerns had to be taken more seriously. Their first determination was to vote against the rule, and then, unless concessions were made, against final passage. Marge Roukema said later that though the leadership had been accessible throughout the year—the reason many moderates gave to explain their loyalty to Gingrich—"they refused to mediate with us." She continued, "In the end, we were always in the defensive position, and in the end we had to give in in the name of party unity." The moderates decided, Roukema said, "to hold together as a group and send the defining message that they had to come to us before the fact."

As the House leaders struggled to get almost all the appropriations bills

—plus a big telecommunications bill—through the House before the August recess, scheduled to begin on the fourth, they made concessions to moderates and conservatives alike, including, of course, the freshmen, allowing them to offer certain amendments to both bills. Many conservatives simply wanted to vote against a bill appropriating funds for domestic programs they didn't like—in the past, a number of Republicans had opposed those two appropriations bills.

That the leadership had in fact overreached was made apparent in a stunning vote on Friday afternoon, July 28, when fifty-one Republicans, most of them moderates, joined with Democrats to adopt an amendment, offered by Boehlert and Louis Stokes, Democrat of Ohio, killing all seventeen riders—DeLay's handiwork—that would roll back enforcement by the E.P.A. A great cheer went up on the Democratic side when it was clear that the amendment had a majority. The Democrats hadn't had much occasion to cheer all year. Though the vote was close—212–206—it represented a strong warning to the Republican Party. The tenuous coalition within the party had finally come apart. There were, after all, limits to the moderates' loyalty.

While the moderates took their stand, with Northeasterners and some Midwesterners voting for the amendment and Westerners against, the large majority of the Republicans felt increasingly distant from the environmental movement. And, of course, one of the House leaders had run a pesticide company. As they saw it, the environmental groups had ceased to be bipartisan. Therefore, most of the more senior Republicans, plus the freshmen, thought there was nothing to lose in opposing the environmental groups. Vin Weber thought that this was a risky strategy because there was probably a broader environmental constituency. "Republicans assume that 'left-wing activist organizations' don't speak for anybody," Weber said, adding, "On the environmental issues, that could be a misreading."

In the floor debate on the Boehlert amendment to remove the riders, DeLay called the E.P.A. "the Gestapo of government agencies." Another view was presented by Charles Wilson, Democrat of Texas, who said that the voters the previous November were "not voting to get arsenic in their drinking water."

The leadership was taken by surprise by the House's adoption of the Boehlert amendment. There had been no formal whip count before the vote. Gingrich and Armey were preoccupied with other matters. DeLay's staff had told him the day before the vote that there was trouble, but DeLay was juggling other issues and didn't pay much attention. With only a week left before the August recess, the leaders were overloaded. The day before the Labor-H.H.S.-Education bill was to be brought to the floor, Republican conservatives and moderates still hadn't agreed on the rules of engagement. Gingrich called them in and told them to do so. "It was crisis management," Dan Meyer said. In addition, Gingrich was holding hour-long briefings with groups of Republicans—again—on how to talk about Medicare during the recess. And he spent Wednesday evening at an extraordinary town hall meeting in the District of Columbia, whose near-collapsed condition Gingrich had decided to take on. It would be a lab for some of his ideas. On July 27 he had to appear before the Ethics Committee. Gingrich was exhausted, and, according to several observers, at his wit's end trying to hold together the various factions of his party.

In a meeting in Gingrich's office following adoption of the Boehlert amendment the leadership decided to shut down the House for the afternoon—they feared that another anti-committee amendment would be adopted. Gingrich expressed interest in negotiating a compromise with Boehlert, but DeLay was passionate about the importance of preserving the riders. "I was just livid," DeLay said later, "because the Boehlert amendment gutted all my regulatory reform that I had been working on all year."

On Monday, the Republican leadership tentatively decided to try to reverse the vote. Such "revotes" were rare, and this was a risky decision, because the leadership didn't know whether it could win, and to lose twice would be a major embarrassment. And the leaders had found no Republicans willing to change their vote from for the Boehlert amendment to against. DeLay said, "Unfortunately, Republicans got locked in and couldn't switch their votes. We tried over three days." (Some members of the leadership staff couldn't resist spinning a frustration into a virtue: suggesting that the leadership, out of some noble motivation, hadn't actually tried to switch votes.) But Armey and DeLay argued that in order to get enough votes from Western Republicans and conservative Democrats (who didn't like other things in the bill as well) for passage, they had to try again. Also, the floor staff for Armey and DeLay noticed on Monday afternoon that more than a dozen Democrats hadn't got back to town yet, and they figured that, as was usually the case, if the Democrats weren't back by then, they weren't going to be back that day. (Despite the supposed cultural change in the House, there were generally no roll call votes on Mondays until 3:00 P.M. and no votes on controversial issues until after 5:00 P.M. that day.)

On Monday, Boehlert called his allies, and sixteen environmental groups, from the National Wildlife Association to the American Lung Association to Trout Unlimited, co-signed a letter that was faxed to all members. The National Rifle Association, which wouldn't seem to have any direct interest in the legislation—but did have a tight relationship with the House Republican leadership—faxed a letter to every member, saying that the E.P.A. imposes "overburdensome and costly requirements on individuals and small business."

That afternoon, Armey called Boehlert to tell him that the leadership was going to try to turn the vote around. The decision angered Boehlert and several other moderates. Boehlert replied, "I'm not going to lose if I lose. The party is."

Boehlert and his allies made the argument against restoring the E.P.A. riders on the basis of both content and process—the latter, Boehlert said later, was "our strongest argument." A man of equable temperament, who had been largely deferential to the party leaders, he was now getting worked up. On Monday afternoon he said, "They're assuming that people are voting one way or the other that has nothing to do with principle, that people are like clay that can be molded." He added, "For forty years we were in the minority and we complained about Democratic 'high-handed' tactics. Now we're in power and we're doing the same thing."

The leadership didn't want to take the vote until they were sure they would win. At about 8:00 P.M. Armey and DeLay met off the floor to compare notes and decided to go ahead. The vote was taken at 8:30 P.M. Boehlert's amendment went down on a vote of 210–210. (A tie vote kills an amendment.) Now it was the Republicans' turn to cheer. Boehlert managed to hang on to all the Republicans who had voted with him on Friday (with the exception of one, who was out of town—but then, so was Gingrich, who would have voted to kill the amendment); the difference was caused by the fact that fourteen Democrats were out of town. While some charged the Democrats with failure on this vote, the Democratic leaders had taken a deliberate decision. Since House Democrats were of differing views on whether to "improve" a bill or let the Republican leadership win a "worse" bill—a dilemma they had faced all year—the Democratic leadership decided to make no effort to win on the revote on the Boehlert amendment. The White House took no position, as well. The President and the House Democrats were hoping to defeat a couple of appropriations bills in the House—the one now pending, covering the Department of Veterans' Affairs, HUD, and other agencies, and the Labor-H.H.S.-Education bill. Gephardt and Clinton had discussed this strategy in a meeting at the White House on July 21. Such defeats would presumably put the President in a stronger position going into the endgame. Panetta said, "To the extent we can show they're beginning to break down in their march to the sea it will give us more leverage."

But the bill was passed even without the anti-environmental riders in it, 228–193.

Boehlert made the best of the reversal, saying he still considered himself the winner. He said, "Washington does not make major changes in public policy based on a tie vote." He also took heart from the fact that Mark Hatfield, the Senate Appropriations chairman, had said that the Senate had to "clean up" the House bills.

An indication of the multilevel thinking of Gingrich—as opposed to Armey and DeLay—was that at the same time that the internal rebellion was going on, Chris Shays, with Gingrich's blessing, had quietly formed a group of moderates, most of them from the Northeast, to try to see to it that their reelection chances weren't sunk by what the majority of the party was doing. It was understood that several items in the Contract and the social issues (abortion) now coming to the fore were more attractive to the South and the West than to the Northeast. Someone who participated in this group said, "Newt understands that the Contract didn't play as well in the Northeast as in other parts of the country."

The competing philosophies about the role of government came into the greatest collision over the appropriations bill for the Departments of Labor, Health and Human Services, and Education. The House Appropriations Committee went hardest at reducing spending in this area—eliminating 170 programs. It was an all-out onslaught against the Great Society and much that followed. It eliminated or drastically reduced Clinton's "investments." Nothing like this had happened before—if much of it stayed intact. Nixon had succeeded in killing off some programs, but instituted others. Reagan and his budget director, David Stockman, had wanted to drastically reduce the size of the federal government, but weren't able to do much about it. George Bush had compromised with the Democrats on spending on social programs.

The bill eliminated Clinton's Goals 2000 and his national service program, and cut substantially the program directing education funds to schools whose students were very poor and also cut funds for Head Start, and cut job training by thirty percent. It eliminated the summer jobs program for low-income youth (to keep them off the streets and give them some training). In all, the bill provided $9.1 billion less in funds than its counterpart the year before. It was a dramatic turnaround in spending on social programs, which usually went up, at least to take account of inflation. (It did increase funds for the National Institutes of Health, which enjoyed bipartisan cachet—for its research itself and its research projects in particular congressional districts.) It also made the kinds of sophisticated cuts that furthered conservatives' purposes, but were all but invisible to the public: about 250 administrative jobs in H.H.S. were abolished, seriously damaging the capacity for managing the department.

In the Appropriations Committee and on the House floor, there was a strong sense of revenge. The liberals had prevailed for a long time, and now came the chance to undo their work. A liberal defense of this or that program would often be met with the argument that the liberal Democrats were seeking "to defend the status quo," or that they didn't "care about reducing spending." Though sometimes there were substantive rebuttals, and arguments that a program was no longer needed (the Low-Income Home Energy Assistance Program, LIHEAP, begun in the 1970s during the energy crisis), or didn't work (aid to schools with concentrations of poor children), most of the cuts didn't arise from careful study of a program. Most of them arose out of differences of philosophies.

The moderates won an early victory on the Labor-H.H.S.-Education bill when on Wednesday night, August 2, they (with the help of Democrats who voted with them) won an amendment to restore the funds for the family planning program that the committee had eliminated. Their victory infuriated conservatives who had considerable animus toward Planned Parenthood, which administered many of the funds and which had subsidiaries that ran abortion clinics. And, as conservatives saw it, Planned Parenthood was a liberal organization that took positions on campaigns. In the debate, Tom DeLay charged that over $30 million of the program went to Planned Parenthood, "the nation's largest abortion provider." A moderate Republican said later, "There is a fury toward Planned Parenthood that I didn't realize." The leadership worried that adoption of the amendment would cause conservatives to kill the bill. The next day, an amendment by Jim Kolbe, Republican of Arizona, to overturn a committee provision that permitted the states to bar the use of Medicaid funds for abortions even in the case of rape or incest was defeated, 206–215. (The committee provision overturned a Clinton administration requirement that the states spend Medicaid funds for such purposes.)

The rule for debate barred what would have been a more easily accepted version of this amendment from being offered. Ernest Istook, who had held off offering an abortion rider to the rescissions bill, had thrown a fit at the idea that the more acceptable version of the Kolbe amendment would be allowed to be brought up, and the leadership owed him one. (Alluding to this, Gingrich said in an interview later, "Armey has a great rule. He says, 'In this business every solution creates two new problems.'")

The Rules Committee's rationale was, of all things, that the original proposal would constitute legislating in an appropriations bill. (The committee, which marched to the orders of the leadership, allowed twenty-nine such legislative items in the bill.) A member close to the leadership said of the rape and incest provision, "I think we'll get it worked out in conference. We look bad on this."

Gingrich told some colleagues that he was bothered by the sweep of this anti-abortion measure, and of other anti-abortion measures pushed by Republicans. He was angry with the right-to-life members for pushing these kinds of amendments, and he told Christopher Smith, of New Jersey and a leader of the group, that if they continued to push them, the movement would become marginal, and it would be increasingly difficult to fashion a "majoritarian" coalition. Gingrich, once a Rockefeller Republican, wasn't a social conservative of the stripe of right-to-life members; also, his sister was an avowed lesbian and his two daughters were pro-choice. As a pragmatist, he worried about the House going too far on social issues. But he owed the Christian Coalition and the right-to-life members because of their earlier restraint. Also on Thursday, another pro-choice amendment failed: this one, offered by Greg Ganske, a freshman, would have overturned a committee provision barring the federal government from withholding funds from medical schools that didn't train in abortion.

On Thursday morning, DeLay told Gingrich that if the Labor-H.H.S.-Education bill was to be saved, he would have to devote much of his schedule for that day to it. Gingrich agreed. Meetings were set up with conservatives, with the roughly thirty Republicans with large labor constituencies (the bill curbed the N.L.R.B. in several respects and overturned Clinton's executive order barring federal contractors from replacing strikers), and with other Republican moderates. Gingrich gave each group essentially the same message: we can go home as having had the most successful seven months anyone can remember, and have people have a positive view of how we work as a team, or we could lose the bill, with people spending a month saying that we are falling apart. Gingrich added, It's incredibly important for the fall battle with Clinton. He closed by saying, "As in the case of other teams the mystique matters." His point was that the House Republicans had developed a mystique and that if they stuck together, if they kept that up, they could keep on winning. Gingrich believed in the power of the mystique and stoked it all he could.

The House Republicans were now in a situation very much like the earlier one when the tax bill—the last major item in the Contract—was pending, also just before a recess. The arguments made to recalcitrant Republicans in both instances was that a defeat would be extremely damaging to the leadership and the party.

In talking with the moderates Gingrich emphasized that the bill had come from the subcommittee headed by the moderate Porter. Porter commented that he wished he'd been allocated more money to work with—the allocations to the various subcommittees, which were now the subject of controversy, had been made by Livingston and the committee staff—but that given the amount allocated to him, these were the priorities.

At eight-thirty that evening, a nervous Dan Meyer asked for a whip count and was told that fourteen Republicans had said that they definitely opposed the bill and that forty members—a large number at that point—were undecided. A big factor for many conservatives was whether the rider concerning lobbying by nonprofits was going to stay in the bill. Then, a proposal by David Skaggs to strike it set off the angriest debate of the night, with Bob Walker, whom Gingrich had put in the chair because of his faith in Walker's abilities at this most dangerous moment, gaveling down George Miller so hard that the gavel flew apart. Miller accused the Republicans of being "fascists" and had refused to stop speaking when his time expired. What set Miller off was that this amendment fit into what he considered a thought-out pattern of destroying voices that opposed Gingrich's ideas and agenda.

Miller said the next day, "What got under my skin were the suggestions that these nonprofits are the real lobbyists that are evil in the public mind. *Excuse me.* These aren't people who hire law firms. They take buses to the Capitol. They're talking about the Red Cross, Girl Scouts, any nonprofit organization that gets federal money. It's an attempt to stifle the ability to petition government from the center-left. They feel comfortable that they can fund all of their voices through the political contributors."

So important was this provision to getting the entire bill passed that Gingrich was on the floor, rounding up votes during the roll call on it. Gingrich, in fact, "worked the floor" for nearly four hours that night. Also, Gingrich had asked Haley Barbour to come work on some Republicans who were planning to run for the Senate.

At midnight, still uncertain about the votes, Gingrich met in his office with some moderates—including Sherwood Boehlert and Marge Roukema— who had told the whips that they intended to vote against the bill. Haley Barbour was also there. Gingrich once again made the pitch to consider the big picture, to give the party credibility for the fight with Clinton in the fall, and he also argued that since some freshmen from unsafe districts were going to vote for the bill, it wasn't right for more senior members from safe districts to vote against it. Gingrich told the group that the leadership had "messed up" on the bill, and recognized that, but that now they had two choices: "We could lose a major vote on the eve of leaving and for three weeks get attacked by the media, or we could win and continue what is almost a mystical capacity to keep getting things done."

In an interview later, Gingrich said he recognized that the bill was "overloaded with too many restrictions, we got a little beyond ourselves." He went on, "It's got to be a cybernetic system, you've got to listen to yourself, you can't just run straight forward. You've got to modulate, you've got to know what you can get done. You can go right to the edge but you can't go over it." He added, "There were lots of little sloppy things. Part of the rule was written wrong, part of the conversations were wrong, some people were bad about other things. There were lots of different pieces of it. But you just had to listen to people all day and you had to try to sort out what was going on and why. We knew all along this would be the hardest bill and we had been preparing for this for three or four weeks. I mean, this was not an overnight experience."

In his midnight meeting with the moderates, Gingrich promised to see to it that in the conference on the bill funds for education, job training, and LIHEAP were increased. Roukema told Gingrich and Barbour that the issue wasn't the funding for specific programs but that the social policies in the bill were driving their party to extremism, and if that didn't stop, the base of the party would be narrowed. Boehlert—who as a moderate had faced several difficult moments during the year and had occasionally broken with the leadership—decided to vote for the bill. He said later that he was swayed not only by the pledge of restored funds, but also by the fact that "the psychology of it all is of extreme importance." He added, "It would have sent a devastating signal if the bill had been voted down." Besides, Boehlert said, "I like being in the majority and I want to stay that way."

By this time the determination of the moderates to hang together on the bill and bring it down if their concerns weren't adequately met had collapsed. The "defining moment" to tell the leadership that it had to consult the moderates early had come and gone. Once that was the case, the bill became for some, such as Roukema, simply a budget issue, and she, too, decided to vote for it.

About fifteen minutes before the final vote, DeLay told Dan Meyer that enough votes were in hand to pass the bill.

Much was made later by Gingrich of the fact that on the final roll call vote, some moderates as well as hard-right conservatives helped round up votes. The tally was indeed close through much of the final roll call, as several members held back to see if their votes were needed for passage. In the end, the final vote, at just before 1:15 A.M., was 219–208—just one more than the Republicans needed for passage. Eighteen Republicans voted against the bill and six Democrats for it. Leadership aides said that others would have switched if their votes had been needed. In his dramatization of the event later, Gingrich said, "We got the last four votes as people walked on the floor."

After the vote, an exhausted but exultant Gingrich dropped by Armey's office for beer and a recap. A late night beer or two was a not infrequent occurrence in the House leadership offices. Gingrich especially appreciated the opportunity for "team-building," camaraderie. Gingrich talked a lot about the leadership team, of the House Republicans as a "family." Someone who knew him well said, "When Newt finds an opportunity to bond with someone it's a big thing—he doesn't have friends." It was often said of Gingrich that he loved it when the House was in session "because there's nowhere else he wants to be."

The victory on the Labor-H.H.S.-Education appropriations bill had been a hugely important one. This was the one he had most worried about thus far all year, his closest brush with defeat. (Term limits didn't count because everyone knew the proposal wouldn't carry.) Losing the Labor-H.H.S.-

Education bill would have been a major blow to Gingrich's goals. DeLay was called and asked to join them, plus a number of staff members, in Armey's office. Typically, Gingrich reviewed what hadn't been done right on the Labor-H.H.S.-Education bill, and what had worked and what hadn't in the session thus far.

Also typically, he talked about where they were in trying to reach their goals. And he likened his situation to the Duke of Wellington's in the Peninsular Campaign—the relevance being, in Gingrich's eyes, that like Wellington when he was fighting Napoleon's army in Spain, he himself had to make both strategic and theater decisions, and couldn't delegate all operational responsibilities to others. (This was at variance with Gingrich's usual description of his role.) Tony Blankley explained later that Gingrich had started reading about Wellington in the spring, because he thought Wellington might be a more preferable "management model" than George Marshall, who, faced with a mammoth undertaking, was a delegator and up to then Gingrich's primary model. Gingrich's switch of models, Blankley said, stemmed from the fact that "Wellington had a smaller organization, and couldn't delegate everything—as Newt began to sense he couldn't." Blankley added an interesting revelation: "When the school lunch issue popped up, he thought maybe he was delegating too much, and that Wellington was a better model because he was operational as well as a delegator."

Gingrich said that what the Republicans believed in—lower taxes, smaller government—was shared by the majority of Americans, and if they didn't mess up, make a catastrophic misstep (which he thought was possible on Medicare), they would win, whereas the Democrats had a much tougher challenge because a minority of the country shared their beliefs.

The following morning, despite Gingrich's fatigue and lack of sleep, the "Five Amigos"—Lott, Mack, Weber, Kemp, and Gingrich (Armey was also invited), who used to dine together once a month, but now there was little time—met in Lott's Capitol office for coffee and rolls for a couple of hours, and talked about what had happened in Congress thus far, and what lay ahead.

At a gathering of the Republican conference at 1:00 P.M. that day (and decided on at the spur of the moment at 2:30 A.M. in Armey's office), Gingrich, with the moderates' near-rebellion in mind, said that four issues "have to be talked through with much greater sensitivity": affirmative action, the environment, dealing with the labor movement, and social issues —"particularly abortion." He told the conference that during August he would "design systems" to make sure that such issues got talked out among Republicans. He said, "We have to practice listening skills." He said that he would begin with himself. This becoming modesty, displayed from time to time, wasn't to be constant.

Starting early the next day, an exhausted House debated the giant and complex telecommunications bill, which would allow previously separate industries (cable, telephone, and broadcasting) to compete with each other, and loosened all sorts of restrictions on ownership. (A Democrat, sitting in the reception room behind the House floor, nodding toward the door to the Chamber, said, "There aren't six people in there who understand this bill.") Vast amounts of money had been spent on lobbying by the competing economic interests—long-distance telephone, regional Bells, cable, Hollywood, broadcasters (big broadcasters versus small broadcasters). What got lost in the contest of the titans was the public interest. Gingrich had wanted to "jam" the bill through because it was a big part of his vision of a revolution in telecommunications, the views he shared with the Tofflers and Jeff Eisenach, the head of the Progress & Freedom Foundation, and it also reflected the results of his talking to corporate interests. (Later in the year, the *Wall Street Journal* disclosed that a telecommunications executive, Donald Jones, who had interests in cable and Internet services, served as a "volunteer" in Gingrich's office from December 1994 through late July 1995. Jones's lawyer stated that Jones hadn't advised Gingrich on the substance of the telecommunications bill. In a memo to associates, Jones described himself as "a trusted listener and companion" to the Speaker, often spending "2 to 3 hours daily" with him, and cited four instances in which he had influence over "huge matters." (An ethics complaint about this was filed.)

The leadership lost its first recommittal vote of the year when liberal Ed Markey, of Massachusetts, and conservative Dan Burton, of Indiana, teamed up to offer a recommittal motion that ordered the inclusion of a provision requiring that a "violence-chip" be built into all new television sets so that parents could opt to block unacceptable programs (as defined by a board that would rate programs). The House leadership had sought to avoid a vote on the "V-chip," which was opposed by an odd combination of the broadcasters, Hollywood, and the Christian Coalition (which felt that the federal government shouldn't take the place of parents). With the "V-chip" provision quickly added, the bill passed by a vote large enough to override a veto—which Clinton had pledged on the bill as a whole—and the House of Representatives went home for August on Friday afternoon.

Sitting in his office that Friday afternoon, Gingrich, looking very tired, described his mood as one of "exhausted satisfaction." On the table at which Gingrich sat—there was no desk in his office—were piles of autographed copies of his book *To Renew America,* which was now number one on the *New York Times* best-seller list. He was about to set off on a book tour again. The year had taken its toll: long a bit thick in the middle, Gingrich now had a pronounced potbelly.

Asked how far along he thought he now was toward the goal he had mentioned on opening day, of "having a whole new debate, with new terms," he replied "sixty" percent. He explained, "On Medicare, for example, you very seldom now see a reporter write the word 'cut.' That's an enormous transition. On welfare, it's mostly now fought on our terms. The President's conceded we need to balance the budget." He continued, "For this year, I would say we are explicitly on track and are laying a very firm foundation to then set up next year. I think frankly having a book that's number one helps—in the sense that there are about 300,000 copies out now so people are learning the language direct. You can convey much more complex ideas in 250 pages than you can in a traditional speech. So I think we're gaining ground. I don't know of anyplace where we have lost ground."

But, Gingrich added, "It's just very hard. It is unrelentingly hard. That's one of the great lessons of this year." Conceding that it was much harder than he had expected, Gingrich explained, "Part of it's just scale. When you're in the opposition you pick your fights and then you rest and think. When you are governing, you do things all day, every day, and there's a positive, affirmative need to act.

"Second, what we're doing is a cultural revolution with societal and political consequences that ultimately changes the government. That is a vastly bigger agenda than has been set by any modern political system in this country.

"Third, we are a brand-new majority with a remarkably narrow margin undertaking extraordinarily bold gambles and having to pull every one of them off.

"And, fourth, since we're all brand-new, none of us has a clue how to do these things and so we're having to learn, because we're not doing what people used to do. We don't resemble any previous syst m. There are no comparisons that make sense because you've never had ai informa- tion-age, grassroots-focused, change-oriented structure."

Asked whether, and how, he intended to keep the revolution going, he said, "Of course, we intend to complete it. And we'll do that next year, but we intend to keep the revolution moving forward one day at a time until it's done."

Asked what the nature of the ongoing revolution would be, Gingrich replied, "It's continuing to rethink the shape of American society and the nature of American culture, and derive from that the political and govern- mental consequences. In some places, it's bigger government. We're spending more money on N.I.H., not less, because we're in an age of molecular medicine. We will, intriguingly, end up spending more in D.C. because we are the first modern Congress to recognize that we have the obligation to D.C. that a state has to its cities. And we can't shirk it." (The House cut funding for the District.)

Asked how much energy he thought his revolution still had, he answered, "That depends on whether you're accelerating. If you're accelerating it's endless, because we have 260 million people to draw in. I don't think we'll crest before 2000 or 2004; as long as you're in the recruiting phase, you're adding, you have more energy every week, more people sign up. People try to understand us as a reformism within the old order. Reformism in the old order has very limited energy and can only win very limited battles. Reagan was brilliant at this. I mean, Reagan knew he could do three things—that he couldn't do six. He was exactly right."

Gingrich then shed light on his strategy of all-out onslaught against the administration. He said, "One of my key decisions in November of 1994 was to launch a revolutionary rather than a reformist effort. A revolutionary launches sixty battles. Two things happen: each battle attracts its particular group, so you can increase your total energy level enormously, and you spread the opposition—the establishment, the decaying old order. You spread their attention so they can't focus. They can beat you on any five things. They can't beat you on sixty. You want to launch every possible fight simultaneously so that they are so distracted, and then they get together in a room because they're an organized establishment. We are a disorganized revolution."

Referring to "the old left, the reactionary left, the Democrats in the House and Senate and the White House, the labor unions, the trial lawyers, the various left-wing activist groups," he said, "What happens is because they know each other, they get in a room and they try to set priorities. Which things should we fight to save? So they then burn up more energy trying to establish where to focus. Meanwhile, we don't try to focus anything. We just move on it all simultaneously.

"If you're control-oriented and somebody walks in and says, 'Can we do X?,' you have to say, 'Gee, you're only allowed to do four things this week.' If you're a revolutionary, and somebody wanders by and says, 'I want to go and do X,' you say, 'Sure.' Doesn't cost me anything. So you can have people piling on every day. And the general principle is simple: if the revolution is going that way, is the thing they want to do going that way? If the answer is 'Sure. Why not?' that increases their energy level. They go do it. They have a little victory. They feel better.

"So you have all these different fights erupting and they can't figure out how to cope with them."

Gingrich, never one to think small, said he was looking beyond the

Congress and the coming collision with Clinton in the fall. He would soon be addressing a conference of state legislators: "They'll have seven thousand people there. Every state in the country will have state legislators there. My goal there will be to get sort of a general vision of where *they* should go in fifty states simultaneously. So the whole notion is you keep every front moving and, by the way, we use vision, strategies, projects, tactics. The collision with the White House is a project but it's a tiny part of what we're doing. I mean, we'll do that *en passant.* That will not be a major part of my planning operation." But despite this bit of braggadocio Gingrich knew that the outcome in the fall was extremely important, that it held big stakes for him and his party, and he was giving the matter a lot of thought.

But Gingrich wasn't content to think only about the legislative agenda. He had recently signed up a just-retired Air Force general, Charles Boyd, to think about what the legislative branch could contribute to the world. Similar to other arrangements Gingrich had made for receiving advice, Boyd was to be based at the Congressional Institute, a nonprofit foundation, established by Bob Michel.

When asked what he wanted Boyd to do, Gingrich's response was as revealing as anything of the way his mind worked. First, he said, he wanted Boyd to be "thinking through how do you achieve honest self-government." (He said this with no apparent irony.) Next, he said, "If somebody from Somalia calls and says, Gee what is it you guys do that works, we ought to have something to send. Networking worldwide elected officials and designing a training, both an electronic worldwide network and a training institute here in Washington so that for example we'll bring the Chileans in to talk about privatizing Social Security and invite anybody who's a freely elected official on the planet to come and learn or we'll bring in the Dutch and the Finns and the Swedes to talk about privatizing post offices so you create a world learning center here in D.C. Third, he's supposed to look at what's a twenty-first-century legislative branch. Fourth, we want to look at how the United States leads the planet. And fifth we want to look at how you retrain the legislative branch for foreign policy and defense. So there's five jobs."

He continued, "I asked myself, If I serve seven years and five months longer as Speaker—this is a hard enough job that I count the months—I'd want to know what I'd leave behind. And part of what I want to leave behind is a worldwide system. Let legislatures talk to legislatures. And if we do that we'll change something."

Publicly, Gingrich continued to affect nonchalance about the ethics investigation, but he was anything but nonchalant about it. Further, as he must have known, the committee was at the time engaged in delicate negotiations about calling in an outside counsel. Democrats argued that the issues were so complex that outside help was needed. Outside pressure—in the form of editorials, calls for action by such groups as Common Cause—was building on the Republicans, and Nancy Johnson, the chairman of the Ethics Committee and a fervent Gingrich supporter, was in a tight spot. Some way of reaching closure was needed.

Gingrich's anger over the Democrats' attacks on him, and over the fact that he had to endure the ethics investigation, was apparent in comments he made about David Bonior in the interview. "Boniorism is a big problem. Boniorism is a process by which an intolerant, ideological elite drives people out of its party. And the virus could affect us the way it's affected the Democrats." On another occasion, Gingrich said, "Bonior dominated the left wing of the House." In late June, when Dick Gephardt went to see Gingrich about a dispute over the Republicans' giving their latest recruit, Greg Laughlin, of Texas, a seat on the Ways and Means Committee, thus giving Laughlin something the Democrats had denied him and changing the party ratio on the committee, after keeping Gephardt waiting four days and then keeping him cooling his heels outside his office for a while, the first thing Gingrich brought up, heatedly, was the harassment he was feeling over ethics. He said that if Gephardt wanted his help, Gephardt had to help him on this. Gingrich seemed to fail to understand that if Bonior weren't leading the effort, someone else would. Gingrich's chief of staff often made a similar appeal to Gephardt's chief of staff.

Bob Dole's bill to apply risk assessment tests to regulatory laws ran into sufficient opposition in the Senate that he was forced to modify it, and, at that, in late July he failed in three attempts to shut off a Democratic filibuster. The trouble he was having doing so shed a less-than-lustrous light on his leadership, and suggested that he had put himself to the right of the mainstream on these kinds of issues. (In an illustration of his own lack of definition, or core, Dole told an R.N.C. meeting in July, "If that's what you want, I'll be another Ronald Reagan.") It also showed the difficulty of finding a center in the Senate Republican caucus.

Phil Gramm sent out a fund-raising letter in July attacking Dole, comparing his leadership unfavorably to Gingrich's and saying that "Republicans cannot waffle on this Contract and expect to win the confidence of Americans in 1996."

Earlier, the Senate had passed a securities law "reform" bill (that didn't go as far as the House bill did), but several other Contract items were stalled in the Senate. The crime bills passed by the House hadn't been taken up in the Senate, though new limits on habeas corpus were included in the anti-terrorism bill passed by the Senate in the wake of the Oklahoma bombing. But the House had passed no anti-terrorism bill, because both liberals and conservatives objected to what they saw as legally sanctioned intrusive investigative behavior. By summer, Dole had awakened to the fact that the line-item veto, embodied in widely differing bills passed by both Chambers, would give Clinton enhanced veto powers and what was the point of that? So a conference to work out differences between the two Chambers' bills was stalled. A Republican senator said that Clinton's veto of the rescissions bill dampened interest in giving him the line-item veto.

In late July, the Senate Republican conference accepted some rules changes proposed by the insurgents. The changes imposed term limits for the elected party leaders and for committee chairmen. The changes may have seemed dry, but they had tremendous implications for the transfer of power from senior senators to the more junior ones—and for the chemistry of the Senate itself. No longer could senior senators disregard the views of their juniors. The changes provided that chairmen would be chosen by secret ballot—"now every chairman is always at risk," a senior Republican senator said.

Dole and Gingrich continued their tenuous but mutually useful courtship. Dole supporters made much of the fact that the two men met in Dole's Capitol office suite for dinner on June 26. The only two others there were Joe Gaylord and Scott Reed, Dole's campaign manager. (Gaylord and Reed were longtime friends.) Reed said, "Keeping Dole and Gingrich together was a big political goal of ours for the year."

But passing a welfare bill was proving far more difficult than Dole had anticipated. Governors Engler and Thompson—with Gingrich's encouragement—had in March put on their by now familiar performance, telling of their wondrous deeds, for the Republicans on the Senate Finance Committee. Haley Barbour, the great go-between, was also present. It was convenient for the committee Republicans to believe Engler and Thompson, since it would save them money and grief. Committee Chairman Bob Packwood had come out for block grants early, disappointing supporters of maintaining the principle of entitlement. But even if Packwood had been otherwise inclined—and there was no evidence that he was—he was no longer a free agent. Dole had become his protector in his ordeal over charges of sexual harassment by seventeen women, including some former employees.

Decisions about Packwood's fate lay largely in Dole's hands until that was superseded by the insistence and perseverance of Barbara Boxer—after the Senate voted 48–52 not to hold hearings—that hearings should be held. Packwood gave in, thinking that he had bought himself time. But hearings on Packwood's sexual peccadilloes (plus his evident seeking of help from lobbyists in supporting his ex-wife) were about the last thing his Republican colleagues wanted, and on Capitol Hill self-preservation is the strongest instinct. John McCain, Republican of Arizona, to whom Packwood had turned for advice during his long ordeal, watched Packwood, in television appearances after the committee on September 6 voted six to zero that he should be expelled, and issued a merciless, stunning report on Packwood's misdeeds—the most damaging evidence being his own if expurgated diary. Packwood was taking an aggressive approach to the matter. McCain concluded that there was no way that Packwood would win. He felt that Packwood would put the Senate and himself through a bloodletting that would serve no purpose. Now Packwood had become an embarrassment to the institution, and he had to go. On the day after the committee voted, McCain phoned Packwood and said they should talk. The two men met at twelve-thirty in Packwood's Capitol hideaway, where they were joined by Alan Simpson, of Wyoming, who had been defending Packwood. McCain said, "You've got to go. You've got to go now. There's going to be blood all over the floor if you don't go, and it would just be prolonging a painful experience." Simpson said nearly the same thing, and Packwood reluctantly agreed. Dole, who arrived to deliver essentially the same message, suggested that Packwood make an announcement on the Senate floor after a roll call later that afternoon. Packwood agreed to that as well. In the end, this once-powerful, influential, respected senator, brought low by his own doings, was a confused and pathetic figure when he offered his resignation tearfully on September 7.

The welfare reform bill reported by the Finance Committee, which Packwood said he'd prepared with the help of Engler, Thompson, and Weld, turned A.F.D.C. into block grants to the states, and had few strings attached —as the governors had sought. (Dole had promised the governors at Williamsburg a block grant welfare bill without strings.) The governors were still dictating national policy, concerning themselves less with what kind of protection welfare recipients would have than with getting control and, perhaps, saving money.

Then the bill fell into the deep chasm caused by the division within the Senate Republican caucus (which Presidential politics underlined). On the right, the inevitable Phil Gramm, but also Lauch Faircloth, of North Carolina, Lott, and Santorum wrote to Packwood complaining that the bill didn't have strings (like the ones passed by the House), which would, they claimed, reduce illegitimate births. Seven moderate senators wrote to Dole, saying that they would "strenuously object" to such strings. A fight over the formula for distribution among the states—with senators from states experiencing strong population growth, such as Texas and Florida, complaining that the existing formula, which rewarded states according to their current contributions, would shortchange them—was also in part a proxy

Presidential fight. (The administration had fanned the flames by pointing out the large disparities in the distribution among states.) Gramm had bragged during the year that he had led the fight to stop the Clinton health care program in 1994—while Dole was negotiating on it—having said it would pass "over my dead body," and he now had an opportunity to stop Dole's welfare reform.

The vehemence of the formula issue took Dole by surprise, and in mid-June, worried about signs of contention within his party, he called Engler one morning to come address the conference and Engler dropped everything and flew in. The choleric Faircloth, angry over the formula and the lack of strings, which he—rightly—attributed to Engler's influence, objected to his addressing the conference (but he was outvoted by the conference). Santorum and fellow freshman James Inhofe, of Oklahoma, objected that the bill was too moderate, prompting a more senior senator to say later, "You have groups of freshmen who don't know anything about what it takes to get a bill passed in the Senate." The conference further deteriorated into a shouting match between Alfonse D'Amato, of New York, and Faircloth over the formula issue. Another senator said, "It was as close to a fistfight as the conference has ever seen."

Dole had planned to bring the welfare bill before the Senate in mid-June, but, a moderate Republican senator said, "the wheels came off it." The search for a compromise went on.

Meanwhile, the Democrats had drafted a bill of their own, and were proceeding with remarkable unity. The Democratic bill was drawn up by John Breaux and Barbara Mikulski, of Maryland, working with Daschle's staff. (Breaux, who worked closely with the White House, was trying to find a welfare bill that Clinton would sign.) In essence, the bill replaced A.F.D.C. with contracts with individual welfare recipients requiring them to start out right away to seek a job or training, and said that if they didn't comply, benefits would be reduced. The contract was, therefore, a "conditional entitlement." But welfare recipients could stay on the rolls for only five years. By contrast, the Republican bill froze funds at 1994 levels, which meant that a person seeking benefits might be turned away because the state had run out of money for the program.

Under the Democratic proposal, children wouldn't be cut off if the parents failed to comply. The bill also contained funds for child care and for training and jobs. The fact that the Republican bill called for the states to put fifty percent of their welfare population into jobs by 2000 but offered no funds for jobs made it, Breaux said, "the mother of all unfunded mandates."

Clinton endorsed the bill in a meeting with the relevant Democratic senators on June 14, and reendorsed it in his radio address and in other appearances. Though Clinton later issued a strongly worded criticism of the Republican bill—saying it "falls short of the central goal of real welfare reform, moving people from welfare to work . . . [and it] does not provide the level of child care resources necessary to support the imposition of tough work requirements"—his statement contained no veto threat. (Nor did it mention a "safety net.")

The Democrats knew that Clinton wanted badly to sign a welfare reform bill, and that if a final bill wasn't as strong as theirs—and it wasn't likely to be—he might well sign it anyway. Though Clinton was still avoiding the word "entitlement," he did call for the states to maintain the same level of effort they had made in the past; White House aides said this went a long way toward "entitlement," but it didn't guarantee that all people in like situations in a given state would be treated the same way. Such a requirement for "maintenance of effort," contained in neither the House-passed bill nor the bill pending in the Senate, would be the strongest protection—once Congress changed the program into a block grant—against states "racing to the bottom."

The bill also had the support of Senate liberals such as Edward Kennedy and Christopher Dodd and of conservatives such as Howell Heflin, of Alabama, as well as senators in the middle.

This Democratic unity complicated the situation for Dole.

On July 31, Clinton and Dole both addressed the Governors Conference, meeting in Vermont, on welfare. Dole gave the more effective speech. He argued that it was time to turn the issue over to the states and that governors shouldn't have to come to Washington and say, "Mother, may I," and he was indignant at Clinton's suggestion that the states would engage in a "race to the bottom." Rather than join in the issue, Clinton gave a rather mechanistic speech in which he said that he would give expedited treatment to state requests for waivers, and announced four more waivers (bringing the total to thirty-two). Clinton, with Morris's guidance, had begun a phase of showing that he could do things and draw attention to himself through executive actions—be President—while Congress was in irons over welfare reform. The Dole camp was thrilled with this first face-off with Clinton.

Dole kept the Senate in session for another week after the House's adjournment in the hope of getting a welfare bill passed, and brought up a revised version of the Finance Committee's bill in an unusual Saturday session on August 5. This was an issue on which Dole's dual roles—as Senate majority leader and Presidential candidate—came into conflict. If he bowed to the right wing of the party, which—with Gramm growing ever warmer to the role of leading it on this issue—was demanding strings along the lines of those passed by the House, he lost the votes of moderate Republicans. And of course the reverse was also true. And Daschle told Dole that the Democrats had a united front and would stand behind their own bill.

Moderates were angry when Dole had made a couple of concessions—albeit minor ones—to Gramm. Then, at the leadership meeting that followed, Trent Lott, in front of the others, angrily confronted Dole for considering changes requested by the moderates without clearing them with him. Lott repeated these charges at the policy luncheon that followed the leadership meeting.

So, on Tuesday afternoon, Dole announced that he was dropping the bill for now and would take it up again when the Senate returned in September. The administration delightedly played this up as a Dole failure. Gramm said that Dole wasn't trying hard enough to get a welfare reform bill through the Senate. A Republican senator said, "There are so many motives driving this."

Much was made of the fact that by the time of the August recess action had been completed on only two items in the Contract: the law requiring Congress to live by the laws it imposed on others, and the curb on unfunded mandates.

But in a much larger sense Gingrich had set the agenda: the Senate and the President had acquiesced in his proposal to produce a balanced budget within a fixed number of years—a decision from which a great deal else followed. Now Clinton and the Senate were working within Gingrich's frame of reference. The direction of the government had been turned around. If Gingrich had overinterpreted the mandate there could still be a price to pay. But the main problem he was facing at the moment was a sense on the part of the public that the Republican Congress hadn't done very much.

21

THE SYNTHESIZER

"One from Column A and
One from Column B"

As had happened before, Clinton's poll ratings began to improve in the course of the summer. This was in part a result of his own determination and in part a judgment on his opponents. In head-to-head matchups, Clinton beat Dole. (In a July 20 CNN/*USA Today*/Gallup poll, the score was 50–44.) Dole was, it was thought, making all the right moves to win the Republican nomination. But his campaign had little rationale except that he "deserved" the nomination, that it was his turn, that he had suffered a grievous wound in World War II. Dole said several times, "I've been tested and tested, and tested."

Gingrich's poll ratings continued on their downward trajectory. By early August, according to an NBC/*Wall Street Journal* poll, forty-two percent of Americans had a negative view of him (as opposed to thirty-one percent in January).

Clinton had had such revivals before, but now some Republicans and political commentators weren't writing him off for 1996 as they had at the beginning of the year. Clinton's resilience, and his real political talent, were being paid new respect. Still, everyone (including the White House) understood that his electoral college challenge was daunting, and that just as Clinton had a way of bouncing back, he also had a way of tripping himself up. And, as in any Presidential contest, there would be exogenous factors that neither side could do much about.

•

By mid-July, Dick Morris had progressed from establishing himself in the inner circle to working regularly with other staff members. He functioned out of Curry's small office, in the Old Executive Office Building, which Curry shared with his executive assistant. Sometimes Mark Penn, of Penn & Schoen, Clinton's favorite new pollster, also worked out of that office. The four consultants—Stan Greenberg, Paul Begala, James Carville, and Mandy Grunwald—who had swept from the campaign into the inner circles of the 1993–94 White House were all but gone. Greenberg still did some polling for the Democratic National Committee; Carville was writing a book and could still return as an adviser. Carville enjoyed a special place with the Clintons because of his shrewd instincts and because, as one person in the Clinton entourage put it, "The President believes that there are very few around him who when they get up in the morning are willing to kill for him. Two of them are Carville and Morris. It has nothing to do with politics; it has to do with loyalty."

But Morris was in charge. There were long "message" meetings on Tuesday, Wednesday, and Thursday—but, one White House official said, "You don't know who's running the meeting. It's weird." (Theoretically, the Chief of Staff should.) But, this official said, "We feel more included, and we get a sense of closure." Morris, this person said, helps by standing "a step away" and thinking through such matters as how to position the President versus the Congress—in Morris's view, Clinton shouldn't get mired in Democrats versus Republicans—how to make better use of the Saturday radio addresses, how to position Clinton for the Presidential campaign. The influence of Morris and Curry was reflected in the President's decision to make Don Baer, until then the head of speechwriting, the Director of Communications, replacing Mark Gearan, who had been nominated to head the Peace Corps. Baer was one of their own, and they overrode a tentative decision to give the job to Ann Lewis, a prominent liberal. (Lewis was made deputy campaign manager of the Clinton-Gore campaign in charge of communications.)

Despite efforts on the part of White House spokesmen to get across the idea that the new combined team was working together harmoniously, the level of distrust and resentment remained high. The White House staff was still riven. The Morris, Curry, Quinn, Baer, and Schoen camp considered themselves a group apart and kept in virtually daily touch. Morris's and Curry's early claiming around town that they were in charge had got back to the White House staff. An administration official said, "The only thing that has changed is that we know the name of the person who has the authority to veto ideas." He added, "There is a procedural distance between those who come up with ideas and those who veto ideas." Some White House aides referred to Morris as "Jack-in-the-Box," for his constant popping up with ideas.

But Morris had the confidence of the President, buttressed by the fact that Clinton was doing better in the polls. Morris hadn't taken him anywhere he wasn't comfortable—and it seemed to be working. Morris acolytes, and Morris in particular, spun from this a grand theory that Clinton had "taken his Presidency back," but they were being a bit expansive. And when Morris described the phenomenon he was slightly if unintentionally patronizing. Morris said in an interview, "The overarching theme of the developments that have occurred since 1994 is the President's increasingly putting his stamp on this administration. He's better when he does it himself—when he adds up numbers for a budget on a pad, when he phones up foreign leaders. He has gone through the process of finding out he could do this himself."

In July, Clinton set out to define himself through a series of speeches. There had been several such efforts before, but now there was to be a concentrated one. Clinton wanted to use the month of July to talk about "values." An adviser said, "Clinton had a great psychic urge to get out who he was, and Morris wanted to get out who he was."

The idea behind the speeches was to put the President "above the fray" as he was moving toward the center. An adviser said, "Tone is very important." Thus Clinton began to speak of "common ground." This was both a defensive and an offensive move. The polls continued to reflect that Clinton had a substantial problem with the public's view of his character. Also, he was seen as tacking too often, which was considered a product of vacillation and weakness. Also, according to an adviser, people saw Clinton as an adolescent. Clinton knew all this, and worried how to change these impressions. One adviser said, "He wanted to show his ability to synthesize, to think, to balance things, to put a heroic dimension on things that were considered unheroic." He also understood that there had been too much public discussion of strategy. He said that people didn't want to hear that he had a "third way," they didn't want to hear about strategy.

Mike McCurry said, "The President has given more and more thought about what the fundamental disconnect is between him and the public right now. People tell him that much of the public is anguished about their future, and is angry about crime, decline in moral standards, and politics. They say the Democrats have shut themselves off from the subject of values, and that he'd better get in the discussion. He wants to show that the Republicans are way off to the right on values. He's setting up the argument he wants to take into next year: what is the government's role?"

Morris, offering a novel view of the Presidency, explained in an interview in early August that Clinton was striving for a role as the synthesizer—"of being the person who elaborates to the public the conclusions we've all come to in the past three years." He continued, "That means both activist government and the conservative view of government. Thesis is an active government, antithesis is the Republican, negative view of government. By synthesis he means the middle ground, the experience we've had with activist and inactivist government in the last three years. It has to do with being in the lead on this." Thus, Morris explained, Clinton had figured out where the country was on welfare: it didn't want orphanages, but, "We do want teenage mothers to live at home; we want time limits; we want welfare recipients to work." And that had become the heart of Clinton's position on welfare. (One night in the summer, Morris, upon reading some data on public opinion about welfare, got very excited, and told colleagues, "Once you deal with welfare the whole country becomes Minnesota on race.")

"What the President is trying to do," Morris explained, "is take one from Column A and one from Column B." He continued, "It's been described as centrism, as triangulation, but it's not those. It's common ground. It's a synthesis of the common wisdom of this country in the last forty-eight months." Thus, Morris said, Clinton had arrived at synthesis on health care: a set of reforms that most people agreed on. This was an odd view of leadership: it didn't appear to countenance that a President should get out in front of public opinion, educate the public. What was the difference between a synthesizer and an ink blotter?

Clinton's July speeches were punctuated by his battles with the Congress and his veto threats—undermining somewhat the goal of showing him "above the fray." Morris explained that there was no inconsistency between Clinton's saying he didn't want to have "a pile of vetoes" (as he had said in April) and the numerous veto threats because many of the threats had been made in order to avoid a veto. Clinton himself said in an interview with National Public Radio, "They're really sort of veto notices." Also, some of the speeches were obviously poll-driven. Though the set of speeches that emerged looked as if they had a logic to them, an aide said that "up until the week before it all there was no agreement on the progression of them." Aides later described the July speeches as the "common ground speeches," imputing to them more architecture than they had. But though almost everything that happened in the White House in that period was attributed to the fine hand of Dick Morris, Morris didn't initially see the point of some of the speeches Clinton wanted to give, including a speech at Georgetown on "civility" and one on religious freedom, which Morris out-and-out opposed for a while.

The Georgetown speech, on July 6, was a nearly hour-long, rambling excursion that left some of his aides thinking that there must be a speech in there somewhere. Morris said later that two-thirds of the speech was extemporaneous. He also said that the Georgetown speech "was the first articulation in public of the synthesis." As he said in the speech, Clinton was intent on having "a conversation" with the American people. Clinton liked at times to give discursive speeches, engaging in themes rather than specifics, and at the same time positioning himself as the unpartisan preacher/doctor tending to, or at least diagnosing, his country. The problem was that such speeches—especially after he and his aides got done overloading them with meaning—sometimes came off as so much blather. If Clinton had been more disciplined—if he simply talked less—they might have had more impact. And he was saying and doing so many things in July—there was a week dedicated to events on the subject of Medicare and one on education—that he and his topics became a blur.

In the Georgetown speech Clinton returned to a theme he had unveiled in his State of the Union speech—the importance of civility in society—but hadn't paid much attention to since. He offered up the vision of a society that wanted to "move beyond division and resentment to common ground." He was also responding to polls that said that people were tired of partisan politics. The positive response he had received to his speeches at the time of the Oklahoma City tragedy caused him to want to speak again about the country's soul. He also dwelt on the subject of the frustrated middle class, and the rationale for an activist government. A conference on "common ground" had been seriously considered and even scheduled for July, but the idea was so fuzzy and unfocused that the President gave the Georgetown speech instead.

Another White House adviser said, of Clinton's speeches about civility and common ground, "he sees this as a way to combat the character problem. He's trying to talk his way out of it. He was trying to keep the post-Oklahoma feeling going." (By mid-May, Clinton's approval ratings had gone back down to their pre-Oklahoma levels.)

Clinton's Georgetown speech was full of analysis of what was bothering the public, a line of inquiry he had been following since the 1994 election. But there is a thin line between speaking to what's bothering the public (as measured by polls) and pandering to its every complaint. Not all of them are well founded. And of those that are, there are limits to what a President can do. Of course he can use the bully pulpit, but that's different from a psychiatrist's couch. And the bully pulpit isn't very effective if it isn't used with consistency. Seeking sources of alienation can be a useful exercise, especially to the extent it can inform policy making. But some of the alienation came from a lack of information, and some of it from a lack of proportion. Years of demagoguery—in the media, by politicians themselves—about the unworthiness of politicians and politics was bound to build a public cynicism, and make it more difficult for the good guys (and there were some) to function. Some of it came from wanting conflicting things: lower taxes and a lower deficit; smaller government and all the services government can provide. The lack of knowledge had several origins, and was becoming greater with the decline of standards in the mass media. A President shouldn't let people think he can make them feel better on all scores—and he shouldn't try to.

In a July 10 speech in Nashville, at a conference convened by Gore about the family, Clinton tried to retrieve the issue of violence on television. He had mentioned the matter in his State of the Union speech and was irritated when Dole seemed to snatch it away. Clinton flanked Dole by endorsing the V-chip, which Dole had opposed. In the Nashville speech Clinton actually said little about violence on television—the Hollywood community of Democratic donors had reacted badly to his State of the Union message—and talked more about the problems of families, and defended public broadcasting. Morris cited it as another example of "synthesis": Clinton came out against excessive violence on television without coming out for excessive regulation.

Clinton's speech on school prayer, given July 12 at James Madison High School in Vienna, Virginia, just outside Washington, was the most troubling one. In his effort to defuse the issue of a Constitutional Amendment permitting group prayer in schools by citing the kinds of religious activities that had been approved by the courts and saying that he disagreed with "those who do believe our schools should be value-neutral and that religion has no place inside the schools" he seemed to be pandering (as well as erecting a straw man). He clearly thought he was being sensitive to minority religions, but it didn't come off that way. Clinton had discussed "spirituality" before (nearly a year before) and then, as with other subjects, essentially dropped it, making this speech seem opportunistic rather than from the heart. Morris said that when he first saw the speech "I looked at it and said, Holy cow! Seventy to seventy-five percent of the people want a school prayer Amendment." He worried that Clinton was going against this strong opinion. But Clinton replied that he had a way of reaching the goal without an Amendment, that he could document what could be done at school without violating the Constitution. "As he began to explain that idea to me," Morris said later, "I switched from being opposed" to being in favor. "School prayer reflected his thinking," Morris said. "His thinking and my polling show there are a lot of very religious people who don't accept the Christian Coalition." Morris went on, "He wants to articulate a nonpolitical, deeply religious way of having religion in the schools, of having people feel they don't have to send their children to religious schools." So Clinton's school prayer speech was "synthesis," too. Morris supplied some of the language for the speech.

But the most important speech of the series—accidentally part of the series, because it had been postponed several times—was Clinton's speech a week later, on July 19, on affirmative action.

This divisive and emotional issue wasn't something the Clinton White House wanted to have to confront in 1995—or 1996. There had been clear signs in 1994 that the Republicans might use it as a "wedge" issue in 1996 —something that could produce more white flight from Bill Clinton. No issue seemed as poised to divide the Democratic Party. But it took off in early 1995—largely because of Republican Presidential politics—and there was no way to not face it. Besides, Clinton was looking for ways to win back some of the "angry white male" vote.

The issue got its liftoff in California, where Governor Pete Wilson had endorsed a petition to put on the state ballot in 1996 a proposition to eliminate all state affirmative action programs. The White House was concerned that such an issue on the ballot in 1996 would affect the Presidential race—negatively for Clinton, as those opposed to affirmative action felt strongly motivated to turn out. In February, Phil Gramm started talking about the need for "color-blind" programs. Also, in early February, Dole said on *Meet the Press* that "affirmative action has to be looked at." (In March, in a speech on the Senate floor, Dole said, "The American people sense all too clearly that the race counting game has gone too far.") Inevitably, Gramm chastised Dole for coming later to the issue than he had. In mid-February Lamar Alexander, another Presidential candidate who had shown himself to be flexible, said that affirmative action as it was currently practiced should be eliminated. Around the same time, Gingrich said in a press briefing, "I'm very interested in rewriting the affirmative action programs."

The issue had been given added bite by the stagnation of middle-class incomes over the last decade and by "downsizing" by corporations. Polls indicated that a majority of Americans felt that granting preferences in jobs or education on the basis of race, sex, or ethnicity—what opponents termed "reverse discrimination"—was no longer necessary.

In his February 23 appearance before the House Democratic caucus— where the big issue was school lunches—Clinton said that he had ordered an "intense, urgent review" of affirmative action. He told the caucus, "Let's see what we can defend and what we can't." Clinton ordered up a study by his staff, putting Stephanopoulos in charge.

Clinton was worried about finding a solution that was workable in both substantive and political terms: was there a way of satisfying angry whites without losing his black constituency? Stephanopoulos thought it was a "no-win" situation.

The very announcement of the study was seen by some in the civil rights community as a sign that the President was prepared to back away from at least some aspects of affirmative action. At a conference in Ottawa the next day, Clinton said, "What we need to guarantee is genuine equality of opportunity," and added, "We shouldn't be defending things we can't defend."

While the study, which for a while could displace action, went on, Clinton not atypically gave off differing signals. At a press conference on March 3, he said, "Where we can move ahead based on need we ought to move forward." This set off a flurry of speculation that Clinton was seriously considering moving away from traditional affirmative action programs and embracing one based on economic need—and the evidence is that he was. In discussions with his advisers, Clinton talked about white people he had grown up with who felt as excluded economically as blacks. He said that the issue wasn't as much anger or lack of anger as it was about opportunity. One person close to the process said while it was underway, "He has a set of hunches and intuitions about some promising avenues to explore and this is one of them." For some time, a sentence about basing affirmative action on need cropped up in Presidential statements. Another person involved in the process said, "It crossed through the President's thinking that if you reallocated on economic grounds and were rewarding poor whites versus middle-class blacks that might be worth considering."

While the study fell behind schedule as those conducting it found that the subject was far more complex than they had anticipated, and the data were hard to collect—a speech in April had been anticipated—Clinton was under increasing pressure to state a position, and out came a series of confusing statements. In a meeting with college journalists in late March Clinton seemed to move away from economic need as a factor for affirmative action. But in a speech in Sacramento on April 8 to the California Democratic Party, he talked of growing up in segregated Arkansas, and said that affirmative action had provided opportunities for minorities and women. He added that this was "psychologically, a difficult time for a lot of white males—the so-called angry white male."

At the White House, Stephanopoulos and White House Counsel Abner Mikva convened a number of meetings and asked questions—questions that alarmed the civil rights community. Should women be covered? Should Hispanics continue to be covered? Should affirmative action be based on economic disparity rather than on race, ethnicity, or sex? Civil rights supporters worried that these were indicators of where the President was headed. Stephanopoulos said, "At a minimum, these were questions that had to be answered." At the time of these deliberations, there was in the public debate a line of argument that affirmative action should be limited to covering African Americans; there was another that affirmative action should be class-based.

While Christopher Edley Jr., an African American legal scholar and associate director of the Office of Management and Budget, ran the interagency group that put together the study, Stephanopoulos worried about reaction on Capitol Hill, about "outreach" to black and other minority communities, and communications.

During all of this, civil rights groups and the Black Caucus weren't passive. Ralph Neas, of the Leadership Conference on Civil Rights, made sure that certain voices, such as those of prominent businessmen who favored affirmative action, were heard at the White House, and that the White House understood that the civil rights community and the Black, Women's, and Hispanic Caucuses would consider any rolling back of affirmative action a retreat. Vernon Jordan, the Washington attorney and former head of the Urban League and close friend of the President, made his presence felt in the White House and pushed the view that affirmative action had been valuable.

Some people in leading positions, such as Gephardt or Kweisi Mfume, who headed the Black Caucus task force on affirmative action, made public statements about the importance of Clinton's not wavering. Gephardt was very concerned that Clinton would undo some of the affirmative action programs, and would thus split the party. In mid-March Gephardt quite specifically took on the concept (aired by Clinton) of moving toward an economic standard, saying that the U.S. had no history of "discrimination against people who are in poverty" comparable to the difficulties encountered by racial minorities and women. The Black Caucus was very worried, and in part Gephardt was demonstrating to it that he, too, was concerned.

Leaders of the centrist Democratic Leadership Council also made their presence felt at the White House; while not monolithic, the D.L.C. leaders urged a phasing out of set-asides—the reserving of certain contracts for minorities—and their replacement with programs encouraging economic empowerment. A strand of the D.L.C. wanted the President to make a public break with his traditional constituencies, and argued that even if some programs were defensible, there was a philosophical tension between seeking equal opportunity and making decisions on the basis of race. Bill Galston, formerly of the D.L.C. and a Presidential adviser until he resigned in late May, argued in the White House meetings that the President had to show an understanding of this moral tension.

Clinton began to toy with the idea that where there wasn't objective evidence of discrimination, a community-based program might be a recourse. Bill Curry had the idea early in the year of replacing the controversial set-asides with a form of empowerment zones—awarding contracts to businesses which were located, or that relocated, in economically deprived areas—and Morris bought it. Morris thought that the idea was good politics and good policy. Morris said later, "I was persuaded and enthralled at first by Clinton's idea and Curry's idea and I became a passionate advocate." Stephanopoulos didn't take Curry's idea very seriously, but then Stephanopoulos didn't take many of Curry's ideas very seriously.

In any event, one participant said as the deliberations proceeded, "the debate raged" on class versus race.

A participant said that the "overarching question" was what was the legitimate rationale for affirmative action: how much was compensatory for past discrimination, or seeking diversity and some sort of equality of outcome—a question which divided traditional liberals from moderates. Stephanopoulos was in search of what could be given full-blown defense.

Certain Cabinet members—Cisneros, Shalala, Reno, Reich, Brown, and Energy Secretary Hazel O'Leary—got involved early, and pressed their view that affirmative action was a valuable program substantively and politically. They argued that politically the President had to both energize his base and expand it, that if women and minorities had turned out in 1994 in the force that they had in 1992, the last election wouldn't have been such a debacle.

As time went on, Black Caucus members were becoming increasingly anxious. Stephanopoulos gave no clues—to them or anyone—as to what he was thinking or where the policy was headed. The Clintons and the Gores held dinners with civil rights leaders and other thinkers on the subject.

The Supreme Court decision *Adarand Constructors v. Pena,* issued on June 12, applying strict new standards for affirmative action programs, came as a salvation to the administration. The White House had known that a decision was coming in June, and saw no point in issuing its own conclusions (whatever they would be) in advance of the Court's—but it was far from ready to do so anyway. The Court's implicit approval of affirmative action while at the same time setting forth tough new guidelines provided the administration with a useful framework. On the day after the decision, Clinton made a noncommittal statement—which infuriated blacks, who wanted him to repudiate it—and ordered a review of all government affirmative action programs to see whether they conformed with the Court's ruling.

By showing respect for the *Adarand* decision, issued by a conservative Court, the administration could say to the conservative Democrats and others who wanted affirmative action reined in that it was complying with the law of the land. "It bought us a little time, and the legal review helped move the process of deciding affirmative action policy along," one adviser said.

Mike McCurry said later, "The affirmative action equation changed dramatically with *Adarand,* which mandated the kinds of changes the D.L.C. had wanted." He added, "Also, *Adarand* meant that he could bring blacks and women and Hispanics into the tent because they had to accept that there had to be changes in these programs as a result of the Court decision." At the same time, Clinton could reject unpopular "quotas." In effect, McCurry said, the President was "flanking" the Republicans on this issue.

•

According to some people close to the process, Clinton's leanings did shift along the way. (Clinton had long said that he favored affirmative action as long as it didn't result in quotas.) Close observers of the process believed that Stephanopoulos had modified his thinking too. According to this view, Clinton at an earlier point was indeed headed toward a broader definition of affirmative action—one that was based on class as well as race.

A participant said, "The question was, do you get anything out of ending little things here and there—do you help yourself that much if you weren't ready to do major surgery?"

Informed speculation in one camp suggested that if the President's speeches had been in a different order—if the affirmative action speech had preceded the balanced budget speech—the President would have come out at a different place. But, according to this theory, other factors prevailed: after a while it became clear that Republicans were divided on how far to go on affirmative action (Gingrich was urging caution); the President's speech on June 13 announcing he was for a balanced budget had set off a stronger negative reaction from Democrats than had been expected; in the wake of the balanced budget speech, Jesse Jackson was making more serious threats about running against Clinton (and a challenge by Jackson as an Independent in the Presidential race could draw crucial votes from Clinton); and the *Adarand* decision placed a boundary on how far the President could go in tempering affirmative action policies. Also, according to a senior White House official, "as time went on, the polls we were seeing suggested that this was an issue the public didn't want retreat on." And the result of the study did have an impact. Someone who had been for a significant change in the programs said, "There had been few facts. When the review was done there wasn't a person in this process who didn't think there were fewer instances of discrimination against white males than they had thought." Also, all the consulting with various groups convinced the President that too large a bow in the direction of the "angry white male" would alienate important Democratic constituencies.

Further, there was a view that it would be better politics to base the resolution of the matter on principle—because, an official said, "If it was perceived as a political act it was doomed." Finally, a White House aide said, "Once you decide to stand for the programs and defend them, that is a powerful moment, and the President was drawn to that part of it. This was a chance to please people with a speech, a chance to respond to people who said he's always muddling through. He chose that moment."

Leaks of the study in late May pointed to where Clinton would come out: that hiring or other preferences based on race or sex were justifiable, but that some set-aside programs for government contracting raised questions. In particular, it said that programs seeking a greater share for minorities of government construction contracts that allowed minority "fronts" for winning these contracts should be adjusted.

Toward the end, the big argument within the White House was over the tone of the President's speech. This was a subject on which subtleties could make a big difference. One adviser said, "The real argument was over to what extent do you discuss the pain, how much do you allow those who feel aggrieved to identify with the speech. It was a difference in political sensibility. The issue was, When does the acknowledgment of that pain become pandering?" This person added, "This was where George won."

Morris and Curry argued that the President should express real sympathy with the grievances of the angry white male. Others, particularly Stephanopoulos, argued that this would come across as pandering, and would undercut the general endorsement of affirmative action. (Stephanopoulos was concerned in this context as well as others that the President look strong—that he not be seen as wavering.)

Gradually, Morris, who had numerous conversations with Stephanopoulos on the matter (even though they were no better friends), came around. Another participant in the process said that Morris had "thought there had to be replacement of the racial standard with an economic one, but then thought it would be a mistake," adding, "it wouldn't be consistent with the President's past, and would be interpreted as doing away with affirmative action." But Morris and Curry also wanted Clinton to put more emphasis on the finiteness of affirmative action than did other advisers.

Clinton's speech, delivered at the National Archives on July 19 to a specially invited audience, came off as a more ringing endorsement of affirmative action programs than it was. His endorsement of the concept was clear enough, and, as was to be expected, news programs chose as its sound bite Clinton's statement, "Let me be clear, affirmative action has been good for America." He also called the approach "a moral imperative, a Constitutional mandate, and a legal necessity." Clinton said that "affirmative action did not cause the great economic problems of the American middle class."

But there were other things in the speech that reassured his centrist supporters. Clinton's ordering that all programs be in conformance with the Court decision, and his setting forth criteria for programs—no quotas; no illegal discrimination, including reverse discrimination; no preference for people who are not qualified; retirement of programs that have succeeded—were taken by party centrists as signals that several existing affirmative action programs would be pared back. And in the end he added a program of incentives to businesses located in economically deprived areas, regardless of ownership. (Curry believed that affirmative action policy would move in his direction as programs were found not to meet the Supreme Court criteria.) Clinton's Jackson-like slogan, "Mend it but don't end it," gave comfort to both camps. Civil rights supporters were by and large quite pleased with the President's speech. It was almost a matter of which set of thoughts the President chose to put in bold type in his speech —and how differing camps heard it.

Clinton's dealing with this highly charged subject was a political tour de force of sorts—of the type that had made him President. He managed to please a large segment of the party's base without driving away its center. Al From, the D.L.C. chairman, said, "I'm not sure that that speech was his final word on affirmative action." (A major Pentagon contracting program was suspended in October.) Though Morris had started out somewhere else, he and his allies came to see that Clinton's coming out for a balanced budget, suggesting an expansive approach to school prayer, and endorsing V-chips gave him the leeway to identify himself as on the side of affirmative action. In any event, the alternative would have been costly: dampening or even alienating civil rights supporters without much chance of winning over those adamantly opposed to affirmative action. And Clinton came across as principled—something he badly needed to do.

A senior White House official said, "Morris thought the reporting on the speech came out a little more left than he would have liked." Morris said that the press coverage didn't pay enough attention to the development zones and that he, too, believed that administration policy would be headed more in that direction. Of the outcome, he told me, "It was pure synthesis."

The hearings on Whitewater in the House and Senate had been anticipated with apprehension at the White House. But while the hearings held by the Senate Banking Committee, chaired by a now subdued, even gallant D'Amato, and by the House Banking Committee, headed by Jim Leach, of Iowa, revealed a few things embarrassing to the Clintons there was nothing very damaging. (Gingrich had urged Leach to hold hearings during the August recess, so as to keep up the pressure on Clinton.)

The ghoulish nature of the Senate hearings, dwelling on the events in Vince Foster's office the night of his suicide—with senators waving about the dead man's briefcase—showed some senators at their most tasteless. The picture that arose from this phase of the hearings—though not from the testimony of those closest to Mrs. Clinton (former White House Counsel Bernard Nussbaum, close friend and adviser Susan Thomases, and Chief of Staff Maggie Williams)—was one of panic, and perhaps poor judgment, on that terrible night, but not criminality. It seemed clear that Mrs. Clinton wanted files on the first couple's private financial dealings removed from Foster's office, and that she saw to it that that mission was carried out—

either that night or in subsequent days. The remaining question—after the hearings—was whether any documents pertinent to any investigations were destroyed, and the answer to that would still leave the question of what the panic was about. At that point (June of 1993), the Whitewater story hadn't really got much attention. It was learned after the hearings that a loose-leaf notebook containing notes about the travel office brouhaha had been found in Foster's briefcase but not turned over to investigators.

Though her close friends might well have decided to protect her, the sense one got was that as a result of the odd, near-lethal, mix of inexperience and arrogance that marked so many things that happened in the Clinton White House, especially in the early days, Mrs. Clinton wanted the papers retrieved. There were conflicting stories from 1994 to 1995 about what happened to the papers after Maggie Williams removed them on one night or another. (Mrs. Clinton said that she hadn't seen the papers.) The testimony also brought out that though Nussbaum had handled the matter ham-handedly, he was within his rights to prevent the Park Police, who were investigating Foster's death, from rummaging wholesale through his files. The papers, some of which were leaked to the press by Mrs. Clinton's counselors in preemptive moves before the hearings, did contain some information that was at odds with some of what the Clintons had been saying, but there were no major disclosures.

And try as it did, the House committee failed to establish that there had been a cover-up of the case against the now-famous Madison Guaranty, the Arkansas thrift institution owned by James McDougal, the Clintons' partner in the Whitewater investment. This didn't definitively rule out that one had been attempted—the Justice Department did resist and delay bringing action—but no cover-up attempt was brought to light. The House committee hearings did produce one of the more hilarious, though little-noticed, moments of the hearings, when Jean Lewis, the Resolution Trust Corporation officer who brought the Whitewater case to light, and argued, but did not prove, that there had been an attempt to block prosecution of it, explained her secret taping of a conversation with a Washington-based official by saying that her tape recorder didn't work right and had switched itself on automatically in the course of that conversation.

Yet the hearings did leave some questions. Evidence was presented that the Clintons, despite their statements that they lost money on the project, did benefit from Whitewater, that they may have taken questionable tax deductions, and that Governor Clinton did favors for James McDougal. And people around Clinton were falling like so many extinguished June bugs. Their close friend Webster Hubbell, former high official in the Justice Department and former law partner to Mrs. Clinton, was in jail (not on Whitewater charges, but for false billing of the law firm's clients), the harshness of his sentence seeming connected with his unwillingness to help the Independent Counsel as much as the investigators had hoped; the McDougals were indicted. So, while nothing major seemed to have involved the Clintons, the picture wasn't edifying. And the Independent Counsel, Kenneth Starr, was continuing his broad investigation.

In the couple of weeks leading up to his August vacation Clinton took a number of executive actions. The idea, backed strongly by Morris, was that this would show leadership, stature, would be Presidential. It was a way of demonstrating that the President could act even though there was little he could get through the Congress. Morris said that such actions were to give him "loft"—"while everybody is down fighting in the trenches, the President can take action." McCurry said, "Not coincidentally," these actions could "show the President as a strong leader, and that in turn strengthens his hand in dealing with the Congress in the fall." Also, an official said, "There is a conscious effort to find places where he can act. The American people get tired of him talking and want to see him doing things." Eventually, what sort of executive actions Clinton could take became a subject in every strategy meeting. As one official put it, the White House wanted to show that "there are many ways to act and achieve other than being legislator-in-chief." He continued, "It involves speaking out clearly and engaging in moral issues—affirmative action, prayer—taking executive action." And he added, revealing the kinds of trade-offs that had been considered: "If you make the proper adjustments on welfare, then you can do affirmative action."

Morris believed that Clinton's speeches on school prayer and affirmative action took those subjects "off the table," and freed Clinton to do some other things, one of them the normalization of relations with Vietnam, on July 11. Clinton also announced the halt of underground nuclear testing; ordered that companies with federal contracts had to file reports with the government on their pollution levels and clean-up plans (striking a blow for the E.P.A.); imposed new disclosure requirements on lobbyists; and barred the sale of cigarettes to minors and controlled advertising of the product to attract minors.

The action on cigarettes was extremely controversial in the White House. Stephanopoulos and Pat Griffin, at a minimum, were against it—on the grounds that it would alienate three states: North Carolina, Kentucky, and Tennessee. (In 1992, Clinton lost North Carolina narrowly, but carried Kentucky and, with Gore's help, Tennessee. Tennessee went Republican in 1994.)

But Gore strongly supported taking action against cigarette companies. His sister had died of lung cancer, and he admitted in meetings that this wasn't a subject about which he was objective. Though Clinton's mother had died of breast cancer, he believed that smoking had aggravated her condition. Morris saw this as an issue that could help define Clinton—and the polls indicated that taking on cigarettes as regards young people would be popular. Morris explained later that this, too, was a place where the President had found "synthesis": people didn't want the government regulating smoking, but they'd like less smoking, so start with children.

Clinton was acting more confident now. Even if much of what he did seemed synthetic, he now had a plan, and in the view of his centrist advisers he was back on his original course, where he was more comfortable, and was now showing consistency. He had put down his marker in many places, and, when he wasn't calling for finding "common ground," he was ready to fight.

22

READYING FOR BATTLE
"No, I Am Not Going to Blink"

Gingrich saw prevailing on Medicare in the fall as crucial to continuing Republican control of the House. In an interview, he told me the Republicans had to "Win on Medicare, win the public relations—the serious public discussion that it does need to be fixed and that we can offer a better system that's more secure at lower cost than the government bureaucracy." His other two goals were to: "Win this fall in getting a balanced budget and [getting] welfare reform signed." He also said he wanted to: "Make sure every member is doing the fundamentals, going back home, paying off their campaign debt, organizing. If we do those things and then if we fight 1996 on our terms rather than Clinton's, we'll win. In fact, we'll increase our membership by at least twenty seats."

On Medicare Gingrich said, "I think the left understands it is the only issue emotionally strong enough and appealing to a wide enough bloc of people, that if they could ever turn the corner and convince them we were bad people, it would lead to a substantial shift of votes against us."

Gingrich then tried to appear nonchalant, saying, "I don't have any worries. It's like carrying nitroglycerin on a hot day: if you're a real expert, if you pay attention, you can carry nitroglycerin all day and it won't blow up. If you get clumsy, if you get arrogant, if you trip, you're going to blow yourself up. So you have to pay attention. A real expert with nitroglycerin never worries about carrying it, but they're very respectful of it."

When he wasn't imagining himself to be carrying nitroglycerin, Gingrich saw himself again as another great general: "I try to stay three to six months ahead of the curve. In an ideal environment—this was Eisenhower—by the time you get to the problem you don't notice it because you'd already solved it. There are very seldom crises in a system like this because you're just always out ahead of the curve. While your opponents don't even know the issue's developed, you've already thought it through, trained the team, and got them moving.

"I believe we are at the vision-and-strategies level, so much superior now on Medicare to the sort of nihilistic negativism of the Democrats, that I'm not worried except about execution. If we calmly and methodically execute, we're going to do fine. I mean people are going to look back on this and say, 'That must have been easy.' "

Gingrich didn't rule out other problems. He said, "Next year, if we're insanely stupid we could self-destruct."

Gingrich was aware—or some part of him was—of the danger of his party's going too far. At times, he expressed to friends worries about the hard-right orientation of the freshmen, and concern that Armey and DeLay were too far to the right—that these factors could jeopardize the Republicans' majority status in the Congress.

But at the same time that Gingrich worried about excesses by his party, he encouraged his troops to be "revolutionaries" and gave them their head. And he was pleased that two days after the end of the session, another Democrat, Billy Tauzin, of Louisiana, as had been long expected, would defect to the Republicans. (That made three House switches so far in 1995.) Gingrich valued such switches for more than the added votes they provided. In the television interview with Charlie Rose in July, Gingrich said the party switches were "tremendously demoralizing to the Democrats." He added, "I think the morale loss will leave you a tremendous number of retirements."

(The demoralization of the Democrats was compounded by the sixth declaration of noncandidacy for reelection by a Senate Democrat, this time by Bill Bradley, in mid-August, and then Sam Nunn, in October, said he would retire. This string of departures made it seem unlikely that the Democrats could recapture the Senate within the century.)

As the August recess loomed, a great deal of positioning for the fall began to take place. No one wanted the blame for any prolonged stalemate—or "train wreck"—that might occur. Though there had been seven brief shutdowns of some government agencies in the past ten years and the Republic had stood, there was now an understanding on both sides that this time the public would have little patience.

At a meeting with the bipartisan leaders at the White House on July 12, Clinton said that he would very much like to avoid a "train wreck."

Republicans felt at once that they were being set up—which they were. He asked the Republicans to stay in session to work out their reconciliation bill earlier than planned (late September)—this was another setup—but Democrats suspected Republicans of deliberately delaying the reconciliation bill so as to not allow much time for scrutiny of their Medicare proposals, which they had yet to make. Gingrich flatly ruled out a summit, telling Clinton at the White House meeting that he was "unalterably opposed" to a summit. (In Republican dogma, the 1990 summit at Andrews Air Force Base, which resulted in George Bush's acquiescence in a tax increase—despite his "read my lips" campaign pledge—and which Gingrich up-ended, occupied a place of infamy.) Gingrich told Clinton that there could be no speed-up on reconciliation unless there was a deal on Medicare, and that the House leaders couldn't send their members home having cut Medicare without the Democrats sharing the blame, that the only other choice was to "jam" it through as late as possible.

Gephardt, rubbing it in, said that the Republicans should be able to arrive at a reconciliation bill by sometime in August. Gingrich candidly admitted that Medicare was his biggest problem, and he told Clinton that the Republicans would be prepared to "take a lot of other risks" if there was a bipartisan agreement on Medicare. Gingrich complained that the Democrats were slowing things down on the Hill, which was true from time to time. Wendell Ford, the Senate minority whip, said that the tax cuts were the "culprit" in making an agreement difficult. Gingrich responded that "tax cuts are going to be part of the final package."

Clinton summarized by saying, "We want to make an honest effort to avoid a train wreck," and that the Republicans could get much of what they wanted if the reconciliation bill took the budget on the path to balance, the tax cuts were for families and to encourage economic growth, and that there be slow growth in entitlements. He also listed the things on which they differed: the targeting of the tax cut; the timing on balancing the budget; and education, Medicare, and Medicaid. Two Republicans who attended the meeting wondered afterward whether Clinton was summarizing what he understood the Republicans to want, or that, in his ambiguity, was suggesting the broad outlines of a deal.

Gingrich and Dole had agreed that it was important to have a plan for the endgame and asked some outside advisers to work out a strategy. Dole and Gingrich held two meetings on the matter during the last week of the House session.

By mid-summer, research was being conducted for the White House and Republicans alike over what would be the effect of various contingencies, including a partial or even full shutting down of the government.

On Saturday afternoon, August 4, at Clinton's invitation, Clinton and Livingston played golf, at the Tournament Players Club at Avenel, in nearby

Maryland, a situation that lent itself to conversation. They casually discussed whether there was ground for compromise, talking in broad parameters. Livingston saw what Clinton's interest was—more money for education, appropriations bills he could sign—and passed that along to Gingrich. The two men agreed that after people went away for August and came back and settled down the spending matters would be worked out. It was the opening of a channel—or seemed so.

Gingrich was supremely confident that he could outwit and outlast Clinton. He also believed he could outwait the Republican Senate, forcing it to come around to his view of things. He spread the word that he didn't care when the Congress went home. He said, with a broad smile, in an interview, "I have told our members to prepare to buy Christmas trees, just for here." He added, "If the administration knows we're very comfortable being here, they will agree sooner, whereas if they think that we are anxiety-ridden to leave, they might think they gain something by waiting." Speculation trickled out of the White House that perhaps a coalition of Democrats and moderate Republicans could be put together in the fall. Gingrich, of course, had by then had a lot of experience at keeping the moderates in camp.

Before everyone fled for their August vacation—to the great relief of White House aides Clinton left for Jackson Hole on August 15—there were numerous White House meetings to discuss the vast number of possibilities of the way things could go in the fall.

There was a large school of thought within the White House that the Republicans wouldn't be able to agree on the necessary cuts in Medicare and Medicaid to meet their seven-year balanced budget, which included their tax cut. But the White House had been predicting for much of the year that Gingrich would be in a corner on Medicare—but thus far Gingrich had been adept at getting out of corners.

In the abstract, resolving the differences between the Congress and the White House shouldn't have been difficult. The mid-year review of the budget by the Office of Management and Budget said because of an improved economic outlook, the administration's new budget would be in balance in nine years. But too many people were dug in, had struck poses, were under political constraints—and, to be sure, there were things each side felt strongly about—for a compromise to be reached as easily and rationally as might seem possible.

Morris shared the prevailing White House view that the Republicans wouldn't be able to produce a reconciliation bill, and he predicted the unraveling of the Republican position and the unraveling of Dole in the fall. "It will be the exact mirror image of what happened to Clinton on health care reform," Morris said. In that case, he added, "Those developments will put Clinton in the driver's seat—all the way to the '96 election."

Clinton said on National Public Radio on August 7, "No, I am not going to blink." In an interview, Gore said, "I think the Republicans are in danger of a very serious miscalculation if they believe they are going to make the President blink on his priorities in this confrontation. They're in very great danger on that."

Thus, two wily men—Clinton and Gingrich—headed into the August recess amid vows not to blink, and with the question of how much combat the public would tolerate in the fall.

23

ENDGAME

"The Largest Domestic Decision We've Made Since 1933"

Shortly before the August recess, Trent Lott, worried that there could be a prolonged crisis over the budget, called the President. Lott said to Clinton, "Mr. President, we really don't have to have a train wreck. Mr. President, you're the leader. Are you going to lead or are you going to leave it to third-level people like me?" In his own mind, Lott wasn't sure that Clinton was up to the challenge—that he would be focused enough, that he had the right people to do it. Lott was in effect suggesting himself as a channel to the White House, through his friend and political consultant, Dick Morris, for working out a solution on the budget—just as they had on the rescissions bill.

Lott and Morris had stayed in fairly frequent contact throughout the year, and now agreed that they could work out a solution that would avoid a big confrontation in the fall. They felt that it would be in the interest of both the President and the Republican Congress, and Morris was eager to work with Lott toward a solution.

Morris felt that the President could give the Republicans two things to cover their inevitable retreat (as he saw it) from the steep Medicare cuts they were proposing: a cut in the capital gains tax, and a balanced budget in fewer than nine years (the administration's latest proposal).

Lott told the White House that he could convince Gingrich to agree to whatever deal he and Morris came up with. Morris led Lott to believe that he could deliver the President.

Still, it was widely assumed, on Capitol Hill and in the White House, that in order to preserve their bona fides, the Republican congressional leaders would have to send Clinton a bill that reflected the views of the rightward Members of Congress, and the President, to preserve his bona fides with his party, would have to veto it. Also, many of the President's advisers believed that a veto would increase Clinton's leverage with the Congress. Gingrich had said to Clinton in a meeting in August, "It may be in your interest and our interest that there be a veto."

Nevertheless, Gingrich told me in an interview later, "My sense in September was that we were on the edge of a deal that would have been worked out and been done by Thanksgiving. Just talking to the President, Lott's conversations with Morris, other things that were going on—you just had a feel that this was all do-able."

Lott tried to keep his project a secret, so that his colleagues wouldn't get out of joint. Only three people were to know: Lott, Morris, and Gingrich—whose support was critical to any deal. Lott wouldn't even have conference calls with Morris and Gingrich for fear that such a means of communication might spring a leak. Eventually, Lott understood, Dole would have to be involved, as would the two Budget Committee chairmen, Pete Domenici and John Kasich. But Lott considered both men wonks likely to get bogged down in the numbers. And Dole and Clinton had a prickly relationship (one of the reasons Lott and Morris had established a back channel).

Lott felt that if there was a shutdown of some part of the government, or the government went into default because Congress hadn't agreed to lift the ceiling on the amount of debt that the government could incur—causing embarrassment to the United States as well as threatening the economy with higher interest rates and instability in the financial markets—the public was likely to blame both the Congress and the President. He was also worried about the Republicans getting hurt on the Medicare issue.

Lott told his co-conspirators that "everyone loses if there's a train wreck": the majority of the Congress would lose, he said, "if while we're standing on principle the economy went bad."

Clinton expressed interest in Lott's proposal and turned Lott over to Gore, while he himself maintained a backchannel communication with Gingrich.

In fact, Clinton and Gingrich had kept up a tightly held communication all year, speaking to each other about once a week. Sometimes Clinton spoke to Gingrich from the Oval Office, sometimes from the residence late at night. Much of the communication was about routine matters: when a meeting might be held at the White House, the timing of other events. Some of it was about Bosnia. Gingrich told me later, "We had a passable ability to get things done and talk to each other."

In late summer, their conversations turned to the subject of the budget. A senior White House official said in early October, "I never got the sense that there was negotiating going on. It was more, 'What do you think you need to ultimately put a deal together? Here's what I need.' They seem to have a fairly cordial relationship on the phone." But this wasn't to last. Gingrich was becoming frustrated by his talks with Clinton—so much so that he told others that he was getting fed up with Clinton's "lies." Gingrich—like a lot of people—mistook Clinton's agreeableness for agreement, and even a commitment. A Gingrich adviser said, "Newt always tells me that he likes Clinton, but he just doesn't ever know whether he'll keep his word. He thinks Clinton knowingly misleads him and then hides behind staff."

By early September, Lott was growing concerned; nothing had happened to bring the two sides closer to an agreement. "We've been spinning our wheels for a month," Lott said in an interview in his office in mid-September. He felt that one of several "windows of opportunity" (as the Republicans prepared to pass their own reconciliation bill) was being allowed to slip by. He worried that this would happen with other opportunities. "If we fail," he said, "the light at the end of the tunnel will truly be the light of an oncoming train." He added, "I think it would be stupid to get to that, because it's not necessary."

Then Lott let the situation get out of hand. In his efforts to work out with Morris one of the key issues—the differing economic assumptions on which the Congress and the President were proceeding—he talked to too many people. (The fact that the administration's assumptions were more optimistic had been crucial to Clinton's coming up with his balanced budget in June.) The result of the difference between the assumptions amounted to $475 billion over the seven years. Several officials didn't see how they could lop that much more off the President's proposal and still have an acceptable budget.

Never having been involved in the intricacies of the budget, Lott had to turn to others for information. He asked Kasich for advice on the numbers, and Kasich kept the secret, thus helping Lott work around Domenici. A few other people, including members of Gingrich's staff, knew about Lott's efforts. But then a member of Lott's staff went to Domenici's staff to talk about ways to work out the differences. "Trent didn't realize how close Domenici and Dole are," an adviser to the Senate leadership said. In short order Dole let Lott know that his efforts weren't appreciated. "I got the message loud and clear," Lott said. He told Gore that Dole had yanked his credentials.

Meanwhile, many other conversations had been quietly taking place between Capitol Hill and the White House. Members of Panetta's staff talked to members of Domenici's staff (they had worked together when Panetta was chairman of the House Budget Committee), trying to reach an accommodation on the economic assumptions. Panetta himself held private conversations with Domenici and Kasich, and he also had conversations with Gingrich. Dan Meyer, Gingrich's chief of staff, was talking to Pat Griffin, who headed the White House's legislative liaison office. Robert Rubin, the Treasury Secretary, talked to Gingrich about the debt limit. Tony Blankley even had a conversation with Jack Quinn, Gore's chief of staff. Despite all these contacts, there weren't as many or as good lines of communication between the Clinton White House staff and key figures on Capitol Hill as there had been in past times when they were dominated by different parties—and this became a problem.

Gingrich said later, "We had absolute indications at every level—every level communicated that they wanted to get this done, that it was all very serious, we would be very pleased how much things moved."

But most of this talking turned out to be so much buzz—no real negotiations were going on, and no real progress was made.

Still, in these conversations, the "parameters" of any deal were made clear: the President had to have more spending on education, the environment, Medicare and Medicaid, and on other discretionary spending. Gingrich had to have a balanced budget in seven years and a sizable tax cut.

In a conversation in early October, Panetta told Gingrich that it would be better to get an agreement sooner rather than later, that a veto wouldn't help either side. "I'm trying to figure out where the votes are, Newt," Panetta said. "There's no point in cutting a deal if the votes aren't there."

Gingrich replied, "My tax cut has to be healthy. It has to be at least two hundred billion for me to get it through the House." He told Panetta not to worry so much about getting enough votes in the House, that he would have a harder time in the Senate.

Panetta said that he had thought he'd have an easier time in the Senate, where he might pick up the votes of moderate Republicans.

"No," Gingrich said. "You should deal with us, and I can get you the votes." Panetta told Gingrich that Clinton couldn't sign onto a compromise budget that didn't have the support of at least a hundred House Democrats and a majority of the Senate Democrats. The President, Panetta said, wouldn't get in the position of Bush in 1990 (whose compromise with the Democrats, raising taxes, was rejected by House Republicans led by Gingrich). Panetta said that Clinton wouldn't allow himself to be seen by Democrats as selling out his principles, as Bush had been seen by Republicans, when he abandoned his famous "read my lips" pledge to not raise taxes. White House aides were very conscious of this precedent.

Clinton's aim was to win the support of a hundred conservative or centrist Democrats. The plan in the early fall was to start with the Coalition—twenty-three conservative Democrats (also referred to as "Blue Dogs")—

and work toward the center, gaining the support of moderate Democrats who didn't want to go home not having passed a balanced budget. ("Blue Dog" was a play on the old term "Yellow Dog," formerly used by those Southerners, now nearly extinct, who said that they would vote for a Democrat even if it was a yellow dog. The number of Blue Dogs decreased as Southern Democrats switched parties—in all, five in 1995.) Clinton wasn't aiming to get the support of such liberals as David Bonior, because he couldn't see how to build a coalition that included the left yet made up a majority of the House. (This assumed he could win over some moderate Republicans.) Besides, working toward a centrist budget fit Morris's "triangulation" theory. Clinton was also aware that the House Democratic liberals wanted a major confrontation with Republicans over the budget, and he already had some repair work to do with them.

In meetings in the fall, Morris told the President and other senior officials that he thought he could see a way to settle matters. He and Lott cheerfully reached a number of agreements—about the economic assumptions, about Medicare, about domestic discretionary spending (nonentitlements) —all of which Panetta rejected as unrealistic or unwise, or off the mark. (Panetta was still no fan of Morris.) Lott and Morris had decided, for example, that the two sides could compromise on Medicare by the administration's accepting more cuts and the Republicans accepting fewer. Panetta told Morris that the administration couldn't just throw in more Medicare savings at that point.

But the White House was under pressures, too. There was embarrassment over the President's comment to a dinner of Houston donors in mid-October that he wished he hadn't raised their taxes so much in 1993. (This was actually the fourth time he had made a remark along these lines to wealthy donors, but the press hadn't picked it up before—and neither had the White House staff.) The President's explanation at a press conference—that his mother had told him never to speak after seven o'clock, especially when he was tired—helped not at all. Just as Clinton had begun to rise again in the polls, one of his more troubling traits had conspicuously reemerged: his great desire to tell people what they want to hear. When he then called the conservative Democratic author Ben Wattenberg and said that his own 1994 welfare proposal hadn't been tough enough, and criticized himself for excessive liberalism, Clinton further reinforced the alarming impression that he was confused about who he was and what he stood for and even what he should appear to stand for. For these reasons —and because of some articles in the press very critical of Morris and saying, among other things, that when he had worked for Republicans in the past he had been scathingly critical of Clinton—Morris had to lie low for a spell. As Lott put it, "The White House people basically had to cool their jets for a while."

Clinton, for his part, and not atypically, felt misunderstood. His aides had a whole spiel for reporters about why the Houston remark wasn't being portrayed accurately, but they knew, as one said, that the Houston remark was "a *big* problem."

In early October stories in the papers, particularly the conservative *Washington Times,* said that there had been contacts on the budget between Gingrich and the White House, and also between Gingrich's staff and the White House. These stories stirred a negative reaction in the Republican conference, especially among the freshmen. Some freshmen had already told Gingrich that they would tolerate no backsliding on key elements of their agenda. In a meeting with Gingrich shortly after their return from the August recess, the freshmen told him that a balanced budget in seven years as measured ("scored") by the Congressional Budget Office was nonnegotiable.

Kasich said in an interview later that the House freshmen and then the Republican conference as a whole became dug in on seven years "because it's in the Balanced Budget Act [the Republicans' new name for the reconciliation bill] and the numbers in this plan are so reasonable there isn't a reason to go beyond seven years." In fact, Kasich, a hero to the freshmen, tried in early September to encourage more flexibility, telling some of them in a meeting in his office, "You can't say that at the end of the day it's going to be a hundred percent our way. It could be seven years and one hour." Sam Brownback, one of the leaders of the freshmen, recalled, "We said, 'No, John, not an hour.' "

In the minds of some Republicans—especially freshmen, sophomores, and part of the leadership—the culture of "split the difference" was a thing of the past. One stood one's ground until the other side gave in. Even when it was essential to compromise, that didn't mean "split the difference."

Such digging in hadn't been the congressional norm—but the Republican freshmen weren't interested in norms or compromise. They hadn't come to Washington for that. Like Gingrich, the freshmen were bent on changing the Washington culture. Brownback said, "You're seeing now more of the clash of cultures of the old Washington and the new group. The old culture was more hierarchical and disciplined, and the new is more horizontal." In general, the freshmen got more support from the leadership than from other senior members, especially the committee chairmen. Brownback said, "They waited a long time to run this place and now that they've got there we're trying to blow it up." Gingrich himself told the conference on several occasions that he would refuse to agree to any more than seven years—to wild applause. But he would add that, as long as the agreement was held to seven years, the Republicans would have to give Clinton more funds for education and the environment.

One question often raised over the course of the year was how much control the freshmen had over Gingrich, or vice versa. One Gingrich ally summed it up best by saying, "Newt moves the freshmen more than the freshmen move him. But he has to constantly gauge their reaction. He can't afford to lose. He has to figure, 'Is this one they will stay with me on?' " It was also the case that Gingrich used the freshmen—their potential defection—as a weapon.

Gingrich did lose one with the freshmen in October. When Appropriations Committee Chairman Bob Livingston, with Gingrich's concurrence, sought to switch Mark Neumann, a freshman from Wisconsin, from the national security subcommittee to a less important subcommittee, as punishment for voting against a House-Senate compromise defense bill backed by Livingston and the leadership, a rebellion by the freshmen and sophomores, who formed a majority of the conference, forced Gingrich to unmake the switch and for good measure Gingrich even appointed Neumann to the Budget Committee. Roger Wicker, of Mississippi, the president of the freshman class and a Gingrich loyalist (Gingrich had worked to block someone who was thought to be more of a troublemaker, while Wicker called himself "a GOPAC product"), said later, "to let stand what happened to Neumann wasn't possible." He added, "That had the potential to destroy our message. We didn't come here for business as usual."

Word was reaching Gingrich in early October that White House aides were telling the press that his overtures to the White House were a sign of weakness, that the Republicans were in great trouble over putting together a reconciliation bill. The reports Gingrich was hearing were true. The White House continued to believe that the Republicans might well founder over the reconciliation bill, especially over Medicare. And they saw Gingrich beginning to have more trouble in the House and in the polls. They happily talked to the press about all this.

In fact, Gingrich *was* interested in reaching an agreement with the White House before the House took up the reconciliation bill, and the House Republican leadership *was* concerned about delivering the votes for any compromise with the White House following a veto. The Republican leaders tried to convey the point to the White House that an early compromise was in its interest as well. Gingrich wanted talks with the White House while the reconciliation bill was going through the Congress, and had so indicated to the White House. (The freshmen got wind of this and were concerned.) Tony Blankley said, "We are to a certain extent preconferencing the reconciliation bill." He added, "It's our last chance to work on a nonconfrontational basis." Len Swinehart, Gingrich's top legislative aide, made a "time line" for finishing the budget. The goal was to get a reconciliation bill to the President by mid-November; meanwhile, there would be conversations with the White House, and the whole thing could be done by November 17, when Congress was to leave for its Thanksgiving recess. (Senate leaders thought this was unrealistic.) Otherwise, Swinehart said, "There'll be chaos."

The Republican leaders felt misused when they learned that the White House was spreading the word that the Republicans were in trouble. Gingrich and his allies wanted a signal from the White House that it had overplayed the business about Republicans' weakness—but no such signal came.

"It all began to just fall apart in September," Gingrich said later. "I don't know whether that was a decision on their part to go left or their fear of a primary challenge or what happened." He added, "And you had the clear sense that they felt we couldn't get the budget act through so they were saying, Why cut a deal when these guys can't get the job done. So then they backed off and at that point we just decided, Fine, we'll get the job done."

After a long series of meetings at the White House, it was decided to not engage with the Republicans before they passed their own reconciliation bill—if they could—so that the White House wouldn't share the authorship of various controversial provisions. The President was also under strong pressure from House and Senate Democrats not to make a deal before the Republicans had to cast votes on Medicare and other matters that would give the Democrats grist for TV ads in the fall. And they wanted (as they had wanted in June, when the President offered a balanced budget) more time to attack the Republicans on Medicare. (The June budget turned out not to have been an impediment.) While Pat Griffin thought it would be awkward to refuse to negotiate at that point, Stephanopoulos was particularly opposed to entering into such talks. One view held that the President would have more leverage to get an acceptable deal in any negotiations after he had vetoed the Republicans' bill. Another view held that any deal would be a loser for the President because he didn't have enough leverage, and there was growing evidence that the Republicans' budget was becoming unpopular. A White House official said, "So whether you wanted a stalemate or a deal, you didn't negotiate yet."

Besides, one White House official said, "A veto would be good for us." A veto would not only give the President more leverage but would bring more unity to the Democratic Party. Dick Morris, on the other hand, thought a veto could be avoided.

In fact, in his press conference trying to explain his Houston comment, Clinton seemingly out of nowhere said he thought he could agree to balancing the budget in seven years. This remark came as a surprise to his top aides, including Panetta and Griffin. But it was of a piece with Morris's strategy—he believed that the President should make some moves toward the Republicans around this time. In any event, other aides backed Clinton away from this comment—at that time. Thus the Clinton negotiating strategy was running on at least two tracks—the Morris track and the Panetta/ Stephanopoulos/Harold Ickes track (they didn't completely agree)—with no clear plan. An aide said, "They haven't figured out where they want to end up."

The President and his advisers had taken pains to ensure that Clinton had no major political distractions during this period. By early October, he had raised all the money he could use during the primaries period, and had made sure that he had no primary opponent.

On Monday, October 9, the Columbus Day holiday, Gingrich gathered a small group in the "Dinosaur Room," his reception room. Among those present were some staff members and some outside advisers, such as Ken Duberstein, who had been asked to help the Republicans on endgame strategy. There were two items on the agenda: the difficulties with the White House, and the difficulties with Dole.

"Newt blew up," an attendee said later. "While we were spending a month trying to deal with them they were out trashing us." In that meeting, Gingrich and his advisers resolved to break off the informal contacts with the White House. "We have to stop all this crap," Gingrich said. "We don't want to send any more signals that get misinterpreted."

Lott told me that he had spoken to Gingrich over the weekend—during which Gore had called the Republicans "extremists" and that "Newt took it very seriously that he was being called 'extremist' and that the White House was taking our willingness to talk as a sign we're in a weak position."

Then the group gathered in Gingrich's suite on Columbus Day addressed Dole's worrisome signs of independence. There had been two serious breaches. The first was when Dole said on *Face the Nation,* on October 1, that the tax cut didn't have to be as high as $245 billion. "Newt was furious that it hadn't been coordinated," a Gingrich ally said later. The second was Dole's supporting John Chafee's effort to keep Medicaid (which provided medical care for the indigent) an entitlement program, rather than turn it into a block grant, as the House had done. The House leaders had worked out this policy with the Republican governors. When it looked like the Senate would balk, the governors "became unglued," in the words of one House Republican leadership aide, and there ensued an angry set of phone calls between them and Dole. Dole's campaign staff was very upset.

Gingrich and his advisers decided to rein Dole in by setting up a bicameral Budget Steering Group, consisting of the leadership of both chambers and the chairmen of the key committees: Ways and Means and Finance, the two budget committees, and the two appropriations committees. This group was obviously too large to make critical budget decisions (or keep them secret), but now Gingrich had Dole where he wanted him—or so he thought. (At the same time, Gingrich remained comfortable with the idea of Dole as President, because he continued to think he could control the agenda from Capitol Hill. But he thought he wouldn't be able to manage Colin Powell in the same way he thought he could Dole. In fact, conservatives had suggested that Powell might kill the "revolution." Therefore both Gingrich and Dole—like Bill Clinton and his advisers—were relieved when Powell on November 8 announced that he wouldn't seek elective office in 1996.)

Tony Blankley said that another reason for the Columbus Day meeting, and the decision to break off talks, was "a misreading by the White House about what's going on here," in light of the recent losses on the two appropriations bills. But perhaps most important of all was the concern, Blankley said, "of how our members are reading the polls." (A recent *Washington Post*/ABC poll showed for the first time that the public trusted Clinton more than the Republican Congress to handle its problems.) Blankley said that the cross-tabs showed that many of the large number who disapproved of the job the Congress was doing believed that it wasn't keeping its promises.

But some Republicans did worry that the public was in fact seeing them as going too far. Even Tom DeLay had told his colleagues after the August recess that the Republicans were in trouble on the environment. He blamed not the bills and riders that the House had passed (with his strong backing) but the failure of the Republicans to get their "message" across.

DeLay told me in the fall, "What I said was that we had lost the debate on the environment." He continued, "Their people have outdebated our people. It's like school lunch." He added, "The environmental extremists have lied about what we're doing. Our friends out there haven't supported us enough. I've told them they want these things done but they don't want to do it. They want us to do it, and get our hands dirty."

Gingrich and his advisers said often that he and others found solace about their loss of public esteem in Governor John Engler's story of a fall in the polls and then a reelection. But the Engler precedent could turn out to be misleading. Engler had three years to repair the damage. Still, Engler's story was convenient.

On the day after Columbus Day, Gingrich and Dole announced a break-off of the talks, citing Gore's remark. But this was a ruse. The reports about the contacts were causing too much trouble for them to continue; this was far from the first time Gingrich had been called "extremist." A close adviser to the Republican leaders said, "The statements by Newt and Dole about why they wanted to break off the talks were excuses, because of the pressure on Newt."

•

Having taken so much time earlier in the year to pass the Contract, and having passed some appropriations bills that were so controversial that they were stuck in the crosswinds on Capitol Hill, the Republican Congress fell far behind schedule in passing the annual appropriations bills by September 30—the end of the fiscal year. The internal congressional deadline for passing the reconciliation bill, which covered taxing and spending policies for the rest of the government, kept slipping.

On September 28, the Republican leadership and the White House agreed without great difficulty on a continuing resolution to keep the government operating until midnight November 13. But well before the new deadline, it was clear a collision was coming. If all of the appropriations weren't passed by then—no one thought they could be—another continuing resolution would be needed, as would authority to raise the debt limit. Gingrich had made it clear that he would use those extensions as leverage to get his way on both the spending bills (with their numerous policy implications and riders) and on the budget as a whole. In one leadership meeting, Gingrich banged the table and said, "I'm not going to schedule a second continuing resolution."

Yet, some significant legislation was passed in the course of the fall. After making compromises with both a bipartisan group of moderates, and also with conservatives, Dole exacted a welfare bill from the Senate. The concessions to the moderates included adding more funds for child care and tightening the requirements of state spending on welfare in a block grant. Like the House-passed bill, the Senate measure limited the time people could be on welfare to five years, and required that fifty percent of the recipients be working by the year 2000, but proposed no funds for training or jobs. And, as in the House bill, it abandoned the principle of entitlement. Nonetheless, Clinton praised the bill, which passed on September 19 by a vote of 87–12, despite the importunings of Daniel Patrick Moynihan, Democrat of New York, and Edward M. Kennedy that Democrats vote against it. Many Democrats voted for the bill because they anticipated that Clinton would support it, and didn't want to be left out there alone. (Clinton did warn that he would veto a conference compromise if it moved too far in the direction of the House bill.)

While the Senate was debating the welfare bill, the administration was sitting on a report by the Department of Health and Human Services estimating that the Senate bill would throw about a million children off welfare. The White House released it under pressure from Moynihan, who made scathing remarks on the Senate floor about the President's role in the welfare debate.

Just days before the Medicare bill was to be brought up in the House—on October 19—the Republican leaders thought they might lose it. Representatives of rural areas were dropping away, as were some members from New Jersey, because of feared effects on their constituencies.

Gingrich had been deeply involved in the details of the Republican proposal. On September 11, a meeting in Gingrich's office with the relevant subcommittee chairmen and Gingrich advisers, including Joe Gaylord, had gone on until 1:45 A.M., where the group went through the proposal line by line. On October 14, Gingrich spent two hours going through the details of the bill and making changes. It was rare for a Speaker to become so engaged in a piece of legislation, but Gingrich knew that this was the crucial one. In part Gingrich's role had increased as a result of his downgrading the committee chairmen; in part it was a result of his confidence in his powers as a leader.

Gingrich was aware he was taking a big risk. Dan Meyer said, "We have spent some political capital. Our unfavorable ratings are going up. But there is a strong belief, and Newt shares it, that this will change and be to our credit. The White House is misreading where the public will be on this." He added, "But if we turned and ran, our problem would be worse, because people will conclude that this Congress is just like all the rest. That's why the only option we have is to see it through. But we're following the John Engler model."

Gingrich had worked hard to mollify or win the support—or at least the neutrality—of various interest groups. The American Association of Retired Persons made a political decision to not attack while the program was being developed—this lasted into October. Moreover, the A.A.R.P. was a provider (of Medigap insurance), and in the discussion Gingrich made the benefit structure slightly more generous. In the end, it still opposed the bill, but with striking restraint given its activities in previous years. The American Medical Association endorsed the plan after Gingrich agreed to trim the reductions in fee-for-service payments. The Republican proposal also made it easier for doctors and hospitals to establish their own managed-care plans, to be reimbursed by Medicare. Representatives from rural areas demanded, and received, a guaranteed minimum reimbursement to managed-care providers in their locales. To pay for his deals, Gingrich squeezed payments to other providers all the more.

The debate over the Republicans' cuts in Medicare—or, as they insisted, reductions in its rate of growth—was fraudulent on both sides. The $270 billion cut allowed the program to grow at a rate of 7.2 percent, down from the 9.9 percent under current law. The Democrats attacking the Republican plan didn't acknowledge that the 1993 Clinton proposal had sought to reduce spending by six to seven percent. Nor did they point out that in terms of spending, Clinton's and the Republicans' plans weren't very far apart. The Republican plan contemplated spending $289 billion on Medicare in 2002, while the administration's plan would spend $295 billion. Starting shortly after he was elected, Clinton had argued strenuously that health care costs had to be brought under control. Medicare and Medicaid now constituted one-sixth of the federal budget. In 1995, the Clinton administration essentially took a pass on the hard questions about Medicare.

Republicans insisted that they were *increasing* spending for Medicare, by at least twice the rate of inflation. Technically, they were correct, but it was also the case that a combination of more beneficiaries and increased costs would require $270 billion more to maintain its current level of benefits and services. To save the money, the Republican plan raised the costs of premiums and reduced the rates of reimbursements to providers. Democrats, indulging in overstatement, argued that the Republican plan would "decimate" Medicare. Clinton said that the Republican plan would "eviscerate" Medicare. This was the school lunch argument revisited once more, in a new and highly sensitive political context.

The policy changes in the Republican Medicare plan were at least as important as the much-discussed reduction in funding. The Republicans effectively proposed to change the nature of Medicare. At the heart of the policy changes was the concept of luring the elderly, through more "choices," under a voucher system, into private plans—Health Maintenance Organizations, and the like—and out of Medicare. The proposal also allowed people to set up tax-deductible medical savings accounts with which to pay for certain coverage—or make a taxed withdrawal. (The Clinton plan had encouraged enrollment in private plans, but didn't appear to go as far toward dismantling Medicare.)

And the Republican plan placed hard caps on how much the federal government could spend each year on providers and on benefits. If costs rose faster than the amount the government would spend, providers and beneficiaries would have to absorb the difference. In essence, the federal guarantee of adequate health coverage for the elderly was removed. And no limits were placed on how much insurance companies could charge for policies to fill in the gaps in coverage left by Medicare.

The Republican plan didn't deal with reform of health care coverage—the heart of the 1993 Clinton plan—to make it universal and more certain. The Clinton plan came a cropper over the complexities—not all of them essential—proposed to bring that about, but the Republicans didn't try to expand coverage to the uninsured, or protect those who had insurance from losing it. The Republican plan was likely to result in a Medicare population of the poorer and the sicker—not the makings of a powerful constituency to protect the program. (In June 1995, Clinton offered, along with his new balanced budget, a Medicare proposal, making net cuts of $98 billion, based almost entirely on curbs of payments to providers. The proposal offered incremental reforms—including increased portability and limits on penalties for preexisting conditions—that were quite important, but Clinton's proposal was politically irrelevant and didn't become part of the debate.)

Gingrich was furious when the Democrats ran an ad quoting him as saying, in a speech to Blue Cross/Blue Shield, on October 24, that Medicare should be left to "wither on the vine," as the fee-for-service system disappeared. With the kind of candor he was capable of, Gingrich said in the speech, "We don't get rid of it in round one because we don't think that's politically smart." He insisted that the phrase applied to the Health Care Financing Agency, which ran the Medicare program, rather than the program itself. Not everyone saw a big distinction. On the same day, Dole said in a speech to the American Conservative Union, referring to the establishing of Medicare in 1965, "I was there fighting the fight, voting against Medicare . . . because we knew it wouldn't work."

Gingrich later described the Medicare battle as "the hardest thing all year," and also "the greatest achievement of the year"—in terms of writing the legislation. "The drafting of that was the hardest single creative act—to put together Medicare, have it work, build a coalition around it," he said. At the time, Gingrich was focused, almost obsessed, with Medicare, and the strain on him was beginning to show. He was becoming tired and snappish. But he was also keeping his eye on the larger victory he was determined to achieve. Losing the Medicare fight or the reconciliation battle to come would be a crushing defeat, leaving Clinton in a far stronger position. Gingrich had to prove wrong the White House officials who were saying that he couldn't succeed on these issues.

After some fits and starts, the House Republican leaders brought up the Medicare bill on October 19. They had decided to separate it from the reconciliation bill of which it would ultimately be a part because they didn't want it to be in the same bill as the tax cuts, giving the Democrats an obvious target—and they didn't want to lose votes on the reconciliation bill because of Medicare or vice versa. An adviser to Gingrich said, before the Medicare debate in the House, "They're all very nervous that the argument connecting Medicare with the tax cut has got through." Gingrich had told associates all year, "If we can handle Medicare without getting killed politically, we'll be fine."

In the debate, the Democrats of course repeatedly linked the bill to the tax cut. They protested that the bill was being rushed through: there had been only one day of hearings by the Ways and Means and the Commerce Committees, and the floor debate was limited to three hours on the Republican plan and an hour on a Democratic substitute. Clinton vowed to veto the bill.

David Bonior said, "With this vote, we turn back thirty years of progress." Bonior mocked Republicans for saying, "This will be a courageous vote." He added, "For thirty years, they have waited for this moment to dismantle the system." John Lewis cried, "How long? How long until they realize what they're doing to our seniors?"

The plan was that Gingrich would close the debate with calming and magnanimous remarks. He was, after all, winning. But, as he sat on the floor for an hour listening to the debate, the attacks by the Democrats got to him, and he responded angrily. "I regret that this debate is ending at the same level of misrepresentation with which it began," Gingrich said. "There are no tax cuts today. . . . This is about Medicare." The Democrats hooted at him. There were deep lines under his eyes. He attacked Democrats as "pathetically incapable of saving this system."

Still, as a result of Gingrich's intense involvement, the Medicare plan was passed by the House with apparent ease, by a vote of 231–201, with only six Republicans voting against it. Four conservative Democrats voted for it. But a lot of Republicans were uneasy about their votes.

Senate Republicans included their Medicare proposal in the reconciliation bill; their proposal also reduced Medicare spending by $270 billion and was similar to the House proposal in other respects.

The House and Senate took up their reconciliation bills in late October. Both bills affected a large number of programs, and touched the lives of virtually all Americans. Both constituted a radical turnabout in government policy—which the balanced budget had been intended to bring about. They not only made deep cuts in Medicare but also in Medicaid; the House bill turned Medicaid into a block grant, ending its entitlement status (as the Republican governors had sought); the Senate bill contained a limited entitlement. (The Medicaid cut was proportionately higher than the proposed cut in Medicare.) Both bills cut taxes by $245 billion, but the Senate cut off the child tax credit at adjusted gross incomes of $110,000, while the House set it at $200,000 (but expected to compromise). Any possibility that the Senate would go for a smaller tax cut ended when Dole, having no real choice, named Phil Gramm to the Finance Committee, filling Packwood's seat, and William Roth, of Delaware, a champion of tax cuts, became the new chairman. Both bills made a large cut in the Earned Income Tax Credit, in effect raising taxes on the working poor—the Senate cut being the larger by far. Other programs for the poor, such as nutrition aid, were cut by both chambers.

The President had already vowed to veto the Republicans' plan.

The House passed its reconciliation bill on October 26 by a vote of 227–203. Ten Republicans voted against it. Sherwood Boehlert and some other environmentally sensitive Republicans did so because it contained a highly controversial provision to open the Arctic National Wildlife Refuge, in Alaska, to oil exploration.

An alternative budget offered by the Blue Dogs received the votes of sixty-eight Democrats (and four Republicans), and supporters of the proposal thereupon became the "swing group" that both sides would court in their efforts to prevail on the final budget. The Coalition's proposal, which had the support of the Budget Committee's ranking Democrat (and former chairman), Martin Sabo, of Minnesota, and a liberal, made smaller cuts in spending than the Republican proposal, and contained no tax cut. "The Blue Dog proposal may be something we can work with," one White House aide said. The fact that it contained no tax cuts, White House officials thought, would prevent a compromise between the Blue Dogs and the Republicans.

Though passage of the reconciliation bill looked fairly easy, Gingrich had undergone a great effort to see that it came about. He had had to deal with members representing agricultural interests, dairy concerns (struggling over milk marketing orders), conservatives, moderates. Gingrich was said by an adviser to be annoyed by the incessant demands, but he had let it be known that such tactics worked.

Gingrich said later that while Medicare had been the most difficult creative act, reconciliation "was the greatest legislative effort."

Immediately following passage of the bill, Gingrich said, at a rally of outside backers of the bill held in a basement room of the Capitol, "It's the most decisive vote on the direction of government since 1933." (The rally featured children—real children and pictures of children—to emphasize the Republicans' argument that these steps were being taken for the benefit of the nation's children. "Children" was on the GOPAC list of "positive words.") But then he did an odd—but by now somewhat familiar—thing. At what should have been a celebratory event, with many television cameras present, Gingrich launched an attack on White House press secretary Mike McCurry. Looking very angry, Gingrich assailed remarks McCurry made earlier in the day—and immediately retracted—that Republicans were slowing the growth of Medicare "because eventually they'd like to see the program just die and go away. . . . That's probably what they'd like to see happen to seniors, too. . . ."

If there was to be a rebuttal to McCurry, it should have been made by someone at a lower level, and shouldn't have interrupted and inevitably taken over the coverage of a victory party. This was similar to what Gingrich had done at the end of the Medicare debate. It seemed that he just couldn't control his anger.

The Senate passed its reconciliation bill in the early hours of October 28, after a lengthy debate. Moderate Republican senators did force some changes in the Senate bill as it came from the Budget Committee. William Cohen pushed especially hard for restoration of nursing home standards which had been repealed—at the behest of the Republican governors— leaving the way open to go back to the lax practices and horrendous abuses of patients that had led to enactment of the standards in 1987. Nancy Kassebaum got changes in funding for subsidies for college loans. The Senate bill would slow the growth of the direct student loan program

—a Clinton program that let beneficiaries borrow directly, at less cost, from the government rather than through commercial banks and other lenders —while the House bill would end it. (Banking institutions opposed the program.) The final vote on the Senate bill was 52–47. Cohen was the sole Republican to vote against it, saying that this was no time to cut taxes. Though Chafee was bothered by many things in the bill, he said, "You've got to remember one driving force that is pushing this: we've got to get these deficits under control." He added—speaking, it seemed, for many moderates, in both chambers, on many issues in the course of the year— "So we've been able to swallow a lot of things to achieve that goal." Kennedy, stating what would become a strategy of a number of Democrats, said, "These cuts were not what the 1994 election was about, but it will be what the 1996 election is about."

To Gingrich's great irritation, a meeting between the President and the congressional leaders on November 1, called on the subject of Bosnia, was also to take up—at Dole's unilateral suggestion the night before—the subject of the debt ceiling. Dole had been becoming unhappy about looking like Gingrich's lapdog. He told a few people that he was weary of Gingrich's trying to take charge of everything.

In the meeting, Clinton asked the Republican leaders to send him a "clean" extension of the debt ceiling and continuing resolution—ones not carrying any conditions or policy changes. But neither Republican leader was in a position to do this, even if he wanted to. Gingrich told Clinton, "You have to understand the situation we're in. We have very fired-up members. We don't have the votes for a stand-alone extension of the debt ceiling or continuing resolution."

White House aides made much of this meeting, telling one and all that the President had been very "strong," and that it had been very candid. Clinton and Gore were seated in the familiar gold wing chairs; Gingrich was seated to Clinton's left, Dole to his right. (The meeting began with close to a punch-out between Gingrich and Gore. Gingrich, replying to the President's question of where they were on the debt limit, said, "Nowhere. How can we get somewhere when you call us extremist?" Gore responded, "At least we didn't accuse you of killing two children before the election.") Clinton told the Republican leaders, "I've accepted all of your principles— a balanced budget, welfare reform, saving Medicare—and you haven't accepted any of ours. Do you think you're the only ones who have principles? How can we talk when you don't even acknowledge our principles?" Clinton added, "I worry that hidden behind your Contract is that you want to destroy the federal government."

Then, Clinton said, "I don't want to break *my* contract with America," and, dramatically pointing to the chair behind his desk, "I'll let Bob Dole do that if he's in that chair." (Morris was the author of this and similar lines.) Clinton told the Republicans, "I have strong feelings about your budget. I didn't run for office for the things in your budget."

After the meeting, Tony Blankley said, "Newt feels that these encounters with the President are always interesting, but that imputing any meaning to them may be a fool's errand."

In an interview shortly after this meeting, McCurry said that the President wanted to fight on the issues of Medicare, Medicaid, education, and the environment in 1996. "Clinton would prefer to fight it out in the elections next year," McCurry said. "That's a hell of a lot better than seeing the federal government dismembered. We'd rather have no deal than a bad deal." He continued, "Gingrich and Dole saw that in Clinton for the first time at the meeting."

At this point the President's advisers—including Morris—felt that it was important to show him as strong, as standing for principle. The backflip in Houston on taxes and all that it conjured up were still on people's minds. That there were things that Clinton did care about, such as education, was undeniable. But the theatrics tended to undermine that point, as did the extent to which his list of priorities reflected the polls.

Over a period of the few days before the continuing resolution was about to expire on November 13, a new one, and an increase in the debt limit, bounced back and forth between the House and the Senate—and some unusual baggage was added to them. (The Democrats had added policy matters to past continuing resolutions, but not to this extent.)

The debt limit bill had a provision that removed some of the Treasury Department's powers to deal with the matter. And House Republicans also added to the debt limit bill a version of the regulatory reform bill (which was stuck in the Senate), and a bill limiting habeas corpus (which was stuck in the House). The debt limit bill also carried a provision committing the President to a balanced budget in seven years, as measured by the C.B.O. Tom DeLay said in an interview, "If he shuts the government down we'll keep it shut down until he signs a bill or an agreement in writing about what he will do. You can't trust their word on anything." Both bills became pork barrel legislation, as votes were sought to get it passed. Oddly, both bills contained a provision having to do with allowing Medicare to pay for certain oral hormonal drugs—at DeLay's suggestion in order to please some moderates who were pushing for this. Dan Meyer said, "The House and Senate leadership were worried about getting into fighting between the two chambers. The leadership was together, but they had trouble maneuvering."

But in writing the continuing resolution, the House Republicans committed a big blunder—and made another miscalculation. The Republicans put in their continuing resolution a provision eliminating a scheduled (for technical reasons, having to do with the resetting of computers) drop in Medicare premiums—which would have to go back up even higher under the Republicans' Medicare proposal. When Bill Archer, the Ways and Means chairman, made the proposal at a leadership meeting in the Dinosaur Room, Eddie Gillespie, Armey's press secretary, started waving his arms in distress at Bill Paxon. In that meeting and others, Kasich strongly opposed putting such a proposal in the continuing resolution, predicting, presciently, "They're going to kill us with that." A leadership aide said, "We made a conscious decision to put the Medicare premium in the continuing resolution because politically it was better to debate it this year than next year." Besides, he added, the Republicans expected Clinton to sign both the continuing resolution and debt limit bills.

Many conservatives, especially the freshmen, were upset that the now-peripatetic Istook amendment—to curb lobbying activities by groups receiving federal funds—didn't make it into the final versions of these bills. Some freshmen had crossed the Capitol to encourage the Senate to support both the Istook amendment and the elimination of the Commerce Department, but there weren't enough votes in the Senate to kill the Cabinet department, and it wasn't prepared to make the Istook amendment a demand.

As Kasich had predicted, the White House pounced, saying that the Republicans wanted to cut Medicare benefits in order to balance the budget. In the debate on the House floor on November 10, Dick Durbin, of Illinois, said, "The Speaker wants to shut down the government so that he can raise the Medicare premium." Under the Republican plan, Medicare premiums would end up in seven years at $85 a month, and at $77 a month under the administration's proposal (they were currently $46 a month). A frustrated Gingrich often pointed out the similarity between the proposed premium increases.

The two chambers approved the debt limit bill and the continuing resolution on November 8 and 9 and on Friday, November 10, Clinton said in the briefing room, "Last night, Republicans in Congress voted to raise Medicare premiums, cut education . . . and [broke with] three decades of bipartisan environmental safeguards." (Riders limiting E.P.A. enforcement had been added.)

Clinton added, "I believe this budget debate is about two very different futures for America," a valid comment with which Gingrich agreed.

Beneath all the noise and the posturing, and despite the fact that in some specifics the Republicans and the administration weren't very far apart, and despite the compromises Clinton had already made, two very different views of the role of government *were* driving the debate.

The atmosphere in Washington was keyed up and edgy. The people on

Capitol Hill were tired and frustrated. There had been shutdowns of the government in previous years (five of them on weekends and none of them laying off federal workers for more than one weekday—though monuments were closed), but no one could be sure where this would lead or what the public reaction would be. At the White House, staff members stayed close to their television sets as Congress completed action on the continuing resolution and the debt limit.

And something that the House Republicans hadn't expected to see all year was suddenly before them. An adviser to House Republicans said in early November, "They're watching their poll numbers fall deeper and deeper. For the first time, there's real concern about their reelection." On that same day, a *Wall Street Journal*/NBC poll (taken more than a week earlier) said that the public would blame Congress more than the President if there was no budget agreement. Gingrich's own support had been dropping all fall. On November 10, a Gallup poll said that his favorable rating was twenty-five percent and his unfavorable was fifty-six percent. The same poll also said that a large majority of the public thought that the Republican proposals to cut spending went too far. And it gave Clinton his highest approval rating—fifty-two percent—in eighteen months. This was a swift reversal of fortunes.

And then the Republicans made what Gingrich and others later realized was another mistake. After the President on Friday called on the Congress to stay in session over the weekend and work to resolve the impasse, he had gone off to play golf. Dole and Gingrich held a press conference at which each carried a golf club and made light of the situation. (The President's outing may seemed unwise, but he very rarely played golf during the week, and aides explained that on Saturday, Veterans Day, he would be tied up with official duties.) Gingrich realized later that the golf club stunt was inappropriate.

The Republicans believed that a shutdown would hurt Clinton more than it would them, because a shutdown in 1990 had hurt President Bush. Still, having convinced themselves that Clinton would accept whatever they proposed, they were surprised by his resistance. In fact, the communications between the Republican leaders and the White House were so poor by that weekend, and Gingrich was sufficiently puzzled by Clinton's recent behavior, that he asked a Republican friend to find out through his own Democratic ties what was going on at the White House. Gingrich assumed that the "hard-liners"—by whom he meant Harold Ickes and Stephanopoulos, as opposed to Morris—had taken over.

The lack of any real contact, or understanding, between the Republican leaders and the White House led to a number of miscalculations—on both sides—in the course of the year. A leading Washington Democrat said,

"The Republicans feel that there's no one at the White House to talk to. Leon could have been that person if he hadn't over time become rough and personal. You can be tough about proposals as opposed to calling the Republicans terrorists with a gun to the head of the President," as Panetta did in the course of the argument over the continuing resolution. This person continued, "So there's nobody left for the Republicans to talk to, and that's serious." (Over the course of the Thanksgiving week, an effort was made by go-betweens to get Clinton and Gingrich on the phone with each other, to smooth things out. But neither Clinton nor Gingrich—both being capable of churlishness—was willing.)

Over the weekend of November 11–12, with the shutdown scheduled to begin at midnight on Monday, each side strove to place blame on the other. Republicans charged that Clinton wasn't willing to work with them to avoid a crisis. On Saturday, Dole and Gingrich complained that in a brief phone conversation with them the President had done almost all of the talking, and then, having said he would call them back after a Veterans Day event, didn't. Dan Meyer said later, "They felt set up because the President did a monologue and they weren't able to say why they were making the call."

On the Sunday television talk shows, administration figures denounced the Republicans' proposals. That afternoon, Mike McCurry said that the President was willing to talk to the Republican leaders in the Oval Office the next day if they would drop the "Medicare fee increase."

The Republicans also used the shows to defend their position. On *Meet the Press,* Gingrich said, "The President basically hung up on Senator Dole and me yesterday . . . and apparently is prepared to close the government down rather than sit down and talk to us." Dole brought a cellular phone to *This Week with David Brinkley,* joking that he wanted to be available if the President called.

A White House official said that it "wasn't an easy call" for the President to veto the Republicans' continuing resolution and the raise in the debt limit, which he did on Monday morning. A Presidential adviser said, "He has to convey that he has good reason to veto. If the public just thinks it's bickering, that doesn't work. It's important for the President to be clear about what he's standing for."

In the Oval Office ceremony, Clinton put the issue in large terms. Wearing his reading glasses (he almost never did this in public), Clinton said, "Our country has to choose between two very different options—two very different visions of our future." He added, "The Republican Congress has failed to pass most of its spending bills, but instead has sought to impose some of its most objectionable proposals on the American people by attaching them to bills to raise the debt limit and to keep the government running."

Clinton had long believed that, in the end, both Gingrich and Dole would want to be able to say that they had produced a final agreement, but now he saw that reaching that point was more difficult than he had thought. Panetta was now according a higher probability to the idea that there might not be one. Stephanopoulos was unperturbed, since he preferred to fight over the issues—on which he felt that the public was on the Democrats' side—all the way to the 1996 election. With no deal, the President could take to the election five big issues: Medicare, Medicaid, the environment, education, and taxes on working people (the E.I.T.C.). By mid-November, the White House people came to believe that Gingrich had been seized by his hard-right members (just as Gingrich believed that Clinton had been seized by his liberal hard-liners).

Virtually lost in the commotion over the continuing resolution was completion of work by the House and Senate on a compromise reconciliation bill. The final bill, cutting spending by $894 billion over seven years, was approved by both chambers on Friday, November 17. (A few details had to be ironed out on Monday.) Overall, it redistributed the benefits of federal programs from the less wealthy—especially the poor—to the better off. Some of the programs needed to be brought under control, and liberals couldn't have done it (or hadn't done it), but the Republicans' proposals had a clear class impact. They would expand the already growing gap between rich and poor. By one estimate, almost half the savings in the reconciliation bill were in entitlement programs for the poor, though such programs accounted for about a fourth of all spending on entitlements. (At the same time, in separate appropriations bills, numerous programs that were supposed to benefit the poor were being sharply cut.) In an interview, Gingrich rejected as "liberal fantasy" the idea that spending could increase "unending forever and crush your children in debt." He argued that liberal critics "start with a fantasy baseline and claim cuts." In the Republican program, he said, "Spending goes up. We improve the delivery services, we decentralize away from Washington, we cut out red tape and bureaucracy, and we have a different moral purpose. Our purpose is to get people to work and to strengthen families, not just to transfer wealth to people as they destroy themselves." Gingrich had a point in arguing that programs couldn't just keep growing unchecked, and also that in some instances alternative approaches should be considered—but those points didn't address the issue of disproportionality.

Medicaid was turned into a block grant program, removing its entitlement status, and its rate of growth was cut nearly in half. For this and other reasons, the White House had already said that the President would veto the bill. Having undergone so much criticism from his own constituency—including a powerful public letter from the Clintons' longtime friend Marian Wright Edelman, head of the Children's Defense Fund, published in the *Washington Post* on November 3—over his going along with welfare being turned into a block grant, Clinton dug in on not allowing Medicaid to be turned into a block grant. Moreover, Medicaid was an issue for the middle class as well as the poor, since the Republican proposal allowed states to go after the assets of children of nursing home residents. It also cut the states' matching requirements. Thus, welfare recipients could be twice (or more) hit as a result of the changes in welfare and Medicaid. The final bill cut the Earned Income Tax Credit substantially—about eighteen percent at the end of seven years.

It also cut spending on food stamps, school lunches, and foster care. And it denied legal immigrants Medicaid, food stamps, and other benefits.

The final reconciliation bill still cut taxes by $245 billion, but only for families with adjusted gross incomes under $110,000 a year. Those who were too poor to pay taxes wouldn't receive the benefit of this cut. The family tax credit was made retroactive to October 1, 1995, at the behest of conservative family groups who wanted something to show for their efforts before the year was out. Other tax cuts went for capital gains and business —mostly small business, the House Republicans' key business constituency. And tax benefits of Individual Retirement Accounts would be increased—a boon to the wealthy.

Medicare spending was still reduced by $270 billion. A few tax preferences (Robert Reich's "corporate welfare") were ended so as to lessen the cut in Medicaid, which was still substantial. A ceiling was placed on the direct student loan program. The final bill did take on a couple of powerful Republican constituencies: subsidies of some major commodities (but not of sugar, peanuts, and dairy products) were reformed and lowered. Some veterans services were reduced.

The ultimate result was to make some changes that needed making, and also to change the direction of government. Spending would no longer keep up with inflation and the number of recipients. The Republicans played to their own constituencies, which did not include the poor. They played suburban politics. The Republicans' program also made a strong start on referring programs to the states, where the legislatures were dominated by suburban interests. It marched in the direction of Gingrich's goal of breaking the national power of the liberal lobbies by making them scramble for their programs in fifty state capitals. There was little in the Republicans' final budget that reflected the magnanimity in Gingrich's opening day speech. Gingrich would and did argue that only by curbing the federal government could people realize their potential, but even if this was the case his program didn't address the gaps that would occur in people's lives. It would be a long time before charities could make up the difference, as Gingrich often suggested—if they ever could. (Of course, the spending cuts would reduce the federal funds that charities had to work with, and the Republicans were also seeking to reduce the charities' political power.) Even some of Gingrich's closest advisers thought that his program had a problem of fairness.

Gingrich also argued that the welfare state had failed, but this was an oversimplification. Some programs worked; many were never fully funded. Other industrial democracies were also struggling with the problem of how to meet the needs and demands of its citizenry. Certainly in the case of the United States, the demands were contradictory: for less government but against reductions in services and benefits to one's own group.

In a press conference with Dole on Saturday, the day after the reconciliation bill was passed, Gingrich said, "This is the largest domestic decision we've made since 1933. . . . This is a fundamental change in the direction of government." Gingrich was right to see it in such historical terms, if the Republican position held.

With a shutdown looming on Monday night, Domenici, who was experienced at negotiating budget compromises, and, like Dole, was more inclined than the House leaders to resolve issues, put forth the idea of freezing the Medicare premium at the existing rate. The Gingrich quarters weren't pleased that it learned of this proposal through the press. A House leader said, "Enough of us threw cold water on it that Pete knew it wasn't going to fly with us." When Gingrich in the Republican conference late that afternoon raised the possibility of passing a new continuing resolution without the Medicare provision, most members went along, but a large enough number opposed dropping the Medicare provision, on the grounds that it would appear that they had done something wrong and were making a concession, that the idea went nowhere. The Republicans were stuck with an untenable position.

The House and Senate were kept in session Monday night while Dole and Gingrich went down to the White House to meet with Clinton—in case they came back with some understanding that could avert a government shutdown.

Clinton had offered to meet with the congressional leaders on Monday night because some aides worried that he wasn't looking willing enough to try to work something out. They had a point. He had been brusque with the congressional leaders, and his staff appeared to take pleasure in giving them the runaround.

In the meeting, Gingrich warned that he would never let a centrist budget get to the House floor. He also allowed that he had some problems with the C.B.O. numbers, too, and that was something the two sides could work on together. Gingrich said, "I'm as infuriated with them as I am with you guys sometimes." He said he'd be willing to have some well-regarded outside experts, such as Alan Greenspan, advise the C.B.O. on its assumptions. Rubin replied that that wouldn't be appropriate. Armey, who was in the meeting, agreed. (Later in the week Gingrich was insistent on basing any agreement on C.B.O. assumptions.)

White House officials said afterward that they got the impression that Dole was eager to make a deal, that Gingrich was interested, but that Armey was very hard-line. In fact, Armey and Clinton got into a dustup over Clinton's being so negative about the Republicans' plan, and the Republicans' total opposition to Clinton's 1993 economic program and Armey's attacking Mrs. Clinton in 1993 (saying that "her thoughts sound a lot like Karl Marx—she hangs around a lot of Marxists").

When Clinton insisted to the group that there were some programs he felt strongly about, Armey—who by now had a record of bluntness with Clinton—said, "I don't believe you." "I didn't expect you to," Clinton snapped. Gingrich's concern of earlier in the year, which he had expressed to his friends, that Armey and DeLay were too far to his right still held. But Armey was a very important figure because of his influence with conservatives, including the newer members, who had pushed for him to be on the negotiating team. Armey could sell or sink any agreement that Gingrich made. When Gingrich came to some tentative agreement with Dole on a move, he would say he had to "shop that around," meaning, an aide said, he had to talk to Armey.

The whole business about the "assumptions" was, of course, absurd—"a joke" as one administration official put it. There was no way to predict the state of the economy seven years hence—or even before that—and small differences in numbers could make a big difference in how a budget turned out. The official said, "The average difference in our growth rate over seven years is smaller than an error in a one-year forecast. There's always an error in a forecast. You can't know at that level of precision what's going to happen—to health care costs, to profits versus wages. The differences in our forecasts are very small. The problem is that over seven years small differences grow because of the effect of compound interest. Therefore the assumptions were a crucial part of the bargaining."

But the debate wasn't about that. It couldn't by any logic be about at what stage the C.B.O. scored a budget, or what profit shares (the share of national income that goes to profits) would be in seven years—one of the ostensible issues in the argument over assumptions. It was a test of strength, with the Republican leaders wanting to make a point, to defeat the President, and to squeeze spending as much as they could, and the

President's side leaning on assumptions that would cause its programs less hardship.

George Stephanopoulos said at one point in the fall, "The whole ball game is economic assumptions and the tax cut and Medicare." He continued, "If they insist on their assumptions there can be no deal. We can get to seven or eight years using our numbers. We can't get to ten years with their numbers."

Another bit of farce was that though the Republicans' proposal put the budget in balance in year seven, the deficit would rise in the first two years and it was only to come into balance in the seventh year—and was then to go back up, largely because of the tax cuts. The Republicans postponed the pain—at least for their own constituencies, since the tax cut was to begin right away and be retroactive, and defense spending was to rise right away, and amount to $7 billion more than the Pentagon had asked for. In political terms, seven years was a century, so if the goals weren't met—as most budget goals weren't—the politicians could think about that later (if they were still around).

At the end of the Monday night meeting, the President suggested that all those present tell the press that the meeting had been constructive, though no agreement had been reached, and that there would be further meetings of Panetta, Kasich, Domenici, and Alice Rivlin.

At about midnight, Dole, Armey, and Gingrich came out of the White House and told the press, somberly, "We don't have an agreement," but they adhered to the President's request. Then Daschle and Gephardt followed, and were much more negative. Daschle said that there had been "no progress at all," and talked about the President's firm stand on Medicare.

The next day a furious Domenici denounced the Democrats for their comments, saying that an agreement had been made in the Oval Office to be constructive in their comments afterward but that the Democrats had violated it. Dan Meyer said, "Newt felt very set up." The next time that Panetta and Kasich and Domenici met, when Panetta suggested that they take a certain line after the meeting, the Republican Budget Committee chairmen refused.

The shutdown, which began at midnight on Monday, November 13, created an eerie feeling in Washington. There was some giddiness over the question of whether one was "essential," and was to keep working, or "nonessential." There was status in one, time off in the other. But the furloughing of 800,000 federal workers left many families with uncertainties. (It was decided later that they would receive back pay, but this didn't alleviate short-term hardship.) In the government offices it was as if numerous people had simply disappeared. There were also inconveniences for

Members of Congress, who had to put up with smaller staffs, whose switchboard was a sometimes thing. The Senate dining rooms were closed, but the House dining room, which had been contracted to private purveyors, wasn't. On the first day of the shutdown, Daniel Inouye relied on a can of soup in his office; Nancy Kassebaum lunched on a granola bar. As the shutdown went on, some senators deigned to eat in the House dining room. The closing of the national parks and some buildings in Washington to tourists who had long ago made plans was the most visible—and embarrassing—part of the picture.

While each side was trying to blame the other for the shutdown, Gingrich's complaining about the snub he felt he had been given on the President's plane to the funeral of Yitzhak Rabin, who had been assassinated on November 4, and saying that that had affected the fate of the nation, gave the Democrats a great boon—and the Republicans a headache. His telling reporters at a Wednesday, November 15, breakfast that that was "part of why you ended up with us sending down a tougher interim spending bill," set off an explosion of derisive laughter from his opponents.

Gingrich complained that the President hadn't bothered to discuss matters, in particular the budget, with him and Dole during the entire trip, and that the Republican leaders had to leave the plane by the rear exit. (According to one passenger, Gingrich, seated next to Dole—Gingrich's wife, the only spouse allowed to come, after Gingrich made a fuss, was across the aisle—talked at Dole almost all the way to Israel.) The scene in the photograph gleefully released by the White House showing Gingrich and Dole and a lot of other people seemingly in conference with the President was actually a briefing for all the passengers on the situation and logistics in Israel.

A key House Republican said that the continuing resolution had in fact become tougher as a result of Gingrich's pique.

The fundamental question was why Gingrich would say such a thing—especially since he knew it could cause trouble ("Tony is going to tell me later that I shouldn't have said this"). The resourceful Blankley later explained that Gingrich had simply been making the point that the White House had passed up another opportunity to make progress on the budget issue. Gingrich told Joe Gaylord that he just thought it was very interesting historically that such things can affect policy.

But Gingrich wasn't so detached at first, when colleagues tried to tell him that he had made a big mistake. According to two witnesses, when in a meeting John Boehner tried to tell Gingrich that he had erred he got "screamed at" by Gingrich for fifteen minutes for suggesting such a thing. When Gingrich went on to say in a leadership meeting that he had been trying to make the serious point that the Republicans had been reaching out to talk to the President but the White House didn't seem to want to talk —this was following the Veterans Day weekend as well—according to a colleague, "The rest of us around the table kind of rolled our eyes." It was some time before Gingrich would acknowledge that he had made a mistake.

This incident came just as Republicans were moving to drop the Medicare provision from the continuing resolution—and adding the seven-year budget/C.B.O. term—and getting back on the offensive. They said that Clinton wouldn't accept their new proposal because he didn't want to balance the budget. Republicans who knew better—and in some cases knew that their listeners knew better—seemed to have no difficulty in purveying this falsehood.

Gingrich, the former misfit who had now achieved great power and fame, seemed to be especially sensitive to what he saw as slights from people who were more accepted. But he also had a point (as a few people in the White House recognized). It wouldn't have made sense or been appropriate for the President to negotiate the budget on a plane trip and without the relevant aides, but it would have made sense, and been more polite, for the President to have schmoozed with the Republican leaders for a while. And someone in the President's entourage should have been smart enough to see to it that the congressional leaders left the plane from the front door—seemingly a small matter but the kind of punctility that helps hold Washington together. The President did seem to be giving the congressional leaders the back of his hand. And for the White House to put out the word, as it did after Gingrich's complaint, that Clinton was too much in mourning to deal with earthly matters was silly, especially since according to several witnesses he had spent a fair amount of the time on the plane playing hearts, his favorite card game.

A Presidential adviser said later, "This all came at a time when people in the White House were anxious that the President spend as little 'face time' as possible with the Republican leaders—that he should look 'strong.' The prevailing view was 'Don't spend time with them. Send the message that you're sticking with principles.' You show that by treating it as a bad Gary Cooper movie."

A Clinton adviser said that the President was now coming across strongly because he truly believed in what he was saying: that one can be fiscally responsible and be a Democrat.

Clinton and his aides believed that he was finally getting through to the public, and getting across the idea that there could be deficit reduction and also some increases in spending at the same time. To his great frustration, he hadn't been able to achieve this in his first two years in office. The adviser said, "This is a very good debate for him." Besides, this position put him between the wings of his party. Now he was both "triangulating" within his own party, and, at the same time, mending relations with the liberals who had angrily split with him over his offering a balanced budget in the first place.

But the President carried the argument to melodramatic lengths, saying, on CBS, "If the American people want the budget that [the Republicans] have proposed to be the law of the land, they're entitled to another President." He also threatened on CBS to take the issue into the 1996 election. (The week before, Cabinet members filed out of a meeting with the President and praised his determination and quoted the President as saying several times, "I cannot, I will not, back down." This was getting embarrassing.) At a gathering of the Democratic Leadership Council on November 13, Clinton became Churchillian, saying of the Republican budget, "I will fight it today, I will fight it next week, and next month. I will fight it until we get a budget that is fair to all Americans."

Some people in the White House, and at times also Morris, thought that the President needed to look more like a calm leader than the feisty combatant. But at this point, a White House aide said of the often-feuding Stephanopoulos and Morris, "George's and Dick's temperaments converged—each brought a pugilistic temperament to the discussions." For a while, Morris even sided with Stephanopoulos and others who didn't want an agreement. But that didn't last.

Clinton came to enjoy his new approach. One of his aides said, "He likes standing up. Once you get used to it, it's kind of fun." Clinton still tended to be more accommodating than some of his aides, but when they brought him certain specifics—such as turning Medicaid into a block grant or making heavy cuts in education—he would say, "I won't sign that."

Gingrich had some difficulty on Wednesday in persuading his flock to back a new continuing resolution without the Medicare provision. Many of the freshmen had been unhappy with the first continuing resolution, which they felt was too easy on the President. Now, when it came to removing the Medicare provision, Tom DeLay, who was whipping the issue, told Gingrich that a rebellion was brewing. So, while a regular party conference, called for 6:00 P.M., was being conducted in the Ways and Means Committee room, in a side room Gingrich was working on about twenty-five freshmen whom DeLay had delivered to him, explaining his reasoning. He told them that it was very important to "get back on message," dropping the Medicare issue and talking about balancing the budget. Kasich worked on the freshmen as well. But the freshmen were insistent on keeping the Medicare provision. Kasich said, "I told them that we had lost that fight, that seven years and C.B.O. were the most important things we could get. It was a long conversation." Dan Meyer said later, "Newt was determined we were going to do it. We told Armey's and DeLay's staffs, 'Bring the House back in. Ring the bells. Start whipping.' "

The House leaders didn't realize how worried the White House was that the House might pass the new continuing resolution by a large margin. It was opposed, of course, to the resolution's demand that the Republican budget terms—seven years with C.B.O. scoring—be met. The President and the Vice President were on the phone to Democratic members. Panetta and Stephanopoulos went to the Hill.

In the end, forty-eight Democrats supported the Republican resolution, which passed by a vote of 277–151—nearly enough to override a veto. (Two-thirds of those voting were necessary for an override—290 if all 435 members voted.)

Going into the weekend, both sides were under considerable pressure to make a deal on the continuing resolution—though they wouldn't admit it. Polls were now showing that the public blamed the shutdown on the Republicans rather than on the Democrats by margins of about two to one.

The paradox that the politicians had been facing all year—that the public wanted them to both stick to principles *and* work together to get things done—was now making itself felt forcefully. The polls also indicated that the public was growing tired of the bickering in Washington, and could at any moment turn on both parties.

Clinton was in danger of being overridden on his next veto of a continuing resolution. Several Democrats who had voted with the President were making it clear to the leadership that they couldn't continue to appear to be voting "against a balanced budget." After the November 15 vote, David Skaggs, the Colorado Democrat, said, "I voted against the continuing resolution but there are probably forty Democratic votes that are hanging with the President by a thread." Several Senate Democrats felt the same way. Dole told House leaders that he thought he could win an override of a Presidential veto on the next vote.

The particular problem for the House Democratic leadership was that more than eighty members of their caucus had voted at one time or another for a balanced budget in seven years. And now that the Republicans had removed the Medicare issue, and were making the simple argument that Clinton didn't "want to balance the budget," Republicans were beginning to win the public relations fight. Mike McCurry said, "The Republicans lose the debate on the budget itself, but when they keep it on the continuing resolution, it's about balancing the budget."

Dick Gephardt believed that it was time for the President to make a deal on a continuing resolution—that Clinton could sign anything and it wouldn't matter because it wasn't enforceable. It was too hard for his members to get across to their constituents why they weren't voting "for a balanced budget"—the talk about C.B.O. numbers versus O.M.B. numbers made no sense to the general public. "You can't explain this to anybody," Gephardt said. Gephardt pressed his view on Panetta and Stephanopoulos that the President should sign *something,* and let the government reopen. Everyone from the liberal Rosa DeLauro to the conservative Charles Stenholm thought that the President should sign a continuing resolution. Some Democrats—and also a few Republicans—had large numbers of federal workers in their districts and were under strong pressure to end the shutdown. Even some black Democrats who represented a lot of government workers had voted for the most recent continuing resolution. A Democratic leadership aide said, "For us, it didn't make sense to keep the government closed."

Gephardt believed that it would be better to take the issues to the public in the 1996 election than settle on a budget agreement. Gephardt said, "My view is that we should take the bigger argument to the public. This is not a trifling event. These are huge changes in programs and huge tax cuts and we should let the public in on that." A close associate of Gephardt's said, "Dick wants to be Speaker, and the best way for the Democrats to regain control of the House is through these issues."

Toward the end of the week, Clinton's approval ratings, as measured in the administration's own polling, began to drop—a fact Lott passed on over the weekend to his Republican colleagues, who were under the clear impression that it had come from Morris. (Asked about this later, Lott said, "I'm not denying, but I'm not admitting it, either.") Lott suggested to his colleagues that the new numbers meant that Clinton was ready to buckle.

The Republican National Committee ran a damaging ad all weekend showing clips of Clinton citing the various time periods—ten, nine, eight, seven, and even five (during his Presidential campaign) years—within which he could see getting to a balanced budget. This ad was in part designed to help Gingrich, who had been hearing from peeved members that his airplane saga had taken him—and the Republicans—"off message." Tony Blankley said, "We told members that he would get back 'on message.' " Gingrich was publicly insistent that "there's no compromise on seven years and on having an honest number scored in an honest way." John Boehner said, "We've finally found something that Bill Clinton stands for: he doesn't want to balance the budget." On Saturday morning, Gingrich, Haley Barbour, Blankley, and Eddie Gillespie and other communications advisers gathered to discuss how to win the propaganda war. The primary conclusion, Blankley said, was to "make sure we keep the message on the balanced budget and don't get in the weeds on process." (In the fall, Dole had Barbour removed from his conferences with Gingrich, feeling —with reason—that Barbour's role was to reinforce Gingrich and get Dole to go along.)

The next step was for the House Republicans to convince the White House that they really weren't going to yield. This was an odd way to "negotiate," but by now, because of the freshmen, and the House leaders' own feeling that they had pledged a balanced budget by 2002, and because of their sense that Clinton was in a weakening position, they weren't about to budge. Gingrich had told Clinton in a meeting at the White House that he and his fellow Republicans were prepared to use the continuing resolution and debt limit to get their way.

Gingrich was doing no less than trying to weight the Constitutional system of checks and balances—of shared power between the President and the Congress. If the President had the veto power, Congress had the power of withholding funds. The Constitution was, in the Constitutional scholar Edward S. Corwin's words, "an invitation to struggle." In the end, the two branches were to compromise but a number of House Republicans rejected a system dependent upon consensus and compromise. And if one doesn't believe that the federal government should have much power, one doesn't mind the consequences of strangling it, or shutting it down, in order to prevail (even if there are short-term negative polls). In a Senate speech in early January, Paul Sarbanes, Democrat of Maryland, said, "To make our Constitutional system work requires a certain amount of restraint and good judgment on the part of all decision-makers. It must be an essential premise of our system that one is not willing to subvert everything, in effect to bring the whole building crashing down, in order to get your way."

In Gingrich's view, he said in an interview, the Constitution favored the Congress on domestic issues. "All the advantages a Commander in Chief gets in foreign policy the Congress gets in domestic policy." He added, "The Federalist Papers describe it that way. It's what Reagan and Bush discovered to their chagrin—that owning the Congress is much more powerful than owning the White House in terms of defining America domestically. What's shocking people is this is the first time you've had a center-right majority that was serious in a very, very long time." Gingrich was certain he had the weapons to help him prevail. "If we don't provide the money, in the end they run out of options," he said.

Dole and Domenici were more willing—the House leaders thought them too eager—to compromise than Gingrich and Kasich, and suspicion between the two chambers' leaders deepened as the budget crisis continued. John Boehner said of the dealings during this period, "The White House played a role, but our greater concern was the Senate. They wanted to balance the budget, but being loved was more important to them. They wanted to do what they'd done all these years—cut a deal." Even Trent Lott, who was involved in the events of the weekend before the continuing resolution was about to expire, was a problem for his old friends in the House. In a meeting on Saturday morning, Gingrich said, "No, Trent, we're not going to cut a deal. It'll be seven years and C.B.O. or we'll all sit here for a long time."

All weekend, the Capitol was the scene of rolling meetings, one after the other, some consisting of just the Republican leaders alone, some including Panetta. On Friday the White House offered language setting a "goal" of a balanced budget in seven years, which the Republicans wouldn't accept.

The matter remained stuck until well into Saturday, after Dole returned late in the afternoon from a straw poll in Florida (which he won, but not by an overwhelming margin) and urged his colleagues to make a deal with the White House. Dole said, "We've got to send them some language. We can't just sit here and not respond." Domenici said that Panetta would laugh at a proposal that said the C.B.O. should reach its decision after consultation with the O.M.B. and others, because that already happened—but a proposal adding this to a demand for a seven-year budget, scored by the C.B.O., was sent to the White House late Saturday.

By now, relations between the House and Senate leaders were quite frayed. Dole had even taken to avoiding when he could standing next to Gingrich for the cameras, figuring—not without reason—that Gingrich's sinking popularity was rubbing off on him. Kasich, who did want a budget deal, felt that the senators—Dole and Domenici—were too eager to bend. Dole and Domenici had been more willing than their counterparts to accept the White House offer. Kasich remembered that Domenici had started off thinking that the budget couldn't be balanced. "The Senate wasn't going to get us to cave in," Kasich said later.

A House leadership aide said, of Dole and Domenici, "While they couldn't do anything without us, we didn't want a rupture with the Senate." He continued, "They felt that we weren't getting the better of the argument. They judged that we might overplay our hand, and the longer it went on the less we might get. So we had to manage that relationship." Blankley said later, "It was a judgment call based on the character traits of the institutions. The Senate prefers to avoid conflict, but we feel comfortable with using it to achieve our goals."

(Blankley later made a comment that few Washington figures would admit to—and many wouldn't have the sophistication to understand. Of the back and forth over the weekend, Blankley said, "Often you have to communicate within the chatter with insiders—the jockeying back and forth on the language. It's a moment in Washington time in which we play with words. But you don't necessarily want to get that to the country.")

Dole's aides later made a big thing of his role in pushing for a compromise. They suggested that Dole was concerned about the effect of Gingrich's intransigence on Gingrich's own dropping poll numbers—which the Gingrich people didn't much appreciate.

In any event, Gingrich felt that by now he had a good majority within the Senate Republican caucus. Paul Coverdell, of Georgia, with whom Gingrich had struck a close alliance, and Connie Mack and Trent Lott even attended meetings of the Speaker's Advisory Group—sometimes Coverdell chaired them.

On Sunday morning there was a vigorous argument within the White House over whether the President should stand his ground and accept an override rather than agree to a firm seven-year time limit. Some Clinton aides—in particular Stephanopoulos, Laura Tyson, and Gene Sperling, a deputy to Tyson, were opposed.

Tyson argued for allowing the President to be overridden and taking a stand on principle: that there wasn't an acceptable way to balance the budget in seven years. Stephanopoulos shared that view. It was argued that this strategy would provide unity with the congressional Democrats. Gore, who was traveling back from Japan, was upset about the prospect of a seven-year deal, and preferred accepting an override. Panetta was inherently against letting the President be overridden, but that morning felt it might be necessary in order to get the budget talks going. Griffin was very opposed to an override.

The argument over whether to accept an override was a reflection of a larger debate within the White House. The President's aides were divided over whether an ultimate deal—at least of the kind that could be gotten with the Republican Congress—was in the President's interest. Stephanopoulos was of course against a deal, feeling that the President was doing well in the current debate, especially on Medicare, and that these issues should be taken into the 1996 election—and that there was no decent agreement to be gotten, given the distance between the Republicans and the President. Ickes agreed that the issue should be taken to the election, as did Sperling. Morris was for getting a deal, because he felt that the country expected Clinton to be able to govern, get things done. Panetta was of mixed views: he was used to dealing and took some pride in reaching agreements, and thought one should be reached, but he was concerned about the impact on specific programs of any deal. Those of the no-deal school also felt that in that instance the Republicans would be in a worse political situation than Clinton: that Clinton could run on having stopped the Republicans from doing dreadful things. And the Republicans would have failed to enact the centerpiece of their program.

Clinton himself wanted to end up with a budget agreement, provided it wasn't one that made it seem that he had sold out on his priorities. That was why, a senior official explained, Clinton felt that he had to have a hundred Democrats behind any agreement he made.

In one of the White House meetings that morning, deputy chief of staff Erskine Bowles argued that the White House should get away from discussions of C.B.O. and O.M.B. and get back to talking about Democratic values. (Bowles had agreed to stay on the job until Christmas.) Besides, he argued, it would look bad if the White House flatly refused the latest Republican offer, and pressure from congressional Democrats to sign *something* was increasing.

Clinton asked that Stan Greenberg, who still did polling for the Democratic National Committee, the results of which were still sent to the President (and read by others in the White House), be asked his view. Greenberg, who was against a deal, was nevertheless of the view that the President would be weakened by an override. He also thought that the Republicans needed a deal more than the Democrats did. James Carville, who was still in touch with the White House (and close to Stephanopoulos, as was Greenberg), also thought that it would be better to take the issues to the 1996 election.

Bowles drew up a list of programs that the President would insist be adequately funded. And it was decided to add this as a condition to the Republicans' latest proposal—that "if and only if" there was adequate funding for Medicare, Medicaid, education, and the environment would the White House agree to a seven-year budget. (Some White House aides thought that the "if" clause would be meaningless.) The proposal hedged on how the assumptions would be arrived at. A second proposal sent by the White House said that it was the "sense of Congress" that the budget be balanced in seven years. White House aides believed that both proposals were "nonstarters"—but ones that would give the White House an "exit strategy" (this term came into much use in the last months of 1995, in both domestic and foreign affairs). It could say that two offers had been made and rejected by the Republicans.

When Panetta and Stephanopoulos met with budget negotiators on Sunday afternoon, Domenici took the proposal with the list of programs to be given priority and turned the sheet of paper over, saying that that proposal would go nowhere. Kasich made a big point of telling the White House representatives that the Republicans wouldn't move. Kasich told Stephanopoulos, "We're not going to budge. We're not going to change on seven years and C.B.O." (Kasich thought that Panetta had brought Stephanopoulos to the meeting to show him how dug in the Republicans were.) He added that on the next vote on a continuing resolution the Republicans would pick up at least sixty votes. Kasich believed that Panetta really wanted to settle the matter. On Friday, Panetta had chased him down in the gym. Kasich told him, "Leon, we're not going to budge." Kasich also warned Panetta not to try to make an end run around the House leaders and strike a deal with the Republican senators.

With Dole pushing for a deal on the continuing resolution, Gingrich felt that the White House proposal offered an opportunity. Besides, the Republicans felt that the White House had caved on the big issues. Kasich said later, "We took the two proposals and looked at them, and the more we looked at the one with the list, we could see that they had accepted our bookends—seven years and C.B.O." In fact, as Gingrich had told Clinton in the Monday night meeting, the Republicans had $150–$180 billion in funds they could spare for the administration's desires. (There had been some other extra funds at one time in the fall, but when Gingrich became angry with how he was being treated by the White House, he took the money off the table and spent it on other programs.) They were already considering lowering the tax cut and the cuts in Medicaid and Medicare.

So on Sunday afternoon the Republicans changed the words "if and only if" to "and." They could argue that they *were* protecting Medicare and Medicaid, and they were already privately planning to give Clinton more funds for education and the environment. The Republicans added a few priorities and hortatories of their own—making the list almost meaningless —and faxed their counterproposal back to the White House. (Interest group politics lived: the White House added agriculture and the Republicans added veterans programs. So many subjects were being added to the list that at one point Dole joked, "Why don't we add ethanol?"—an industry he had worked hard to protect.) White House aides insisted that they were surprised that the Republicans had responded positively to their proposal.

In the end, both sides agreed to a resolution saying that the President and the Congress "shall enact" a budget that balanced by 2002, and that the agreement would be estimated by the C.B.O., "following a thorough consultation and review" with the O.M.B. "and other government and private experts." The C.B.O. had long followed this approach.

Everyone, of course, claimed victory in Sunday night television statements. Clinton said, "This agreement reflects my principles." He added, "This is the way our government ought to work," and, summoning up a phrase from the past, that "We ought to be able to find common ground." Gingrich, speaking, along with Dole, Domenici, Armey, and Lott, from the Senate radio and television gallery, called the agreement "one of the great historic achievements in modern America."

But Gingrich's euphoria was short-lived. Following their statements, the Republican leaders walked downstairs to Dole's second-floor office and watched as Panetta, appearing along with Daschle, Gephardt, and Stenholm, offered his interpretation of what had happened. Emphasizing the President's priorities, Panetta said, "If we can achieve it in seven years, fine. If it's eight years, fine."

Gingrich said later, "Four to six minutes after our press conference we were already angry because we felt they were explicitly distorting a signed, written document." He added, "We walked into Dole's office and watched Panetta misdefine it. I mean, standing there saying seven years could mean eight years. I mean, go back and read the text. It was an amazing moment. We're standing in a room thinking we've just created a deal that is in writing that's about to become law. In retrospect maybe we should have blown it up at that moment, and said this is not going to pass. The government's not going to reopen, unless we get an agreement where you actually keep your word. But we didn't."

On the next morning's *Today* show, Panetta repeated the thought that balancing the budget might take "seven years or eight years"—thus confirming Gingrich's worst suspicions. He also said, "I don't think the American people ought to read a lot into what was agreed to last night." Early Monday afternoon, Gingrich complained by phone to Clinton, and Clinton managed to calm Gingrich down. Gingrich told the *Washington Times* that Clinton had agreed "that seven years means seven years." Clinton told McCurry that he had told Gingrich that he had agreed to a balanced budget in seven years and to address all of the priorities.

Gingrich claimed later that "on Monday afternoon, the President was telling me in a telephone call that he did not know why Panetta was using these words. And he was astonished." Gingrich added, "That's sort of why I decided those phone calls weren't as useful as they could be."

The continuing resolution calling on the Congress and the President to enact the new budget by the end of the first session was passed by the Senate that Sunday night, and by the House the next day. It funded government agencies without new appropriations at the lowest of the amount in the Senate or House appropriations bill or the prior year's funding, or, for agencies or programs slated to be abolished, seventy-five percent of the previous year's appropriation. After a six-day shutdown, the longest thus far, government workers returned to their jobs. The new continuing resolution was to last until midnight, December 15.

Clinton had given away a lot, and the Republicans very little. He may have resisted the idea for a while, and signed the agreement with misgivings, but Clinton was now effectively locked into seeking a balanced budget in seven years—having gone from no balanced budget to a balanced budget in ten years, then nine years, and then seven, meeting the Republicans' original demand. In their November 1 meeting, Clinton had told Gingrich that he wouldn't agree to seven years and C.B.O. scoring. But Gingrich's strategy of sitting tight and waiting for the administration to move toward him had worked.

24

DENOUEMENT?

"Newt, This Isn't Going to Work"

Despite his triumph over the President, Gingrich went off to Georgia for the Thanksgiving break feeling very low. By the time the reconciliation bill was passed, he was exhausted—"I was out on my feet," as he put it later. He was now all the more prone to being snappish and losing his temper (another trait he shared with his counterpart down Pennsylvania Avenue); his staff was tense and tired. Gingrich sometimes took on so much, adding his enthusiasms to his already staggering workload—appointing task forces at the drop of a hat—that his staff would turn to Gingrich allies for help, saying, "Newt's out of control." His tendency to pronounce on almost everything had led to new problems, and he was on the defensive in several respects.

Gingrich's complaints about the plane trip to Israel were followed six days later by his remark about a recent tragedy in Chicago in which a young woman was murdered and her unborn child was cut from her body and stolen. Gingrich said that this was "what the welfare system has created." The reaction against his remark was made all the stronger by an emotional comment by the woman's cousin that Gingrich should "remove our family tragedy from his political rhetoric." In an interview later, Gingrich pointed out that in "the great era of the Muckrakers and the Progressives, if you had a serious problem dealing with the poor there was a systemic analysis behind the problem. Now it is inappropriate to have a systemic analysis because it would be too shattering. So it's simply ruled out."

Joe Gaylord said in an interview, "He believes that if you don't talk about these things in terms of right and wrong it gets brushed aside as a random example of violence, and he believes it isn't random."

And Gingrich's victory on the continuing resolution on November 19 was followed by anxiety and disappointment. He had hoped that the continuing resolution could lead quickly to a budget agreement with the White House, just before Thanksgiving, but this was unrealistic, if not naive. The numbers were proving hard to compromise on, and even if they could be agreed on there would still be a large number of important policy differences. The Republicans were demanding that Clinton say how much more he wanted to spend and tax. The White House saw this as a trap. Panetta said in an interview, "We're not going to do that." Panetta said later, "We knew eventually that we would get to a seven-year budget scored by the C.B.O." But White House officials weren't inclined to make such a concession with nothing in return. They hoped that the trade-off for accepting seven years could be the Republicans giving something on the disputed economic assumptions. Panetta maintained that in demanding that they agree on the assumptions first the Republicans "clearly want to put us in a box." He insisted that the November 20 agreement on a continuing resolution stipulated that the measurement of an agreement by the C.B.O. would come at the end; Republicans refuted that. (The words of the agreement supported the Democrats' position.) This seemingly arcane argument could have substantive ramifications, as both sides knew.

Gingrich's worry, according to a close ally, stemmed from the fact that "he saw Phil Gramm opposing the continuing resolution and felt that if Republicans let it go on too long the right would harden, and pounce on any compromise."

When Gingrich returned from Thanksgiving, having rested and contemplated his situation, he told colleagues that he was going to put himself on the sidelines for a while. "I've thrown two interceptions," he said, referring to his comments about the trip to Israel and the Chicago murder. Gingrich explained in the interview that he had used that metaphor, "Because the defensive line established by the elite media made it impossible to complete either pass, so it was a dumb pass." A smart quarterback, he went on, "would have thrown the ball out of bounds or would have just taken the loss. I was throwing right into the teeth of the defense. I was dumb."

Gingrich knew that he had been overexposed (again) and was aware that the grumbling about him within the Republican conference was spreading, in part out of concern that he could be a liability in reelection races, that his garrulousness was taking the Republicans dangerously "off message." Just before he returned to Washington, Gingrich, inevitably, took himself out of the Presidential race.

But Gingrich's mood took another dive when, later in the week after

Thanksgiving, the Federal Election Commission filed a lawsuit against him, saying that in his 1990 reelection race (which he won by less than a thousand votes) GOPAC had given him $250,000 in "Newt support," at a time when GOPAC wasn't legally qualified to participate in federal races. The F.E.C. issued two thousand pages of documents about GOPAC—which an angry Gingrich considered a fishing license for the press and for his enemies on Capitol Hill. The press did find evidence of a GOPAC contributor asking Gingrich to intervene with the E.P.A. on its asbestos policies. (Gingrich did write the agency a letter.) Gingrich dismissed the F.E.C. report, calling it "a false and malicious charge," and a Gingrich ally said that Gingrich was very unhappy and worried about the F.E.C. report. (In a press conference, Bonior called GOPAC "a personal multimillion-dollar slush fund.")

And when, the following week, with resistance by the Republicans no longer an option, the House Ethics Committee called for an outside counsel to investigate whether Gingrich was aware that the Progress & Freedom Foundation had contributed to his college course, Gingrich's office put out a statement that he was "pleased" by the committee's action on other charges, and "confident" that "the remaining charge . . . will be dismissed." Tony Blankley said, "This can only be very gratifying for us." Actually, in a letter to Gingrich the committee said that in three instances Gingrich had violated the rules of the House, and it also chided him for exploiting his position to get a large advance on his book. The softpedaling by his office notwithstanding, Gingrich was in fact upset about the report.

The next day Gingrich's fellow leaders appeared on the House floor and were all over the television programs to celebrate his putative exoneration —saying that the Ethics Committee had "dismissed" all but a narrow tax charge. Democrats were also in a celebratory mood, saying that the committee's calling for an independent counsel on the one matter was just the opening wedge, and pointed out that the investigation of Jim Wright had begun in a similar way. (The committee's Democrats had wanted the independent counsel to investigate broader charges.)

Gingrich tried to lie low the day after the Ethics Committee letter was issued, staying out of camera range. But, caught in a hallway, he said, "I think I've been dramatically strengthened." In fact, Gingrich felt that the committee's investigation wouldn't be a short-term matter but a major distraction lasting some time, and spreading to other matters.

In early December, DeLay said, "The revolution will continue even if they brought him down." Billy Tauzin, of Louisiana (one of the five House Democratic converts to the Republican Party that year), said, "Our job is to convince the voters that [the 1996 election] is not a referendum on Newt Gingrich, it's a referendum on ideas."

•

Budget talks between high-level congressional figures and senior White House aides began on Capitol Hill on November 28—with an argument over what they were to talk about. This argument was to last for a long time. There was also, of course, an argument over who was to be at the table—a common beginning to negotiations. But the plan, arrived at in a meeting among Dole, Gingrich, Kasich, and Domenici the evening before, was to force the administration to offer a budget that was in balance in seven years, as scored by the C.B.O. Dan Meyer said, "Our thinking was that if we got them to do that, it would force them to come a long way in our direction."

But the first round of talks, characterized by acrimony, broke off three days after they began—ostensibly to await new economic estimates by the C.B.O., which hadn't revised its figures since January.

When the talks resumed on December 5, the administration made another big move in the Republicans' direction by agreeing to submit a seven-year balanced budget (though not one necessarily based on C.B.O. assumptions).

The President's latest move was privately explained by White House officials as inevitable—they had known that they were going to have to do it, but hadn't planned on doing it yet. Now the idea was to make a positive offer just before the President vetoed the reconciliation bill the next day, December 6 (using a pen that Lyndon Johnson had used to sign Medicare into law in 1965). The White House hoped that by making a new offer it could get the discussion back to the subjects of Medicare and Medicaid rather than let the Republicans go on attacking Clinton for not offering a seven-year balanced budget. The Republicans had been arguing that in the agreement about the last continuing resolution Clinton had committed himself to submitting a seven-year, C.B.O.-scored budget; he had acutally only committed to trying to reach one with the Congress. White House officials were also concerned about the approaching deadline for the continuing resolution (December 15). They didn't expect a deal by then, but, as one official put it, "It was important to appear responsible." (A House Democratic aide, asked how House members felt about Clinton's now offering a seven-year budget, sighed and said, "People are sort of used to this by now.")

Besides, congressional Democrats, with whom Panetta was in constant touch, felt that it was important to keep the process going. Otherwise, there was the danger that the President would be overridden if he opposed the next Republican continuing resolution (which many Democrats didn't want to vote against). And for those—in the White House and out—who didn't want a deal, the President's offer of a seven-year budget could be an "exit strategy," because it could be cited as evidence that the White House had tried to get a deal. And some of the President's advisers, including Alice Rivlin and Bob Rubin, found a seven-year budget an acceptable idea. Gore was opposed.

The administration's new proposal, offered on December 7, proposed the same cuts in Medicare and Medicaid as did his June budget, and made most of its cuts in discretionary domestic programs. Domenici called the proposal a "warmed-over" version of the President's June budget. Kasich said, "The bottom line is the administration came up to Capitol Hill today and gave us the Clinton plan that is at minimum $400 billion in the hole." Administration officials shot back that the Republicans appeared to not want to talk about Medicare and Medicaid. They also vowed that they would not be "blackmailed" into accepting the Republicans' terms—a seven-year/C.B.O.-scored budget—in order to avoid another shutdown. It was a while before Gingrich realized that they meant it.

Because of his involvement at the time in various foreign policy matters, Clinton was for a while less than fully engaged in the White House discussions about budget strategy. More immediately important was the need to sell a very dubious Congress on implementing a peace agreement on Bosnia by dispatching twenty thousand troops as part of a sixty-thousand-member force. Officials recognized, and some worried about, the complexity and fragility of the agreement—reached on November 21, after twenty-one days of peace talks at Wright-Patterson Air Force Base, in Dayton, Ohio—that Bosnia was to be a single country divided in nearly equal parts into a Bosnian-Croat federation and a Serb republic, with a central government to supposedly manage overall affairs. The chief worry was whether the Bosnian Serbs would ultimately accept it, even though Slobodan Milosevic was behind it. To deal with the strong congressional pressure to help the Bosnian Muslims rearm, the administration privately (outside the agreement) promised the Muslims that it would see to it that they were rearmed—by other nations, so as to maintain the United States's "neutrality."

Bob Dole drew criticism from within the Republican Party for supporting the administration; Gramm was of course critical, but so was Trent Lott. John McCain, the former P.O.W. in North Vietnam, also drew heat from within the party for supporting Dole, but his position was a great help to Dole. Dole's reversion to the bipartisan statesman, a role he had played well in the past, made him stand out. In the end, both the Senate and the House grudgingly voted to support the troops (the Senate also said the President could send the troops, provided he also promised to beef up the Bosnian Muslim forces).

The debate reflected division and confusion over American foreign policy in the post–Cold War era. It also reflected the unpopularity of sending troops into an area where the outcome is not a sure thing. Even with a volunteer army, Americans had low tolerance for casualties. Surveys showed that a majority of Americans didn't approve of sending troops to Bosnia. In that sense, Clinton was taking a big risk—and being a leader.

In the House, which had earlier voted against the administration's policy in Bosnia, Gingrich took an essentially positive position ("I think most Americans don't want us to fail to lead NATO"), adding that the burden was on the President to make the case. One night, Boehner felt compelled to seek Gingrich out in his office and tell him that between his "interceptions" and his statement on Bosnia there was a furor on the House floor, with several Republicans questioning his leadership. After that, Gingrich remained quiet about Bosnia. A House leader said, "Newt and Dole got out ahead of their troops."

Clinton's trip to Ireland later in November provided excellent television pictures of rapturous crowds, celebrating a relative calm (even though the I.R.A. had yet to fulfill its pledge to disarm). From there, Clinton went to Paris to sign the Bosnian accord and to Germany to visit troops that would be sent to implement it.

In contrast to the first years of shaky foreign policy management, Clinton was now looking decisive, in command, and even seemed to enjoy dealing with the subject. Success became him, and he was coming to appreciate that this was an area where, with the exception of Bosnia, he could act without the oppressive Congress.

Without much notice, a new Republican demand had been introduced into the budget struggle: that unless the administration submitted a budget that balanced in seven years as scored by the C.B.O. there would be no new continuing resolution. The Republicans' drumbeat of "where's your budget" was analogous to their earlier one, saying that Clinton didn't want to balance the budget. (The widely held impression that the new hard line began later with a freshman rebellion against Gingrich was far off the mark.) When Clinton returned from a short trip to Arkansas on December 10 he had called Dole and Gingrich and said that he wanted to reach a deal and wanted his people to work for one and that he would push the process along. This was one of many instances where the congressional leaders' hopes were raised by Clinton's words—only to be dashed.

Dole began to split openly with Gingrich in mid-December, agreeing with Clinton that when the current continuing resolution expired on the fifteenth, there should be an extension for another week, to give negotiators time to reach an agreement and the House and Senate time to act on it. House leaders objected. John Boehner said, "I love Bob Dole, but I'm not sure I agree with that strategy." Clinton complained that the new C.B.O. numbers, issued on December 11, were still too pessimistic—but they did narrow the overall difference between the Republican and administration budgets. On Wednesday both sides agreed to offer new balanced budgets according to the new C.B.O. numbers on Friday—or so the Republicans claimed. Panetta said later that he had only promised to try to do so (one House Republican source supported his version).

In the Capitol one night that week, Domenici, Kasich, and Panetta were having an agreeable conversation, and in the course of it Domenici told Panetta that he had to bring a new budget on Friday. "I'll lay our plan down and you'll lay your plan down."

"I'll get back to you," Panetta replied.

In a meeting in Daschle's office on Thursday night, Panetta told Dole and Domenici that he would try to bring a seven-year/C.B.O.-scored plan. Back in Dole's office, Dole and Domenici and Kasich debated whether they should try to get a memorandum of understanding from Panetta— mistrust of the White House was increasing—but instead Kasich called him and said, "Leon, this has to pass the smell test if you want another continuing resolution." Panetta said the President's proposal might not be absolutely in balance, and Kasich said that that would be all right as long as it met the "smell test." After a while, Panetta called back and said, "I'm going to get my CR, aren't I?" Kasich replied, "Only if it passes the smell test." His anger rising, Panetta said, "Now you're trying to tell me that I'm not going to get a CR unless I prove something tomorrow."

Domenici suggested that Kasich get off the phone before things got worse.

When, the following day, Panetta showed up with a budget that was part based on C.B.O. assumptions and part on O.M.B.'s—and wasn't very different from his previous budget (the Medicare and Medicaid numbers were the same)—the emotional Kasich felt personally disappointed by Panetta. Kasich had once thought he and Panetta could work together. Panetta told the Republicans, "Look, this is a negotiation, this isn't a surrender." He wasn't going to give them the administration's bottom line before he gave them the top one. Domenici privately told Panetta that he could see why he wouldn't want to accept all of the C.B.O. assumptions yet. Domenici also recognized that Gingrich and Kasich weren't free from constraints from the House Republican conference, that proposals he thought made sense couldn't be offered because he had to cater to what the House Republicans would or wouldn't accept. (At the meeting on the fifteenth, the Republicans also offered a new budget, which, on the basis of the new C.B.O. estimates, contained an additional $135 billion in spending. It reduced the size of the tax cuts from $245 billion to $240 billion, reduced the cuts in Medicare and Medicaid, and added funds for child care and for the Earned Income Tax Credit and domestic discretionary spending.)

At a press briefing afterward Kasich and Domenici expressed indignation. Kasich, expressing a view that was growing in his and some other Republicans' minds, said, of the White House, "They're afraid they're going to lose their base." Dole, too, was feeling burned by Clinton. Dole had told him in a phone conversation that he had been out there taking fire on Bosnia, and after the conversation had felt reassured by Clinton that the President would be forthcoming on the budget. From this point on, Dole was skeptical that the White House wanted a deal.

That afternoon, in an appearance in the White House press briefing room, Clinton said, "It is wrong for the Republicans to insist that I make deep cuts in Medicare and Medicaid or they'll shut the government down." He added, "I would not give in to such a threat last month, and I will not give in today."

In fact, Panetta had wanted to submit a seven-year, C.B.O.-approved budget. He believed it was necessary in order to move the negotiations forward. But he was overruled. Gore, who remained upset that the President had accepted a seven-year budget at all, opposed further yielding at that point. Even some of those who wanted a deal thought that tactically this wasn't the time to put down a seven-year/C.B.O. budget, which would be close to the administration's last offer. In fact, experienced negotiators in top levels of the administration—Bob Rubin, Alice Rivlin, and Erskine Bowles among them—were unhappy about the way the White House had dealt with the Congress thus far. They felt that the President had given away too much. Stephanopoulos and Ickes were, of course, against the President's meeting the Republicans' terms. At this point, the President still wanted a deal, but felt he couldn't be seen as accepting a variation on the Republican budget. And Clinton and his team resolved not to yield on the seven-year/C.B.O. issue as a result of coercion by the Republicans.

At the same time, the White House group knew that it would have to offer a seven-year/C.B.O. budget eventually, for credibility. "We wanted to hold out as long as we could," a Presidential aide said. They knew that once they put down a budget, the split-the-difference talk would begin. The aide said, "What the Republicans didn't realize was that the longer we held out the better it would be for us." The assumption was that holding off would bring pressure on the Republicans to move toward them.

Within the White House, there was much discussion about whether there was a deal the President could make with the Republicans that would have the support of a large number of congressional Democrats. The idea of a centrist budget—supported by moderate Republicans and conservative and centrist Democrats—would have to confront two realities: few Republican moderates were ready to abandon Gingrich at such an important moment (which the Clinton people didn't understand for some time); and Gingrich had told Clinton that he wouldn't let a centrist budget pass the House. "He said it with great certainty, and the message resonated in the room," an administration official said. Panetta had called Sherwood Boehlert, the New York Republican who had broken with the leadership on some issues, mainly environmental, a couple of times to see if he might back a Democratic budget. Boehlert told Panetta that his vote wasn't available.

By now Gingrich was coming under heavy pressure from within his own conference, even from his fellow House leaders. In a dramatic and unusual leadership meeting on Friday, December 15, in H 227, the conference room in Gingrich's suite of offices, Bob Walker and Dick Armey were seated at the head of the table. Gingrich was meeting with Dole in Dole's office as the leadership meeting began, at 3:30 P.M., but word got around that Dole and Gingrich were talking about offering a new continuing resolution—which didn't sit at all well with Gingrich's fellow leaders. Barry Jackson, the House Republican Conference's executive director, had found out about the discussion of a new continuing resolution, and spread the word, pulling members of the leadership aside and saying, "They're going to do a CR."

When Gingrich arrived and took his seat, he said, "Where are we?" Boehner, who had been alerted by Jackson, replied, "Newt, this isn't going to work." Bill Paxon, a moderate but also a Gingrich loyalist, also spoke against the idea of giving Clinton another continuing resolution, as did Sue Myrick, of North Carolina and a freshman representative to the leadership. Paxon said that they had made a tactical error the month before in giving Clinton so much time to comply with the agreement in the continuing resolution, and that nothing had happened. "They have shown no good faith," Paxon said. Gingrich sent for Dole, who arrived looking very agitated. Dole wanted a continuing resolution. He felt that the current strategy of tying up the government and refusing to negotiate wasn't working. He wanted to wrap up a deal and get out on the campaign trail. Besides, his poll numbers were dropping. He would say in budget strategy meetings, "I'm nineteen points down in the polls." A House Republican leader said, "He thinks he's getting killed by the public, and he's probably right about that, but we have different motivations."

Gingrich asked the House leaders to tell Dole what they thought. He also asked John Engler, the omnipresent governor of Michigan, who was also attending the House Republican leadership meeting, to say what he thought. Engler told the group, "You've fought the battle this far. You can't cave. A new CR would be seen as a capitulation."

Dole remarked that he thought it had been decided to pass a new continuing resolution. To Engler, Dole commented, "Remember, we're shutting the federal government down, not the states."

It was decided at that meeting that, without a seven-year, C.B.O.-scored

Clinton budget, there would be no new continuing resolution. "I think that was the turning point," a member of the leadership said afterward.

Gingrich's fellow leaders thought he was being too reasonable with the administration. One of them said later, "Newt was willing to give them the benefit of the doubt all week." Another said, shortly after the December 15 meeting, "Newt would have been much more flexible than the rest of us. Newt has to live with Dole." And then this person made it clear that despite appearances almost all year—despite Dole's apparent submission to Gingrich on the Republican agenda and on many strategic decisions—it was Dole who was now dominating the relationship. A member of the House leadership group said, "Dole is beating up on Newt. He has a way of being the senior statesman, the leader of the Senate, holding his cards against his chest. Therefore, Newt is more willing to be accommodating than the rest of us."

The following week, Gingrich told two confidants that he had a problem with Dole, that he related to Dole the way he related to his stepfather—he wanted his approval.

On Saturday, the day after the meeting in which the leadership told Gingrich that another continuing resolution wasn't acceptable, Gingrich, after meeting with Dole again, proposed to the other House Republican leaders a new plan for opening up the government (which had officially closed as of midnight the night before). "We all just laughed," a member of the leadership said. "We told him there isn't any way."

And because a large swath of the House Republicans now felt that Gingrich was too accommodating toward Clinton, he faced another rebellion—on the part of far more than just the freshmen—the following week.

Gingrich and Dole, at their request—it had been Dole's idea—were to meet with Clinton in the Oval Office on Tuesday afternoon. Kasich felt strongly that Dole and Gingrich shouldn't negotiate with Clinton on anything, since the administration still hadn't laid down a seven-year/C.B.O.-scored budget. After all, Kasich had been following the instructions of the leadership in refusing to negotiate until the administration did that. In Dole's office on Monday night, he urged that the two leaders do nothing at the White House the next day except demand a proper budget. He believed that they had agreed to this.

In a cordial conversation lasting two hours, Clinton offered options on how to proceed. They could start negotiations if there were no preconditions; he could offer a seven-year/C.B.O. plan if the Republicans agreed in advance to his Medicare and Medicaid numbers; they could negotiate from one of the now-multiple plans that had been put forward (by Daschle and other Senate Democrats, by a bipartisan group of conservative Senate Democrats and moderate Senate Republicans). Clinton said that if the administration put down its own plan, the Republicans would simply attack it. The Republicans concluded that Clinton was still unwilling to offer his own plan.

When Clinton brought up the possibility of another continuing resolution, Gingrich said, "If I go back and try to get a long-term CR without a budget from you, the next time you'll be dealing with Speaker Armey." But Gingrich agreed nevertheless to try to obtain a short-term continuing resolution if it was agreed that negotiations at the White House would follow.

The meeting ended without an explicit understanding as to whether the administration's plan could be on the table, along with other proposals, even if it wasn't entirely scored by the C.B.O., but it was agreed that Panetta would resume discussions that night with Domenici and Kasich to work out a "framework" for moving forward. If those talks went well enough, the "principals"—Clinton, Dole, and Gingrich and other House and Senate leaders of both parties—would meet. In the car on the way back to Capitol Hill, Gingrich's conviction that the President's budget would have to be scored by the C.B.O. before it could be on the table hardened. He felt that the administration was stalling in order to avoid tough choices.

In a press conference held by Gingrich and Dole, after they returned to the Hill, Gingrich went beyond what had been agreed upon in the meeting, saying that "everything on the table will have been scored by C.B.O." He also mentioned that a new continuing resolution would be considered if enough progress was made on the structure of the next meetings.

After the briefing, Gingrich joined a meeting of the Republican conference, which was already underway. He reported what had taken place at the White House, mentioning that a continuing resolution was under consideration. A number of members of the conference—not just freshmen —stood up at microphones placed around the room and said that there should be no continuing resolution until there was a budget agreement. One member said, "Why would we trust them on getting a balanced budget after what they did to us after the last CR," and was applauded. Gingrich asked for a show of hands of those who agreed with that statement. Almost everyone raised a hand.

While the Republican conference was meeting, Gore went to the White House briefing room to take issue with a couple of things Gingrich had said in his press briefing. With Gephardt and Daschle standing beside him, Gore said that it hadn't been agreed that the President's proposal had to be scored by the C.B.O., nor had it been agreed, contrary to what Gingrich had suggested, that a deal would be reached by the end of the year. (Even a Republican who had been in the meeting said privately that Gore's remarks were accurate.)

Nevertheless, Gore's performance set off an explosion among the House Republicans, in part because they didn't understand that Gore was being truthful, in part because they were ready to explode, and in part because the incident reminded them of Panetta's attempt to reinterpret the November 19 agreement.

At a meeting of the Speaker's Advisory Group (SAG), held early that evening in the Dinosaur Room and attended by nine House members and three Senators (Trent Lott, Connie Mack, and Paul Coverdell), Gingrich's fellow leaders were unanimous and adamant that there be no further continuing resolution.

As Gingrich reported on what had happened at the White House meeting, he described with some puzzlement and admiration Clinton's ability to win people over. He spoke, as he sometimes did, of Clinton's charm—which was real enough when he turned it on. Gingrich would say that the President had charmed him, that when he met with him he felt he was "getting sucked in," and that he had to "go through detox" for a couple of hours afterward. Clinton even worked his magic on Armey. Toward the end of the talks, which usually concluded with the "big three"—Clinton, Gingrich, and Dole—standing in a circle, Clinton reached for Armey and pulled him into the circle, and said, "I want to say that I misjudged you," and told him he saw that he really cared about his country, and apologized for the sharp words he'd aimed at him. In the Republican meeting in the Capitol afterward, Armey commented, "He was probably blowing smoke but it was nice of him to do it." At another meeting, Clinton took Armey's cup and offered to pour him some more coffee. Armey was charmed.

At the White House meeting that day, Gingrich told his colleagues, the President had complimented him on his tie and told him that he missed their chats. "I fell for it," Gingrich said. Early in the meeting, Gingrich said, "I knew that he had half of the money in my wallet, and I was reaching for my wallet to give him the rest of it." Gingrich was now feeling that the White House meeting had been surreal, because it never got down to the issues. The assembled Republican leaders then talked about Clinton, agreeing that the President seemed to honestly feel he was doing something substantive when he wasn't, and could bring people into his "fantasyland."

Still, during a spirited discussion about a new continuing resolution, Gingrich for a while resisted the idea of turning the President down flat. "I think that you're wrong," Gingrich told the others. ("I think he was thinking about having to tell Dole," one leader said later.) Then, in the course of this meeting, a videotape of Gore's comments was played. Gingrich, visibly upset, threw his pencil on the table and said, "I'm tired of being snookered. Every time I discuss something with them I get taken. These people are just not honest." Agitated, he said that the incident reminded him of Panetta's behavior after the last continuing resolution was agreed upon. The others at the meeting became exercised over Gore's statement as well. They were reinforced in their view that Clinton couldn't be trusted. Dan Meyer tried to explain to them what had actually happened at the White House meeting, to show that there was a basis for what Gore had said, but the others were too worked up by now to pay him heed.

The feeling was growing among House Republicans that in his dealings with the administration Gingrich was "gullible," as one top House Republican put it, or "too amiable," in the words of another—a notion that Gingrich himself, capable of objectivity, had testified to in the meeting. He had also said, "Whenever I go into a room my tendency is to like and trust the people in the room."

Like Clinton, Gingrich was especially eager to please people. A House Republican said, referring to the negotiating team, "That's why Armey is in the room." This picture of Gingrich was of course at wide variance with the public impression, encouraged by the administration—which didn't much understand the dynamics within the House Republican conference. But Gingrich was a useful foil in any event. During this period, Clinton was shining as the anti-Newt; he was campaigning against the most unpopular national political figure. Clinton, an effective campaigner, always preferred a target. "Gingrich" became the shorthand for the House Republicans' intransigence, but he wasn't really the reason for it.

On Wednesday morning, Gingrich called Panetta into his office and told him that there wouldn't be another continuing resolution.

At a SAG meeting that morning, Gingrich proposed that the House Republicans say that there would be no new continuing resolution until a budget deal had been reached. The Speaker and his advisers agreed that such a resolution would give Gingrich "cover" with Dole and with the White House. Barry Jackson, Boehner's aide who had been so active in this matter, went off and drafted the resolution with the new demand, Gingrich approved it, and then Jackson tracked down Scott Klug, a third-term moderate from Wisconsin, to suggest that he offer it. The leaders wanted a moderate to do this, rather than one of their zealots, and Klug had his own reasons for wanting to help.

So, at the conference that afternoon, Klug offered the resolution against any further continuing resolution until a budget agreement had been reached. Klug explained in an interview later that *the moderates* had been looking for a way to respond to the public suggestions out of the White House that perhaps they would break away from Gingrich and support Clinton on a final budget. (He and his good friend Boehner had discussed this on the House floor the day before the conference.)

Klug said in the interview, "The frustration had been building up for a long time." He continued, "It was a message to Leon and also to the Senate Republican leadership." Klug said that the moderates—some forty to fifty members—also wanted to send a message to Gingrich that the Republicans shouldn't keep passing a series of short-term continuing resolutions. "We felt that the only way to get the White House to be serious was by keeping the government closed," Klug said. Thus the moderates and the more zealous Republicans were thinking the same way.

Most of the moderates—such as Klug and Chris Shays—were fiscal conservatives. They might differ with the leadership on the environment and on social issues, but that didn't mean they would abandon Gingrich on economic matters, especially on the heart of the Republican program.

At the end of a rowdy conference meeting that afternoon, after passing the Klug resolution almost unanimously, the House Republicans sang "Jingle Bells."

Gingrich, according to witnesses, was frustrated. One key House Republican said, "Newt felt very boxed in." Gingrich was in fact ambivalent about the shutdown issue. Though he at times agreed in White House meetings, or in a meeting with Dole, to seek a short-term continuing resolution, he still saw the power to shut down federal agencies as an important weapon. In an interview on December 28, he said that as long as there was no deal, the administration would get no long-term continuing resolution ("They're not going to get one"), and that increasingly the public would blame the President, the chief executive, for the shutdown. He said that some governors had assured him of this.

Dole was also unhappy. He said on the Senate floor, "It is my hope we will get a continuing resolution today from the House" that would end the shutdown for at least a few days, while a deal was sought. Most of the House Republican leaders continued to think that the President would "cave" if for no other reason than that he'd want to get the government reopened for fear of being blamed for the shutdown. This was another Republican miscalculation. (For their part, White House officials believed that Gingrich wouldn't want a shutdown over Christmas.)

By this time, Dole had come to believe that the House Republican leaders were engaging in "inspeak" as they sat around congratulating themselves on what a good position they were in. He didn't think that what they were saying fit what he was picking up when he did go out and campaign; he thought that the shutdown was overshadowing the Republicans' issue of balancing the budget. Dole, as he habitually did, watched the nightly news broadcasts and the weekend talk shows and saw that the emphasis was not on the balanced budget but on "Day X of the shutdown," and stories of hardship for federal workers and people affected by the closing of national parks (a bobsled driver, an inn), the freeze on federal contracts, the loss of patronage by federal workers. Dole also felt it wasn't right to keep federal workers home when they wanted to work, and penalize them by postponing their pay. That they were going to be paid anyway made the whole thing, in Dole's view, absurd. The House Republican leadership, however, believed that since the government was shut down they'd might as well keep it shut down in order to avoid continually opening and closing it, which they thought would subject them to even more criticism. But many Republicans still held the view of government workers they had held before the tragedy in Oklahoma City, and said that their "base" couldn't see why federal workers should be paid for not working.

This time, 280,000 federal workers were furloughed, but many more went to work with nothing to do, since agencies that hadn't been funded couldn't incur any additional expenses. The halt on government contracts would have a direct impact on the private economy. State governments didn't know how to plan for the coming year. As Christmas approached, there were news stories about federal workers who depended on their paychecks and now couldn't meet their mortgage payments or other expenses. Not only was the passport office closed, but U.S. embassies abroad were threatened with loss of security protection by foreign nationals, who weren't getting paid. The normally docile foreign service rose up in rebellion, spilling the goods on Members of Congress who were planning foreign trips at government expense while most of the government was shut down. Even if park service personnel could go back to work, they couldn't fill up with gasoline because that would incur a new cost. E.P.A. enforcement of various laws was slowed or halted.

Shortly after the House Republican conference voted to deny a new continuing resolution, Clinton moved to exploit the growing split between the House and Senate Republicans, charging in a press briefing that "the most extreme members of the House of Representatives" had voted to keep the government closed.

Despite the apparent impasse, on December 22 Clinton and congressional leaders began a series of extraordinary meetings at the White House. The Republican delegation included Gingrich, Dole, Armey, Kasich, and Domenici, and the Democratic group included Gore, Gephardt, Daschle, and the senior Democrats on the Budget Committees, Senator James Exon, of Nebraska, and Sabo. Such a large group would make it more difficult to reach an agreement, even if the top leaders on both sides wanted to. Gephardt and Daschle would be the enforcers from the liberal wing of the party, while Armey would play that role for the right. (Armey, concerned about his reputation for being the heavy in White House meetings, said not a word at the December 22 gathering. But he wasn't always to be so restrained.)

With the President and Vice President along with the House and Senate delegations and key administration officials seated around the table in the Cabinet Room—and staff members from the Hill and the White House arrayed along the walls—Clinton conducted a seminar on the federal government. (Dan Meyer referred to it as "Renaissance North," after the annual New Year's weekend the Clintons attended in Hilton Head, South Carolina, where earnest seminars were held.) Each side presented its problems with the other's proposals and wandered into a philosophical discussion about government. Both Clinton and Gingrich loved that sort of thing, and both —Gingrich in particular—indulged their loquaciousness, and desire to show off. An expert staff member presented the facts and issues on a certain subject and then the "negotiators" discussed it. Sometimes the staff members themselves chimed in, even interrupting the President and Gingrich. Despite his earlier opposition, Gingrich was participating in a "summit" after all. Dole, who was largely silent throughout these sessions, thought them a waste of time.

Gore, too, talked a lot at the meetings, and Republicans complained privately that he played "the heavy"—taking a hard-line position for the administration, sometimes seeming to pull the President back from a more flexible one. The Republicans were annoyed by Gore's behavior but thought that it stemmed from a "good-cop-bad-cop" agreement with Clinton. But Clinton was in fact willing to go further than Gore to get a deal. Gore was actually restraining him. Another factor may have been the never buried rivalry between Gore and Gephardt.

Gingrich was surprised by how "rejectionist" Gore was, and by how much the administration seemed to be pulled around by the Democratic congressional leaders, whom he thought—accurately—didn't want a deal. "It was obvious that Gore was going to be an impediment to a deal," said one Republican who attended these sessions. At one point, Gore said that if permission to drill the Arctic National Wildlife Refuge, in Alaska, for oil was still in the package—even if every other part was agreed to—it would be vetoed. When Gingrich said in one meeting that, "Just as you said, Mr. President, that we'd have to get another President before you would sign our Balanced Budget Act, you'll have to get a new Speaker if you want us to schedule a bill without capital gains," Gore said that the Republicans had to understand that for the Democratic Party, for twenty-five years opposition to capital gains tax breaks had been a "theological" tenet. At the same time, Clinton offered a capital gains break.

At the end of the first meeting, a smaller group adjourned to the Oval Office, where Panetta suggested that they meet again in another week. Some Republicans were startled, wondering why the White House was allowing so much time to pass, but felt that they couldn't protest in the President's own office. (When many key White House staff members, including Panetta, went off for several days around the Christmas holiday, Republican aides were suspicious that that was the reason for the delay.)

The seminars resumed on December 29, ending around noon on New Year's Eve. While some attendees described the long and long-winded seminar as useful, in essence, as one White House official said, "Nothing happened."

Dole came away impressed with Clinton's political skills. Clinton, for his part, felt that Dole was more flexible than Gingrich, readier to cut a deal, and he ended up feeling closer to Dole, more able to communicate with him, than with Gingrich. This was a reverse of the situation in the early months of the year, when Clinton found it easier to deal with Gingrich.

At a meeting of the Republican negotiators on January 2, the day that more serious talks, with only top officials present, were to begin, Domenici argued that Clinton couldn't move far enough toward the Republican positions to get a deal, that his party's politics prevented that. In Domenici's view, Clinton's insistence that he would approve no deal that didn't have a hundred House Democrats behind it gave the liberals a veto power. Further, through his insistence on what he considered adequate funding for Medicare, Medicaid, education, and the environment, Clinton was gaining in the polls. ("We're killing them," a White House aide said at about this time.) Another factor in the polls, it was widely believed, was the public's disapproval of the tactics of the Republicans, on whom they placed the greater blame for the shutdown, which as it dragged on was becoming increasingly unpopular. So at their meeting on January 2 the Republican negotiators resolved to "blow up" the talks that night if there was no progress.

There was at this time a polling war among the President's advisers. Morris and his allies argued that their data showed that the President's recent rise in the polls wasn't due to his "principled" stand on Medicare and other popular programs (Medicaid, education, and the environment) —but that, rather, his rise had begun before he became combative. Stan Greenberg's polling, on the other hand, indicated that the President's ratings had gone up since he became confrontational, and had fallen during his periods of trying to erase the differences with Republicans, such as the Claremont, New Hampshire, talkathon. Greenberg had warned the White House that the President was in bad shape with low-income workers—on whom, he argued, the election would turn—while Morris argued that Clinton had secured his base so should reach for the center, and give up "class warfare." But in taking a strong stand for the liberal Democrats' favorite programs, Clinton had gone some way toward mending the rupture with them that had occurred in June over his offering a balanced budget, and in October over his remark in Houston about taxes. "Triangulation" was at least temporarily in remission. A White House aide (not one in dead opposition to Morris) said, "The need or ability to triangulate has lessened. You can't easily triangulate on Medicare. The more this became up or down on specific issues, the more the President took traditional Democratic positions." A congressional Democrat said, "Ultimately, he couldn't triangulate on the tax cut. All of his supporters wanted a low tax cut, and the Coalition didn't want one at all."

Clinton was receiving conflicting advice from within his staff, from congressional Democrats, and from outside advisers over whether and what sort of a deal would be in his interests. He and Morris remained the two people in the White House who most wanted a deal. Morris believed that if Clinton struck one, enough congressional Democrats would support him. Clinton, too, seemed to feel that if he cut a deal the Democrats would follow. The liberal congressional leaders, Gephardt and Daschle, thought that Clinton wanted a deal too badly and warned him in the course of the negotiations that he had already moved beyond the point where most congressional Democrats would support him. Clinton discounted Daschle's and Gephardt's advice as coming from Democrats who didn't want a deal. Gephardt and Gore were in accidental alliance; Stephanopoulos and Gore were in rare harmony. A number of Democrats felt that Clinton would come under strong attack from within the party if he went as far as he seemed inclined to—that his fate would be like Bush's in 1990. They warned that he would so damage himself with his base as to jeopardize his reelection chances. Morris continually pushed Clinton to be flexible enough in the negotiations to get a deal; Stephanopoulos continually worried that he would.

At the meeting at the White House in the late afternoon of January 2 and into the evening, the administration said it couldn't move any further, and Panetta, pointing to a flip chart, said that by agreeing to reach a seven-year, C.B.O.-scored budget the administration had already given the Republicans nearly $500 billion, so the Republicans had to give on the remaining big matters. "We have to win on Medicare and Medicaid," Panetta said. Now just the top negotiators met, in the Oval Office. John Engler was present as well on January 2 as a sort of fourth branch of government (he was there to discuss Medicaid entitlements). While the talks in the Oval Office proceeded, Domenici and Kasich and Republican staff members waited in the Roosevelt Room; when the Republican principals took breaks the Republicans would come to the Roosevelt Room to talk strategy. On occasion, the top negotiators would return to the Oval Office upholding a stronger position than when the break was called. Kasich was concerned that while the President and Panetta were steeped in the budget, the Republican negotiators weren't. He felt that the Republican negotiators weren't firm enough with the administration, that they didn't stick with the agreed-upon strategy, and he urged them to cut the chitchat in the Oval Office and to demand numbers. At one point the Republican negotiators came into the Roosevelt Room and said that the administration had laid out a new proposal—drawing arrows on the whiteboard that was in constant use—and that they were encouraged, but when the Roosevelt Room team asked for the numbers it concluded that the administration hadn't moved at all.

While the Republicans caucused in the Roosevelt Room, Clinton met with aides in the Oval Office to discuss strategy. Clinton was often in a very good mood when the breaks began, because he believed he had moved his opponents, only to be disappointed when they returned to the Oval Office. When the Republican principals came into the Roosevelt Room on Tuesday, January 2, Dole said, referring to the waiting group, "I don't think we should tell them what went on because if we did it would blow up the talks." When asked where they thought they were on a scale of one to ten in terms of getting a deal, Dole replied "Five," and Gingrich said, "Four." But the Republicans didn't walk out.

At a leadership meeting at the Capitol later that night, Gingrich told the others that the talks weren't succeeding, and urged that they agree to a continuing resolution. Gingrich said, "One of the biggest problems we have right now is the exhaustion of our members. If we don't solve it we will break. We need time off in January and February. Our team is tired. Vince Lombardi used to say, 'Fatigue makes cowards of us all.' " Gingrich continued, "We're a cumbersome party, but when we're a team we're virtually unstoppable." He said, "We made a mistake. We miscalculated the effect our pressure would have on Clinton in December."

And then Gingrich made a stunning admission. "One thing we didn't recognize that I should have seen," he said, "is that I always believed in talking to you about Engler and Weld, that we could survive low poll numbers if we accomplished what we set out to do. Our polls would come back when the people saw that we kept our promises. The mistake was that we only read the poll numbers from our side. We expected that there would be a slump in our poll numbers, but we didn't calculate that a surge in Clinton's numbers would cause him to dig in even more."

Gingrich was sufficiently disturbed by the way things were going that afterward he spoke to staff and advisers on the phone, and spoke to Armey twice, once at five-thirty the next morning. He conveyed his view that "they came in and gave us nothing." At a meeting with some advisers—including members of his staff, Engler, Joe Gaylord, and Chuck Boyd, the retired Air Force general who had now joined Gingrich's circle—on Wednesday morning, he said, "We've got to recognize that our plan for 1995 [to get a seven-year/C.B.O. balanced budget signed into law] didn't work because they resisted more than we expected." By this time, there were people on both sides who thought that the talks should end soon, but weren't sure how to bring that about without being blamed for the failure.

•

While the White House talks were going on, so, off to one side, was a struggle over whether the Republicans could get essentially their budget passed by the House by a veto-proof number (normally 290, but, because of a vacancy, at the time 289 votes). Though the White House felt that this was difficult to unlikely, it didn't want to take chances. So, as Kasich in particular worked with the Blue Dogs—especially his close friend Gary Condit, of California—to see what they would accept, White House aides worked to retain the support of conservative Democrats. (Friendly Blue Dogs reported to the White House on the Republicans' overtures.)

Highly placed House Republicans admitted privately that they didn't really think that they could find enough votes for a budget proposal to survive an override—or that even if they did Senate Republican leaders could find the needed sixty-seven votes. (But some Republicans thought that if they got sixty votes to shut off a filibuster and pass a bill that would be impressive enough.) Yet most of the talk of trying to pass their own bill was a way, as one House leader put it, "of putting pressure on the White House."

At the same time, the Clinton White House was trying to put together a budget that had the support of as many Democrats as possible. White House officials were working with Daschle and his staff on a budget that met the criteria of seven years and C.B.O. scoring, but protected the President's priorities. The administration had argued that it didn't object in principle to seven years; the problem was mathematical—how to write a seven-year balanced budget without cutting too deeply into programs the Democrats held dear. Though the White House had hoped that in return for agreeing to try to reach a seven-year budget the Republicans would give them some leeway on the economic assumptions, not hold them strictly to the C.B.O. numbers, the Republicans had held firm. (The House leaders had no leeway on this.)

The administration managed to shape a seven-year/C.B.O. budget by proposing a much lower tax cut ($17 billion net, having added substantial cuts in "corporate welfare") than the President's earlier one ($80 billion net) and ending ("triggering off") the child tax credits and college education credits after five years if the C.B.O.'s more conservative economic assumptions turned out to be right. Of course, no one involved believed that the tax credits would be dropped in the fifth year, the year 2000— even if that weren't an election year. The administration plan made smaller cuts in the entitlements than it had previously proposed, but large ones in discretionary spending. And it did most of its spending in the first five years, saving the heavy cuts for the last two—to an even greater degree than the Republican budget. "This is what the country wants," a White House official said later, "a liberal balanced budget." But many liberal Democrats opposed the cuts in domestic discretionary programs. And the

Coalition had difficulties with the Daschle budget. By working through Daschle, the administration preserved some "deniability" in response to Democratic complaints that it went too far in one direction or another. It also gave the Clinton side its best starting point from which to move toward the center. The administration officials felt that if they started "splitting the difference" from the Coalition budget, that would bring them too close to the Republican side. This way, they could move toward the Coalition bud-get—if they chose to—and call that a compromise.

Administration strategists considered their latest budget their trump—to be brought out at the right moment—perhaps in the President's State of the Union address if no agreement was reached by then.

"We've known since December 16–17 [when there were meetings at Blair House and on Capitol Hill in which Democrats and administration officials tried to find a unified Democratic position] that there were ways to get to seven years and C.B.O. scoring, and it came down to what was the best negotiating strategy," the official said. Once the Daschle/adminis-tration budget was formulated, this person said, "We had it in our back pocket." The President would then be able to argue that the budget could be balanced in seven years without steep cuts in Medicare and Medicaid or in the President's other priorities.

The Republicans believed—or talked themselves into believing—that the President wouldn't want to deliver a State of the Union speech without having reached a budget deal. But the State of the Union address would be an excellent platform for the President to carry forward his struggle against the Republicans.

For a long time, Gingrich was optimistic—another trait that he and Clinton shared. In a strategy meeting in December (Kasich and Domenici got their instructions from Dole and Gingrich in these meetings) Gingrich was pre-occupied with looking through a stack of history books from the Library of Congress. When Domenici asked, "What are you looking for, Mr. Speaker," Gingrich replied that he was looking at the period before the Second World War for Winston Churchill's philosophy "of being cheerfully optimistic and wear 'em down." In meetings he would urge, "cheerfully wear 'em down." Gingrich had thought that in the end Clinton would see the benefits of a deal and would respond to the pressure to get one, and to keep the government open. But in the first week of January, as he was riding back from the White House to the Capitol, Gingrich said, "I didn't realize that they would be so committed to their liberal base." There had been division among Republicans as to whether Clinton was serious about getting a balanced budget. "A lot of them are getting to the point where enough is enough," a Republican source said. Armey, untypically, said that he saw some reason for optimism. "But that may be because of skunk-at-the-picnic fatigue," he said.

•

In an unusual scene—much about the year had been unusual—on January 3, Gingrich, in the chair, gaveled the first session of the 104th Congress to a close at 11:59 and gaveled in the second session at noon. Normally the Congress checked in on the third and checked out again until the President's State of the Union speech later in the month.

At the end of the first session of the 104th Congress very little had been accomplished legislatively. As public opinion and pressure groups caught up with the Contract items that had been speedily approved by the House, a backfire began against many of them. Also, the Senate's relatively more moderate Republican caucus wasn't prepared to slavishly follow the House. The filibuster rule lent strength to those who wanted to fight House-passed legislation.

In the end, only three Contract items, none of them major, became law: the Congressional Accountability Act; limits on unfunded mandates; and constrictions on securities litigation, which passed over the President's veto. The product liability bill, much watered down by the Senate, was still before a conference committee. The line-item veto remained hostage to the Republican leaders' belated realization that they didn't want to give Clinton this additional power. Dole never found the sixty-seventh vote for the Balanced Budget Amendment, but of course through Gingrich's persistence a balanced budget became a requirement anyway. The tax cuts were caught up in the unresolved budget battle. It was Clinton's good fortune that the welfare bill, which covered much more than the Aid to Families with Dependent Children program, was moved in conference sufficiently toward the House-passed bill and away from the Senate-passed bill, which Clinton had praised, that he could veto it. Clinton's particular problems with the conference bill were that it put the food stamps program into an optional block grant and cut its funding substantially; cut severely into assistance for disabled children; turned a number of child protection programs into block grants; allowed a certain number of states to convert their child nutrition programs (including school lunch) into block grants; and created a serious mismatch between the work requirement for welfare and the funds available for child care. Clinton's good fortune was that the final bill was sufficiently objectionable that by vetoing it he could repair relations with an important constituency. (Republicans were gleeful at the prospect of charging that Clinton had killed welfare reform.) The crime bills passed by the House were stalled in the Senate or killed by a Presidential veto. In all, Clinton used the veto power eleven times.

Many of the policy changes that were to be wrought through riders on appropriations bills ended up in limbo because the bills were vetoed or didn't make it to the President's desk.

Six appropriations bills hadn't become law: three as a result of vetoes, two because congressional Republicans couldn't agree among themselves, and one, the Labor–Health and Human Services appropriations bill, was being blocked by Senate Democrats because it overturned an executive order regulation forbidding government contractors from hiring replacements for strikers. The anti-environmental push hit a wall. Such restraints on environmental enforcement as survived the Congress—the Senate did vote to limit the E.P.A.'s power to designate wetlands—died with a Presidential veto of the appropriations bill for Veterans Affairs, HUD, and independent agencies. The congressionally approved provision to kill the national service program died in the same bill. The Istook amendment, which put limits on lobbying by recipients of federal funds, was still looking for a home. The Clean Water Act ran into John Chafee's opposition in the Senate and was moribund at session's end. (The Republicans' final budget did propose to cut E.P.A. enforcement funds by forty percent.)

The Commerce Department lived, though its funds were cut substantially; the same held true with Legal Services. As for other conservative targets, the severe cuts in the funding for the National Endowment for the Arts and the National Endowment for the Humanities were caught in the vetoed Interior appropriations bill. Funding for PBS was caught up in the stalled Labor-H.H.S. appropriations measure. The complex telecommunications bill was suspended in the cross-pressures of different parts of the industry and political interests. (It was approved on February 1.) The only agency to die was the Interstate Commerce Commission. (Even Clinton had proposed killing that one.)

Lobbyist registration and strict gift ban bills were passed by the House and Senate—the House leadership was pushed by the freshmen to bring them to the floor. But the most important political reform, of campaign financing, got nowhere—despite Gingrich's avowals in Claremont.

The Republicans' propaganda war about Medicare hadn't worked—Gingrich, aware of this, would claim it hadn't worked *yet*. But Democratic polling said that fewer people believed in December that the Republicans were trying to "protect" Medicare than did so when the Republican campaign started. The Republicans thought that they had found politically salient words, but the Democrats had used a more politically potent (if somewhat misleading) argument. As the Republicans had the year before, Democrats succeeded in raising people's fears about their health coverage.

The 104th Congress was also noteworthy for the number of members—thirty-five in the House and thirteen in the Senate as of January 16—who chose to depart it. Among them were some truly distinguished and thoughtful senators, such as Nancy Kassebaum, William Cohen, Sam Nunn, Bill Bradley, and Mark Hatfield—whose independence had been threatened by freshmen. (The new rules adopted in the Senate Republican conference were going to make all chairmen subject to the will of the new conservative bloc.) The reasons people gave were varying—some wanted to establish a professional life in the "real world" before they were too old, some wanted to pursue politics in a different form, some simply wanted to retire. Some Democrats, particularly in the Senate, left because they couldn't see regaining majority status for a long time. But something deeper was afoot.

As William Cohen said early in the year, the demands of serving in the Congress were ever greater and the satisfactions ever diminishing. The need to raise increasing amounts of money, the instant demands on the part of the instant electronic electorate, and the declining comity were all factors that had been increasing in recent years. But the highly partisan atmosphere of the 104th Congress and the further decline of civility and institutional self-respect made the job less satisfying than ever. Centrists, which most of the Senate retirees were, felt squeezed out, even though they did form a swing bloc in the Senate.

These departures, and the ascendancy of the more recently elected classes, with their own views of how things should be run, could change the nature of both institutions for a long time to come.

By the middle of the first week in January, Gingrich himself was looking for a way to end the shutdown. He felt that it was putting the Republicans on the wrong side of the issue by asking people to work without pay and not letting people work who wanted to, and was also distracting attention from the Republicans' program. The public was blaming the shutdown on the Republicans by margins of two to one.

But Tom DeLay argued strongly that to pass a new continuing resolution would be seen as "caving in." Armey was also opposed, as was David McIntosh, a representative of the freshmen to the leadership. But by now some of the other leaders agreed with Gingrich that the strategy of shutting down the government wasn't working, indeed was backfiring. A party strategist said at the time, "Republicans can't sustain being in this position much longer. We're taking a beating." Dole, reading the tea leaves, had already broken loose and on Tuesday got a continuing resolution passed by the Senate (only he and Domenici and John Warner, Republican of Virginia, where a lot of federal workers live, were on the Senate floor). "Enough is enough," Dole said. The resolution would send all federal workers back to their jobs, but pay only those whose agencies had been funded. (By this time, Kansas was running out of unemployment compensation funds.) Phil Gramm of course attacked Dole for this move, as did some right-wing groups. But in the end Dole looked the wise, mature leader (and his poll ratings began to climb).

Gingrich learned about Dole's move only after he returned to his office, having just come from a long private meeting with him. ("That's Dole," a

House leadership aide said with resignation.) But in a meeting in his office with John Boehner, Joe Gaylord, and some staff members, Gingrich indicated that he didn't agree with the strategy of keeping the government shut down, that it was taking too long to get a resolution, that it was proving more difficult than they'd expected to break Clinton. Aware that a large segment of the Republican base had objected to paying federal workers for not working, Gingrich wanted to get them back on the job.

Besides, Gingrich was facing a crisis of his own: the possibility of losing control of the House floor. In a conference meeting on January 3, fifty-four Republicans, most with large numbers of federal workers, or national parks, in their districts, voted to end the shutdown. Marge Roukema, a moderate who had wavered in her support of the leadership, had enlisted the support of more than thirty House Republicans behind a reopening of the government. John Boehner said, "All of us in the leadership sensed that our grip was slipping." He added, "The biggest problem we were facing was members who didn't like the pictures on TV and didn't like the fact that we were sinking, even though Clinton was sinking faster."

Clinton, welcoming any opportunity to drive a wedge between Dole and Gingrich and bring pressure on Gingrich, issued a statement praising the Senate for voting to reopen the government and attacking the House Republicans for the shutdown ("this is not how a great country behaves").

The House Republicans' uncertain situation led to a series of leadership meetings over a two-day period. Gingrich preferred meetings of the larger leadership group to SAG meetings, one of his colleagues said, because he was "more likely to get his way" in the larger meetings. On Thursday afternoon, January 4, Gingrich pushed through a leadership meeting a provision—to bring all federal workers back to their jobs and pay them until March 15. From there he went to a series of meetings, picking his way through the arrayed factions within the House Republican conference: the freshmen, the whip organization, the Tuesday Lunch Bunch, the CATs. (Talks scheduled at the White House for that night were called off while Gingrich tried to find a solution to his troops' resistance to ending the shutdown crisis.)

But Gingrich met strong opposition in the Republican conference that evening. "Newt was very forceful," a colleague said. "He said, 'All right. Apparently the strategy I've outlined is not acceptable to our conference. So I'm going to sit here and we're going to listen.' " One of Gingrich's problems was that members had come back from the Christmas holidays having taken seriously the one-sentence boilerplate announcements of "progress" in the White House talks. In that case, members thought, Why switch gears on the strategy? So Gingrich sat there for two and a half hours on Thursday night, listening to at least thirty speakers. After the meeting, Gingrich told the leadership, gathered in Armey's office, that he would propose a shorter continuing resolution, letting it run out on January 26. The furloughed workers could go back to their jobs, with pay, but with a few exceptions their agencies wouldn't be funded to resume their activities. A second resolution would allow a full resumption of activities if the President offered a seven-year/C.B.O. budget. This was a backing away from the demand that there be an actual deal. But it was a way, Boehner said, to "take the hot potato and put it squarely in Bill Clinton's lap." When freshman David McIntosh objected to giving furloughed federal workers back pay—the Republican leaders figured that Clinton wouldn't sign the bill without that—Gingrich responded sharply, saying, "We can't deal with that at this point."

With Gingrich's decision reported in the Friday morning papers, a lot of members, particularly the freshmen, were grumbling. At a conference meeting, Gingrich put all the elected leadership in a semicircle in front of the room, to share the incoming fire. Tired and angry, he told members making noise in the back of the room to "shut up," and said, "There aren't going to be any questions or any comments. This is what our strategy is going to be, and why. We're going to get the shutdown off the front page and get back to the balanced budget." He'd had enough of collective decision-making, of brattish defiance. "You don't like the job I'm doing as Speaker, run against me," Gingrich said. He told the Republicans that they were about to lose control of the floor, that "we came here as a team and we're going to act like a team today," and "I'm going to keep a list of who wants to be on our team and who doesn't." The room was dead silent.

When Gingrich finished, he received a standing ovation. Afterward, he told McIntosh, to whom he had given a great deal of authority, that if he didn't vote for the leadership proposals his letter resigning from the leadership would be expected. Some freshmen went to work on other freshmen.

In the end, after a raucous floor debate on Friday, January 5, fifteen Republicans, including twelve freshmen, voted against the leadership proposal for a continuing resolution. Gingrich pocketed a list of their names. (He subsequently canceled fund-raising appearances with four of them.) Dick Gephardt said in the debate that a provision to supply workers at unfunded agencies with crossword puzzles should be added to the bill, "for them to have something to do." Shortly afterward, the Senate passed the bill. The House and Senate also passed legislation to fund certain sensitive or politically popular programs, such as veterans benefits, the Peace Corps, Medicaid, parts of Medicare, "Meals on Wheels" nutrition for the elderly, visitor services in national parks. (The list grew longer as the logs were rolled.)

Also on Friday, Gerald Solomon, of New York and as Rules Committee chairman a member of the leadership, suggested that Rubin, who had been finding ways to stave off default in the face of no new debt ceiling—be impeached. Rubin was a respected alumnus of Wall Street, and the market dropped fifty points.

Following the House action on Friday, Gingrich went to Dole's office to propose "pulling the plug" on the White House talks—to provide a dramatic moment to highlight the failure of the administration to put a seven-year/C.B.O. plan on the table. Dole didn't like the idea; neither did Armey nor Boehner nor the leadership staff. They all felt that pulling out of the White House talks, which was a real possibility, had to be done very carefully. Otherwise, Clinton was certain to bash them for walking away because they wanted to "gut" Medicare.

In the White House meeting on Saturday night, Gingrich suggested that the White House offer anything that could get scored by the C.B.O. as being in balance. To the administration that was the clue that the Daschle budget, being assessed by the C.B.O. at that moment, would meet with its approval. Until then, they had feared that anything they offered would be ruled not in balance. So in the Oval Office on Saturday night Clinton put forth the seven-year/C.B.O.-scored balanced budget, as drawn up by Daschle and the White House—but first it had to have the C.B.O.'s imprimatur. (The night before, Bill Hoagland, chief of staff of the Senate Budget Committee, had phoned C.B.O. director June O'Neill, and asked her to get the C.B.O. staff in on Saturday to score the Daschle budget. "This is about the President of the United States, this is about reopening the federal government," Hoagland said.) The Republicans caucused in the Roosevelt Room for two hours while they waited for the C.B.O.'s report and went through the Daschle budget proposal and, using the whiteboard, worked on their own response to it. They felt that the Daschle budget was a disappointment. Kasich considered the proposal "phony." (The fact that on paper it balanced, even according to the C.B.O., didn't impress him, though that was what the Republicans had been demanding.) Dan Meyer worked on getting the bill allowing a reopening of the government if Clinton offered a seven year/C.B.O.-scored budget enrolled and down to the White House from Capitol Hill.

While the Republicans deliberated, Clinton watched a Western in his study next to the Oval Office. A football game was on in the office of his secretary. Panetta commuted between the two.

By Saturday, the Republicans had a letter, signed by forty-seven House Democrats, saying that they would support cuts of $168 billion in Medicare (this was down considerably from the original Republican proposal of $270 but still too high for many Democrats). Thus they held a large majority of the House on this issue. The Republicans also on Saturday night lowered their amount for tax cuts (to $185 billion), and they lowered their Medicaid cut (to $85 billion, the Coalition's figure) and their welfare cut (to $60 billion, the amount in the Senate-passed bill, which had received eighty-seven votes). Thus they argued that they had presented a "bipartisan" offer. After the fax arrived from the C.B.O. saying that the Daschle budget was in balance, Gingrich and Gore (as President of the Senate) signed the continuing resolution for the Congress, and then Clinton signed it. After twenty-one days, the shutdown was over.

Later, White House officials crowed that the Republicans had buckled, and said that the President's offering a seven-year/C.B.O. budget was no big deal, nothing it had been coerced into doing. White House officials privately bragged that the administration had outsmarted Gingrich. Even Gingrich was to concede that the strategy of holding the government hostage had failed. But while it had outrun public acceptance, it still succeeded in making the seven-year/C.B.O. budget the ticket to reopening the government, and Clinton paid the price for the ticket.

Gingrich understood that shutting the government down again wasn't an option. House Republicans spoke of "targeted" shutdowns after January 26—keeping open only those agencies they approved of—but the President still held the veto pen. Those Democrats who favored taking the issue to the elections knew that any continuing resolutions the Republicans gave them would restrict spending considerably, but they preferred that to accepting important structural changes in their pet programs. (The new resolution, like the previous one, funded them at the lowest of the amounts in the House and Senate appropriations bills or the prior year's appropriation, or, for agencies that were targeted for elimination, seventy-five percent of the previous year's amount.)

On Sunday, Washington lay buried in a blizzard of snow, and the highest officials in the land couldn't get together to continue their negotiations. (On Monday, the Capitol Police went to fetch Gephardt, who lived in Virginia, but their car broke an axle and Gephardt remained stranded.)

Both sides had expected for days that the talks might well break off on Tuesday, January 9. On Monday, McCurry said that the next day would be "the be-all and end-all." There was only so far either side could go, and they were still far apart, and to sit there wasting more time seemed pointless. They were, simply, tired of it. Besides, all of the major figures had other things to do. Gingrich was to go on a ten-day, twenty-five city fundraising trip. Dole was to get out and campaign. Clinton was to go to Bosnia over the weekend of January 12–13. But Clinton's projected overnight trip to Bosnia wouldn't have interfered with negotiations for very long. There simply had come a time, White House aides said, to set a deadline. This strategy particularly suited those Democrats, in and out of the White House, who didn't want a deal.

Sometimes the talks had gotten into considerable detail, such as on Medicare policy, what to impose new user fees on, what to put spectrum fees on. There was a search for how to lower the Consumer Price Index, which would save a lot of money on cost-of-living adjustments, but neither side wanted to legislate on this subject, since it would affect Social Security and it would cut the amount by which taxes were indexed (Armey wouldn't stand for this). A tentative decision was made to have the Bureau of Labor Statistics, which doesn't have to face the voters, lower the C.P.I. by .3 percent. This was far less than the amount by which some experts (including Alan Greenspan) thought the C.P.I. was out of kilter. But none of this mattered much as long as the two sides remained far apart on the big issues.

The Republicans, angry with Clinton, felt that they were being strung along. The Democrats felt that Gingrich couldn't come close enough to what they were proposing. There were serious philosophical differences between them. But both sides were locked in a fatal embrace: politically, neither could afford to be seen as having been the one that broke off the talks.

Both sides made pro forma offers over the next two days. On Monday, the Republicans suggested that the Republicans' total savings in entitlement programs be put in "a box," and the administration could rearrange the pieces any way it wanted. But this still put the Republicans and the White House $131 billion apart on the total to be spent on entitlements, and several big policy issues—on Medicare, Medicaid, student loans, agriculture—remained unresolved. Anticipating that Clinton might propose that they reach agreement on the numbers and put off the policy issues, thus finessing the Republicans' proposed policy changes until after the election, House Republicans were adamant that they wouldn't agree to this. They argued, with some justification, that a balanced budget plan without entitlement reform wasn't credible. They also had big stakes in the reforms they'd proposed. (In a January 11 press conference Clinton did propose simply agreeing on numbers.)

In the Monday talks, the discussion also got around to what would happen if the Republicans agreed to drop ("trigger off") their child tax credits for the last two years, as the Daschle plan did. It was estimated that doing that would bring the Republican tax cut down to a net $103 billion. Of course, the idea of dropping the tax credits at that point was fanciful. This discussion went on for some time. Gingrich didn't offer any strong objection to the idea. Armey, confident it would go nowhere, was silent.

At the end of the meeting on Monday, Republicans concluded that the administration wouldn't move very far from its Saturday night budget. Clinton told them, "I suggest that you come back with your last best offer and an exit strategy."

Gingrich replied, "We think you're right."

Tuesday morning, the Republican leaders, meeting in Dole's office, agreed to tell Clinton that the talks weren't going anywhere so they might as well break them off, and discussed how to behave publicly after the inevitable breakdown. Gingrich, from whom all optimism had drained, was in low spirits. Boehner recommended that when they make their statements Dole and Gingrich appear sad, and that Kasich and Domenici could then come on stronger. Gingrich snapped at Boehner for telling him what to do. Dole said that he wouldn't be combative but he didn't mind if others were. Trent Lott, who had kept his line to Morris open, had information from the White House about what the administration would do in the talks that afternoon, including that it would offer a new number on Medicare. Lott told the assembled group that his information was that "the Shiites" at the White House (by which he meant Stephanopoulos and Ickes) were "looking for a way to blow this up," but that "the typical two" (by which he meant Clinton and Morris) were trying to get a deal.

At the Tuesday meeting at the White House, both sides, though they knew the talks were over, probably for good, put new offers on the table, wanting to seem as reasonable as possible to the public. The Republicans lowered their tax cut figure to $177 billion, which, they pointed out, was half the amount voted in April, when the House was voting on the Contract. But in the talks, Gingrich suggested that he could move to $152 billion, an amount a House Republican leader said privately that the leadership could probably sell to the conference. This was still a higher amount than Congressional Democrats were willing to accept. Kasich had privately cut a deal with Pat Robertson, head of the Christian Coalition, which strongly backed the child tax credit. In prayerful phone calls, Kasich and Robertson had agreed that the child tax credit could be limited to couples with incomes of up to $70,000. This was a big change from the Christian Coalition's early position that there should be no cap, and its subsequent insistence that the cap not go below $200,000; it would reduce the size of the tax cuts by $30 billion. The Republicans didn't offer this position in the negotiations.

The administration began moving away from the Daschle budget on Tuesday and made its own suggestions for the record: if the Republicans reduced their tax cut, the administration might raise the amounts it would cut in Medicare (from $102 billion to $124 billion) and Medicaid—both of them back to the numbers the administration had proposed in June—and welfare. A Democratic staff member told the Republicans that Clinton might go up a couple more billion on Medicare cuts, but that was all, which echoed something Clinton told the Republican leaders. The new Medicare cut number was too high for liberal Democrats, who also felt Clinton was on the way toward settling for a tax cut that was too high. On the other hand, Kasich and some other Republicans didn't consider the administration's moving back to its original numbers much of a concession, or a real move to the center. Meyer said that while the Republicans had moved in a linear direction, the administration had moved in a circle, staying with its original zone.

But a well-placed Republican said something else was a factor in the breakdown of the talks: that the Republican leaders weren't prepared for Clinton to actually offer a seven-year/C.B.O. budget, and when he did, "we were caught a little flat." Once Clinton showed he could do this without causing himself much pain, without giving up the issues of Medicare and Medicaid, the Republican said, "he had co-opted us on balancing the budget, stolen our year-long rhetoric, and was still in a position to beat us up on Medicare and Medicaid." He added, "We were not prepared to come back and say, 'It's in balance, but not really.' " Finally, the House Republican negotiators were under pressure from the conference not to give up very much. Armey had a clear sense in his own head of how far they could go.

Clinton had wanted to get a deal at the center, but there was no center. He wasn't willing to pay any price to get a deal—but his price was a lot lower than that of the liberal Democratic leaders and of some of his advisers.

The idea that the talks broke off because Clinton had "stood on principle" was something of a myth. Clinton had already moved quite a distance toward the Republicans, and was prepared to move further. In fact, the Republicans' impatience and self-constraints may have saved Clinton from making a party-fracturing decision. There was a happenstance coalition of hard-line conservatives and hard-line liberals against an agreement.

The political math remained difficult: Clinton still wanted a deal that had the support of seventy to a hundred Democrats, but White House officials conceded privately that it was hard to see how to reach an agreement acceptable to that many Democrats as well as nearly half the Republicans. Clinton couldn't accept a deal that had the support of most of the Republicans, but that was the only kind of deal Gingrich wanted (or dared agree to). Dole and Gingrich were coming to the realization that any deal they could get with Clinton wouldn't get past their membership. Gingrich would have to be willing to split his party over this, but there was no sign that he was. And both he and Dole were coming under increasing pressure to stop going down to the White House to treat with the enemy. Kasich said, "There was growing concern inside the conference that things were going too far."

As the Tuesday, January 9, meeting was ending, Clinton tossed out a last-minute (and undiscussed with his staff) offer of $30 billion to spend on unspecified tax cuts. But at this point the Republicans were nearly out the door. In a conference call with the full House Republican leadership afterward, Gingrich called that proposal "totally irrelevant." He also told the other leadership members, "Armey and I are committed to being restrained, but the rest of you don't have to." After the conference call, Gingrich, in the words of a colleague, "looked whipped." He'd had enough, and he was disappointed with the outcome. Most of his program —the heart of the "revolution," the repeal of the New Deal—was in the budget and now there was no budget.

When Dole, Gingrich, and Armey came into the Roosevelt Room on Tuesday afternoon to report on the four hours of talks that had taken place, Domenici and Kasich told them that they weren't making any real progress. Gingrich, agreeing, said that they would "go back in there and say that we're going to suspend the talks." Dole said, "If you feel that way, why don't we go back in there and tell them right now?"

In the Oval Office discussions that followed, Gingrich said that the talks should be suspended. Clinton suggested that they all be circumspect about the breakup of the talks, lest it have an untoward impact on the financial markets. The administration negotiators said that "recess" would be a less disturbing word, and the Republicans, won over by Clinton once again, agreed. After another hour, the Republican leaders returned to the Roosevelt Room and asked that their press aides be brought in to work with them and Panetta on a statement. Panetta, in the Roosevelt Room, said that they had agreed that the talks be "recessed" for one week, that there had been significant narrowing of differences, that the staffs should work on various issues in the meantime.

After Panetta left the room, Gingrich exploded. He demanded, "Why are we wasting our time and saying we're recessing for a week?" He continued, heatedly, "We should suspend the discussions, as we originally agreed. I don't see any reason to be down here in a week. We agreed to suspend. Why are we talking about a recess? We're wasting our f—ing time down here dealing with the White House."

Gingrich insisted that Panetta return and when he did, Gingrich said, "We don't want a recess, we want to suspend."

Panetta said that they had agreed on "recess" and they should consider the markets. The Republicans could say what they wanted, Panetta said, "but we're going to say 'recess,' " and that the staffs will continue to work.

After fifty hours, the talks had broken off.

Tuesday wasn't one of Clinton's better days, anyway. A federal appeals court ruled that Paula Jones's suit against him for sexual harassment while he was still governor could proceed. Clinton's lawyers were trying to get the case postponed until after Clinton left office. Mrs. Clinton was coming under increasing attack from some quarters—especially the Republican-led Senate Whitewater Committee—over the credibility of some of her explanations of her past activities in Little Rock and Washington. Part of the problem was the sudden coming to light of long-sought documents that turned out to be in the family quarters of the White House, and in addition some contradictions. But the Whitewater Committee was ranging far and wide in its inquiry, mostly into matters that did not appear to be of great moment and might not have existed if Mrs. Clinton had been candid about them in the first place. Though Mrs. Clinton may have cut some ethical corners back in Arkansas, most of the issues seemed to be about covering over embarrassments rather than violations of the law. The danger lay in actions taken while in the White House to conceal prior actions. (The White House had inadvertently given charges about Mrs. Clinton's honesty far more circulation than would have been the case by responding to a column by William Safire in the Monday *New York Times* calling Mrs. Clinton "a congenital liar"—through a statement by McCurry that if Clinton weren't President he "would have delivered a more forceful response to that on the bridge of Mr. Safire's nose.")

In the budget talks, both sides had compromised, up to a point, and logically there was a way to compromise on the numbers, but the issues between the two sides weren't really about numbers or logic. As Dole said when the talks broke off, "It's not about numbers, it's about policy." He also said, "It's not a narrow difference, it's a wide difference."

The soft-pedaling of the breakdown by Gingrich, Dole, and Clinton in their statements to the press confused a lot of people. Clinton said, "recessed"; Gingrich said, "We think that this is a good time to take a deep pause." (But the Republicans felt tricked once again when the President in his statement attacked them for wanting to cut Medicare too much.) The talk of a meeting a week hence was window dressing. The next day, Gingrich—speaking candidly, as was sometimes his wont—said, "I am, for the first time in a year, pessimistic about the likelihood of our getting agreement." Gingrich believed that the talks were over. The same day, the stock market fell ninety-seven points. Clinton and Gingrich would then get into a blame competition.

Clinton felt that he was in the stronger position. Gingrich had set the terms of the debate, but Clinton, as he often had in his political career, coopted them. White House aides felt that the Republicans had been so busy talking to themselves, making a seven-year/C.B.O. budget the be-all and end-all—and, other Republicans felt, sounding like bookkeepers rather than visionary leaders—that they didn't see that they were setting a trap for themselves.

The extent to which Gingrich felt cornered was revealed in an angry press conference he held in Seattle shortly after Clinton's concluded. Standing at an easel, Gingrich heatedly and repeatedly attacked Clinton for calling the Republicans' proposed reductions in the growth of Medicare and Medicaid "cuts." This was of course an old argument.

Gingrich's setting the terms of the debate in 1995 was a big, even historic, achievement. But without an actual balanced budget containing various policy changes, and with other changes stalled in unsigned appropriations bills, he had little specific legislation to show for a year's work. He had set himself up by declaring a "revolution" and had outrun his mandate. His big weapon against the veto was now gone. A few days after the first session ended, Gingrich said, "It takes two elections to make the revolution real."

Though Clinton was now impassioned in public about how easy it should be to get an agreement ("in fifteen minutes") and the closeness of the two sides—playing down many differences—in fact the two sides were far apart on policy questions and in some important instances on numbers. Administration officials didn't expect an agreement unless great pressure was exerted from the outside and the Republicans gave up on their key policy changes. In the end, Gingrich had provided Clinton with the means for resuscitating his Presidency.

However they resolved matters in the interim, the next big decision was up to the electorate.

Epilogue

After the White House talks broke off on January 9, the Republicans decided to not return to the table the following week, as Clinton had suggested. Dole still thought the talks a waste of time and was under pressure in the primaries, and Gingrich was sick of the whole thing and under pressure from other House Republicans to yield no further. (In a meeting in Dole's office on whether to go to the White House, Gingrich referred to Clinton as an "S.O.B." and a "liar," and said, "Physically, I don't want to be in his presence.") The Republicans preferred to take the heat for staying away to being used, as they saw it, as props.

Clinton's clever if uninspiring State of the Union speech on January 23, stealing a number of their themes ("The era of big government is over"), left the already discouraged Republicans even more dispirited. The fact that they had defined the frame of reference didn't give them the satisfaction it should have. Dole's calamitous response to the State of the Union—not just the much-criticized poor delivery but also the text, with its attacks on "liberals" and "elites," which revived the impression of the mean, visionless Dole—demoralized Republicans even more.

The next day, Gingrich, aware that there could be no more shutdowns and that the budget talks were over, said, "We do not believe now it is possible to get a budget agreement."

Now that the glow was off Gingrich, and his strategy of remaking the federal government through the budget and his tactic of forcing a deal from Clinton by shutting down the government had failed, the House Republican conference was in disarray. Members spoke openly of a post-Gingrich world, with Tom DeLay and John Boehner maneuvering outright for advancement. The Republicans now had no strategy for dealing with Clinton, which frustrated Gingrich greatly and led to turmoil over what to do about new continuing resolutions and about extending the debt limit. Many Republicans wanted to make a "down payment" on balancing the budget part of such legislation, but weren't in agreement about how to do this, or even whether it should be done.

After negotiations with the White House, the Congress in late January voted a new continuing resolution, to last until March 15. It contained an anti-abortion provision to soothe the Christian right, which was upset that none of those adopted the previous year had made it into law. Ten minor programs were eliminated, and those still without appropriations were to be funded at various levels (some of the President's priorities at the lowest level, seventy-five percent of the previous year's appropriations). The result was a hodgepodge that would cause uncertainty among recipients of federal funds, including the state governments that the Republicans had done so much to cultivate. House Republicans hoped to come up with a more long-term strategy after a long February break.

There was some talk about finding a bipartisan agreement on the budget —Clinton still wanted one—but the differences were still great, there was still much bad blood as a result of the previous negotiations and the shutdowns, and the election year was underway. Some Republicans still thought they needed a deal, to have more to show for their efforts, while others wanted to move on; within Republican ranks criticism of making a balanced budget the Holy Grail was increasing.

Thus, the government was likely to lurch along until the voters had their say.

Afterword

The showdown between Newt Gingrich and Bill Clinton was the predicate for the 1996 election. Clinton ran for reelection as much against Gingrich as he did against Bob Dole, his actual opponent. Clinton's ads contained pictures of Dole and Gingrich (which Dole after a while had tried to avoid) and talked of the "Dole-Gingrich Congress." And Clinton based much of his campaign on the four issues that he had stressed during the budget talks: Medicare, Medicaid, and education and the environment. Dole paid a price for having lined up with the Contract with America despite his misgivings—notwithstanding his efforts to separate himself from Gingrich later on.

House Democrats also ran against Gingrich. They desperately wanted to win the House back and the Republicans just as desperately wanted to keep it. The Republicans actually hoped to increase their margin of nineteen House seats, and were optimistic that they would. Republican members believed to be vulnerable, especially a large proportion of the original seventy-three freshmen, were bombarded by ads linking them to Gingrich and citing their votes "with Gingrich" on such key issues.

In the spring of 1996, the House Republicans decided that they needed a more positive record to present to the voters and, sometimes over the objection of the Dole campaign, they passed legislation that Clinton could sign into law. At the same time, House Republican moderates were becoming more independent of the House leadership, and many of the freshmen had become more pragmatic. Gingrich himself admitted to having made mistakes. (In October he said, "In retrospect, if I were doing it all over again, we would consciously avoid the government shutdown. It was clearly wrong.") The shutdowns had left a more lasting impression and had more resonance in the House campaigns than Gingrich and a great many others had expected.

Eager to get home to campaign, and wishing to avoid any more such collisions with Clinton, the Republicans settled with him on appropriations bills, but no overall budget was ever agreed to.

Among the major pieces of legislation sent to Clinton for his signature were a welfare reform bill, a bill to curb illegal immigration, a bipartisan measure "incrementally" expanding health care protection, and even a bill raising the minimum wage. The minimum wage bill came about after House Republican moderates threatened to go their own way and vote with the Democrats.

The welfare bill, which eliminated federal guarantees of support, was the most controversial, and Clinton's decision to sign it nearly rent the Democratic Party. His Cabinet and White House advisers were deeply split in their advice to him on whether to sign it.

In the end, fewer than half of the major items of the Contract were signed into law, but Gingrich had scored significant victories in forcing Clinton to adopt the concept of a balanced budget in seven years and to sign the welfare bill, which undid one of the key components of the New Deal.

With Dick Morris's encouragement, Clinton continued his march toward the center. Through a series of proposals, most of them small and some of them symbolic—calling on school systems to require school uniforms, stressing his support for the V-chip and for putting 100,000 new police on the streets (often with a group of policemen as a backdrop), proposing curfews, relieving pressure on the 911 emergency number, and advocating a Constitutional Amendment on victims' rights—Clinton co-opted the Republicans on the crime issue and identified himself with "family values." Much of his campaign was aimed at middle-class working families, and to appeal further to that group he advocated new tax credits for two years of community college and expansion of other programs to aid families who want to send their children to college.

In advocating these "targeted" and modest programs—and having announced in his 1996 State of the Union address that "the era of big government is over"—Clinton was acting on the public's indisposition toward large new programs. (The political calamity that had befallen his and Mrs. Clinton's ambitious health care reform proposal in 1994 was still impressed upon his mind.)

•

That Bob Dole ran a hapless campaign should not have come as any surprise. He had, after all, said that he wanted to run because "it's my turn." His lack of vision had already been apparent. He was out of his element and up against a master campaigner. His surprise choice of Jack Kemp as his running mate—wildly popular among Republicans at their convention in San Diego—ended up doing him little good. Dole's proposed 15 percent tax cut didn't sell. Clinton's ideological flexibility blunted Dole's effort to paint him as a "liberal," now an epithet. His attacks on Clinton's "character" were of little avail, in part because of Clinton's astute reading of what was really bothering the middle class, and because to most of the voters Dole himself wasn't a viable alternative. Trying to defeat an incumbent President in the midst of a good economy would have been a daunting task for anyone. Republicans worried that Dole's probable poor showing would have a negative effect on their campaigns for House and Senate seats.

In the end, though the Republicans held the House, they did so with a net loss of nine seats. Of the eighteen House seats that the Republicans lost, thirteen were held by freshmen. Republicans had a net gain of two Senate seats, and some of the new Republican senators who filled open Republican seats were more conservative than their predecessors. Clinton's overwhelming Electoral College victory—379–159—didn't translate into the majority of the popular vote that he had coveted (Clinton received 49.2 percent of the popular vote, Dole 40.8 percent, Perot 8.5 percent).

Though Gingrich had survived the 1996 election as Speaker, he could never return to the position of power that he held at the beginning of the 104th Congress—even if he wanted to. Too many Republicans had become restive under his rule, and too many had had to fight off election charges that they had been excessively associated with him. Further, he was facing a continuing investigation by the House Ethics Committee on a number of issues, including the new and dangerous question of whether he had misled the committee. (Other House members took notice of the fact that Ethics Committee chair Nancy Johnson narrowly escaped defeat for reelection; her opponent in the race for her Connecticut seat had charged that she had been too protective of Gingrich.)

On election night, Clinton vowed to govern from the "vital center." After the election, the Republicans were proceeding under the dual imperatives, as they saw them, of working with Clinton to rack up more legislative accomplishments and conducting investigations into various White House scandals, including the one that arose shortly before the election of allegedly illegal financial contributions to the Democratic National Committee. Further actions on the part of the independent counsel, Kenneth Starr—who had let it be known that he would bring no indictments in the weeks leading up to the election—on Whitewater and other issues were awaited. Though foreign policy was barely discussed in the Presidential campaign, a number of potentially serious problems were pending, including continued strife in Bosnia. (Clinton had held off until shortly after the election the widely expected announcement that the United States would have to maintain forces in Bosnia past the December 20 deadline.)

As the new year approached, both President Clinton and House Speaker Gingrich were facing potentially turbulent second terms.

Author's Note

This book is based on interviews with the figures in the White House and on Capitol Hill who were involved in the struggle, as well as some who were very close to the action. They ranged from leaders of the Congress to lesser-known staff aides—who are often the best-informed and most candid participants—to people in the private sector with a range of important contacts and a wealth of information. Always, the reporter must test the facts and hypotheses with a number of people in order to get at the truth.

In many instances, people spoke on the record, but some, particularly some staff members in sensitive positions, could not be quoted by name. All quotations are from direct sources. Any thoughts or views attributed to anyone came from someone with direct knowledge. In all cases, I sifted what I was told and asked myself, "Why is this person telling me this?" A reporter must be on the lookout for things that might be said out of self-aggrandizement, a desire to boost the role of the boss, or rivalry.

I consider this a genre of middle-distance journalism, intended to catch events and people's involvement in them or reactions to them while they are still fresh and before they have been prettied up, fuzzed over, or retouched for any number of purposes. It is also intended to offer the analysis and perspective of someone close to the events, seeing them unfiltered, but not under the demands and restrictions of daily or weekly journalism.

Acknowledgments

Any book of contemporary journalism is by definition a collaborative affair. It depends on the willingness of sources, usually very busy people, to share their time and insights with the author. I was quite fortunate in the number of people, in all sorts of roles in this drama, who were generous with their time. They made the experience extremely interesting, and I learned a lot—and had fun as well.

I talked with people at both ends of Pennsylvania Avenue, at the epicenters of the battle. They all know who they are, and they have my gratitude for their help in telling this extraordinary story.

This book was also a collaborative affair in the sense of those whose help, advice, and support were crucial to my getting it done. My assistant, Amy Brennan, did a lot of everything, and came to have a command of the subject herself that was invaluable to me. She brought to the task all that one could ask for: intelligence, willingness to work very hard, and a fine sense of humor. She was simply a joy to have around.

Former assistants Kathleen Glover, Christine Haynes Myers, and Melissa Price, whose continuing loyalty I find very moving, also played a role in producing this book—by reading proofs, by tracking down elusive facts, and by helping to keep my little enterprise afloat. John Bennet once again showed that he is as good at friendship as he is talented. Leslie Sewell (also a former assistant) and Jim Jaffe, who are practically family, helped in all sorts of ways, as they always do. My friend Michael Beschloss offered crucial moral support and good advice. As usual, Tom Oliphant was there when I needed him. I'm also grateful for the help of Colette Rhoney, Olwen Price, Ana Romero, and Marilee Steele, and of Roger Labrie, who shepherded the manuscript at Simon & Schuster.

My agent, Sterling Lord, was once again a sympathetic ear and wise counselor. And my editor, Alice Mayhew, again provided enthusiasm, tough-mindedness, and energy to this book.

As always, my husband, David Webster, was the total partner, involved at every stage. Without him as a sounding board—testing ideas, helping me search for the truth—I can't imagine what I'd have done.

Index

Printed in the United States
72305LV00004B/99